A Literary Guide to Dublin

Endpapers: John Rocque's
Plan of the City of Dublin and the Environs (1756).

College Green c. 1910, with the Bank of Ireland on the left
and Trinity College straight ahead.

A Literary Guide to Dublin

Writers in Dublin: Literary Associations and Anecdotes

Vivien Igoe

Methuen

Published by Methuen 1999

3 5 7 9 10 8 6 4 2

First published in the United Kingdom in 1994
by Methuen London

This edition published in the United Kingdom
in 1999 by Methuen Publishing Limited
215 Vauxhall Bridge Road, London SW1V 1EJ

Peribo Pty Ltd, 58 Beaumont Road, Mount Kuring-Gai
NSW 2080, Australia, ACN 002 273 761
(for Australia and New Zealand)

Copyright © 1994 by Vivien Igoe

Copyright details for all the photographs and
illustrations are included on the Acknowledgements page

Vivien Igoe has asserted her right under the Copyright, Designs
and Patents Act, 1988, to be identified as the author of this work

Methuen Publishing Limited Reg. No. 3543167

A CIP catalogue record for this book
is available from the British Library

ISBN 0 413 69120 9

Printed and bound in Great Britain by
Biddles Ltd, Guildford and King's Lynn

For my mother,
Eileen Corr Veale

Contents

List of illustrations   xi
Acknowledgements   xiii
Preface   xv
Introduction: A brief history of Anglo-Irish literature   xvii

Joseph Addison (1672–1719)   1
Æ [George Russell] (1867–1935)   2
Jonah Barrington (1760–1834)   5
Samuel Beckett (1906–89)   8
Brendan Behan (1923–64)   14
George Berkeley (1685–1753)   16
John Betjeman (1906–84)   19
Isaac Bickerstaffe (1735?–1812)   24
Dion Boucicault (1820?–90)   25
Elizabeth Bowen (1899–1973)   26
Henry Brooke (1703–83)   30
Christy Brown (1932–81)   32
Edmund Burke (1729–97)   35
William Carleton (1794–1869)   38
Austin Clarke (1896–1974)   44
Padraic Colum (1881–1972)   49
William Congreve (1670–1729)   54
George Darley (1795–1846)   55
Thomas Davis (1814–45)   57
Mrs Mary Delany (1700–88)   59
Thomas De Quincey (1785–1859)   63
Charles Dickens (1812–70)   64
George Farquhar (1678–1707)   65
Samuel Ferguson (1810–86)   66
Percy French (1854–1920)   70
Monk Gibbon (1896–1987)   74
Oliver St John Gogarty (1878–1957)   76
Oliver Goldsmith (1728–74)   82
Lady Gregory (1852–1932)   84
Lafcadio Hearn (1850–1904)   88
Felicia Dorothea Hemans (1793–1835)   92
F.R. Higgins (1896–1941)   95

Contents

Gerard Manley Hopkins (1844–89)   99
Douglas Hyde (1860–1949)   105
John Kells Ingram (1823–1907)   109
Thomas Caulfield Irwin (1823–92)   110
Denis Johnston (1901–84)   112
James Joyce (1882–1941)   113
Patrick Kavanagh (1904–67)   123
Thomas Kettle (1880–1916)   128
Charles Kickham (1828–82)   132
Rudyard Kipling (1865–1936)   135
Maura Laverty (1907–66)   139
Emily Lawless (1845–1913)   140
Joseph Sheridan Le Fanu (1814–73)   143
Charles Lever (1806–72)   148
Lord Longford (1902–61)   153
Samuel Lover (1797–1868)   155
Denis Florence MacCarthy (1817–82)   159
Donagh MacDonagh (1912–68)   161
Thomas MacDonagh (1878–1916)   162
Micheál MacLiammóir (1899–1978)   164
James Clarence Mangan (1803–49)   166
Edward Martyn (1859–1924)   170
Charles Robert Maturin (1782–1824)   173
George Moore (1852–1933)   177
Thomas Moore (1779–1852)   184
Lady Morgan (1776–1859)   187
T.C. Murray (1873–1959)   191
Cardinal John Henry Newman (1801–1890)   191
Sean O'Casey (1880–1964)   195
Frank O'Connor (1903–66)   199
Sean O'Faoláin (1900–91)   201
Liam O'Flaherty (1896–1984)   203
John O'Leary (1830–1907)   204
Brian O'Nolan (1911–66)   206
Patrick Pearse (1879–1916)   209
Joseph Plunkett (1887–1916)   213
Lennox Robinson (1886–1958)   215
Sir Walter Scott (1771–1832)   217
George Bernard Shaw (1856–1950)   219
Percy Bysshe Shelley (1792–1822)   222
Richard Brinsley Sheridan (1751–1816)   224
Annie M. P. Smithson (1873–1948)   226

Contents

Thomas Southerne (1659–1746) 231
Edmund Spenser (c. 1552–99) 233
Richard Stanyhurst (1547–1618) 234
Sir Richard Steele (1672–1729) 237
James Stephens (1880–1950) 239
Bram Stoker (1847–1912) 243
L.A.G. Strong (1896–1958) 249
Jonathan Swift (1667–1745) 254
John Millington Synge (1871–1909) 260
William Makepeace Thackeray (1811–63) 267
Thomas Tickell (1686–1740) 269
Anthony Trollope (1815–82) 271
Katherine Tynan (1861–1931) 273
Oscar Wilde (1854–1900) 277
William Wilde (1815–76) 282
Jack Butler Yeats (1871–1957) 284
William Butler Yeats (1865–1939) 286

A selection of literary and historical pubs in Dublin 293
Suggested literary routes and maps 301
Mount Jerome Cemetery 331
Glasnevin Cemetery 335
Useful information: transport and places 342
Select bibliography 345
Index 352

List of illustrations

Endpapers. John Rocque's *Plan of the City of Dublin and the Environs* (1756).
Title spread. College Green c. 1910.
1. Æ (George Russell).
2. 17 Rathgar Avenue, home of Æ.
3. 14 Harcourt Street, the home of Jonah Barrington.
4. Cooldrinagh, Foxrock, birthplace of Samuel Beckett.
5. 6 Clare Street, the offices of Beckett's father.
6. The anemometer on the East Pier, Dun Laoghaire.
7. Brendan Behan.
8. George Berkeley, Bishop of Cloyne.
9. John Betjeman in Fleet Street.
10. 15 Herbert Place, birthplace of Elizabeth Bowen.
11. Bronze statue of Edmund Burke.
12. William Carleton.
13. Grave of William Carleton.
14. The Black Church, St Mary's Place.
15. The Railway Cottage, Glasthule, home of Padraic Colum.
16. Padraic Colum.
17. The *Irish Independent* offices.
18. Sir Samuel Ferguson.
19. 35 Mespil Road, home of Percy French.
20. 24 Sandycove Road, home of Monk Gibbon.
21. Oliver St John Gogarty releasing a pair of swans into the Liffey.
22. Portrait of Lady Gregory.
23. Lafcadio Hearn.
24. Felicia Hemans.
25. St Ann's Church, Dawson Street, burial place of Felicia Hemans.
26. Portrait of F.R. Higgins.
27. Burial place of Gerard Manley Hopkins.
28. Portrait of Douglas Hyde.
29. 41 Brighton Square, Rathgar, birthplace of James Joyce.
30. James Joyce.
31. The Martello Tower, Sandycove.
32. 19 Raglan Road, home of Patrick Kavanagh.
33. Patrick Kavanagh with Milo O'Shea.

34. Bust of Thomas Kettle, St Stephen's Green.
35. Kickham's last home, 2 Montpelier Place, Blackrock.
36. Grafton Street at about the time of Kipling's visit.
37. Emily Lawless.
38. Portrait of Joseph Sheridan Le Fanu.
39. The House by the Churchyard in Chapelizod.
40. Miniature of Charles Lever.
41. The Gate Theatre, Cavendish Row.
42. Portrait of Samuel Lover.
43. Kilmainham Gaol, where Thomas MacDonagh was executed.
44. 4 Harcourt Terrace, home of Micheál MacLiammóir.
45. Bust of James Clarence Mangan in St Stephen's Green.
46. Portrait of Edward Martyn.
47. Engraving of Charles Robert Maturin.
48. The Shelbourne Hotel.
49. Engraving of Thomas Moore.
50. Portrait of Lady Morgan (Sydney Owenson).
51. Newman House, 86 St Stephen's Green.
52. 422 North Circular Road, home of Sean O'Casey.
53. Portrait of John O'Leary.
54. St Enda's, Rathfarnham, now the Pearse Museum.
55. Portrait of Lennox Robinson.
56. 3 Upper Synge Street, birthplace of George Bernard Shaw.
57. Oxmantown from Moll's Map of Dublin, 1714.
58. The remains of Stanyhurst's Tower in Little Ship Street.
59. The National Gallery, Merrion Square.
60. 15 Marino Crescent, Clontarf, birthplace of Bram Stoker.
61. Bram Stoker, the author of *Dracula*.
62. The Forty Foot Bathing Place, Sandycove.
63. St Patrick's Cathedral, Dublin.
64. The bust of Dean Swift in St Patrick's Cathedral.
65. Drawing of John Millington Synge.
66. The old Abbey Theatre.
67. The new Abbey Theatre.
68. Thomas Tickell's House, Botanic Gardens, Glasnevin.
69. 6 Seaview Terrace, Donnybrook, home of Trollope .
70. 1 Merrion Square, home of the Wilde family.
71. Oscar Wilde.
72. 18 Fitzwilliam Square, home and studio of Jack B. Yeats
73. 5 Sandymount Avenue, birthplace of William Butler Yeats.
74. Cartoon of W.B. Yeats and Æ.
75. McDaid's pub in Harry Street.

Acknowledgements

Special thanks are due to the following for their assistance and courtesy: Mary Kelleher the Librarian, and the staff at the Royal Dublin Society Library; also the staff of the National Library of Ireland, in particular Niall McNamara.

For some points of information I would like to thank the following: Dr Benedict Kiely, Douglas Bennett, Ciara Byrne, Penny Cabot, R. Dardis Clarke, Peter Costello, Simon Curran, Joseph C. Gallagher, Sheila Gallagher, Professor Conal Hooper, Michael Johnston, Major Eric Lanning, John McCullen, Iseult McGuinness, Ken Mawhinney, Ken Monaghan, Val Mulkerns, Robert Nicholson, Tony O'Doherty, Frederick O'Dwyer, Máire O'Sullivan, Jim Reynolds, Séan G. Ronan, Mark Rutledge, Dr Gillian Sheehan and Dr Patricia Sheehan.

I would also like to thank Alan Bryan and Don Holder at Mount Jerome Cemetery, and the staff at Glasnevin Cemetery, especially Joe Kenny.

For the bulk of the photography in this book, I would like to thank Paddy Tutty, who waited patiently at various locations for the sun to shine at the right angle. I would also like to thank Michael Gleeson for his dedicated work on the eight maps.

To my husband Michael must go my thanks for his help and support throughout.

Last, but not least, many thanks are due to Mary O'Donovan, my editor at Methuen, for her careful and sensitive treatment of the manuscript.

My thanks go to the following for permission to reproduce individual photographs: The Abbey Theatre for number 26 of F.R. Higgins; Mary Cosgrave for number 21 of Oliver St John Gogarty; the Dublin Writers' Museum for 61 of Bram Stoker; Candida Lycett Green for number 9 of John Betjeman; the National Gallery of Ireland for numbers 8 of George Berkeley, 12 of William Carleton, 22 of Lady Gregory, 28 of Douglas Hyde, 38 of Joseph Sheridan Le Fanu, 40 of Charles Lever, 42 of Samuel Lover, 46 of Edward Martyn, 47 of Charles Robert Maturin, 50 of Lady Morgan, 53 of John O'Leary, 55 of Lennox Robinson; the National Library of Ireland for numbers 36 of Grafton Street and 74 of Yeats and Æ, and for the photograph of College Green reproduced on the title spread and John Rocque's *Plan of the city of Dublin and the environs* (1756) reproduced on the endpapers; the Governors and Guardians of Marsh's Library for number 37 of Emily Lawless and 57 of Oxmantown from *Moll's Map of Dublin* (1714); Máire O'Sullivan for number 16 of Padraic Colum; Sean Ronan for number 23 of Lafcadio

Acknowledgements

Hearn; Mrs J. Solterer for number 30 of James Joyce; and Elinor Wiltshire for number 33 of Patrick Kavanagh. Finally, my thanks to Ordnance Survey of Ireland, Phoenix Park, for permission to reproduce maps of Dublin and to the Board of Trinity College Dublin for permission to use their photograph of Trinity College Library.

Preface

Since the seventeenth century, Dublin has probably produced more writers of international stature than any other city of comparable size. In this book it is portrayed as a writers' city and its literary geography is delineated by showing its connections with various authors: where they were born, the places they lived in and the areas they frequented in their everyday lives as well as some of the locations in which their works are set. Most of the places referred to still exist and, where possible, they have been pinpointed exactly for the reader's convenience, both in the text and in the suggested literary routes.

Only deceased writers are featured, the earliest being Richard Stanyhurst who was born in 1547, and the latest Christy Brown who was born in 1923, and most of them are Anglo-Irish, that is, Irish authors who wrote in the English language. Authors who wrote in the Irish language have, for the most part, been excluded as most of them were concentrated in areas other than Dublin. The selection of ninety-one writers includes those born in Dublin, such as James Joyce, William Butler Yeats and Brendan Behan; some who had a Dublin connection, such as Oliver Goldsmith, William Carleton, Douglas Hyde and Padraic Colum; some who came from overseas and settled for a time in the city, such as Mrs Delany, Felicia Hemans and Lafcadio Hearn; some who came or were sent to work there, such as Joseph Addison, Anthony Trollope, John Henry Newman and Gerard Manley Hopkins; and a few who simply visited the city, such as Percy Bysshe Shelley, Charles Dickens and William Makepeace Thackeray. All had literary links with Dublin and these are set out in the biographical sketches which make up this book, together with other details concerning their lives and work.

Certainly the knowledge of biographical detail enhances the understanding of a poem or a work of prose. This *Literary Guide* portrays only some of the literary associations which exist and should be used simply as a guide or stepping stone. More detailed information may be obtained from the biographies, memoirs and other works listed in the bibliography.

The writers are listed alphabetically to help those who wish to visit places associated with the life and work of a particular writer and, where possible, particular works are linked with the localities in question. Exact addresses are given wherever possible to direct the reader to the sites with minimal difficulty. Few of the houses are open to the public (most are now private homes or offices) and their privacy should be respected. There are some houses and buildings which are open to the public, however, and these are listed in the section of Useful Information towards the end of the book. Of necessity, the entries are of uneven length and while this usually reflects the importance of the writer it is not always the case. Some authors tended, because of personal or family circumstances, to move from house to house, like Sean O'Casey and James Joyce, and space is given to detailing all their addresses: others, like Oscar Wilde, had only one or two addresses.

The geographical area covered in this book, with a few exceptions, is Dublin city and its immediate suburbs, and all places mentioned are within easy reach of the city centre by the public transport system. The book includes a selection of literary routes, for exploring on foot. Each walk encompasses a locality in which there are many houses with literary associations along the route so that a wealth of literary richness from different generations can be contained within the same walk. If, for instance, the reader is following in the steps of William Carleton, finishing with the fine memorial to him in Mount Jerome Cemetery in Harold's Cross, it will also be possible, while there, to visit the graves of many other writers included by referring to the separate list and map of the cemetery towards the end of the book. For more detailed information on streets and roads, the reader may find it helpful to consult the Ordnance Survey Street Map of Dublin.

It is hoped that for those interested in one or all of the writers included, this book will provide a useful reference work and guide to their homes and haunts in the city of Dublin, which has one of the richest literary heritages in the world.

Introduction

A brief history of Anglo-Irish literature

In the latter half of the nineteenth century in Dublin, and within an area of a few square miles, were born some of the most famous names in the history of literature and drama in the English language. These include Oscar Wilde, John Millington Synge, Sean O'Casey and James Joyce, as well as four winners of the Nobel Prize for Literature, W.B. Yeats in 1923, George Bernard Shaw in 1924, Samuel Beckett in 1969 and Dublin based Seamus Heaney in 1995. This is a phenomenal record for a city the size of Dublin.

Ireland's literary record starts much earlier, however, and the country as a whole has been producing a remarkable number of notable playwrights, novelists, poets and satirists since the late seventeenth century. While the record has changed in recent times, most of the earlier writers (though by no means all of them) were from Protestant, Anglo–Irish, ascendancy families who formed the ruling classes after the collapse of the old Gaelic order at the Battle of Kinsale in 1601.

The first great Anglo–Irish writer, and the first Irish author of international repute, was Jonathan Swift (1667–1745), often regarded as one of the most devastating satirists in the English language. His most famous satire, *Gulliver's Travels*, was written in 1726 when he was Dean of St Patrick's Cathedral, and his *Drapier's Letters*, in which he supported the Irish in their revolt against Wood's halfpence, greatly influenced the political developments of the time.

William Congreve (1670–1729), a friend of Swift and one of the major exponents of Restoration comedy, was said by Voltaire to have raised the glory of comedy, by dint of his sharp wit and polished dialogue, to greater heights than that of any other dramatist writing in the English language. George Farquhar (1678–1707), a native of Derry, delighted the London stage with his dramas, *The Recruiting Officer* and *The Beaux' Stratagem*, as did Oliver Goldsmith (1728–74) with *The Good-Natur'd Man* and *She Stoops to Conquer*. Another Irish dramatist who was among the most celebrated in the London theatre scene of the time was Richard Brinsley Sheridan (1751–1816), who made his name with his classic comedies, *The Rivals* and *The School for Scandal*. During the same period George Berkeley (1685–1753) and Edmund Burke (1729–97) made important contributions to philosophical and political studies.

The novels of Maria Edgeworth (1767–1849) were among the first to deal with Irish themes and they are said to have encouraged Sir Walter Scott to do for Scotland what she had done for her own country. Charles Lever (1806–72) and William Carleton (1794–1869) were other novelists in this native Irish tradition. Carleton, who unlike most other Irish writers remained in Ireland all his life, wrote of the hidden Gaelic Ireland and its rural traditions in his *Traits and Stories of the Irish Peasantry*. He had an intimate knowledge of his subject matter and was later described by Yeats as 'the greatest novelist of Ireland by right of the most Celtic eyes that ever gazed from under the brow of a story-teller'.

The early nineteenth century was noted mainly for the emergence of what was to become the Irish novel as we know it today. Lady Morgan (1776–1859) established her fame with *The Wild Irish Girl*, and one of the best known poets of this period was Thomas Moore (1779–1852), whose *Irish Melodies* achieved great popularity in both Ireland and Britain. Samuel Lover (1797–1868), author of the novel *Handy Andy*, co-founded the *Dublin University Magazine* with Isaac Butt in 1833. In Butt's words, the magazine was to be 'a monthly advocate of the Protestantism, the intelligence and the respectability of Dublin'. In spite of this it also published some fiction. The magazine was later edited by Charles Lever who wrote such rollicking romances as *Harry Lorrequer* and *Charles O'Malley*. The Irish subject was popularised enormously by both Lover and Lever in the nineteenth century and their novels reached remarkable prominence.

The influence of Irish folklore can be seen in the emergence of the macabre as a major theme in nineteenth–century Anglo-Irish literature. Charles Maturin (1782–1824), most of whose writing was done in Marsh's Library, is best known for *Melmoth the Wanderer*, a classic Gothic novel written on the theme of a wandering Jew. Published in 1820, it had a great influence on contemporary European literature. James Clarence Mangan idolised Maturin to the point of copying his unusual dress and Oscar Wilde, a distant relative, took the name Sebastian Melmoth during his exile in France.

Joseph Sheridan Le Fanu (1814–73) wrote his two best known novels, the spine-chilling *Uncle Silas* and *The House by the*

Churchyard, at 70 Merrion Square. Bram Stoker (1847–1912), born in Clontarf, and for twenty–seven years private secretary to Sir Henry Irving, became the father of the modern horror novel with the publication of *Dracula* in 1897.

In the mid nineteenth century, two notable poets were James Clarence Mangan (1803–49) and Thomas Davis (1814–45), a member of the Young Ireland group and founder of the *Nation* newspaper. *Lays of the Western Gael* by Sir Samuel Ferguson (1810–86), a series of ballads founded on events in Celtic legend and history, can be said to have been a forerunner of the Irish Literary Revival. Dion Boucicault (1820–90) was perhaps the most eminent man in the theatre of England, America and Ireland of his time, with his series of successful touring shows. Among his most popular works are his Irish comic melodramas, *The Colleen Bawn* (1860), *Arrah-na-Pogue* (1864) and *The Shaughraun* (1874).

Oscar Wilde (1854–1900), noted for his brilliant wit, was born in Dublin but left it for London in 1878. He made his mark in the British theatre with such plays as *Lady Windermere's Fan*, and what is generally accepted to be the best light comedy in English, *The Importance of Being Earnest*. George Bernard Shaw (1856–1950) also emigrated to England at about the same time. Born at 33 Synge Street, he went on to become one of the most successful playwrights ever in the English language with a string of successes including *Pygmalion*, *St Joan* and *Man and Superman*, to mention just three.

The late nineteenth and early twentieth centuries witnessed a renaissance in Anglo-Irish literature. Leading writers of the Irish Literary Revival included George Moore (1852–1933), Æ (George Russell, 1867–1935), Padraic Colum (1881–1972) and James Stephens (1880–1950). W.B. Yeats (1865–1939) and Lady Augusta Gregory (1852–1932) founded the Abbey Theatre in Dublin in 1904 in order to encourage Irish drama. One of the theatre's first directors, with Yeats and Lady Gregory, was J.M. Synge (1871–1909) whose *Playboy of the Western World* caused a riot at its first production. It later went on to become one of the classics of the Irish stage. In 1880 Sean O'Casey was born in Upper Dorset Street. As a dramatist he was a late developer and it was not until 1923 that his first play, *The Shadow of a Gunman*, was produced at the Abbey Theatre where it was an immediate success. Brendan Behan (1923–64) achieved an international reputation as a dramatist with *The Quare Fellow*, but later notoriety came from his outrageous behaviour caused principally by alcohol, which contributed to his early death at the age of forty-one.

It is perhaps for the novel, however, that modern Anglo-Irish literature is most famous. George Moore (1852–1933), born in County Mayo, spent the early 1900s living at 4 Upper Ely Place in Dublin. It was here that he produced some of his finest work including *The Untilled Field*, *The Lake* and his 'memoirs', *Hail and Farewell* (1911–14), foreshadowing Ireland's greatest novelist, James Joyce (1882–1941), who was born in the Dublin suburb of Rathgar. Joyce's *Ulysses* is the most celebrated English-language novel of the twentieth century. Samuel Beckett (1906–90), recognised as one of the greatest prose writers of the century, did much of his writing in a garret over his father's office at 6 Clare Street, before he emigrated to France in the 1920s. Brian O'Nolan (Flann O'Brien, Myles na gCopaleen, 1911–66) published *At Swim-Two-Birds* in 1939 which was praised by James Joyce and Graham Greene and can stand comparison with the work of his great predecessors.

The most important poets of the generation following Yeats include Austin Clarke (1896–1974) and Patrick Kavanagh (1904–67). Kavanagh was born in County Monaghan, but lived for much of his life in Dublin's Pembroke Street, near the canal where many of the lyric poems for which he is best remembered found their inspiration. In the same generation, there was a significant development in short-story writing with the emergence of such writers as Liam O'Flaherty (1896–1984), Sean O'Faoláin (1900–91) and Frank O'Connor (1903–66).

With the redevelopment of Dublin, changes have inevitably occurred in the landscape and some of the literary landmarks have disappeared, such as the houses at number 6 York Street where James Clarence Mangan had lodgings, and number 37, home of Charles Maturin, the curate who had a passion for dancing. Some streetscapes have disappeared, such as Dominick Street where Joseph Sheridan Le Fanu was born and where Sydney Owenson, later Lady Morgan, worked as governess for the Featherstonehaugh family. Almost an entire side of Eccles Street has been demolished, including number 7 which, as the home of Leopold and Molly Bloom, must be one of the most famous addresses in literature. Arran Quay, the birthplace of Edmund Burke, has been completely redeveloped. Monto, the setting of the 'Nighttown' scene in *Ulysses*, has vanished as have many of the houses in the older part of Dublin, such as Fishamble Street where Handel's *Messiah* was first performed in 1742. Some streets were destroyed in the 1916 Rising and during the War of Independence between 1919 and 1921, a period vividly portrayed by Katherine Tynan (1861–1931) in *The Years of the Shadow*.

Despite these changes in landscape, however, the birthplaces of many writers such as Wilde, Yeats, Shaw and Beckett are still to be seen, and though the tramlines may have gone, much remains of the Georgian Dublin of Elizabeth Bowen's time. Amazingly, of the many houses inhabited by Joyce in Dublin, all but one of them, the Georgian house in Hardwicke Street, may be seen today.

Joseph Addison
1672–1719

Joseph Addison, statesman, writer and poet, was appointed as Chief Secretary to the Marquis of Wharton, Lord-Lieutenant of Ireland, in December 1708. On his arrival at **Ringsend**, at the mouth of the Liffey, on 21 April 1709, he was met and greeted by members of the Privy Council. Lord Wharton opened Parliament on 5 May, to which, some days later, Addison was returned as Member for Cavan, thus representing the Legislatures of both Great Britain and Ireland.

During his short stay in Dublin, which was only a matter of months, Addison found time to continue his literary work and contributed a number of essays to the *Tatler*, just founded by his friend, Richard Steele, whom he had known since his days at Charterhouse School in London.

Addison's prose was hailed by Dr Johnson as 'the model of the middle style; on grave subjects not formal, on light occasions not grovelling'. Addison himself claims to have 'brought philosophy out of closets and libraries, schools and colleges, to dwell in clubs and assemblies, at tea-tables and in coffee-houses', and to have 'enlivened morality with wit, and tempered wit with morality'.

Addison's coterie of friends in Dublin included Thomas Sheridan, Dr Delany (Mary Delany's husband) and Jonathan Swift, with whom he formed a close friendship and to whom he presented a copy of his *Italian Travels* inscribed, 'To the most agreeable companion, the truest friend, and the greatest genius of his age.'

During his time in Dublin, Addison lived in the official house of the Secretary in **Dublin Castle**. Before his arrival, John Pratt wrote to Addison, 'Your Lodgings in the Castle are in a good forwardness, and I believe will pretty well serve your occasions during your stay here; if you want any room when you come, you may command what you please in my lodgings, which as Constable of the Castle I have next door to yours.'

There is no evidence that Addison lived anywhere else in Dublin. The avenue of yew trees beside the river Tolka, known as 'Addison's Walk', has no connection with the essayist, although it is said to have been planted by the poet Thomas Tickell, a friend and

1

supporter of Addison, when he was in residence at what is now the Director's House in the Botanic Gardens, Glasnevin.

When the Whigs returned to power in 1714, Addison was again appointed Chief Secretary and held this post until 1715, but there is nothing to suggest that he lived in Dublin during this period.

Addison is best remembered for his political essays in the *Tatler* and the *Spectator*, in which he undertook to teach refinements and good taste to the middle class of town and country.

Æ (George Russell)
1867–1935

George Russell, or Æ as he was commonly known, poet, painter, mystic, organiser for the cooperative movement, economist and editor, was born in Lurgan, County Armagh, in 1867. A prominent figure in the Irish Literary Revival, his family moved to Dublin when his father got a job in an accountant's office in **Dame Street** in 1878. 'I have never been sufficiently grateful to Providence for the

1. Æ (George Russell).

mercy shown to me in removing me from Ulster,' he later remarked.

The Russells' first home in Dublin was at **33 Emorville Avenue** off the South Circular Road, where they remained until 1885. It was in this house that George Russell's only sister, Mary Elizabeth, died aged eighteen.

George Russell attended Power's School in **Harrington Street**, and later Dr C.W. Benson's School in **Rathmines**. From March to May in 1880, he attended the Metropolitan School of Art in **Kildare Street** and in 1883 resumed evening classes there where he met the sculptors, Oliver Sheppard and John Hughes, both of whom were later to do busts of him. It was here, most likely, that he first encountered W.B. Yeats. They had endless discussions about occult phenomena and remained close friends for a number of years.

After seven years, the family changed residence to **67 Grosvenor Square, Rathmines**. A couple of years later, Russell started work as a clerk with Messrs Pim Bros., a fashionable drapers in **South Great George's Street**. In 1888 he attended meetings at the Theosophical Society and first used Æ as his pseudonym. (It was originally ÆON, but this defeated a compositor who omitted the last two letters on a collection of his poems and Æ stuck.) In 1890, he became a member of the Esoteric section of the Theosophical Society and the following year moved into their premises at **3 Upper Ely Place**, where he spent the next seven years. Of this time, he wrote, 'The seven years I lived here were the happiest in my life. How fortunate I was to be drawn into the companionship with six or seven others, all I think wiser and stronger than I was.'

In the meantime, his parents Thomas and Marianne had moved from Rathmines to **5 Seapoint Avenue, Monkstown**, where Æ often visited them. It was a pleasant place, close to the sea. (His mother died here in 1897 aged sixty-one.)

In 1895, Æ joined the Irish Literary Society, the aim of which was to advance and promote a new school of literature which would be singularly Irish although written in the English language. Two years later, he left his job at Pim's to join the Irish Agricultural Organisation Society (IAOS), founded by Sir Horace Plunkett to integrate the work of the Irish cooperative units. Russell became editor of its magazine, the *Irish Homestead* (**22 Lincoln Place**), where Joyce's stories, 'The Sisters' and 'Eveline', first appeared in 1904 under the name Stephen Daedalus. Æ later became editor of the *Irish Statesman*, which replaced the former publication. This published the work of many of the foremost writers of the time.

3

In 1898, Æ married Violet North whom he had met at **3 Upper Ely Place**. In the first months of their marriage they moved frequently, living at **10 Grove Terrace**, **6 Castlewood Avenue** and **28 Upper Mount Pleasant Avenue**, all in the precinct of **Rathmines**. In 1900, they moved to **25 Coulson Avenue, Rathgar**, where their son, Brian Hartley, was born. Maud Gonne, the legendary beauty, was their next-door neighbour and the recently married Countess Markievicz lived nearby with her Polish husband, Casimir. It was in 1898 that the Countess founded the republican-suffragette organisation.

The Irish National Theatre was founded in 1902 with W.B. Yeats as its President and Æ as Vice-Chairman. His play *Deirdre* and Yeats' *Kathleen ní Houlihan*, with Maud Gonne in the lead, were first performed by W.G. Fay's Irish National Dramatic Company at St Teresa's Hall in Clarendon Street. Æ's son, Diarmuid, was born the same year.

In 1906, the family moved to **17 Rathgar Avenue**. Æ is associated mostly with this house as he lived here for twenty-five years, the longest period he remained in any house. A plaque commemorates his time here. In 1908, Plunkett House, **84 Merrion Square**, opened as the IAOS Headquarters and Æ had his office on the second floor.

2. 17 Rathgar Avenue, Æ's home from 1906 until 1933, famous for its lively Sunday evening literary gatherings.

From the early days at Mount Pleasant, the various Russell homes became famous for the lively literary gatherings on Sunday evenings where writers met to partake of the hospitality and brilliant conversation. These included Seumas O'Sullivan, James Stephens, Padraic Colum, Frank O'Connor, Patrick Kavanagh, Francis Ledwidge, F.R. Higgins and Austin Clarke (who in 1936 dedicated his *Collected Poems* to Æ). It was said that Æ shook out ideas in dazzling improvisation, and that each of his listeners carried away a spark to light his own fire.

Æ's wife, Violet, died in 1932 at 17 Rathgar Avenue and the following year, he sold the house, gave away most of his possessions and moved to London. He spent the remainder of his life travelling abroad and giving lectures. He died in Bournemouth on 17 July 1935 and his body was brought back for burial in **Mount Jerome Cemetery**, Harold's Cross, Dublin.

In *Hail and Farewell*, Æ's close friend George Moore depicts 'the multiplicity of the man and the variety of his talents'. A bronze bust of Æ by Jerome Connor was unveiled in Merrion Square in 1985.

Jonah Barrington
1760–1834

Jonah Barrington was born at Knapton near Abbeyleix, County Laois, 'the third son of a largely estated but not prudent family'. He spent his early youth living at his grandparents' mansion at Cullenaghmore, County Laois, where his ancestors had resided since the reign of James I.

One of Barrington's first Dublin addresses was a fine house in **Clare Street** which his father had purchased to facilitate the education of his children. They were educated by the famous schoolmaster of the day, Dr Ball of St Michael-a-Powell, **Ship Street**, and later by a private tutor from **Digges Street**. Mr Barrington Senior consented to be launched into the new scenes and pleasures of a city residence. He left a steward in the country to mismanage his concerns there, made up new wardrobes for the servants, got a fierce three-cocked hat for himself, and removed his establishment – the hounds excepted – to the metropolis. His mother had her coach regilted. Four black horses, with two postilions and a sixteen-stone footman, completed her equipage.

According to Jonah Barrington, many pleasurable and whimsical incidents happened to him and other individuals of the family in this house. Stranger things, however, happened in the house directly opposite where Captain O'Flaherty, a most respectable gentleman, lived with his wife and sons, as recounted by Barrington in his *Personal Sketches*. Mrs O'Flaherty had been sending Mr Lanegan, the children's tutor, to several apothecaries' shops to buy a very little rat poison in each, and when she had procured a sufficient amount, she added it to the unfortunate Captain's rice pudding. On his death, the coroner's verdict was 'Poisoned by Arsenic'. Mrs O'Flaherty escaped overseas and was never heard of again, while Mr Lanegan was sentenced to be hanged and quartered for a murder he said he did not commit. He was indeed hanged but when the Sheriff delivered his body to his mother, she poured warm brandy and water down his throat which revived him. He lived to recount the story and escaped to France to a monastery where he spent the rest of his days.

Barrington rejected the opportunity for a military, clerical or medical career and opted for law, which he studied at **Trinity College** and in London. On his return to Dublin, he lodged at a boarding house in **South Frederick Street**, run by a Mr Kyle, an ex-trooper and uncle of the Provost of Trinity College. Mrs Kyle had been a companion to Barrington's grandmother, and regarded Barrington as her own son. The guests at the boarding house consisted mainly of gentry, some of whom were eccentric, and they provided Barrington with constant entertainment by the different pursuits they adopted. One, a Lieutenant Johnson, was, according to Barrington, the ugliest man in Christendom. It was said of him that he need never fire a shot, since his countenance was sufficient to frighten the bravest enemy. Another was Lord Mountmorris whose duel with the Hon. Francis Hely Hutchinson at **Donnybrook** fair green was watched by Barrington from a safe distance (he did not wish to be involved with the coroner's inquest). There was no fatality, and Mountmorris returned to South Frederick Street.

Barrington married a silk mercer's daughter, with a large fortune, and lived at 12 **Harcourt Street** (now number **14**). The house had a bow window which afforded Lady Barrington a view into the garden of Lord and Lady Clonmel on the opposite corner. Mr W.J. FitzPatrick, in *The Sham Squire* (1866), recounts how 'Lord Clonmel occupied the house at the opposite corner, and Lady Clonmel affected to be much annoyed at this window overlooking their house and movements. Here Lady Barrington, arrayed in imposing silks and satins, would daily take up position and placidly commence her survey. Barrington was remonstrated with, but he declined to close the obnoxious window. Lady Clonmel then took the difficulty in hand, and with the stinging sarcasm peculiarly her own, said, "Lady Barrington was so accustomed to look out of a show window for the display of her silks and satins that I suppose she cannot afford to dispense with this." ' The window was bricked up, but today is back as it was.

3. 14 Harcourt Street, the home of Jonah Barrington and his wife. Note the bow window from which Lady Barrington used to keep watch on her neighbours.

In 1788, Barrington was admitted to the bar and served in the Irish Parliament from 1790 until its dissolution in 1800.

The Barringtons moved to 8 **Merrion Square East** (now number **42**). In his *Personal Sketches*, Barrington wrote, 'In 1793 I purchased a fine house in Merrion Square . . . and here I launched into an absolute press of business, perhaps justly acquiring thereby the jealousy of many of my seniors.' The same year Barrington became King's Counsel and was appointed to a sinecure in the Custom House worth a thousand pounds a year. He was appointed Judge of the Admiralty Court in 1798.

In *Sketches of Irish Political Characters* (1799), it was written of Barrington that, 'He does not rank high, either as a lawyer or a speaker, but he has great application, and consequently some business. As a speaker his manner is bold and daring, and to his intrepidity he owes his advancement.'

Barrington lost his sinecure, together with any advancement for his career, in 1800, by opposing the Act of Union. He was knighted in 1807. He went to France some years later to escape his creditors and was stripped of his office when it was discovered that he had misappropriated court funds. He died in Versailles aged seventy-four. Among his works, his three-volume *Personal Sketches and Recollections of his Own Times* (published 1827–32), are perhaps what he is best remembered for; they are an amusing and interesting account of the political and social life of late eighteenth-century Ireland.

Samuel Beckett
1906–89

'I can't go on and I can't get back.'
Beckett, letter to T. McGreevy, 14 December 1953

The second of two sons, Samuel Beckett was born in the fashionable County Dublin suburb of Foxrock in a fine Tudor-style house named **Cooldrinagh** in Kerrymount Avenue. Built by his father William Beckett in 1903, the house stands in spacious grounds. Some of the land has been sold since the family lived there, but the tennis court and larch trees which were there in Beckett's day are still to be seen.

There is some confusion as to the date of his birth, but Beckett liked to claim it was on Good Friday, 13 April 1906. 'My memories begin on the eve of my birth under the table when my father gave a dinner party and my mother presided,' Beckett wrote in his novel *Watt* (1944) which contains some biographical details. There was a great bow window in the room where he was born: 'It looked west to the mountains, mainly west, for being bow, it looked a little south and a little north necessarily, a little south to more mountain, and a little north to foothill and plain.'

In his works, Beckett recalls episodes from his childhood spent in Cooldrinagh and gives descriptions of his surroundings (*How It Is, More Pricks than Kicks, Malone Dies, Company, Molloy, The Calmative* and *Dream of Fair to Middling Women*). He describes the garden with its thrushes and blackbirds where 'the air thrills with the hum of insects', and the lush verbena clustered around the porch; and the summer house to which his father repaired on Sundays after his midday meal with his copy of *Punch*, a cushion and his little son. He remembered too the croquet lawn with its clicking of mallet and ball, and his beloved larches which he saw from his bedroom window.

4. Cooldrinagh, Kerrymount Avenue, Foxrock, County Dublin, the birthplace of Samuel Beckett.

Originally named 'Becquet', his ancestors came from France after the revocation of the Edict of Nantes in 1685, when many Huguenot families sought refuge in Ireland and elsewhere. The family was originally connected with the poplin industry, then changed to building and construction, in which Beckett's grandfather made a considerable fortune.

William Beckett was jovial and outgoing. His wife, May, who worked as a nurse before her marriage, was quite the opposite and was strict and not outwardly affectionate towards her family. She loved animals and kept dogs, hens and donkeys. Some of her dogs appear in Beckett's work. On Sundays, she used to take her two sons to the local Church of Ireland church in the Parish of **Tullow**, a few minutes' walk from Cooldrinagh, on **Brighton Road,** where the family had their own pew. The church bell could be heard from the Beckett home: 'Midnight struck, from the steeple of my beloved church' (*Molloy*). Beckett's brother was to become a deacon here years later.

At the age of five, Beckett went to school at a private kindergarten nearby which was run by two ageing German women named Elsner, whom he later immortalised in his novel *Molloy*: 'The Elsner sisters, were they still living?' Both boys learned music and it was to be a lasting interest with Beckett, his favourite composer being Schubert.

Beckett then attended Earlsfort House School, at 4 Earlsfort Place (now **63 Adelaide Road**). This was convenient as there was a train from nearby Foxrock Station direct to Harcourt Street Station, the terminus on the Dublin and South Eastern Line. Beckett would have used this line regularly during his time in Cooldrinagh. The pleasant scenery which the passengers were afforded from **Foxrock Station** is described in *Watt*, whilst **Harcourt Street Station** of Roman baroque style, designed by George Wilkinson in 1859 and closed in 1958, is mourned by Beckett in *That Time*, from his *Collected Shorter Plays*: 'All closed down and boarded up Doric terminus of the Great Southern and Eastern all closed down and the colonnade crumbling away so what next'. The building is now used for offices.

As a young boy, Beckett often went on long treks with his father in the Dublin mountains which are situated within walking distance of Cooldrinagh. Glencullen was a favourite spot where there were a number of small stone quarries. Beckett later remembered the musical clink of the hammers on the stone and mentions them in *Malone Dies*.

Leopardstown Racecourse, close to Cooldrinagh, still remains as described in *Watt*: 'The racecourse now appearing, with its beautiful white railing, in the fleeing lights, warned Watt that he was drawing near, and that when the train stopped next, then he must leave it.' Horse racing is held here regularly. The racecourse was also the venue in 1910 for the first aviation meeting in Ireland at which the four-year-old Beckett was present with his mother; the event is recorded in *Malone Dies*.

When he was thirteen, Beckett followed his brother Frank to Portora School in Enniskillen, County Fermanagh, where he remained for three years. Oscar Wilde had been a pupil at this school. Beckett was a natural athlete and excelled in all sports. In his first term he won a place on the cricket team, and by the time he had reached his last year he was the star bowler. During the holidays, the brothers were encouraged to take part in tennis, cricket and swimming. By the age of twelve, Beckett had won all the neighbouring junior tennis competitions. For swimming their father took them to **Forty Foot** bathing place in Sandycove, which is immortalised in James Joyce's *Ulysses*. It was expected of the boys that they should dive in to the deep dark water from the high diving board. 'You stand at the tip of the high board. High above the sea. In it your father's upturned face. Upturned to you. You look down to the loved trusted face. He calls to you to jump. He calls, Be a brave boy' (*Company*).

In 1923, Beckett entered **Trinity College,** where he obtained a BA degree in modern languages. He taught for a while, and travelled in France, where he met James Joyce, and then on to Germany. He then lived for a time in London before returning to Dublin where he received his MA degree. After his years travelling, he produced his first novel, *More Pricks than Kicks*, in 1934.

At this time, in the early thirties, he was living on the top floor of his father's office at **6 Clare Street**. He wished to be away from Cooldrinagh, where certain family tensions constantly affronted

5. Number 6 Clare Street, the former office of Beckett and Medcalf. It was in a garret here that Samuel Beckett wrote his first novel *More Pricks than Kicks* and much of his later novel *Murphy*.

11

him, and he wrote much of his novel *Murphy* here in his Clare Street refuge. This address appears in *More Pricks than Kicks* and *Murphy*. A number of places around here and the city centre appear in Beckett's works, such as **Greene's Bookshop**, also in Clare Street, **St Stephen's Green**, and Kennedy's Bar nearby in **Westland Row** which features in *More Pricks than Kicks*.

For the next twenty years, Beckett lived mainly in Paris, returning to Ireland on frequent visits. His health was never robust, despite his athletic youth, and on his return to Ireland it became worse. This aspect of debility is reflected by some of the characters in his works. They live in dustbins and are half-buried in the sand; some of them are blind, some are legless, some are invalided and others, like the unfortunate members of the Lynch family portrayed in *Watt*, have nothing going in their favour at all as regards health.

Beckett was on a visit home in 1939 when war broke out. He returned, nevertheless, to Paris, preferring 'France at war to Ireland neutral'.

'Away to hell out of it all and never come back!'

On his return to Paris he joined the Resistance following the murder of some of his Jewish friends. He and his wife Suzanne fled to the South of France where they remained until the end of the war. Here he wrote his novel *Watt* which he said was an exercise 'to keep my hand in'. It contains many references to his childhood in Ireland.

Beckett was presented with the Croix de Guerre by General de Gaulle in 1945 for his work with the Resistance. He then returned for a brief visit to Ireland to see his mother who was ill. He walked down the **East Pier** in **Dun Laoghaire** where he had a revelation in which the whole course of his literary life unfolded before him. He inserted part of this in *Krapp's Last Tape* where Krapp walks down a similar pier at the end of March in the howling wind: 'Intellectually a year of profound gloom and indigence until that memorable night in March, at the end of the pier, in the howling wind, never to be forgotten, when suddenly I saw the whole thing.' Further along the coast road going southwards past Sandycove are Coliemore Harbour, Dalkey Island and Killiney beach, all of which feature in *Malone Dies*.

With a group from the Irish Red Cross, Beckett returned to France on a mission to St Lô. Then he went on to Paris and in 1946 entered his most productive period, writing some of the most original and haunting prose of the century. This included his trilogy consisting of *Molloy*, *Malone Dies* and *The Unnamable*. His most famous play, *Waiting for Godot*, was written in 1948, the two acts of which were neatly summed up by the critic Vivien Mercier thus: 'Nothing happens, twice.'

6. The anemometer on the East Pier, Dun Laoghaire, on which Beckett is commemorated by a plaque.

Beckett's mother died in August 1950 in the Merrion Nursing Home at **21 Herbert Street**. This is recorded in *Krapp's Last Tape*: 'There is of course the house on the canal where mother lay a-dying, in the late autumn, after her long viduity.' Not far away at **19 Lower Mount Street** was the Elphis Nursing Home which features in *More Pricks than Kicks* and further up the Grand Canal, going west, was the former Portobello Nursing Home which appears in the poem 'Enueg'. Some asylums feature in Beckett's works, but they are outside the city area, such as St John of God's in Stillorgan and Portrane in north County Dublin.

Waiting for Godot was produced in Dublin in 1955 in the **Pike Theatre, Herbert Lane**. In 1956 Beckett wrote his play *Endgame*. He received a Doctorate in Literature, *honoris causa*, from Trinity College and in 1969 was awarded the Nobel Prize for Literature for 'his writing, which – in new forms for the novel and drama acquires its elevation from the destitution of modern man'.

Beckett died in 1989 and is buried in Montparnasse Cemetery, Paris.

To get to **Foxrock**, take the number 86 bus from Fleet Street.

Brendan Behan
1923–64

Brendan Behan, one of the most successful Dublin playwrights of this century, was born in **Holles Street Hospital**, on 9 February1923. The son of Stephen and Kathleen Behan (née Kearney), he had two stepbrothers, Rory and Sean Furlong, from his mother's first marriage. His father was an intelligent man who had studied for the priesthood but changed his mind and became a tradesman. He worked as a housepainter, a job at which he earned enough to keep his family in modest comfort.

7. Brendan Behan.

The Behans lived at number 14 (now demolished) in **Russell Street** off the **North Circular Road,** near Mountjoy Square. The house was rent-free as it was one of the five houses which was owned by Brendan's grandmother, Mrs English, who lived nearby in **Fitzgibbon Street** where she owned a large Georgian tenement. The good-looking, blue-eyed, dark-haired boy was a firm favourite with her. Though not an invalid, she chose to spend most of her time in bed. Brendan ran errands for her which included bringing jugs of porter from the local pub, of which she gave him a sip now and then. She also gave him the odd swig of whiskey, even though it made him slightly tipsy, under the pretext that it would cure him of his worms. This could have been the first step to his later problem with alcohol.

Brendan's education started in his home at an early age. An atmosphere of culture and learning pervaded the household with the father reading to his sons at bedtime extracts from Swift, Dickens, Zola and Pepys. His mother played her part also, bringing her sons on walks through the city and showing them the houses where famous writers and patriots had lived.

When he was aged six, Brendan went to St Agatha's School in **North William Street**, where Sister Monica, the Superior, advised his mother that she was 'rearing a genius'. He then attended St Canice's, the Christian Brothers School on the North Circular Road where he finished at the age of thirteen, deciding to take up housepainting like his father. As he said later, 'After all, I was almost born in a paint-pot.' He became an apprentice at **Bolton Street Technical School**.

In the mid thirties the Behans moved house across the Liffey to **70 Kildare Road** in Crumlin. On and off he was to spend the next twenty years at this address. With his strong Republican family background, Behan became a member of Fianna Eireann and contributed poetry and prose to its magazine, *Fianna: the Voice of Young Ireland*. While still in his early teens, he was arrested in Liverpool while in possession of explosives and was sentenced to three years' borstal detention. He was released in December 1941 and returned to Dublin where he expected a hero's welcome. This did not materialise.

Behan did not have his freedom for long. Following an incident in Glasnevin, after a commemoration of the Easter Rising, he was sentenced to fourteen years' penal servitude. He served his sentence in **Mountjoy**, **Arbour Hill** and the **Curragh Camp**. He wrote his first play, *The Landlady*, in Mountjoy Gaol and had his article titled 'I became a Borstal Boy' published by Sean O'Faoláin in the *Bell*, a literary magazine. During his internment which lasted five years, after which he was released under a general amnesty, he studied the Irish language and became a fluent Irish speaker. He wrote the first version of his play *The Hostage* and started on *Casadh Súgáin Eile* (later to become *The Quare Fellow*). On his release, he went to the Irish-speaking areas of the Galway and Kerry Gaeltachts and wrote poetry.

By the late 1940s, Behan had become well known as a Dublin character. He frequented pubs such as **McDaid's** in **Harry Street** off Grafton Street, and mixed with the literary set whom he met in a basement, known as the Catacombs, in **Fitzwilliam Place**. He hoped he might establish the necessary contacts to have his work published and thus achieve his much desired recognition in Dublin. A brawl outside the Pearl Bar in **Fleet Street** resulted in a brief period back in **Mountjoy Gaol** after which Behan left for Paris where he worked for two years. In 1950 he returned to settle in Dublin and made his living by writing. He wrote radio scripts and a newspaper column and was beginning to be accepted as a writer in Dublin.

In 1954, *The Quare Fellow* was produced in Dublin's tiny **Pike Theatre** in Herbert Lane, where it had a tremendously successful run for six months, making Behan's name as a dramatist. The following year he married Beatrice Salkeld at St Andrew's Church in **Westland Row**. Their first home was in the garden flat at **18 Waterloo Road** from where they moved to **15 Herbert Street**.

In May 1956, Joan Littlewood produced *The Quare Fellow* at the Theatre Royal, Stratford East, London, where it ran for three months. It was a resounding success and brought international fame to Behan. Two years later *An Giall* (*The Hostage*) was produced at the **Damer**, Dublin's Irish-language theatre, and the same year his finest work, his autobiographical novel entitled *The Borstal Boy*, was published. The last of Behan's homes was at **5 Anglesea Road, Ballsbridge**. He could no longer manipulate the media and his long drinking bouts, coupled with his diabetic condition, finally killed him. He died in the **Meath Hospital, Heytesbury Street**, on 20 March 1964 and is buried in **Glasnevin Cemetery**. His funeral is said to have almost equalled that of Charles Stewart Parnell's in size.

George Berkeley
1685–1753

George Berkeley, philosopher and master of English prose, was born on 12 March 1685 at Dysart Castle, on the river Nore near Thomastown in County Kilkenny. The castle is now a ruin. He was the son of William Berkeley, and his mother (maiden name unknown) is said to have been the great-aunt of the famous general, Wolfe.

8. George Berkeley, Bishop of Cloyne.

In 1696, he entered Kilkenny College which had been founded in 1538 by the Earl of Ormonde. Jonathan Swift and William Congreve had been pupils at the college before him, and Thomas Prior, who later founded the Royal Dublin Society, was a contemporary who became a lifelong friend.

In 1700, Berkeley matriculated at **Trinity College** where he went on to study classics, Hebrew, logic and theology. He obtained his BA degree in 1704. At this period he became interested in the philosophy of Locke which had been introduced to Dublin by Molyneux and with a few of his friends he formed a society for the discussion of the 'new philosophy'. In 1707 he obtained his MA degree and was admitted to a fellowship at Trinity College.

In his youth Berkeley was a handsome man of great strength. A story from his college days refers to the fact that he once went to see a man hanged. On his return, he persuaded his friend, Contarini, Goldsmith's uncle, to hang him experimentally. He was cut down when nearly senseless and, on recovering, exclaimed, 'Bless my heart, Contarini, you have rumpled my band!'

In 1709, his classic *Essay towards a New Theory of Vision*, which he dedicated to his friend Sir John Percival, appeared and *A Treatise concerning the Principles of Human Knowledge* followed. During his years at Trinity, between bouts of writing, when his output was large, he held several different jobs, including those of tutor, lecturer, Junior Dean and librarian. He worked as librarian when plans were underway for the new library designed by Thomas Burgh. This library was constructed between 1713 and 1732, and now houses the Book of Kells. This building is now known as the Old Library.

In 1713 Berkeley visited England where he met Joseph Addison, Alexander Pope and John Arbuthnot. He was warmly received by his fellow countryman, Richard Steele, and contributed papers to the *Guardian* which was then under the latter's editorship. Swift did everything possible to assist Berkeley and introduced him to Lord Peterborough whom he accompanied as chaplain when Peterborough was appointed ambassador to the King of Sicily. Berkeley returned to Ireland in 1723 when he was granted the Deanery of Dromore and later that of Derry.

On her death in May 1723, Hester Van Homrigh (Swift's Vanessa), provoked by Swift's rejection of her, left Berkeley half her property, having previously, it is said, accorded it in her will to Swift. She had only met Berkeley briefly on one occasion.

Before leaving for America in 1728, Berkeley married Anne Foster, daughter of John Foster, Speaker of the Irish House of Commons and Lord Chief Justice. He chose her for the fine qualities of her mind and 'her unaffected inclination to books. She goes with great cheerfulness to live a plain farmer's life and wears stuff of her own spinning wheel.' He went to America in an unsuccessful attempt to found a missionary college in Bermuda. He and Anne lived in Newport, Rhode Island, one of the principal cities of the Colonies. Their intention was to remain here for three months before going to Bermuda, but having failed to receive the aid promised towards the establishment of the college, they returned to London in 1732.

On 19 May 1734, he was consecrated Bishop of Cloyne in **St Paul's Church, North King Street**, in Dublin. In 1697 this had been created a parish from part of St Michan's, the only city parish on the north of the Liffey for six hundred years. St Paul's was rebuilt in 1824 in the Gothic style. It was closed in 1987 and is now used for other purposes.

Berkeley spent most of the next eighteen years in Cloyne, County

Cork, with the exception of a visit to Dublin in 1737 to attend the House of Lords (now the Bank of Ireland) in College Green. In Cloyne, he established a spinning school, encouraged local handicrafts and helped the poor. During this period he wrote *The Querist* which dealt with questions of social and economic reform and *Siris* which concerned the merits of tar-water. Berkeley was deeply concerned about the amount of misery and sickness in the Cloyne area at the time and, from various experiments which he carried out, he found tar-water extremely beneficial for a variety of ailments. It became an instant success.

In 1752, Berkeley retired to Oxford where he died on 14 January 1753. He was buried in Christ Church, Oxford. Berkeley was described by his friend Percival as 'a man of noblest virtues, best learning I ever knew'.

John Betjeman
1906–84

> Bells are booming down the bohreens,
> White the mist along the grass.
> Now the Julias, Maeves and Maureens
> Move between the fields to Mass.
> 'Ireland with Emily'

John Betjeman was born in Highgate, London, on 28 August 1906. Of Dutch ancestry, he was the only child of Ernst and Mabel Bessie Betjemann (he later dropped the final 'n'). His early education started locally at Highgate Junior School where one of his teachers was T.S. Eliot. They later became friends in the 1930s.

John's education continued when he boarded at Dragon House School in Oxford. His first published poems appeared in the school magazine, *The Draconian*. Marlborough College in Wiltshire followed, where his contemporaries included the poet Louis MacNeice and the art historians Anthony Blunt and Ellis Waterhouse. In 1925, while still at school, John won the Furneaux Prize for English Verse.

In the autumn of the same year, he entered Magdalen College, Oxford, where he made many interesting and influential friends including the poet W.H. Auden. His tutor in English literature was C.S. Lewis, for whom he had no liking. He mixed with the aristocracy and it was through the introduction of another friend, Lionel Perry, that he met Lord Clonmore, son of the seventh Earl of Wicklow. As a result John stayed as a guest at Shelton Abbey, the seat of the Earls of Wicklow, situated two and a quarter miles from Arklow town on the north bank of the Avonmore river in County Wicklow. This was a magnificent demesne known for its rhododendrons. The house was designed in Tudor style by Richard Morrison (1767–1849). It is now an open prison.

Betjeman also spent vacations with other Oxford friends who lived in Ireland, such as Lord Dufferin in Clandeboye, County Down; the Packenhams in Tullynally, County Westmeath; and Pierce Synnott in Furness, Naas, County Kildare.

Betjeman's childhood, schooldays and college days at Oxford are delightfully recounted in his blank-verse autobiography, *Summoned by Bells*, which was published in 1960.

On leaving Oxford without a degree, Betjeman taught for a short period both at Thorpe School at Gerrard's Cross and at Heddon Court in Hertfordshire. In 1929 he worked as Private Secretary to Sir Horace Plunkett, the politician and agriculturalist who founded the cooperative movement in Ireland to assist with the development of farming. In his diary during this time, Plunkett noted, 'Working in JB is the thing that matters most. The whole trouble is that he cannot concentrate on anything. He reads a bit of agricultural cooperation stuff and then writes a poem or a story which comes much easier than my dull drab toil.'

During the next decade, Betjeman had various jobs. In 1930 he was assistant editor of the *Architectural Review* magazine. This was not a highly paid job but it gave Betjeman the opportunity to indulge himself in the study of old buildings and churches, an interest he had had since his schooldays when, during holidays, he used to cycle around Cornwall exploring churches.

Betjeman's first collection of verse, *Mount Zion*, was published in 1931. In 1933 he married Penelope Chetwode, daughter of Field Marshall Lord Chetwode. The couple moved from London to Uffington in Berkshire which he later commemorates in a poem of that name in his collection *High and Low* (1976). In the late 1930s he worked as film critic for the *Evening Standard*.

When war broke out in 1939, many of his friends joined the forces. Betjeman applied for a job with the Royal Air Force but was unsuccessful, and instead obtained a post with the Ministry of Information in the Films Division.

In 1941 he was posted to Dublin as Press Attaché to Sir John

Maffey in the British Embassy, and remained there until 1943. He later recalled, 'I can't tell you what I was supposed to be doing. It was of no importance, but I had to sign a form saying I'd never divulge anything.' His office was situated at **50 Upper Mount Street**. For the first six months, he and Penelope and their young son Paul lodged at Dunsinea House in **Castleknock** five miles from the city centre and adjacent to the **Phoenix Park**. The house was built by Henry Rathborne in the early nineteenth century. (It now houses the National Food Centre run by Teagasc.)

M.J. MacManus, the Literary Editor of the *Irish Press*, gave Betjeman a car on long-term loan which he drove around viewing property to find a suitable place to settle. In July 1941 the family rented Collinstown House, a large and elegant Georgian mansion near **Clondalkin** in County Dublin. The house belonged to Major Kirkwood, and was formerly known as Collinstown Park. Clondalkin is four and a half miles south-west of Dublin, a picturesque inland village with a tenth-century round tower. At the time, it was in lovely countryside with peaceful winding lanes – idyllic riding country for Penelope who had brought her fine white Arab horse, Moti, with her. Sadly, Collinstown House has since been demolished for a housing development and the area has lost its former rural charm.

The entertaining of distinguished visitors to Ireland was included in Betjeman's work brief but he went far beyond the bounds of any official expenses and many visitors received lavish hospitality at Collinstown House. Notable guests included Leslie Howard, Beverley Nichols and Laurence Olivier, who was engaged in the filming of *Henry V*. The scene for the Battle of Agincourt, which involved one hundred and sixty-five horses used as war steeds mounted by chain-mailed, steel-helmeted soldiers, was shot in the lovely grounds of **Powerscourt Demesne**, Lord Powerscourt's house at **Enniskerry**, County Wicklow.

Many of Betjeman's friends in Dublin were Anglo-Irish, including those he had met during his days at Oxford. His greatest friend was perhaps the poet Geoffrey Taylor, who collaborated with him to produce an anthology of *English Landscape Verse* (1944) and *An Anthology of English Love Poems* (1957). Taylor was poetry editor of the *Bell* which had its offices at **14 Lower O'Connell Street**.

In the Dublin pubs, Betjeman met his friends among the newspaper editors and literati of the time, including Sean O'Faoláin, founder and editor of the *Bell*; short-story writer Frank O'Connor; and Patrick Kavanagh who wrote the lovely poem

'Candida', for Betjeman's baby girl on her first birthday. Candida was born in September 1942 in the **Rotunda Hospital**.

9. John Betjeman (*second from right*) and friends near the Palace Bar, Fleet Street. His wife Penelope is driving her white Arab, Moti, and sitting beside her is R.M. Smyllie, editor of the *Irish Times*.

Along with his many other duties, Betjeman contributed reviews to the *Dublin Magazine* founded by the poet Seumas O'Sullivan. It and the *Bell* were the longest-running and most celebrated literary magazines in Ireland.

Betjeman's passionate interest in architecture and churches continued. With others including the late H.G. Leask, T.J. Cullimore and Eleanor Butler (later the Countess of Wicklow), he was involved with the rescue and recovery of several hundred drawings by Francis Johnston (1761–1829), of whose work he was a great admirer. Johnston had been chief architect to the Board of Works in 1811, and designed the General Post Office on **O'Connell Street** (formerly Sackville Street), St George's Church in **Hardwicke Street**, and numerous other churches and country houses.

Betjeman wrote only a small amount of poetry about Ireland, but it was certainly the inspiration for some of his finest verse. 'Sir John Piers', published in *Old Lights for New Chancels* (1940), was the result of an earlier visit in the 1930s; concerning the Anglo-Irish peerage, this poem was first published in 1938 in the *Westmeath Examiner*, under the pseudonym of Epsilon. It is topographical, like many of Betjeman's poems, and is set in the misty lakelands of County Westmeath. 'Ireland with Emily' was published in *New Bats in Old Belfries* (1945). The Emily referred to in the title was Emily, Lady Hemphill, the beautiful American heiress and brilliant horsewoman, who was married to Lord Hemphill and lived at Tulira Castle, the former home of the playwright Edward Martyn, near Ardrahan in County Galway. She became a friend of the Betjeman family. On a visit to Tulira, John and Emily went on a bicycle ride which John recounts in the poem:

> Has it held, the warm June weather?
> Draining shallow sea-pools dry,
> When we bicycled together
> Down the bohreens fuschia-high.

Other poems with an Irish connection include 'An Impoverished Irish Peer' (*Continual Dew*), 'The Irish Unionist's Farewell to Greta Hellstrom in 1922' (*New Bats in Old Belfries*) and an 'Ode to the Gaiety Theatre'.

Betjeman learned the Irish language and signed some of his books Sean Betjeman or Seán O Betjemán. He was extremely popular and well liked and did much to promote and encourage Anglo-Irish cultural relations. When his term ended in 1943, he received a signed photograph from President Eamon De Valera. His departure was reported on the front page of the *Irish Times* and the accompanying article said that Betjeman took the highest view of his duties as Press Attaché and looked upon it as a duty not only to interpret England to the Irish but also to interpret Ireland sympathetically to the English. He wandered far from the narrow service to which diplomats usually confine themselves and he made friends with writers, poets, newspapermen and clergy. He was at home in every milieu, from the Architects' Society to Maynooth College, from the Society of Antiquaries to the Gate Theatre.

Betjeman was elected to the **Kildare Street Club** as an overseas member in October 1943, a month after he left Ireland.

He was knighted in 1969 and in 1972 was appointed Poet Laureate. In July 1975 he was awarded an honorary D.Litt. by the Senate of the **University of Dublin (Trinity College)**.

Betjeman died on 19 May 1984 in Trebetherick, Cornwall, and is buried there in the churchyard of St Enodoc's.

23

Isaac Bickerstaffe
1735?–1812

Isaac Bickerstaffe, dramatist, was born in Dublin. At the age of eleven he was appointed as one of the pages to the witty Lord Chesterfield, then Lord-Lieutenant of Ireland. During the years of his viceroyalty, 1744–7, Chesterfield left his mark on the **Phoenix Park** by building a new road through it and planting numerous trees. The **Phoenix Column**, which he erected, was recently restored to its original position.

Lord Chesterfield obtained a commission for Bickerstaffe in the marines and in 1755 he went to London where, in addition to his regular duties, he produced many successful comedies. *Leucothoe*, his earliest work, was printed in 1756. His comic opera, *Love in a Village*, which contains the well-known song concerning the Miller of Dee, was produced at Covent Garden in 1762. The music for it was composed by Thomas Augustine Arne, one of the foremost musicians of the London theatre scene in the mid eighteenth century. This work – which has a claim to be the first comic opera – was printed in 1763, and has been included in Bell's *British Theatre* and other collections.

Two years later, *The Maid of the Mill*, founded on Richardson's *Pamela*, was published. This proved very successful in the theatre and ran for many years. Bickerstaffe was at his most prolific as a playwright in the period 1760–71 and had more than twenty plays produced by David Garrick. During these years, he enjoyed the company of some of the most famous men of the time. James Boswell recorded that on 16 October 1769, Bickerstaffe was one of the people who dined at his rooms in Old Bond Street with Dr Johnson, Sir Joshua Reynolds, Oliver Goldsmith and David Garrick.

In 1772, Bickerstaffe was involved in a scandal and was dismissed from his position as officer in the marines. He fled to France where he remained for many years in exile. He died destitute.

Dion Boucicault
1820?–90

The playwright Dionysius Lardner Boucicault, originally Boursiquot, was born at **47 Lower Gardiner Street**, in either 1820 or 1822. It is not certain who his father was – it could have been Dr Dionysius Lardner, known for his 134-volume reference work, *The Cabinet Cyclopedia*, or it could have been Samuel Smith Boursiquot, at one time his mother's husband.

Gardiner Street, where Boucicault was born, has early origins and appears on *Rocques Map* of 1756 as Old Rope Walk. Named after the Rt Hon. Luke Gardiner (1745–98), it was one of Dublin's most fashionable streets. It deteriorated after the Act of Union in 1800 when the rich and titled moved back to London and elsewhere.

Boucicault spent his earliest years in Dublin which were followed by his formal education in London. He worked for a short time as an apprentice in civil engineering, but left to join the theatre. His first successful play, a five-act comedy of manners entitled *London Assurance*, first appeared at Covent Garden in 1841 under the name of Lee Moreton, a pseudonym which he used both as an actor and playwright before eventually changing to Dion Boucicault. He then went to France where he adapted many French plays. His first wife, Ann Guiot, died mysteriously. He then married the actress, Agnes Robertson, and in 1852 they moved to America and toured extensively, where Agnes played the lead in five plays which he wrote for her. They acted together on the stage for thirty years.

Boucicault returned to Ireland three times, on occasion to find source material for his works. His play *The Colleen Bawn*, adapted from Gerald Griffin's novel, *The Collegians*, was produced in Dublin in 1861, after successful runs in New York and London. Boucicault was responsible for many innovations such as having the copyright laws in the United States changed to bring greater rewards for the playwright. He also started a touring company which brought professional theatre to remote provinces. He acted as manager, actor and playwright and created many lavish productions, and with his list of successful plays earned up to five million dollars during his lifetime.

In 1864 his play *Arrah-na-Pogue* was staged at the **Theatre Royal** in **Hawkins Street**. Henry Harris, patentee of the London Theatre Royal, opened this theatre in premises which had originally been occupied by the Royal Dublin Society. The building, which was completely remodelled by the leading theatre architect of the time, Samuel Beazley, was opened in January 1821 and it remained Dublin's main playhouse until the end of the nineteenth century.

Boucicault's play *The Shaughraun* was given its first production in Dublin in 1874, and he himself played the hero Conn. The play was then produced in New York in 1875 where it ran for one hundred and forty-three performances, earning him half a million dollars.

Boucicault was certainly the giant of mid nineteenth century theatre in the English-speaking world. He was a big spender and during the last years of his life lived in poverty in New York. He died there in September 1890. His funeral was held at the Little Church Around the Corner and he was buried in Mount Oak Cemetery, New Jersey.

Elizabeth Bowen
1899–1973

'Between the middle of Dublin and Herbert Place
lies a tract of Georgian streets and squares'

Elizabeth Bowen, Anglo-Irish novelist and short-story writer, was the only child of Henry Bowen and Florence (née Colley). She was born on 7 June 1899 at **15 Herbert Place**, Dublin 2. The street, once a quiet backwater, with only the sound of the trams going over the bridges in the distance, runs along the side of the Grand Canal from Lower Baggot Street to Warrington Place. Number 15, which has three storeys over a basement, is set in an elegant Georgian terrace comprising twenty-eight houses. Originally there were small rear gardens, each of which contained a mews or coachhouse leading on to a back lane.

Elizabeth spent her first seven winters here and always regarded it as her winter home. In the summer, the family moved to Bowen's Court, Kildorrery, in County Cork. Colonel Harry Bowen, an ancestor, had come to Ireland with the Cromwellian army in the middle of the seventeenth century and was given land in this area on which the ancestral home was built. The family returned to winter in **Herbert Place** in late October in time to 'see the leaves fall and lie clotted on the sleepy and dark canal'.

26

10. 15 Herbert Place, birthplace of Elizabeth Bowen and where she spent her first seven winters.

There was a saw-mill on the opposite bank of the canal, and during working hours its singing hum could be heard, wafting across the water with the scent of the new-planed wood. Barges plied their way up and down the canal and deposited logs at the timber yard. Apartment blocks now overshadow the canal and occupy the former site of the saw-mill.

It is interesting to note why Henry Bowen chose to live in Herbert Place in the first instance. Having studied law at Trinity College, he was more interested in following a profession than acting as landowner of over eight hundred acres, much to the chagrin of his father, so he settled for the house in Herbert Place, and furnished it lavishly. In her book *Seven Winters*, Bowen recalls the furnishings in the drawing room, which contained Florentine mirrors, wreathed in spiked gilt leaves between which hung sketches in gilt frames. Sheraton chairs, tables and sideboards that had been the work of eighteenth-century Cork cabinetmakers occupied the rooms of roughly the same date. The family silver was divided between the winter and summer homes.

In *Seven Winters*, Elizabeth Bowen gives a powerful sense of period and an evocative picture of the Dublin areas she frequented at the turn of the century. She was taken on weekday walks by Miss

Wallis, who was her first governess. She dressed Elizabeth up in her gaiters (sometimes pinching her calves with her buttonhook) and her outdoor coat, with a cream silk scarf inside the collar which sometimes made it difficult to turn her head. They came down the ten granite steps from the house and walked up by the canal as far as **Leeson Street Bridge** and on the way passed **1 Wilton Place**, off Wilton Terrace, where the Vernons lived. Mr Vernon was a barrister and agent to the Earl of Pembroke and his son, Humphrey, was a friend of Elizabeth and taught her how to stand on her head.

Sometimes Miss Wallis and Elizabeth walked across **Baggot Street Bridge** to the Pembroke Township and to the lovely wide roads which she called the 'Red Roads', on account of the plum-red colour of the brick houses with their elegant porches, bow windows and gables. The names of many of these roads have military connections: there is **Waterloo Road**; **Raglan Road** is named after Lord Raglan, General in the Crimea; **Elgin Road** from James Bruce, 8th Earl of Elgin and Governor-General of India in 1861; and **Clyde Road** after Lord Clyde who relieved Lucknow. The houses in the area were built between 1846 and 1857. 'Between the mansions the roads ran almost empty, as though a premium were set upon walking there.' This area encompassed part of what was formerly the ancient district of Baggotrath.

The shopping was done in **Upper Baggot Street** which had a splendid selection of shops on either side and opposite the red-bricked Royal City of Dublin Hospital. These included green-grocers, fancy bakers and confectioners, grocers, newsagents, wine merchants, and victuallers with 'sweet dry sawdust' covering the floors. Across the roof lines of **Upper Baggot Street**, Bowen saw a timeless white sky – a sky for the favoured. She recalled that everything about it was classy – the shopkeepers' white overalls were chalky clean and everyone 'had not only manners but time'. The nearby residents made it their village. One side of Upper Baggot Street remains more or less as it was, the other has some modern office blocks replacing older buildings.

Elizabeth's second governess, Miss Baird, was more adventurous than Miss Wallis had been. She was attracted to the city and brought Elizabeth walking as far as **Grafton Street**. She liked **St Stephen's Green** with its lake and footbridge. They fed the ducks here and heard the trams running round outside the trees and railings. This park, one of Dublin's most popular landmarks, was opened to the public in 1880 through an Act of Parliament obtained by Lord Ardilaun. He had the swampy waste transformed into a magnificent park with lakes, lawns, a variety of trees, paths and wildfowl.

Nearby on St Stephen's Green was the **Shelbourne Hotel**, 'an architectural cuckoo', as Bowen described it. In her book entitled *The Shelbourne*, she describes this resort of elegance, a haunt of fashion: 'Celebrities frequented it; local genius did not despise its halls. Bright-plumaged guests from across the water mingled with Irish country families come to town. By the 1880s, all this was in full swing.' It was one big social whirl when the Castle season, a counterpart of the December to March season in London, based at the Vice-Regal Court, commenced. Dressmakers and milliners were kept busy when mothers arrived with their daughters – the vice-regal hospitality was lavish, with regimental balls taking place, and the marriage market brisk.

Bowen recalls the epoch when the first brass plate appeared on the doors of **Merrion Square** signalling the arrival of the professional classes to an area where formerly her Anglo-Irish progenitors had lived, gathering round their Parliament. The lawyers and doctors kept south Dublin witty and sociable and, as Bowen saw it, the post-Union exodus of the bright-plumaged people had not been followed by real decay.

The children she met at her weekly dancing classes at Molesworth Hall at **39–40 Molesworth Street** bore the surnames inscribed on these brass plates. Some of them came also from the 'Red Roads'. Sundays started with the family walking along the canal down to **St Stephen's Church** which was set like an island in the middle of **Mount Street Crescent**. Known as the Peppercannister, it was built in 1824. This fine neo-Grecian church faces down Upper Mount Street to Merrion Square. They went up the steps to the sound of the bells, Henry Bowen in his top hat, Florence with a fine-meshed veil drawn over her face, and Elizabeth attired in her white coat. Elizabeth could not read at the time and mouthed her way through the hymn verses, enjoying the feeling that something was going on. Soon after Sunday lunch, the family took the tram to **Clontarf**, changing at Nelson's Pillar (destroyed in 1966) in Sackville Street (now O'Connell Street), to spend the afternoon with Elizabeth's maternal grandmother Mrs Colley, who lived in a large Victorian house, **Mount Temple**, in **Clontarf**. Clontarf is where the famous battle was fought by King Brian Boru on Good Friday, 1014, which broke Danish power in Ireland.

During Elizabeth's seventh winter in **Herbert Place**, Harry Bowen suffered a nervous breakdown, and while he was being treated, Elizabeth and her mother went to live in England. A few years later he recovered but then her mother died when Elizabeth was aged thirteen. She was taken care of by her aunt Laura in Harpenden in England and was educated at Harpenden Hall School, Hertfordshire, and Downe House School, Kent. She generally spent her summers in **Bowen's Court**.

In 1918 Elizabeth moved to London and became friends with leading writers of the time, such as E.M. Forster and Virginia Woolf. In 1923, she married Alan Cameron and the same year her book of short stories, *Encounters*, was published. Over the next forty-five years she produced almost eighty short stories and ten novels. Her novel *The Last September*, published in 1929, is set in a 'Big House' during the Troubles of 1916–22 and is based on Bowen's Court.

On the death of her father in 1930 Elizabeth inherited Bowen's Court. She was later to publish a book of that name which was an account of the family's history from the mid seventeenth century until 1959 when she was forced to sell the ancestral home for financial reasons. It was later demolished.

In 1949 she was awarded an Honorary Doctorate in Literature by **Trinity College** and in 1956 Oxford awarded her the same degree. Her novel *Eva Trout* won an award from the Irish Academy of Letters in 1970, followed by the James Tait Black Memorial Prize.

Elizabeth Bowen survived her husband by twenty-one years and died in London on 22 February 1973. She is buried in Farahy Churchyard in County Cork, near the former site of her beloved Bowen's Court.

Henry Brooke
1703–83

Henry Brooke, novelist, dramatist and poet, perhaps best remembered for his novel *The Fool of Quality*, was born in Cavan. He was the elder of two sons of the Revd William Brooke, a clergyman and Lettice (née Digby), the daughter of Simon Digby, Bishop of Elphin, County Roscommon. Brooke received his early education at **Sheridan's Academy** in Dublin which was run by Dr Thomas Sheridan, the grandfather of Richard Brinsley and a friend of Jonathan Swift. Brooke entered **Trinity College** in 1720, and then studied law at the Temple in London, where he met Alexander Pope who later revised and praised his poem, 'Universal Beauty', published in 1735.

On his return to Ireland Brooke practised as a lawyer for a time. He married a young cousin, Catherine Meares from Mearescourt in County Westmeath. They were to have twenty-two children, only two of whom survived him.

Swift was impressed by Brooke's talent but advised him against devoting himself solely to literature. Brooke travelled between London and Dublin in connection with his work and when in Dublin resided at the fashionable **South William Street** which had been laid out in 1676. The Society of Artists resided in number 58 (now Assembly House) in the street in Brooke's time. Powerscourt House, which later dominated the street was built in 1771 for Viscount Powerscourt and has recently been sensitively converted into a shopping centre.

In 1739, Brooke's tragedy *Gustavus Vasa* was published. This play, based on events in the history of Sweden, was performed successfully in Dublin, as was his *Betrayer of his Country*, which was staged two years later. Brooke appears to have been one of the first managers of the *Freeman's Journal*, founded in Dublin in 1763 and published at that time at **St Audoen's Arch**. Various people paid Brooke money so that they would not be mentioned unfavourably or satirised in the newspaper.

Three years later, the publication of the first of five volumes of the *Fool of Quality* commenced. Brooke dedicated the first volume 'to the right respectable my ancient and well-beloved patron, the public'. When it was later republished by the Revd Charles Kingsley in 1859, the publisher remarked that, notwithstanding the defects of the work, readers would learn from it more of that 'which is pure, sacred, and eternal', than from any book published since Spenser's *Faerie Queene*.

Brooke retired to live at Cor-fada, or Long Field, in County Cavan, where his father's people had once resided. He was interested in agriculture, a subject on which he wrote numerous essays. Described as a little man, neat as waxwork, with an oval face, ruddy complexion, and large eyes full of fire, he died in Dublin on 10 October 1783.

Christy Brown
1932–81

Christy Brown, novelist, poet and artist, was born in the **Rotunda Hospital**, **Parnell Square**, on 5 June 1932. He was the son of Patrick Brown and Bridget (née Fagan) and one of twenty-two children, four of whom died in infancy. The tenth child in the family, Christy was baptised in the Rotunda Hospital as his mother was ill after the difficult birth.

Mr Brown worked as a bricklayer and though he nearly always had employment, there was poverty in the household due to the size of the family. They lived in the Dublin suburb of **Kimmage** at **54 Stannaway Road** which is off Sundrive Road.

When he was four months old, Christy's mother noticed that there was something wrong with him; he was almost totally paralysed and had no control over his body except of his left foot. She consulted doctors who considered him to be imbecilic and suggested that he be placed in an institution. She refused to believe them and there was no way she was going to let him leave home.

From a very early age Christy displayed a curious interest in his toes. One cold December day when he was aged five and propped up with pillows on the kitchen floor with the family gathered around, he saw his sister and brother, Mona and Paddy, writing on an old chipped slate. He was attracted to the chalk and suddenly reached out and grasped it from his sister's hand with his left foot. He gripped it tightly between his little toes and started to scribble on the slate. His mother noticed and within a year this remarkable woman, who was hard-working and industrious, and made all the children's clothes, had taught him the alphabet. She also taught him to read and write and the first word he wrote was MOTHER. He was later to say of his mother that she was a marvellous inspiration; with her natural intelligence and insight she understood him perfectly. He did not have to express what he was feeling, she just knew it by her instinct.

Christy could not communicate as he was unable to talk and being so disabled he did not go to school. When his brothers returned from school in the evening they took him out to play and he met the neighbouring children. He was pushed along through the various

32

roads in Kimmage in a rusty old boxcar with crooked wheels which they called his chariot. Sometimes they went to the nearby dump where the children collected cinders for the fire. This dump has been transformed into the large and beautiful **Eamon Ceannt Park**. On Sundays, sometimes they went to **Pussy's Leap**, an area on River Dodder just beyond **Templeogue Bridge**. Other times they went as far as the **Phoenix Park** and had a picnic in **The Hollow**. The boys would bring sandwiches and an old billy-can for making tea. When dusk fell they returned home.

As Christy's brothers grew older, they went off on their own and Christy would be left behind. He would sit at the kitchen window and watch his brothers and their pals play football on the road outside the house. They would wave to him and he would try to wave back but when he lifted his arm it would shoot out and bang against the window frame.

Christy was imprisoned in a world of his own. Being creative, he had a desperate urge to communicate. His mother saw that he was lonely and devised little pastimes for him such as writing stories from newspapers into old copy-books. She bought him paints and brushes and he started to paint with his toes and painting became an important part of, and a great love in, his life.

Mrs Brown became quite ill with the birth of Danny, her last child, and was detained in the Rotunda Hospital for a time. While she was there she worried about the eleven-year-old Christy. Katriona Delahunt, an almoner's student in the hospital, agreed to call and see him to put Mrs Brown's mind at rest. She encouraged Christy to enter a painting competition sponsored by a newspaper, which he won; she also arranged for him to visit Lourdes which left a lasting impression on his mind.

Shortly after this, Christy had a visit from Dr Robert Collis, the well-known paediatrician and playwright, who had had two plays produced in Dublin, *Marrowbone Lane* and *The Barrel Organ*. Some years before, Dr Collis had noticed Christy on his brother's back at a film show organised for some charity. He remembered the badly crippled little boy with the blue eyes and set out to find him. He had come to tell him about a new treatment for cerebral palsy and believed he could be helped. At this period Dr Collis was to become the most important figure in Christy's life apart from his mother. It was arranged that initially he would receive treatment at home. This consisted of an intensive programme of physiotherapy. The only room available was the kitchen and it proved to be too small. During the exercises, when Christy stretched out his leg, it would bang against the fire-grate, and when he turned round on his stomach his head would be under a chair and his legs beneath a table. Each time he lifted his head he would get a whack on it. So the resourceful Mrs Brown started to build a special room for Christy on a piece of waste ground in their back yard.

Christy was aged eighteen when he commenced work on his autobiography, *My Left Foot*. It was at this time that he started to attend the Cerebral Palsy Clinic which was located to the rear of the **Dublin Orthopaedic Hospital** in **Merrion Street**. He attended this for six years or more. During these years it moved into new quarters at **Bull Alley Street** and in March 1953 it moved to its own premises, **St Brendan's** in **Sandymount Avenue**. Christy's speech improved enormously from the treatment he received from Dr Patricia Sheehan, the speech therapist.

Collis helped Christy with his education as well as his physical coodination, and encouraged the creative aspect in him. Christy had spent hours and hours, day after day, trying to get his autobiography into shape. Realising that he needed some help, he wrote to the doctor: 'Dear Dr Collis, I'm trying to write a book. If you don't mind, please come and help me. Christy Brown.' The following day Dr Collis came to his house and offered to help. He brought books with him, spoke to Christy about literature and advised him about the techniques of writing. All this resulted in the publication of *My Left Foot* in 1954 when Christy was just twenty-two years old. This was a big achievement as it had been typed out with great effort and courage with the small toe on his left foot. Sadly, his father had died the year before its publication.

When Mrs Brown died in 1968 Christy was absolutely devastated. As a tribute to his mother, he wrote his lovely poem 'Only in your dying, Lady, could I offer you a poem'. He moved from the house at 54 Stannaway Road to live in a purpose-built bungalow which he had constructed next door to his sister, Ann Jones, and her husband and two young children. A special corridor linked both houses and Christy had his own art gallery. His house was named **Lisheen** and was situated in **Stoney Park, Rathcoole**, County Dublin.

Two years later in 1970, his extraordinary novel entitled *Down All the Days*, a fictionalised version of his autobiography, was published. This was an overnight success and became an international bestseller. It was translated and published in fifteen languages. He was now thirty-eight years old and a celebrity.

Christy's brother Sean hosted a party for him at his London apartment in Holland Park following Christy's appearance on the

David Frost Show in 1970. It was here that he met Mary Carr, a dental nurse who was to be his wife. On 6 October 1972 they were married in the Registry Office on **Kildare Street**, Dublin. Christy signed the register with his left foot. Their wedding reception was held in **Sutton** near **Howth** and their honeymoon was spent in the Bahamas. Christy called Mary 'the major miracle of my life'.

Christy published three volumes of poetry, *Come Softly to My Wake* in 1971 and *Background Music* and *Of Snails and Skylarks* in 1973. His novel *A Shadow on Summer* was also published in 1973 and this was followed by another novel, *Wild Grow the Lilies*, in 1976.

The couple lived in Christy's bungalow in **Rathcoole** for a time before moving in 1974 to Mab Cottage, Cliff Road, Ballyheigue, County Kerry. In September 1977 Christy wrote to his friend and former teacher, Dr Patricia Sheehan, 'While I'm not completely rusticated yet to the extent of chewing hay and counting how many eggs the hens lay each morning, I'm well on the way to becoming thoroughly culchified and very happy about it too. Absolutely no regrets about leaving the grey deadness and stultifying inertia of Dublin suburban living – in fact it's hard now for me to imagine I ever lived anywhere else but here, and of course Mary loves it, which makes it all the sweeter . . . Workwise I've never been more industrious, though still far from being totally chained to the typewriter; indeed, the scenery is so lovely it is often a distraction.'

In 1978 the Browns moved to England where they lived at Glastonbury in Somerset. Christy died here aged forty-nine on 6 September 1981. He is buried in **Glasnevin Cemetery**.

In 1989, Christy Brown's autobiography *My Left Foot* was made into a very successful film which was nominated for five Academy Awards, an historic achievement for an Irish film. Directed by Jim Sheridan, it won two Awards for its leading actors, Daniel Day-Lewis and Brenda Fricker, who played the parts of Christy and his mother.

Edmund Burke
1729–97

A bronze statue of Edmund Burke, statesman, orator and writer, stands in front of **Trinity College**. It was executed by John Foley and unveiled by the Prince of Wales on 21 April 1868.

11. Bronze statue of Edmund Burke outside Trinity College.

Edmund Burke was born on the north side of the river Liffey at **12 Arran Quay**. His birthplace has now been demolished and this whole area has been redeveloped. He was baptised nearby in the Church of Ireland **St Michan's** in **Church Street**.

Burke was the son of a mixed marriage. His father, Richard Burke, was a Protestant solicitor and his mother, whose maiden name was Nagle, was a Roman Catholic. Edmund was brought up in his father's religion. He attended the Quaker school in Ballitore in County Kildare which was run by Abraham Shackleton, a Yorkshireman. Burke formed a friendship there with Shackleton's son, Richard, which lasted throughout his life.

Burke entered **Trinity College** in 1743 and while there founded, with three others, a club for 'the formation of our minds and manners for the functions of civil society' which later became the College Historical Society. Burke was conferred with his Bachelor of Arts degree in 1748 and then studied law at the Middle Temple in London. His failure to be called to the Bar annoyed his father who cut his son's allowance. Burke enjoyed the theatre and attended the meetings of various debating societies, and during his years in London met a number of literary and artistic people who included Oliver Goldsmith, Joshua Reynolds, Dr Johnson and David Garrick, and along with these afterwards founded The Club (1763) which was sometimes known later as the Literary Club.

In 1756 he married Jane Mary Nugent, a Catholic and the daughter of his London physician. The same year he published *A Vindication of Natural Society* and the following year *A Philosophical Enquiry into the Sublime and the Beautiful*, which caught the attention of Dr Johnson and won Burke fame. In 1759, with Robert Dodsley, he founded the *Annual Register* to which he contributed for thirty years.

In 1761, Burke returned to Dublin as secretary to William Hamilton, the Chief Secretary for Ireland. During this time he befriended and encouraged James Barry, the Cork-born painter. He remained in the post for two years and before he left Ireland he composed an address to the King, listing the hardships endured by the Irish Catholics. He left this with a friend and fourteen years later it was sent to George III. It is said that this document did much towards reconciling the King to the first instalment of religious toleration in Ireland, although Burke's work on behalf of Catholic rights throughout his life was generally unsuccessful. He became secretary to the Marquis of Rockingham, the Prime Minister, and in 1765 was elected MP for Wendover and became a most distinguished orator in the House of Commons. Burke was tall, with good deportment and a marvellous air of command. (His humble origins, however, and lack of an aristocratic lineage were of no help to him at the start of his political career.)

In May 1768, he wrote to his friend Richard Shackleton, 'I have made a push with all I could collect of my own, and the aid of my friends, to cast a little root in this country. I have purchased a house, with an estate of about six hundred acres of land in Buckinghamshire, twenty-four miles from London, where I now am.' Burke was not a wealthy man and where he got the money to purchase such a property gave rise to some speculation concerning East India stock.

In 1774, Burke became MP for Bristol and his great writings followed on his speech on *American Taxation* in 1774, that on *Conciliation with the Colonies* the next year, and in 1777 *A Letter to the Sheriffs of Bristol*. In 1780 he lost his Bristol seat because of his support of free trade with Ireland and Catholic Emancipation.

In 1787, when Warren Hastings, the first Governor-General of British India, was impeached, Burke opened the proceedings with a speech that lasted four days. Hastings was acquitted after a trial which lasted seven years.

Burke's best known work, *Reflections on the Revolution in France*, appeared in 1790. His friendship with Charles Fox, the Whig statesman and orator, was terminated in a parliamentary debate in 1791 when Fox challenged his views.

Burke retired in 1795, and his son Richard succeeded him in the Commons. He predeceased Burke, who died at his home at Beaconsfield in Buckinghamshire on 9 July 1797.

Edmund Burke is commemorated in **Trinity College** by the Edmund Burke Theatre.

William Carleton
1794–1869

William Carleton, novelist, storyteller and interpreter of the Irish people, was born on 20 February 1794 in the townland of Prillisk, in the Parish of Clogher in County Tyrone. The youngest of fourteen children, six of whom had died before his birth, he was brought up among the Catholic peasantry, on a farm of only fourteen acres. Owing to the educational system at that time, his parents had received only limited education. In his autobiography, Carleton recalls that his father possessed a memory not merely great or surprising, but absolutely astonishing. He would repeat nearly the whole of the Old and New Testaments by heart, and was a living index to almost every chapter and verse in them. He spoke both Irish and English and as a narrator of old tales, legends, and historical anecdotes he was unrivalled. In his early youth, Carleton was surrounded by legends, lore, tales, customs, traditions and superstitions as the area where he lived was teeming with them. It was in his home, and from his father in particular, that he heard all the local lore. His mother Mary (née Kelly) had a good singing voice and when it was known that she would be singing at a wake, dance or festive occasion, people would travel miles just to hear her.

12. William Carleton from the portrait by John Slattery. He is leaning his elbow on a copy of his *Traits and Stories of the Irish Peasantry.*

Because of the Penal Laws, there were no schools where Catholics could send their children. As a result, Carleton was educated at various hedge schools which at that time were widespread. He was aged six when he started at the first one, which had three pupils. It was under the tutelage of Pat Frayne, who had been a 'poor scholar' in his youth. He appears as Mat Kavanagh in *The Hedge School.*

Carleton then studied under Dr Keenan of Glasslough and made considerable progress with his studies of the classics. His parents had in mind that he should be a priest, but after Carleton visited Lough Derg on a pilgrimage, he made a resolution never to enter the Church. Around this time he read Alain-René Lesage's *Gil Blas* which instilled in him a spirit of adventure and a desire to see the outside world.

In 1818 Carleton left Tyrone and walked to Dublin to seek his fortune. He arrived, with two-and-ninepence in his pocket, via the great road that led into **James's Street**, continued down **Thomas**

Street and turned left into Dirty Lane (now **Bridgefoot Street**). He lodged in a house at number **48** and describes in his autobiography an unforgettable night on which he shared a cellar with some of the city's beggars. One thing puzzled Carleton more than any another about them and that was the fluency and originality of blackguardism as expressed in their language.

During his wanderings around the city, Carleton stayed in various lodging houses and had many amusing experiences. With his money almost spent, his circumstances changed rapidly and at times he ran away from some of these. He stayed for a time at **4 Moore Street**, with a man named William Ridge, who was a mailcoach guard. Moore Street, a bustling area with street markets, runs from Henry Street to **Parnell Street**. At this address, Carleton met a Mr McDonagh, a fellow lodger and literary tailor. He was a thin little fellow with black hair 'who had a slight tinge of the gentleman in his appearance and manner'. McDonagh, who worked for thirty shillings a week with a master tailor, spoke fluently and considered himself a man of genius although he had never had any formal education. He approached Carleton to act as his amanuensis in writing his biography, in return for which he would pay for Carleton's lodgings. Carleton agreed and each Sunday for six weeks McDonagh dictated his story, which was composed of the same few facts repeated over and over again. In the meantime, Carleton was asked for his month's rent which was due. He reminded McDonagh who said he would settle the account, but bolted that night. Realising his circumstances, Carleton followed his example and bolted too!

Carleton's next stop was in **Mary's Lane**, which runs from **Church Street** to **Little Green Street**, near the city markets. He boarded here with Mrs Carson, a sagacious and calculating widow aged between thirty-five and forty. She had an eye for him and gave him preferential treatment over the six other lodgers. Every wish of his was anticipated, his word was law, and he found himself a free guest at her table. She had saved an amount of money and intended buying a property in either **Mary Street** or **Henry Street**. She tried her best to lure Carleton into marriage but he felt 'a very uncomfortable sense of degradation at the notion of being tied to such a woman' and decided to make good his escape. Before he managed to do so he was presented with a monstrous bill for all the meals he had been forced to eat under the pretence of hospitality (though he managed to abscond without paying it).

He then moved to lodgings in **Francis Street** which had on the premises a circulating library, and paid the rent in advance on condition that he could use it. Carleton read for twelve or sixteen hours every day and included several of Maturin's novels. He then decided to visit the novelist in his home in **York Street**. Carleton thought that Maturin, who was a thin man, not ill-looking, with good eyes, was dressed in a sloppy fashion. He had his slippers on and was wearing a loose cravat about his neck and a brown overcoat which was much too wide and large for him.

Carleton enjoyed the theatre and was a frequent visitor both to the **Crow Street** Theatre and the Theatre Royal in **Hawkins Street**, often spending his last shilling on a place in the upper gallery.

He tried to get a job as an assistant to a bird-stuffer. When he was asked what he intended to stuff the birds with, he replied, 'Potatoes and meal'. Needless to say, he did not get the job. He also wrote an enlistment application in Latin to the colonel of a regiment, who in turn dissuaded him. He then sought employment in **Peter Street** in Mr Kane's Classical Academy but was again unsuccessful. It was through Mr Kane, however, that he obtained some tutorships. He worked as a classical assistant at Mr Eustace's School in **Lower Buckingham Street**. Around this time he became a friend of William Sisson, the deputy librarian of **Marsh's Library** in **St Patrick's Close**. Carleton read for two seasons here, and claimed that during that time he never saw as many as half a dozen people reading there. Marsh's Library, designed by William Robinson in 1701 for Archbishop Marsh, is the oldest public library in Ireland.

In 1820, Carleton married Jane Anderson, whom he had met in one of Erasmus Smith's schools, in the parish of St Catherine's in **The Coombe**. On marriage he became a Protestant. The couple were not well off in the early years and lived with a family in **The Coombe**. They then moved to a home outside the city at **Dolly-mount**, on the coast road past Clontarf. It was a thatched cottage, or cabin, at a place called 'The Sheds'. On *Perry's Map of Dublin Bay and Harbour* (1728), 'The Sheds', which were used to cure fish, are marked in **Clontarf**. Those in Dollymount were probably used for a similar purpose.

While living here, Carleton had frequent visits from friends and from English visitors who had read and enjoyed his works. One such person was a Cockney, and Carleton later derived great joy relating the story about his dog and the Cockney. Carleton enjoyed going out on shooting expeditions along the strand between Dollymount and Howth, accompanied by his dog. On arrival at Carleton's house, the Cockney espied a gun and a dog in the house.

He enquired whether the dog would go with him on a shoot and Carleton replied, 'He will follow the gun, at any rate.' So off went the Cockney with the dog at his heels. Time passed, and Carleton became anxious, and eventually the dog returned on his own. Some time later the Cockney limped into the house and informed Carleton that the dog had bitten him. Carleton was concerned, and surprised that the dog would bite anyone. 'Did you have any sport?' he asked. His visitor replied, 'No.' He related how he had fired at some birds, and the dog went off to retrieve them, but none had been hit. The dog came back anything but pleased. When he fired a second time, the dog went off, and finding nothing again, came back growling. The third time he fired and the dog found nothing, he came back and took a piece out of the man's leg!

In 1827, Carleton met the Revd Caesar Otway, a Protestant clergyman and determined proselytiser who was co-founder of the *Christian Examiner*, a magazine associated with the established Church. Under the influence of Otway, Carleton contributed sketches of Irish country life to the magazine, including a description of his pilgrimage to Lough Derg. In 1830 the first series of *Traits and Stories of the Irish Peasantry* was published in two volumes. Carleton also wrote for the *Dublin University Magazine* and the *Nation*. He wrote several novels, the best of which include *Fardorougha the Miser*, *Valentine McClutchy* and *Black Prophet*. The year 1845 was the most productive period of his literary career.

In 1847, Carleton gave his address on a letter as 2 Clontarf Crescent, which would appear to be **2 Marino Crescent**, as given by his biographer D.J. O'Donoghue. (William Harrison, in his book *Memorable Dublin Houses*, cites the address as 3 Marino Terrace, Fairview, but this would seem to contradict the address given by Carleton.) Marino Crescent consists of twenty-six houses forming a crescent shape. It was while living there that Carleton was told the good news that he would receive a pension of £200 per annum, due to a petition sent to the government on his behalf by a group of people which included Maria Edgeworth.

Another incident worth mentioning occurred while Carleton lived here. One day, an elderly man called to the house. He said he was Collier, the famous highwayman, and he requested to see Carleton. 'Not professionally, I hope,' observed Carleton. Collier wanted Carleton to write his Life. He said he had given up robbing, and that although he had a bad name, he had never shed blood. Doubting his statement, Carleton declined his offer and Collier departed after a meal.

Carleton's next address was 1 **Rathgar Avenue**, in the well-to-do suburb of Rathgar. The house has since been demolished.

Carleton was a family man and loved being surrounded by his ten children. Later, he was deeply affected by the breaking-up of the family circle. At the close of 1854, when his favourite daughter Rose married, and went to join some of her married sisters in Canada, Carleton became depressed and expressed his feelings in a poem published in the *Nation*. Speranza, Lady Wilde, wrote to him, 'You give a meaning to the Irish character no other writer has done.' He was by then in financial straits as he was now supporting three families, which included the family of his eldest son and that of a married daughter. Around 1861 his health began to decline. He found it difficult to walk and his sight was failing. He was treated by his friend, Sir William Wilde, for cataracts.

Carleton's last address was 2 **Woodville**, on **Sandford Road**. Number 2 no longer exists and was approximately where numbers **83** and **85** now stand. The Ordnance Survey map for 1877 suggests it was a low, villa-type house with an extensive garden. It was close to the entrance of the Jesuit College, **Milltown Park**. Carleton was friendly with the Jesuits and also with the clergy from Sandford Church down the road. It was at Woodville in 1868 that he began in earnest to write his autobiography. This was to contain the general history of Irish literature, including everything connected with it, its

13. Grave of William Carleton, Mount Jerome Cemetery, Harold's Cross.

origin, its progress, its decline, and its natural and progressive extension. Unfortunately, this was never completed. Together with physical pain, Carleton suffered from mental anguish at the thought of leaving his wife and family in dire poverty. He had his dying wish come true when he heard that his wife would receive a pension of one hundred pounds per annum.

Carleton died on 30 January 1869 in his home at 2 **Woodville**. He was attended by the Revd Walsh and the Revd Leet of Sandford Church and was buried with his daughter Rose, who predeceased him by five months, at **Mount Jerome Cemetery**, then on the very fringes of a growing city, now at Harold's Cross.

Some time later, his family placed an obelisk over his grave with the inscription written by his daughter Jane. In time, his memorial fell into disrepair, and was restored by the William Carleton Memorial Committee. At the unveiling on 15 August 1989, Dr Benedict Kiely said in his oration that Carleton, as a novelist, had taken up the issues of tenants' rights, emigration and famine and had put down on record the Irish people as he remembered them before the famine, before they were practically wiped out. Irish people have not much changed, he said.

Austin Clarke
1896–1974

One of Ireland's most distinguished poets, Austin Clarke, was born on 9 May 1896 at **83 Manor Street**, Dublin 7. His birthplace is recalled in the first lines of his poem 'Mnemosyne Lay in Dust'.

> Past the house where he was got
> In darkness, terrace, provision shop,
> Wing-hidden convent opposite

He was the son of Augustine Clarke, an easy-going and generous man who worked for Dublin Corporation, and Ellen (née Browne) who was both strict and stern. He later wrote that 'in the years of adolescent mental struggle, I had felt motherless'. He was to have endless quarrels over religion with his mother. Only four children, Austin and three sisters, Mary, Eileen and Kathleen, survived from a family of twelve offspring. Austin was a delicate child and at the age of three was brought to the Children's Hospital in **St George's Place**, with threatened meningitis. In 1897, he was held up to see Queen Victoria on her visit to Dublin.

Manor Street, where he spent the first three years of his life, was originally included in the area known as **Stonybatter**, and probably comprised part of the ancient road from Tara to Wicklow, built in the second century, which crossed the Liffey at the ford of the hurdles. It was the main thoroughfare into Dublin from the north-west of the city. It was called Bothar-na-Gloch or the road of the stones.

In 1899 the family moved to **15 Mountjoy Street**, near the Black Church. Clarke's bedroom was in a front room on the first floor, and when the blinds were half-drawn at night, he could see the glimmer of the street lamp. The narrow, gloomy hallway of the house was afforded a certain grandeur by family portraits, a bust of Napoleon and a pheasant on the fanlight ledge. In the parlour was a glass chandelier, a painted fire-screen, a large cabinet and a piano. The house was recently demolished.

In the first volume of his autobiography *Twice Round the Black Church*, Clarke recalls his childhood in Edwardian Dublin. The 'gloomy edifice' in **St Mary's Place**, just round the corner from where he lived, and known to all the neighbouring children as the Black Church, held a strange fascination for him and became a central symbol in his poetry. After school the children from the

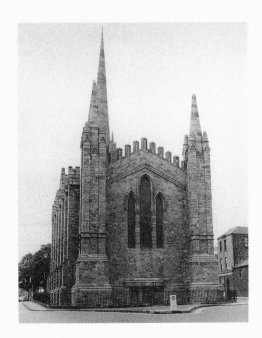

14. The Black
Church, St Mary's
place.

lane which ran parallel to **Mountjoy Street**, behind his house, scampered around the Black Church. But at night the area was deserted, disturbed only by the occasional footsteps of a passer-by or the sound of a horse cab. There was a story that anyone who ran round the church three times after dark would meet the Devil on the third round, but no one had the courage to try it. 'Always, when I came late at night with my parents from the south side of the city, it was an exciting experience to pass that terrible church in complete safety'. St Mary's no longer functions as a church.

While the Clarkes lived in **Mountjoy Street**, a bottle of stout was produced once a month on Sunday for the midday meal. This heralded a visit from his long-bearded grandfather Browne, who had a mysterious past. He had met Fenian conspirators in a grainstore loft in Thomas Street where Lord Edward had been arrested by Major Sirr at the beginning of the century. As a child, Clarke knew this old part of the city well, as he accompanied his sisters shopping in **Thomas Street**. They took various routes by the old city wall in **Cook Street**, past St Audoen's Arch and up by the distillery, returning by **Watling Street** or **Winetavern Street** to the Quays.

He was also familiar with the labyrinth of streets and little lanes close to his home, such as **Capel Street**, **Bolton Street**, **Eccles Street**, **Paradise Place** and **Granby Row**. On Sundays, the family usually attended **Berkeley Road Church**, which has an adjoining triangular plot containing a memorial to the Four Masters, the annalists of ancient Ireland. (*Annála Ríoghachta Éireann*, the *Annals of the Kingdom of Ireland*, were undertaken by a Franciscan friar, Micheál O'Cléirigh, and his three assistants between 1632 and 1636.) Sometimes Clarke went to mass in **St Saviour's Church** because he liked the white robes of the Dominicans. When the secular priests said Mass, he was distracted from his prayers by the glimpses of their black trousers and boots under the hem of the richly coloured vestments. He found it worse at Benediction, when the priest climbed the small stepladder to reach for the Monstrance.

Clarke attended three schools briefly, the Holy Faith School and the national school in **Dominick Street**, and the Christian Brothers' School in **St Mary's Place**, from which his parents removed him on account of the excessive corporal punishment used by the masters. He was then sent to **Belvedere College** in **Great Denmark Street**. According to the college records, he enrolled in 1905 when he was nine and remained at the College until 1912. He recounts his enrolment in the drawing room of the Jesuit house in **Gardiner**

Place, when the rector glanced at him sharply through his bifocal glasses and said, 'Tell me, Austin, what shape is the world?'

'Round, Father, like an orange.'

'And does it move?' he prompted.

'Yes, Father, round the sun.'

'Thou has conquered, o pale Galileo!'

In 1906 Clarke made his confirmation in St Mary's Pro-Cathedral in **Marlborough Street** and the following year, his first communion in **Belvedere College**. On Christmas Eve in 1909, Clarke went to the Volta, Dublin's first cinema, in **Mary Street**, which had been opened by James Joyce four days earlier.

In 1910, the family moved from Mountjoy Street to **2 St Alban's Terrace**, at **221 North Circular Road**. In his writings Clarke recalls how 'great miserable droves from the cattle market of Dublin passed our garden gate every Thursday on their way to slaughter in England and affected me in dreams'. Sean O'Casey and James Joyce also refer to this in their works. The market, which was situated on the North Circular Road, no longer exists.

For four years (1907–11) Clarke made his way every day to the **Rathmines** School of Music where he studied the violin and piano, often practising up to six hours daily. For a term he had a break with Belvedere College when he went to Mungret College in Limerick, but due to ill health he returned to Belvedere. His first known published article, concerning the annual school excursion, was published in *The Belvederian*, the school magazine, in 1912.

In 1913, Clarke went on his first visit to the **Abbey Theatre** to see *The Gaol Gate* by Lady Gregory. After that, he paid frequent visits to the theatre. The same year he entered **University College Dublin**, then situated at **86 St Stephen's Green**. On the way home, he usually took the back streets, crossing from Cuffe Street to Ship Street, Nicholas Street, past Christ Church, down Winetavern Street, over the Liffey Bridge to the Four Courts, along Smithfield, into Red Cow Lane, Grangegorman, and on to his home at St Alban's Terrace.

At college, Clarke was lectured in Anglo-Irish literature by Thomas MacDonagh and in Irish by Douglas Hyde. On the syllabus was the legend of Diarmuid and Grainne and his first book concerned this story. He was awarded a BA degree in 1916 and the following year was awarded an MA Degree with first-class honours in English. The same year, he replaced Thomas MacDonagh and lectured in University College Dublin for the next four years.

Encouraged by Æ (George Russell), Clarke published his first

long narrative, *The Vengeance of Fionn*, in 1917. It was received
with great acclaim. A couple of years later, he spent a brief spell in
St Patrick's Hospital, suffering from a nervous breakdown.

In 1920 the family moved from St Alban's Terrace to **10
Shanganagh Terrace, Killiney**. The same year Clarke married the
writer Geraldine Cummins. He forfeited his job in the University
because he was married in a registry office, and his marriage broke
up not long afterwards.

Clarke went to London in 1921, where he spent seventeen years
working as a professional reviewer writing for *The Times*, the
Observer and other newspapers and periodicals. *The Son of
Learning*, his first verse play, was performed in 1927 at the
Cambridge Festival Theatre.

It was on one of his visits home, in 1930, that Clarke met Nora
Walker, who was to become his second wife. Before he returned to
live permanently in Ireland with his family, he had produced what
he called his prose romances, *The Bright Temptation* (1932) and *The
Singing Men at Cashel* (1936). His *Collected Poems*, with an
introduction by Padraic Colum, appeared in 1936. Colum described
Clarke as a poet 'of the mid-Ireland, the Ireland between legend
and modern history'.

Clarke returned to Ireland in 1937 'determined not to become an
exile'. The family lived at **Bridge House** (now demolished), an
idyllic spot shaded by trees, on the banks of the river Dodder at
Templeogue Bridge. At that time, it was in the country, just on the
verge of the city, but it is now suburbia. The bridge was built about
1800; before that time, it was necessary to ford the river here.
Templeogue was once known for its spa. In its heyday it had its own
newspaper, *The Templeogue Intelligencer*, which reported on the
frolickings of the spa-water drinkers.

Clarke's mother had given him a life interest in Bridge House,
which he recalls in his poem 'Usufruct':

> This house cannot be handed down.
> Before the scriven ink is brown,
> Clergy will sell the lease of it.
> I live here, thinking, ready to flit
> From Templeogue, but not at ease.

The little bridge outside the house, which he mentions in the poem,
changed with the widening of the road. The new, wider bridge was
renamed to commemorate the poet.

Clarke often visited Seumas O'Sullivan, the poet and editor, who lived in nearby **Grange House**, Whitechurch in **Rathfarnham**, and he was within walking distance of his friend F.R. Higgins, who lived at **Lower Dodder Road, Rathfarnham**. He used to drink at the **Palace Bar** in **Fleet Street**, which was frequented by many other writers in the thirties, and later at the **Pearl Bar**. R.M. Smyllie, the editor of the *Irish Times* who started its Literary Page, and who presided over the Palace Bar's literary coterie, employed Clarke as a regular reviewer.

Clarke formed the Dublin Verse Speaking Society in the Peacock Theatre in 1941, the purpose of which was 'to save from neglect the tradition of verse drama left to us by Yeats'. The society moved to the **Abbey Theatre** in 1944 where it became the Lyric Theatre Company, continuing until the Abbey burned down in July 1951. Clarke also had a weekly poetry programme on the radio for a number of years.

Clarke published more than thirty works of poetry, drama, fiction and autobiography and received many awards for his literary work. In 1968 he was awarded the Gregory Medal by the Irish Academy of Letters. At the age of seventy, he was conferred with an honorary D.Litt. by the **University of Dublin** (**Trinity College**). The citation described Clarke as 'the outstanding literary figure in Modern Ireland'.

Austin Clarke died at his home in Templeogue on 19 March 1974. He is commemorated by the **Austin Clarke Library**, housed at Poetry Ireland, the Bermingham Tower, Upper Castle Yard, **Dublin Castle**.

Padraic Colum
1881–1972

'I told my poems, and as they say in stories,
The ford I found, they found the stepping stones.'

Padraic Colum was an outstanding character of the Irish Literary Renaissance. His life spanned almost a century, a period which he described as long enough to be historical. During his distinguished career, he was poet, playwright, biographer, novelist, folklorist and writer of children's books, but it is primarily as a poet that he is remembered.

Colum once said, 'I was born where waifs, strays and tramps

congregated. I heard stories before I could read them, and songs and scraps of poetry before I had to learn any at school.' The son of a Longford father and a Cavan mother, Colum was born on 8 December 1881 in the workhouse in Longford where his father Patrick was a teacher and the master of the workhouse. He was the eldest of eight children.

When Padraic was aged eight, his father lost his job and set off for the United States to join in the Colorado gold rush. His mother Susan moved with the children to live with her family, the Connollys at Grendard, Crossdoney in County Cavan.

When Patrick Colum returned from America after three years he got a position as Assistant Stationmaster at **Sandycove Railway Station**, Eden Road, in **Glasthule**, near Dun Laoghaire, and the reunited family lived in a cottage beside the station which is now

15. The Railway Cottage, Eden Road, Glasthule,
where Padraic Colum lived when his father was
Assistant Stationmaster at Sandycove Railway Station.

commemorated by a plaque. With his brother Fred, Colum attended the nearby Glasthule National School. After school, there was plenty for Padraic to do as he helped his father to deliver parcels which had been sent by rail to their various destinations in the big elegant houses of the neighbourhood. In his spare time he browsed around bookshops and explored the surrounding area of **Killiney** and **Dun Laoghaire** (then Kingstown). At the time, Kingstown, which got its name from King George IV who had disembarked there in September 1821, was an exciting and wealthy seaport town with several hotels, three yacht clubs, pavilion gardens and public baths. The town, which was lit by gas, had an electric tram service and railroad running through it.

Colum's mother died in 1897, and his father lost his job. The family temporarily split up, with the younger members returning to Longford where Padraic, who remained in Dublin, kept in close touch with them. Through them he kept in contact with rural Ireland where a lot of his work is set.

At the age of seventeen Colum finished school and got a clerical job in the Irish Railway Clearing House on **Kildare Street** in Dublin where he remained for five years. Over the next few years he moved around to various houses including **18 Longwood Avenue**, which is situated off the **South Circular Road** between Bloomfield Avenue and Clanbrassil Street. Padraic lodged here with his brother Donald from the late 1890s to the beginning of 1901, when they joined with their father and the rest of the family at **26 Rugby Road**, on the south side of the Grand Canal in **Ranelagh**. They stayed here until 1904, and then moved to **30 Chelmsford Road** in **Ranelagh** where they

16. Padraic Colum as a young man.

remained until 1909 when they moved to Bushfield Villa, **Bushfield Terrace**, off Marlborough Road. Approaching it from Sandford Road, it is the first turn on the left and the house is situated at the end of the road on the left-hand side. It stands alone. They stayed here until 1911 and then moved to 2 **Frankfurt Place, Upper Rathmines Road**. This consisted of two houses (now demolished) just before the turn into Highfield Road.

During these various house moves, Colum began to write and to meet people connected with the theatre, among whom were Yeats, Lady Gregory and Æ (George Russell). The best of his early poems appeared around this time in Arthur Griffith's paper, the *United Irishman*. These included 'The Drover', 'The Plougher' and 'The Poor Scholar' which were later included in his first book of poems, *Wild Earth*, published in 1907, and dedicated 'to Æ who fostered me'. Around the same time Colum produced a number of articles, plays and some beautiful poems which spoke of the land:

> Sunset and silence! A man; around him earth savage,
>   earth broken;
> Beside him two horses, a plough!
>
> Earth savage, earth broken, the brutes, the dawn-man
>   there in the sunset,
> And the plough that is twin to the sword, that is founder
>   of cities!

When Colum was twenty-two a wealthy American, Thomas Hughes Kelly, awarded him a four-year scholarship which enabled him to take up writing as a full-time career.

Broken Sail, Colum's first play (later rewritten as *The Fiddler's House*), was produced by the Irish Literary Theatre. Later, he wrote three of his earliest plays for the **Abbey Theatre**. One of them, *The Land*, was the first successful play staged by the Abbey, owing its popularity to the fact that it dealt with a highly topical situation, the transfer of land from landowners to the tenant farmers. By this time, at the height of the Irish Literary Revival, many playwrights were writing about the country people. 'It was back to the land, the language and the peasants.' Colum had an advantage here in that he was able to write about the situation with which the ordinary people were familiar. Æ wrote of him early in the twentieth century, 'He is in love with the normal. It is his quietly poetic treatment of the normal which has established his reputation in drama, as in poetry.'

Colum became a member of the Gaelic League, an immensely

popular movement at the time, which inspired many literary nationalists. Founded by Eoin McNeill and Douglas Hyde, its principal aim was to revive Irish as the national language through, among other means, the creation of a modern Irish theatre.

James Joyce had known Colum before he left Dublin for Paris in 1904 and they remained friends for many years. In 1912 Colum accompanied Joyce to the Dublin publishing house of Maunsel and Company (which had published the works of Colum, Synge, Shaw, Yeats and Lady Gregory) to negotiate the proposed publication of Joyce's *Dubliners*. The manuscript was rejected by George Roberts, one of the partners, as Joyce would not comply with some alterations that he requested. Joyce left Dublin the same night, and was provoked into writing his broadside 'Gas from a Burner' in which Colum is mentioned:

> Colum can tell you I made a rebate
> Of one hundred pounds on the estimate
> I gave him for his Irish Review,
> I love my country – by herrings I do!

In 1911, together with a few friends, who included Thomas McDonagh, and James Stephens, Colum founded a literary magazine, the *Irish Review*. Due to lack of funds it was short-lived, but during its brief existence published poems, plays, criticisms and reviews by some of the best writers of the time, such as Yeats, George Moore, Æ, Pearse, Gogarty, Corkery, Hyde, Seumas O'Sullivan and Lord Dunsany.

In 1912, Colum married Mary Gunning, also a scholar, whom he first met when she was a student at University College Dublin. She taught at Patrick Pearse's school, **St Enda's** in **Rathfarnham**, County Dublin (now a museum open to the public).

They moved into a brick house, **2 Belmont Avenue**, in **Donnybrook** which Mary recalls in her biography *Life and the Dream* as being 'dampish, largish, uncomfortable.' Here they held frequent parties and their famous Tuesday soirées to which the literati of Dublin used to come.

The Colums spent a short time in a cottage in **Howth** before they left for the United States in 1914 where they remained for the rest of their life together, with the exception of three years, 1930 to 1933, when they lived in France. They renewed their acquaintance with James Joyce in Paris, where Colum helped him by typing and making a few suggestions with his work in progress.

Colum wrote copiously, and both he and Mary taught part-time at Columbia University in New York. After her death in 1957, Colum divided his time between the United States and Ireland. When in Dublin he stayed with his sister at **11 Edenvale Road** in **Ranelagh** where he is commemorated with a plaque.

Apart from his plays he published sixty-one books, and various poetic broadsheets illustrated by Jack B. Yeats and published by the Cuala Press.

Padraic Colum died in Enfield, Connecticut, in his ninety-first year. Micheál MacLiammóir, a lifelong friend, paid him this posthumous tribute:

> Padraic Colum always found gold hidden under the road as well as at the foot of the rainbow. His image is before me as I speak these words: a short, sturdy figure with a face that, for all its smiling and eloquent friendliness, recalls the face of Dante. He was among the earliest poets of the Renaissance that grew out of Yeats' dreams: his lovely *Thomas Muskerry* was among the earliest and the finest of the older Abbey plays.

Colum is buried beside Mary in **St Fintan's Cemetery,** Sutton, near **Howth** in County Dublin. His grave is marked by a Celtic cross. Behind it rises Sheilmartin Hill and before it stretches the whole of Dublin Bay and the city of Dublin. In Æ's words: 'The Giant has come back to his mountain.'

William Congreve
1670–1729

William Congreve, dramatist and master of Restoration comedy, was born at Bardsey near Leeds in England in 1670. His mother's maiden name was Browning, and his father, William Congreve, was from an old Staffordshire family. Shortly after the birth of his son, he was appointed to command the garrison in Youghal, County Cork. He became agent for the estate of the Earl of Cork and eventually moved to Lismore in the bordering county of Waterford.

Like George Berkeley, the young Congreve attended Kilkenny College. Here he met Jonathan Swift, who was two years his senior. After completing his schooling at this college, he entered **Trinity College**, Dublin, in April 1685 and studied under St George Ashe. Swift was also attending Trinity at the time and they formed a lasting friendship.

Congreve left for London to study law at the Middle Temple but soon reverted to literature, publishing his novel *Incognita* in 1691, followed two years later by his comedy *The Old Bachelor*. He said he wrote it to 'amuse himself in a slow recovery from a fit of sickness'. He became a friend and protégé of John Dryden who said it was the best first play he had ever seen. Urged on by its success, Congreve wrote his comedy *The Double Dealer* (1694) followed by *Love for Love* (1695) which was the first play to be performed in the new theatre at Lincoln's Inn Fields. A brilliant success, it was followed at the same theatre by his tragedy *Mourning Bride* in 1697.

In 1697 Congreve was attacked by Jeremy Collier in his *Short View of the Immortality and Profaneness of the English Stage*. The following year he gave Collier his reply in a pamphlet entitled *Amendment of Mr Collier's False and Imperfect Litations*. Congreve's *The Way of the World* was produced in 1700. He always kept on good terms with other playwrights and authors and was regarded by his contemporaries as foremost in his field.

Jonathan Swift, in his *Journal to Stella*, refers to his frequent meetings with Congreve and always spoke well of him. During his sojourn with Sir William Temple in 1693, he addressed a poem to Congreve. Steele also dedicated his *Miscellanies* to him, while Alexander Pope dedicated the translations of the *Iliad* to him. Among the poetical members of the Whig Kit-Cat Club, Congreve was considered one of the 'three most honest-hearted real good men'. Leigh Hunt remarked of him that he had 'the solid reputation of never having forgotten anyone who did him a service'.

In his last years, Congreve was visited by Voltaire, who was surprised that he wished to be referred to as a gentleman rather than as an author. One of Congreve's best friends was the actress Mrs Bracegirdle who generally acted the part of the heroine in his plays.

Congreve died at his home on 19 January 1729 and his constant companion of his latter years, the second Duchess of Marlborough, erected a monument to him in Westminster Abbey.

George Darley
1795–1846

George Darley, poet, mathematician and art and drama critic, was born in Dublin in 1795, the eldest in a family of seven. His parents, both Darleys, were each other's second cousin once removed. His father Arthur Darley is listed as being a grocer in the Dublin Directory of 1807 and became of independent means through an inheritance later in life.

Shortly after their son's birth, the Darleys left for America leaving George in the care of his paternal grandfather, also George Darley, a successful builder who had a house on the outskirts of Dublin at **Ballybetagh** in the hills behind the village of **Kilternan** and later one named **Springfield**, which was situated at **The Scalp** on the road from Kilternan to Enniskerry. The young George remained at Springfield until he was ten years old but always remembered with fondness these years of his childhood. Accompanied by his grandfather, he went out riding on his pony in this lovely scenic area of wooded lands and hills, and some of the poems he later wrote were inspired by his memories of this time.

Darley always referred to **Springfield** as 'the unforgettable home' of his childhood. He recalled that when a child he thought himself miserable, but then realised that by comparison with others he was happy. 'I have been to "la belle France" and to "bella Italia", yet the brightest sun which ever shone upon me broke over Ballybetagh mountains.'

After seven years, Darley's parents returned from America but he remained in his grandfather's care until he was ten years old, after which time he went to live with them in Dublin. In 1815 he entered **Trinity College**, graduating five years later with his BA degree in classics and mathematics. Since childhood he had suffered from a stammer which continued throughout his life and which he termed as 'a hideous mask upon my mind, which not only disfigures but nearly suffocates it'. This handicap severely limited him in his choice of profession and he also shunned most social activities, leading a reclusive life as a result. Darley's three brothers were all talented. William, born in 1798, was a painter and lived in Paris; Charles, born in 1800, was a clergyman, playwright and professor at Queen's College in Cork; and Henry, born in 1802, described as a *bon viveur*, was a land agent. None of them enjoyed good health and they all wore thick slippers over their shoes to help them keep warm.

Darley decided on literature as a career and went to London in 1821. Here he made his living from writing and his first book, a volume of poems entitled *The Errors of Ecstasie and Other Pieces*, appeared in 1822. He was drama critic for the *London Magazine*, a popular non-political periodical something along the lines of *Blackwood's Magazine*. Charles Lamb, an admirer of Darley's work, was perhaps its best-known contributor. Darley was then art critic for the *Athenaeum*. Other contributors included Lamb, Robert Browning, Thomas Carlyle and Thomas Hood. In the period 1826–8, Darley was engaged in writing treatises in mathematics which proved to be popular.

Darley published two plays, *Thomas à Becket* and *Ethelstan*. His best known poem, 'The Loveliness of Love', which starts 'It is not Beauty I demand', was included by F.T. Palgrave in his *Golden Treasury* – Palgrave thought it was a genuine Caroline poem.

Interestingly, Darley's nephew Dion Boucicault had a triumph of the season in 1841 with his play *London Assurance*, which was staged at Covent Garden. Darley's brother Charles had a miserable failure with *Plighted Troth* in Drury Lane the following year and, so far as can be ascertained, the brothers tended to ignore their rather more successful nephew.

Darley spent the summers of 1839 and 1844 in Ireland and revisited the scenes of his boyhood. Two of his last published poems were signed with the name of George Springfield, after the house where he had lived as a boy.

He died in London and was buried in Kensal Green. The flat stone slab bears the inscription:

George Darley
Died 23rd November 1846
Aged 50 years
Poet.

Thomas Davis
1814–45

Thomas Osborne Davis, poet, nationalist and journalist, was born in Mallow, County Cork, in October 1814. He was the posthumous son of John Thomas Davis, a surgeon in the Royal Artillery, and of Welsh origin. His mother Mary (née Atkins), belonged to a well-known Irish family, the Atkins of Firville, whose ancestors included the famous old Gaelic family of O'Sullivan Beare. As his father had served under the Crown, Davis was reared in a household where his family's political opinions were opposite to those which he began to develop as a young man.

When he was aged four years, his family moved to a house in **Warrington Place**, near Mount Street Bridge, beside the Grand

57

Canal in Dublin. Thomas was educated at Mr Mangan's school in nearby **Lower Mount Street**. In 1830, when Davis was sixteen, the family moved nearby to **67 Lower Baggot Street**. As a child he was shy and sensitive and not particularly good at his studies but this changed when he entered **Trinity College**. He read widely and graduated in 1836, following which he studied law. He was called to the Bar in 1838 but never practised, preferring a career in literature and journalism. In 1840, as auditor of the College Historical Society, he gave a particularly fine inaugural address. The same year, he became joint editor with John Blake Dillon of the *Dublin Morning Register*. Two years later, with Dillon and Charles Gavan Duffy, he founded the *Nation*, a weekly newspaper which became the organ of Young Ireland, the nationalist movement led by Davis, Duffy and Dillon. It had a circulation of eleven thousand and the success of the movement was helped by the professional, journalistic approach of the three founders and the excellent editorial content of the paper. As well as being the voice of Young Ireland, the paper sowed the seeds to a revival of Irish literature, the precursor of the Irish Literary Revival which emerged in the late 1800s and early 1900s. A man of vast charm, Davis portrayed great enthusiasm in the national cause and through his essays and patriotic verse, published in the *Nation*, won much popular support for its principles. The *Nation*, which ceased publication in 1891 owing to changing political conditions, had its office on the site now occupied by the *Irish Independent* in **Middle Abbey Street**. It is commemorated with a plaque.

17. Plaque on the wall of the *Irish Independent* newspaper offices, Middle Abbey Street, former site of the *Nation*.

In three years Davis wrote fifty ballads and songs. Among the best know are 'A Nation Once Again', 'The West's Asleep' and 'Lament for the Death of Owen Roe O'Neill'.

Davis died of scarlet fever on 16 September 1845 at his mother's home at **67 Lower Baggot Street**. He was aged thirty. He is buried in **Mount Jerome Cemetery** in Harold's Cross where he is commemorated with a marble statue, the work of John Hogan. There is also a statue of him in the Rotunda Room of City Hall, Cork Hill. In 1977, a memorial to Davis by Edward Delaney was erected on **College Green**.

Davis was remembered by Sir Samuel Ferguson in an elegy written to express his grief on the loss of a friend whose influence concerning movements for political freedom wove its way right up to modern times:

> I walked through Ballinderry in the spring-time,
>   When the bud was on the tree;
> And I said, in every fresh-ploughed field beholding
>   The sowers striding free,
> Scattering broadcast forth the corn in golden plenty
>   On the quick seed-clasping soil,
> 'Even such, this day, among the fresh-stirred hearts of Erin,
>   Thomas Davis, is thy toil!'

Mrs Mary Delany
1700–88

Mary Delany (née Granville), diaryist, member of the Blue Stocking Circle, gifted artist and one of the most remarkable women of the eighteenth century, was the daughter of Colonel Bernard Granville and Mary Granville. She was born in her father's small country house at Coulston, Wiltshire, on 14 May 1700. At seventeen she married Alexander Pendarves, from Cornwall, forty years her senior. She was widowed in 1724 and was not left well off financially, so rejoined her family, though she remained fairly independent and spent time attending court and social functions.

Mary Pendarves first visited Ireland accompanied by her close friend Mrs Sylvia Donellan whose sister Katherine was married to Dr Clayton, Bishop of Killala. They arrived in Dublin in September 1731 and were based with the Claytons at their recently built house at **80 St Stephen's Green** (now part of **Iveagh House**, which houses the Department of Foreign Affairs) until 1733. In a letter to her sister Ann Granville, she describes the house as *magnifique*: 'Stephen's Green is the name of the Square where this house stands; the chief front of it is like Devonshire House. The apartments are handsome, and furnished with gold-coloured damask – virtues, and busts, and pictures that the Bishop brought with him from Italy. A universal cheerfulness reigns in the house. They keep a very handsome table, six dishes of meat are constantly at dinner, and six plates at supper.'

Mary's autobiography and correspondence, which are immensely valuable sources of social history, were published by Lady Landover in 1891–2. She knew many of the most interesting literary figures of her time, and her writings give a clear picture of eighteenth-century Dublin life and the literary, court and social circles in which she moved. She attended many balls and functions in **Dublin Castle**, around which Dublin social life centred: 'The apartments consist of three rooms, not altogether so large as those at St James's, but a very tolerable size.' She attended a review in the **Phoenix Park** about which she wrote that she could not pass over in silence the beauties of the park: 'I never saw a spot of ground more to my taste – it is far beyond St James's or Hyde park.' She visited **Christchurch Cathedral**: 'I cannot say they have much reason to brag of the architecutre of it, but they have good voices and a very sweet organ,' and she found the environs of Dublin delightful: 'The town is bad enough, narrow streets and dirty-looking houses, but some very good ones scattered about: and as for Stephen's Green, I think it may be preferred justly to any square in London, and it is a great deal larger than Lincoln's Inn Fields. A handsome broad gravel walk and another of grass, railed in round the square, planted with trees, that in the summer give a very good shade; and every morning Mrs Donellan and I walk there.'

Mary and Mrs Donellan travelled through Ireland visiting various people and places on their way to Killala where they stayed for three months in the Bishop's house.

In Dublin Mary made the acquaintance of Dean Swift and his celebrated confidant Patrick Delany, the scholar who had just married Margaret Tenison, a wealthy widow. Dr Delany was the Chancellor of **Christchurch** and **St Patrick's Cathedrals**. He also preached at **St Werburgh's Church** in nearby **Werburgh Street**. A genial man, he entertained all the Dublin wits and celebrities of the time, including Swift and Stella, at his home in **Delville, Glasnevin**.

Of Dr Delany, Mary Pendarves wrote, 'The character he bore in the world made me wish to be acquainted with him. He was then married, lived in a very agreeable manner, and reserved one day in the week for his particular friends, among whom were those of the best learning and genius in the kingdom. I thought myself honoured by being admitted to such a set, and Sylvia [Mrs Donellan] and I never failed of making use of a privilege so agreeable to both of us. By this means I grew intimate with Dr Delany and had the opportunity of observing his many excellent qualities.'

In a letter to her sister dated 5 April 1733, Mary wrote that the day before they had left town they had dined at Dr Delany's, and met the usual company: 'The Dean of St Patrick's was there, in very good humour, he calls himself 'my master', and corrects me when I speak bad English, or do not pronounce my words distinctly. I wish he lived in England, I should not only have a great deal of entertainment from him, but improvement.' She became a friend and correspondent of Swift and throughout her life met other eminent writers including Alexander Pope, Edmund Burke and Horace Walpole.

Mary Pendarves went back to London in 1733 and lived in Lower Brook Street quite near to George Frideric Handel who became a close family friend. Handel was in Ireland in April 1742 for the performance of his new oratorio called *Messiah* in the Musick Hall at **Fishamble Street**. Among the four soloists for the performance was the actress Mrs Cibber, who had come to Dublin to escape from a broken marriage and the ensuing scandal. Many of Handel's friends were in the audience of seven hundred people, including Dr Delany who was so moved by Mrs Cibber's rendering of 'He was despised' that he stood up in his box at the end of the performance and exclaimed, 'Woman! for this thy sins be forgiven thee!'

When Dr Delany was widowed in 1741, he was left an income of £1,000 per annum. Two years later, on 9 June, he married Mary Pendarves, with whom he had remained in touch, in London. They returned together to Dublin where they lived at Dr Delany's house at **Delville** in **Glasnevin**. Dr Delany now held the Deanery of Down, the highest position in the Church, through the influence of Mary's relations. They paid occasional visits here but their main home was Delville. The house was built by Dr Delany and Dr Helsham and was originally named Hel-Del-Ville from their combined names. By today's standards it was a big house but Sheridan gives a different impression:

61

You scarce upon the border enter
Before you're at the very centre.

A short time after moving into Delville, Mrs Delany wrote a short description: 'The front of the house is simple, but pretty – five windows in front, two storeys high, with a portico at the hall-door, to which you ascend by six steps, . . . on the right hand is the eating parlour, . . . on the left hand of the hall is another large room, designed for a chapel when we are rich enough to finish it as we ought to do. Beyond the staircase, below, is a little hall, on the right hand is a small parlour where we breakfast and sup; out of it is our present bed-chamber . . . very pretty, and lies pleasantly to the gardens, and as we sit by the fireside we can see the ships ride in the harbour.'

Mary was interested in gardens and their landscapes, but the gardens at Delville were already mature when she arrived. Dr Delany often visited Alexander Pope in Twickenham, returning with the latest in garden design. Mary gives a number of descriptions of the garden: 'The back part of the house is towards a bowling green that slopes gently off down to a little brook that runs through the garden: on the other side of the brook is a high bank with a hanging wood of evergreens at the top of which is a circular terrace that surrounds the greatest part of the garden, the wall of which is covered with fruit trees and on the other side of the wall a border of flowers and the greatest quantity of roses and sweet briars that I ever saw.'

Dr Delany built a miniature temple bearing a motto said to have been suggested by Swift: '*Fastigia despicit urbis*' (It looks down upon the pinnacles of the city). The temple contained a cellar where Swift reputedly printed some of his famous broadsheets. One wall contained a painting of St Paul and the other wall had an inset with a bust of Stella. Mary was an expert botanist and sometimes spent the whole day gardening. The days she spent at Delville were the happiest in her life. Other interests included needlewo.k, at which she was most skilful, shell decoration, drawing and painting.

Dr Delany died in 1768 and was buried close to his beloved Delville in the adjoining churchyard of **St Mobhi's** where he is commemorated by a stone in the north-east corner which bears the inscription: 'Here lies the body of Patrick Delany D.D., formerly senior fellow of Trinity College Dublin, late Dean of Down, an Orthodox Christian believer, an early and earnest defender of Revelation, a consistant and zealous preacher of the Divine laws and a humble penitent hoping for mercy in Christ Jesus, he died on 6th day of May 1768 in the 84th year of his age.'

Mary Delany removed to London and never returned to Ireland. She continued her handicrafts, most notably her flower collages. She associated with the royal family and the court and died in 1788, aged eighty-eight. She was buried in the parish church of St James, Piccadilly, London, and is commemorated by a tablet on the north wall. Among the details written are the lines, 'She was a lady of singular ingenuity and politeness and of unaffected piety.'

Although some of the original trees remain at Delville, sadly the house and its temple were demolished in 1951 with the building of the Bon Secours hospital which now stands on the site.

Bus to **Glasnevin:** Numbers 13 and 19 from O'Connell Street and number 34 from Abbey Street.

Thomas De Quincey
1785–1859

Thomas De Quincey, who made his name with his book *Confessions of an English Opium Eater* (1822), was a writer whose works influenced both Alexander Pope and Charles Baudelaire. He visited Dublin in 1800 to attend the last sitting of the House of Lords in the **Parliament House** in **College Green**, which he described in his *Autobiographical Sketches* (1853–4).

Parliament House, built between 1729 and 1739, was originally the work of Edward Lovett Pearce, who designed the Palladian central block, with temple, portico and flanking colonnaded wings. Sadly, he did not survive to see the completion of the building. In 1785 it was extended with the Corinthian portico to the east by James Gandon, and again it was enlarged in 1794 with the western Ionic portico by Robert Parke.

Following the Act of Union in 1800, when the government of Ireland was moved to Westminster, the building became defunct as a parliament. It was sold to the Bank of Ireland in 1803 and in that year Francis Johnston, another great architect of that time, designed the Cash Office.

While in Dublin, De Quincey stayed with his friend Lord Westport in his house in **18** Sackville Street (now O'Connell Street).

Charles Dickens
1812–70

Charles Dickens, the greatest English novelist of his time, visited Dublin on three occasions as part of the itinerary included on his public reading tours.

His first visit was in August 1858. A notice appeared in the *Freeman's Journal* on 23 August which said, 'As is scarcely necessary to remind the public, a Dublin audience will have the opportunity this evening for the first time of hearing this distinguished gentleman read one of his own inimitable works. Mr Dickens purposes to give four readings in Dublin in the **Rotunda Rooms**. The selected subject for this evening is *A Christmas Carol*.' A couple of days later, the same newspaper reported that, 'We have no doubt that many left the Rotunda last night with softened hearts and minds more disposed perhaps than before to look with earnest sympathy upon the joys and sorrows of those beneath them. The man who can teach such lessons and produce such effects as these deserves to be ranked amongst the benefactors of his kind – and such a man is Mr Charles Dickens.'

The following nights, many had to be turned away from his reading of *Little Dombey* which was based on his book *Dombey and Son*. His readings in the **Rotunda Rooms** were a resounding success. Dickens really enjoyed his popularity with the enthusiastic Dublin people. It was his first visit to Dublin and he was greatly surprised by it. It appeared bigger and more populated than he had thought and had a thriving look about it. The quays on the river reminded him of Paris. He walked around the city and, when tired, he hired a car and went to see the **Phoenix Park**. He found his jarvey, who 'hadn't a piece in his coat as big as a penny roll', intelligent and agreeable.

The Rotunda Rooms where Dickens gave his readings were adjacent to the Rotunda Lying-in Hospital which was founded by Dr Bartholomew Mosse in 1751. John Ensor supervised the construction of the building which opened in 1757. The Rotunda itself was added in 1764 to the right-hand side of the hospital. This comprised a round brick building which was the venue for a number of elegant entertainments including performances by many cross-channel musicians. Subsequently, refreshment rooms were added behind the Rotunda, which now forms part of the **Gate Theatre** in **Cavendish Row**.

Dickens' second visit to Dublin was in the bitter cold March of 1867. He stayed in his usual place which was Morrison's Hotel situated on the corner of **Nassau Street** and **Dawson Street**, about a mile from the Rotunda. (There is an inscription on the present building stating that it is on the site of the former Morrison's Hotel.) On the first night of his readings he had an uproarious welcome. Crowds of people thronged the Rotunda each night with many being turned away.

Dickens' final visit was in January 1869. On some nights, the reading included the Sikes murder from *Oliver Twist* which had an immense drawing power. This proved so popular that on the murder nights, police were brought in to control the crowds around the Rotunda. The *Freeman's Journal* described the performance as 'a masterpiece of reading by the greatest reader and greatest writer of his age'.

George Farquhar
1678–1707

George Farquhar, the dramatist, was born the son of a clergyman in 1678 in Londonderry, where he had his early education. Like a number of other eighteenth-century Irish playwrights who were among the best in the British theatre scene at the time, his main connection with Dublin was **Trinity College** which he entered in July 1694. Not very diligent at his studies, he left Trinity after a year and took to the Dublin stage where he performed in *Othello* in the **Smock Alley Theatre**. Founded in 1661 by John Ogilby, a Scot, who was brought to Dublin by Sir Thomas Wentworth, the Earl of Stafford, as Master of Revels, it was situated in what is now **West Essex Street** near the Temple Bar area. The burial vaults of the Church of St Michael and St John (now no longer used for public worship) were said to be the site of the theatre pit.

Farquhar's acting career in Dublin was shortlived. It came to an abrupt end when he took fright following an incident while he was acting the part of Guyomar in Dryden's *Indian Emperor*. He accidentally stabbed another actor, almost killing him.

Around this time he met a gentleman named Thomas Wilkes in Dublin who later became one of his biographers. Wilkes saw the talent in the young Farquhar and encouraged him to write a comedy, giving him ten guineas to start him off. This paid for Farquhar to go to London where in 1699 his play *Love in a Bottle* was produced at Drury Lane, followed a year later by *The Constant Couple* which was a resounding success.

About 1703, Farquhar married Margaret, a woman who had fallen in love with him and professed she was an heiress to make herself more attractive to him. He later discovered the truth but it made no difference; with his easy-going and cheerful character he never upbraided her in any way for her deceit.

In all, Farquhar produced some eight comedies, the most successful being *The Recruiting Officer* which was first performed in 1706. He would have gleaned some background for this play from the time he spent in Holland on military duty in 1700 as a lieutenant and the period he worked as a recruiter in Shrewsbury in 1704. His last play, *The Beaux' Stratagem*, written during his final illness, was produced in 1707. Despite the success of his plays, Farquhar was always in an impecunious state and fell into severe financial difficulties before his death. He died in poverty in April 1707.

Samuel Ferguson
1810–86

Samuel Ferguson, the distinguished poet and antiquarian, was born in the home of his maternal grandparents, named Knox, in High Street, Belfast. The Ferguson family had originally come to County Antrim from south-west Scotland in the early seventeenth century. Samuel was the youngest child in a family of six children, comprising three boys and three girls. His father, John Ferguson, a spendthrift who was bad at managing his affairs, had gone through most of his property before the last of his children was educated. Samuel's mother, Agnes, known for her intelligent conversation, read Shakespeare's plays and the poetry and novels of Scott, Milton, Burns, Byron, Shelley and Keats to her children. Samuel spent his childhood living at various places which included Cider Court, near Crumlin, later at The Throne, near Belfast, and Collon in Glenwhirry, where 'I received those impressions of nature and romance which have more or less influenced all my habits of thought and sentiment in after-life.' He was educated at the old Belfast Academy and later at the Belfast Academical Institution.

Due to his father's improvidence, Samuel had to earn money while he was studying to be a barrister, so he started to write. By the age of twenty-one he was contributing poems to *Blackwood's Magazine*, the best known of which was 'The Forging of the Anchor'. He was also a contributor to the *Dublin University Magazine* from its first appearance in 1833.

Ferguson studied at **Trinity College** in Dublin, receiving his BA in 1826 and his MA in 1832. He was called to the Irish Bar when he was twenty-eight, and practised on the north-east circuit of Ireland. His home was now in Dublin. When he was not occupied with law he was engaged in literature and poetry. Due to ill health he spent the year of 1846 on the continent and visited the museums, libraries, and architectural remains of the main places in Europe where traces of the early Irish scholars might be found. His travels increased his knowledge on art, archaeology and history.

On his return to Dublin in 1847, Ferguson took rooms adjacent to the **Kings Inns** at **11 Henrietta Street**, off Bolton Street, and continued with his profession. Henrietta Street, developed by the banker, Luke Gardiner, in the 1720s, was a stylish area, whose magnificent town houses were considered to be the finest in the city, and was known as 'Primate's Hill'.

The same year Ferguson met Mary Catherine Guinness, the eldest daughter of Robert Rundell Guinness of Stillorgan. On the occasion of their engagement on 10 May 1848, Ferguson gave his fiancée a copy of *Bunting's Irish Music*, with the inscription 'this happy tenth of May'. They were married in **Stillorgan Church** on 16 August. As they set off on their honeymoon, Ferguson found time to keep an engagement with and defend Richard Dalton Williams, the Young Ireland poet, then in **Kilmainham Gaol** on a charge of treason.

On returning from their honeymoon, the Fergusons remained at **Howth** for a while. Ferguson always loved the promontory of Howth which forms the northern boundary of Dublin Bay. 'I know no more healthful or agreeable place during the summer months,' he wrote. The couple then moved to a house at 9 Upper Gloucester Street (now **Sean MacDermott Street**) which they took for a year, after which they transferred to **20 North Great George's Street**. This street runs from Great Denmark Street to Parnell Street. Steep-sloped, once tree-lined with gates at the southern end, the street was commenced about 1775 by the Archdall family. Most of the houses date from the late 1780s. A number of these at the Parnell Street end were demolished but, nevertheless, the street is a splendid example of a fine Georgian avenue with Belvedere House as the centrepiece on the northern end. Fortunately, many of the houses have now been restored to their former glory including number 35, the former home of Denis J. Maginni, professor of dancing, which is now the **James Joyce Cultural Centre**.

When the Fergusons moved to North Great George's Street around 1850, there were already a number of lawyers residing there. Over the years, a number of famous people lived there. These included Lord Kenmare who lived in number 35; John Pentland Mahaffy who lived in number 38; the eminent physician, Sir Arthur Clarke, who married a sister of Lady Morgan and lived in number 44; and Dr Lawrence, the Protestant Archbishop of Cashel, who lived in number 43 and whose butler was the first Arthur Guinness. Number 45 was the townhouse of the Hon. Mrs Caroline Norton, one of the three stunning Linley sisters. Lady Morgan also lived nearby.

18. Sir Samuel Ferguson at the time he lived in 20 North Great George's Street.

The Ferguson home became a centre for hospitality and was given the name 'The Ferguson Arms' as it was generally filled with guests and relations. 'Plain living and high thinking' was, according to his wife, all Ferguson aimed at. She described the house, where they spent thirty-eight years of their married life, as 'a large and spacious house, and its simple and unpretentious hospitality was readily accepted by the good, the intellectual, and the young.'

It was said of Ferguson by one who was often a guest in his house, that he lived 'in a very atmosphere of kindly friendship'. Musical parties and meetings for the study of foreign literature as well as Shakespearean readings were organised in their home. Ferguson wrote *Shakespearean Breviates*, a volume containing condensations of some of Shakespeare's longer plays, of which he himself made great use. At one of his literary evenings on 19 January 1869, the Prologue of the last three acts of *Cymbeline* was read. Various neighbours and friends took part including Dr William Stokes, Edward Dowden, the Revd Dr George Salmon (Provost of Trinity College), the Revd John Pentland Mahaffy and Mrs Mahaffy, Professor Ball, the Revd R.P. Graves, John Clarke, Miss Stokes, Dr Ingram (President of the Royal Irish Academy), Ferguson and some others. Mrs Parnell, mother of Charles Stewart, regularly called to see Ferguson as did Mrs Robinson and Mrs Butler, the youngest children of Richard Lovell Edgeworth and half-sisters of Maria, who was forty-five years their senior.

In 1863, Ferguson explored the megaliths of Brittany and examined many archaeological sites in Ireland, England, Wales and Scotland. He contributed numerous articles on Irish antiquities to various journals but his most important archaeological work was *Ogham Inscriptions in Ireland, Wales and Scotland*. In 1865, after he published *Lays of the Western Gael*, a volume of collected poems, he received the degree of LL.D. *honoris causa* from Dublin University.

In 1867, on his appointment as Deputy Keeper of the Public Records of Ireland (the first holder of this office), Ferguson retired from practice as a barrister. He was very thorough in his work, and was knighted in 1878 in recognition of his services.

'Congal', an epic poem, which is regarded as his best work, followed in 1872, and in 1880, a third volume of *Poems* was published. In 1882 Ferguson was elected President of the **Royal Irish Academy**, which had been founded in 1785 by the 1st Earl of Charlemont to 'advance the studies of science, polite literature and the antiquities'. When it was established it was housed at 114 Grafton Street before moving to **19 Dawson Street** in 1852.

In 1886 when Ferguson was ill, he and his wife left North Great George's Street for his beloved **Howth** for a change of air. They rented a small house, **Strand Lodge** in Claremont Road, which was close to the sea. It was near **Marine Cottage**, where he had spent the summer of 1860. During his last days, he sat viewing from the bow window of his room the small island of St Nessan, Ireland's Eye. He died at Strand Lodge on 9 August 1886, aged seventy-six, and after a public service in **St Patrick's Cathedral** was buried at Donegore in County Antrim.

Some years ago a plaque was unveiled in St Patrick's Cathedral to commemorate the poet.

Percy French
1854–1920

Percy French, poet, painter, songwriter and engineer, was born into a family of Irish landed gentry on 1 May 1854, at Cloonyquin House, Cloonyquin in County Roscommon. He wrote, 'By the time the doctor arrived I was an accomplished fact.' One in a family of nine children, his father was a landowner, Doctor of Law and a Justice of the Peace, which afforded the family a privileged life. The country had just been through the devastation of the potato famine in the 1840s. The French family, who had been in the area since the seventeenth century, were known to have always treated their tenants well, even keeping a school for their children. Eventually, they too, lost everything.

Cloonyquin House, situated between the towns of Elphin and Tulsk, was in the historic area of Rathcroghan, burial place of the Kings of Connaught. Surrounded by a large estate, it encompassed Lissoy, the home of Oliver Goldsmith. Since it was in a remote area, the French children started their education with a governess. At an early age, Percy, or Willie as he was then known, was writing poetry and stories and sketching. His sister Emily later recalled that she thought it strange that her father, though an intelligent man, failed to realise how talented his son was and did nothing to encourage the development of his talents. Willie had a mischievous sense of fun and was an imaginative child. There was a small stream in one of the fields on which a dam was built, where he played: 'On those placid waters the Spanish Armada, pushed off by Philip II in person, has gone forth to its doom! Columbus, lashed to the mast of a clockwork steamer, has peered anxiously across that watery waste . . .'

Willie attended Kirk Langley School and later Windermere College in England, finishing his schooling at Foyle College in Londonderry. He then attended **Trinity College**, Dublin where he studied engineering, his father's idea. It took him eight years to qualify as he was distracted, and he later said, 'I think that taking up the study of the banjo, lawn tennis, and water-colour painting, instead of chemistry, geology and the theory of strains may have retarded my progress somewhat.' He frequented the recently opened **Gaiety Theatre** in **South King Street** which was staging a season of Offenbach's operas: 'Night after night I was in the pit, marching to battle with General Bloom or listening to the poor little Pericole bidding her lover goodbye.' While at Trinity he wrote and published his first song, 'Abdulla Bulbul Ameer', which was a great success but for which he received no royalties as he had failed to copyright it. (Later he had more luck with publishers although throughout his life he remained remarkably unconcerned about money.) He was soon in great demand as an entertainer in Dublin.

After eventually obtaining his degree, Willie became an apprentice to the Chief Engineer of the Midland Railway Company of Ireland. Here he became a friend of Charles Manners, a well-known professional singer. Once the pair collected pennies from the crowd at the races in Punchestown with one dressed as a negro minstrel and the other playing the tambourine.

In 1881, Willie took up the position of engineer on a drainage scheme with the Board of Works in Cavan. He was paid a generous salary and expenses which amounted to ninepence a mile for travelling and fifteen shillings for overnight food and lodgings, but he chose to ride his bike and stay overnight with various friends. Drains kept him in daily contact with the country people of Cavan and he met many colourful characters in his travels who inevitably found their way into his songs, many of which are the result of actual events. Some of his best songs were written during these seven years in Cavan, including 'Phil the Fluter's Ball' and 'Come Back, Paddy Reilly, to Ballyjamesduff'. Other well-known songs are 'The West Clare Railway' and 'Gortnamona'.

At a tennis party in Cavan, French met the beautiful Ettie Armitage Moore whom he married on 28 June 1890 at **St Stephen's** parish church at **Mount Street Crescent** in Dublin, thereby acquiring an Irish peer (Lord Annesley) as a brother-in-law. Willie and Ettie's honeymoon was spent at Castle Howard, Avoca, in County Wicklow, after which they lived at Victoria Lodge, **3 St John's Road, Sandymount**. At this time French gave up engineering and embarked on a career in journalism, becoming editor of the *Jarvey*, a humorous magazine which was known as the Irish *Punch*. Ettie was an artist and contributed a number of sketches to the short-lived magazine of which one critic wrote, 'Some of the jokes we've seen before and others we haven't seen yet.'

Tragedy struck when Ettie died in childbirth on the first anniversary of their wedding. She was buried in **Mount Jerome Cemetery**, Harold's Cross, Dublin. Sadly, the baby survived her by only a few weeks.

French collaborated with Dr Houston Collisson to produce the first Irish musical comedy which was staged on 27 April 1891 at the **Queen's Theatre** in **Pearse Street** (then Brunswick Street) to a full house. It was called *The Knight of the Road* and was later renamed *The Irish Girl*. Shortly afterwards, the **Antient Concert Rooms** in Brunswick Street staged an entertainment called *Dublin up to Date* devised by French and Richard Orpen, a brother of William Orpen, the painter. French took part in the production. It was a popular success and this encouraged him to take to the stage.

In May 1892, French attended the annual dinner of the Incorporated Society of Authors, the President of which was Lord Tennyson. He drew sketches of a number of the guests attending, such as Oscar Wilde and Dr Todhunter, which were published to great acclaim.

A strong bond of friendship grew between French and Collisson and they collaborated in another musical entitled *Strongbow*, which was staged at the **Queen's Theatre** in 1892. Helen Sheldon, who appeared in the show, became French's second wife in 1894. They settled down in a studio in **Dawson Street** and then moved to **35 Mespil Road**, which runs alongside the Grand Canal, and later still they moved to nearby **Ailesbury Road** in **Ballsbridge**. Their two daughters, Ettie and Molly, were born in Dublin. From this time on French toured regularly with his unique act of sketches and songs throughout Ireland and abroad. In 1906 the family moved to England as it was more convenient for his performances but he returned regularly to Ireland on tour. He loved the country, its people and scenery. He exhibited his paintings, some of which were bought by Edward VII. Percy French worked hard all his life and did not cut down on his work in later years. He never lost his sense of humour or his wit. On a train journey he overheard someone say, 'That can't be Percy French. He died last year in Naples of delirium tremens.' French's comment was, 'As I was practically a teetotaller and had never been to Naples I did not trouble to verify the statement.'

While on a tour of England he took ill and died on 24 January 1920 aged sixty-five. He was buried in Formby churchyard, some

19. 35 Mespil Road, home of Percy French.

ten miles from Liverpool. Coincidentally, his good friend and partner, Collisson, died within the same week in London after holding a memorial service for French. Beloved by all who met him, Percy French added much joy to people's lives with his humour and wit; as he said himself, 'I was born a boy and have remained one ever since.' His books include *Chronicles and poems*, *Racquety Rhymes*, and *More Poems and Parodies*. Katherine Tynan, whose home in Claremorris French often visited, wrote the foreword to the *Chronicles*.

Percy French is commemorated with a seat on the bank of the Grand Canal adjacent to the lock at **Baggot Street Bridge**. It is on the opposite side of the canal to **Mespil Road** where he lived in number 35. On the seat is inscribed:

> Remember me is all I ask,
> And yet
> If remembrance prove a task forget.

Monk Gibbon
1896–1987

William Monk Gibbon, poet and novelist, was born in Dublin on 15 December 1896. He was a notable figure on the Irish literary scene for over half a century and knew most of the leading writers of his time. He was the son of Revd Canon William Monk Gibbon, Rector of Taney parish, near Dundrum in County Dublin and Isabella (née Agnes). As a child, William lived in the glebe house (now demolished) beside the church. The Canon was a keen gardener and his young son witnessed his father interviewing a new curate from the top of an apple tree.

He was educated at **St Columba's College, Rathfarnham**, County Dublin, and at Keble College, Oxford. He served in the First World War from 1914 and was invalided out in 1918. He was in the unenviable position of being present in **Portobello Barracks**, Dublin, on 26 April 1916, the day on which Francis Sheehy-Skeffington, journalist and pacifist, was shot without trial. This incident affected him deeply.

After the war, Gibbon worked as a teacher in North Wales, in Switzerland and in Ireland. His first volume of poetry, *The Tremulous String*, was published in 1926, followed by *The Branch of*

Hawthorn Tree in 1927. In 1928 he won the Silver Medal for Poetry at the Tailteann Games (ancient Irish games revived in the early years of the Free State). The same year, in the Isle of Wight, he married Winifred Dingwall with whom he was to have a family of six children. From 1928 to 1939 the Gibbons were constantly on the move but with the outbreak of the Second World War they returned to Ireland and lived on little means. Monk Gibbon taught at **Aravon School**, then on the Meath Road in **Bray** in County Wicklow. From 1944 to 1948 the family lived in Donegal where his book, *The Seals*, is set. Moving back to Dublin, Gibbon searched for a large house to accommodate his growing family and his father's large bookcase. He bought **Tara Hall** at **24 Sandycove Road**. This house became known for its famous tea parties, where tea and homemade cakes were served between 3.30 and 8.00 p.m., and during this time,

20. Tara Hall, 24 Sandycove Road, home of Monk Gibbon for almost forty years.

75

Gibbon also held poetry recitals attended by Padraic Colum, Austin Clarke, Ulick O'Connor, the Glenavys and other literati of the day. Being the true son of a rector, Gibbon never served any alcohol at these gatherings.

An extrovert by nature, Gibbon liked a wide range of people, especially the young as he relished the freshness of their ideas. He became interested in ballet late in life and knew Massine, Fonteyn, Nureyev and Moira Shearer. He was author of *The Red Shoes: A Critical Study* (1948). His autobiographical works include *Mount Ida* (1948) on which he worked for seven years and *The Climate of Love* (1961).

He had an unusual relationship with W.B. Yeats. When the young Gibbon cross-examined and argued with the older Yeats, the latter's sister, Lily, would tell him that Yeats did not like being argued with. Gibbon was included among the three people Yeats said that he disliked in Dublin, the reason being that he was so argumentative. Gibbon's critical memoir of Yeats, *The Masterpiece and the Man: Yeats as I knew him*, was published in 1959.

Gibbon always wrote in bed and often wandered down to the sea front in his pyjamas to collect driftwood. He was a keen cyclist all his life and could be seen riding his bike around Dun Laoghaire and Sandycove when he was in his late eighties. In 1985, he and his wife left Tara Hall and moved to a smaller residence at **67 Springhill Park**, in **Killiney**. He died on 29 October 1987 in his home in Dalkey and is buried in **St Nahi's Cemetery** in **Dundrum** in the parish of Taney where he spent his childhood. Interestingly, Lily and Lollie Yeats are buried nearby.

To get to Sandycove Road, take the DART to Sandycove Station or the number 8 bus from Burgh Quay.

Oliver St John Gogarty
1878–1957

Oliver St John Gogarty, poet, surgeon and senator, and said by Yeats to be 'one of the great lyric poets of our age', was born on 17 August 1878 at the then fashionable address of **5 Rutland** (now **Parnell) Square East**. Gogarty said it was a good place to be born: 'East is more promising than West.' He was probably born in his mother's room which faced towards the backs of the houses in North Great George's Street, where many notable people lived.

The back garden of the Gogarty home had flowering wild currants and an ornamental urn stood in the centre. At the end of the garden were the stables where the horses were kept.

Gogarty's parents were Dr Henry Gogarty and Margaret (née Oliver). They were Roman Catholic, middle-class and comfortably off. There had been two generations of Gogarty doctors before Henry Gogarty, who qualified in medicine from Trinity College in 1867. He moved to Rutland Square two years later where he developed a substantial medical practice. He also had a magnificent country home, Fairfield, which stood on seven acres of land and was situated close to the Botanic Gardens in **Glasnevin**, about three miles north of the city. To the fields and stream at Fairfield that he had loved as a boy, Gogarty owed all that made him feel at home in the country and restless in the town. In later years he remembered, 'The Tolka is my earliest memory of a river. By its banks, on its islands and in its waters I spent many happy days.' Small boys fished here and Gogarty recalled having seen, on rare occasions, a blaze of bluish green as a kingfisher flashed by.

The house had connections with Dean Swift who is said to have scratched his epigram in praise of a servant girl on a bedroom windowpane there. Yeats' play, *Words Upon the Window Pane*, apparently originated from his reading of the words, 'Mary Kirkpatrick – very young / Ugly face and pleasant tongue.' The house has been demolished.

Oliver's education began at the **Christian Brothers School** in **North Richmond Street**, about two miles from Fairfield. Tom Kettle, later politician and man of letters, was the only child to arrive at school in any class of a vehicle, a little pony carriage with a door at the back. Dr Henry Gogarty never came to collect his son in his light four-wheeled open carriage drawn by two horses; he knew better than to differentiate his son from the other boys who were from less well-off families. At school Gogarty was taught English by Dr Swan, who told the young boy to chisel his words. He never forgot this advice.

When Gogarty was thirteen, his father died from a perforated appendix, and although the family were left comfortably off, according to Gogarty, his father's death heralded a change to misery and servitude. He was sent to a series of Jesuit boarding schools, the first being Mungret, in County Limerick. The prospectus read, 'Situated on a gentle eminence rising from the Shannon.' He later wrote that he would never forget the 'gentle eminence', this being the only thing gentle in the situation. He disliked the school intensely. He was removed and sent to Stonyhurst in England, which he also disliked. When he returned to Ireland he was too young to attend medical school so he marked time at **Clongowes Wood College** in Sallins, County Kildare, the first school he enjoyed. He was fed well and found that 'they did not try to break your will and leave you spineless'. He found it a relief from his English education. He was also pleased to meet Tom Kettle again, a person whom he admired. Here in the summer he played cricket with the First Eleven and became interested in cycle racing. Gogarty had tremendous energy; some days, he would ride thirty miles to play football for the Bohemians in Dublin, and the same distance back after dark.

As the three generations who preceded him had done, Gogarty decided to pursue a career in medicine and entered the Medical School of the Catholic University (established in 1854) in **Cecilia Street**, the building of which still stands. He remained here two years, managing to pass only two out of ten examinations. His time was not wasted, however, as here were friends whom he might not have otherwise met, such as John Elwood, William Cosgrove, and James Joyce's friend, Francis Sheehy-Skeffington, whom he described as 'an opinionated, bearded little theorist in knickerbockers'.

Mrs Gogarty transferred her son to **Trinity College**, which he loved. He spent more time engaged in athletic activities than he did at his medical studies and his sporting ability made him a popular figure. He played cricket and became the Irish champion at cycling.

Gogarty was academically brilliant, with an incisive wit. He had a remarkable memory for Greek and Latin poetry and soon became a friend of some of the dons, such as Dr Robert Yelverton Tyrell, the great classical scholar; John Pentland Mahaffy, who taught Oscar Wilde the art of conversation; and Edward Dowden, the foremost Shakespearean authority at the time. These extraordinary intellectual figures at Trinity College were Gogarty's mentors. He was awarded the Vice-Chancellor's Prize for English Verse on three occasions. During his time at Trinity, he published articles and poems in *Dana*, one of the short-lived magazines of the literary movement.

In late 1902, Gogarty and Joyce met for the first time. Joyce was home on a visit from Paris, where he was living the life of a bohemian student. A conversation at the counter in the **National Library** in **Kildare Street** was the start of their friendship which, however, did not last.

From January to June 1904, Gogarty interrupted his studies at

Trinity College and went to Worcester College, Oxford, hoping to win the Newdigate Prize in poetry, as Oscar Wilde had done in 1878. He came second to G.K.C. Bell, who later became Bishop of Chichester. Joyce in the meantime had returned to Dublin where his mother was seriously ill. Gogarty wrote to him a number of times inviting him to Oxford but Joyce could not afford the passage.

Gogarty was involved with the Oxford Gaelic Society and it was here that he met the Anglo-Irish Samuel Chenevix Trench, who later changed his name by deed poll to Dermot Trench.

In July 1904 Gogarty acquired the lease for the **Martello Tower** in **Sandycove**, County Dublin. Gogarty said it was Joyce who leased it from the Secretary of State for War, but according to the records, it was Gogarty who paid the annual rent of eight pounds. He probably took up occupation around 17 August, which is the date of the covenant. Gogarty was an exceptionally strong swimmer and the Tower was close to the **Forty Foot Bathing Place**, where he swam three or four times a day.

He was joined in the Tower by Joyce and Trench in September the same year. The opening scenes of *Ulysses* occur at the Tower and the three characters are featured in the novel as Buck Mulligan, Stephen Dedalus and Haines, respectively. Joyce left after a few days, his friendship with Gogarty gradually waning.

In 1906 Gogarty married Martha Duane of Moyard, Connemara, County Galway. In 1907, he graduated from Trinity College and went to Vienna, accompanied by his wife, for postgraduate study in ear, nose and throat surgery. He bought a yellow Rolls-Royce, remarking that he was going to drive himself into a practice, and purchased an elegant house at **15 Ely Place**, just off **St Stephen's Green**, for his family residence and consulting rooms. The house has since been demolished and replaced by the Royal Hibernian Academy of Arts.

As neighbours he had Sir Thornley Stoker, the surgeon and brother of Bram Stoker, author of *Dracula*, and George Moore who gives an account in *Hail and Farewell* of evenings held at his home at which Gogarty was always welcome for his brilliant conversation and dazzling repartee. Moore said of him, 'Gogarty is the author of all the limericks which enable us to live in Dublin.' Gogarty held his evenings on Friday, which attended by Moore, Yeats, Stephens, Æ, Tom Kettle, Lennox Robinson and other literati of the day, who could 'affirm his own philosophy'.

Gogarty was attached to the **Richmond Hospital, North Brunswick Street**. Founded in 1811, it was one in a chain of hospitals which included the Whitworth and Hardwick Hospitals. Surgery was taught in the Richmond, medicine in the Whitworth, and fevers in the Hardwick. All these hospitals were sited in the same grounds and none of them now exists. In March 1910, Gogarty became a fellow of the **Royal College of Surgeons, St Stephen's Green**. The following year he was appointed to the **Meath Hospital** in **Heytesbury Street**, as ear, nose and throat surgeon and became one of the best surgeons in Ireland in his day. Noted for his generosity to the poor, he was said to have had the kindest heart in Dublin and the sharpest tongue.

Between 1915 and 1917, Gogarty rented consulting rooms at **32 St Stephen's Green**. He also had a cottage, **Seaview** (now Capri) on **Sorrento Road** in **Dalkey**, a couple of miles south of the Martello Tower in Sandycove.

In 1917, his first play, *Blight*, which influenced Sean O'Casey in his writing of *Juno and the Paycock*, was produced for the **Abbey Theatre**. This was followed two years later by *A Serious Thing* and *The Enchanted Trousers*, both of which were also produced at the Abbey.

Two of Gogarty's close friends died during the Civil War of 1922–3. Michael Collins, who was Commander-in-Chief of the National Army during the struggle, held a key to **15 Ely Place**, which was found on his bloodstained body when he was killed in an ambush at Béal na mBláth in County Cork on 22 August 1922. Arthur Griffith, the journalist and politician, died only days earlier. With Collins, he had headed the Treaty delegation to London in 1921, and was head of government in the new Free State. Their deaths had a lasting effect on Gogarty.

In 1923, when Gogarty became a Senator of the new Irish Free State, he had his own problems. He was kidnapped by republicans on the night of 23 January, when he was alone in his home in **Ely Place**, and taken to an empty house where he was held captive beside the Liffey near the Salmon Pool at **Islandbridge**. He said he wished to relieve himself in the garden, and though he was accompanied outside by guards he managed to escape. He leapt into the icy river which was in flood, was carried downstream and made good his escape. On 24 March 1924, Gogarty fulfilled a promise he had made while immersed in the waters, and presented two swans to the goddess of the river in thanksgiving for saving his life. William Cosgrave, President of the Irish Free State, W.B. Yeats and Mrs Gogarty and her children attended the ceremony. It is said that there were no swans on this stretch of the river before

1924, and that the swans on the Liffey today are all descendants of Gogarty's pair, which came from Sussex. Gogarty's collection of poems, *An Offering of Swans*, commemorated the event. After that he had a strange fascination for 'these calm and lovely things'.

21. Oliver St John Gogarty releasing a pair of swans into the Liffey at Islandbridge in thanksgiving for escaping from his kidnappers in 1922, with (*from left to right*): W.T. Cosgrave, President of the Executive Council of the Irish Free State; Mrs Gogarty; W.B. Yeats and Colonel J. O'Reilly, ADC to Cosgrave.

Shortly after he escaped this attempt on his life, Gogarty's holiday home in Connemara, Renvyle House, which he had bought in 1917, was damaged by fire. His guests here had included Augustus John and W.B. Yeats.

Gogarty's best-known book, *As I was Going Down Sackville Street*, was published in 1937, following which Harry Sinclair, an antique dealer, took out a libel suit against him. The case – which Gogarty lost – received widespread publicity and the costs and damages to him were substantial. In 1939, the year *Tumbling in the Hay* was published, disillusioned with Ireland, he left for America on a lecture tour. With the outbreak of the war, he tried to join the Royal Army Medical Corps but was rejected on account of his age. He returned to Dublin on visits, and stayed at the **Hatch Hotel, Hatch Street**, or with his son Oliver, at **Earlsfort Terrace**. During his years in America, Gogarty derived an income from writing; he contributed to *Atlantic Monthly*, *Harper's Bazaar* and *Vogue*. He also wrote the novels *Going Native* (1940) and *Mr Petunia* (1945). His *Collected Poems* was published in 1950 and his autobiography, *It Isn't That Time of Year at All*, followed in 1954.

Gogarty planned to return to Ireland in 1957, but he died the same year in Beth David Hospital, New York, on 22 September 1957 following a heart attack on one of the city's streets. His remains were flown back to Ireland and interred in Ballynakill Cemetery near Cleggan in Connemara, County Galway. It is said that during the ceremony, Ulick O'Connor, Gogarty's biographer, saw a little swan, 'the whitest of all earthly creatures', in the distance on Shanbollard Lake, move towards the centre of the water and float off into the distance. No one had seen it leave the bank.

Oliver Goldsmith
1728–74

Oliver Goldsmith, the poet, novelist and playwright who, according to Garrick, 'wrote like an angel and talked like poor Poll', was born on 10 November 1728, most probably in Pallas, County Longford. Pallas is mentioned by Dr Johnson in his epitaph to Goldsmith in Westminster Abbey.

Oliver was the second son of the Revd Charles Goldsmith, an Anglo-Irish clergyman. His mother Anne (née Jones) was the daughter of a clergyman, who was master of the Diocesan School at Elphin in County Roscommon. Much of Oliver's childhood was spent in the rectory at Lissoy, County Roscommon, where he arrived at the age of two in 1730, and remained until 1747. It was pleasant countryside watered by the Inny and Shannon rivers, and it was from his memories of Lissoy and the surrounding countryside that the idea of *The Deserted Village* emanated.

Educated at local schools as a small boy, Goldsmith came to Dublin in June 1745, when he was seventeen. He entered **Trinity College**, at a time when Edmund Burke was a student there. Goldsmith was admitted as a sizar which meant that in return for reduced fees, he did work around the College, including sweeping the courts each morning and carrying dishes from the kitchen to the fellows' dining table. His duties also included waiting on the fellows in the hall. In *An Enquiry into the Present State of Polite Learning in*

Europe (1759), his first published book, Goldsmith referred to the sizar system as 'a contradiction, for men to be at once learning the liberal arts and at the same time treated as slaves; at once studying freedom and practising servitude'. His uncle, Contarine, who had himself been a sizar at the college, contributed generously towards his nephew's fees and kept a kindly eye on him, always welcoming him whenever he called. Goldsmith, who was painfully shy, was ugly and physically insignificant. He had a pock-marked face and was of a small and stocky build. He tended to avoid lectures as much as possible and was known to spend his time lounging around the college gate. He suffered real poverty after the death of his father in early 1747, relieved to some extent by occasional gifts from his uncle, by small loans from friends or by the pawning of his books, yet he would take the coat off his back to give to a beggar. One night he even gave the blankets from his bed to a poor woman and her five children.

In February 1749, he graduated with a Bachelor of Arts degree and returned to his mother's home which was now a cottage in Ballymahon, County Longford. His family, including Uncle Contarine, advised Oliver to study for a career in Holy Orders but he was too young and had to wait two years, which were spent at Ballymahon. He occupied himself by helping his brother Henry, master of the village school at Lissoy, to write some verse for their Uncle Contarine and assisting his mother with the household errands.

When he was twenty-three he applied to the Bishop of Elphin for entry into Holy Orders, but was refused. The reason given was that he had neglected his preliminary studies. Another reason was that he arrived to see the Bishop wearing scarlet breeches.

Goldsmith then commenced his travels. He went to Edinburgh to study medicine but took no degree, and then made his way around the continent, arriving back in London destitute in 1756. He tried earning a living by various means including that of a physician in Southwark. Failing to get a medical post in India he applied himself to a writing career starting as a hack writer with Griffith's *Monthly Review*. Goldsmith's coterie of friends were some of the most celebrated men of his day. They included Edmund Burke, Joshua Reynolds, who painted his portrait, and Dr Johnson, of whose famous club Goldsmith was one of the original members.

Goldsmith's first poem, 'The Traveller' (1764), deals with his wanderings through Europe and 'The Deserted Village' (1770), reflects an earlier period at Lissoy. His first book, *The Vicar of*

Wakefield (1766), remains a classic in the first rank of eighteenth-century novels. Goldsmith wrote two plays based in the Restoration Comedy tradition, *The Good-Natur'd Man* (1768) and *She Stoops to Conquer* (1773), which proved a huge success. Although this brought him a lot of money, his feckless practices kept him poor and he drifted around various lodging houses in London.

Goldsmith died in Temple Gardens on 4 April 1774. Dr Johnson and Joshua Reynolds planned a funeral in Westminster Abbey but when it was discovered that Goldsmith had left debts amounting to two thousand pounds, he was interred in the Temple Burying Ground. He was always regarded with great affection by his many friends. A memorial was erected to him in the Poet's Corner in Westminster Abbey and on 5 January 1864, a bronze statue by John Henry Foley was unveiled in front of **Trinity College**, Dublin, where Goldsmith had spent his days in the city.

Lady Gregory
1852–1932

Lady Gregory, playwright and folklorist, was born Isabella Augusta Persse on 15 March 1852 at Roxborough House, County Galway. She was the youngest daughter of Dudley Persse and his second wife, Frances (née Barry), who was related to Standish Hayes O'Grady, 1st Viscount Guillamore (1766–1840). Roxborough, the source of the family income, was a great working estate which comprised six thousand acres. It was fairly self-contained with its own smithy, laundry, dairy, stables, coach-houses, cow-houses, saw-mill, kennels and carpenters' workshops and a three-acre garden. The wall of the demesne measured nine miles in length and during Augusta's girlhood, three or four masons were occupied keeping it in good repair. (Roxborough House was later burnt down during the Civil War.)

Augusta, who was small and slender with fine brown eyes, was educated privately by an English governess. She was, however, influenced to a large extent by Mary Sheridan, the Irish-speaking family nurse who gave her an interest in legends, folklore and the past. Mary remembered the cheering at the news when the French force, led by General Humbert, landed at Killala in August 1798.

During her first twenty-seven years, Augusta did not move far from the confines of the estate and spent her time in an industrious

22. Lady Gregory after the portrait by Jack B. Yeats.

manner, visiting the tenants in the cottages and teaching at Sunday school. She also assisted with the organisation and setting-up of a village library. She learnt the Irish language from local teachers, and started classes for her tenants.

On 4 March 1880, at the age of twenty-eight, she married Sir William Gregory, a widower and neighbour from an estate at Coole Park, near Gort, County Galway. He had lately retired as a governor of Ceylon and was thirty-five years her senior. The marriage took place in Dublin in St Matthias's Church, **Upper Hatch Street**. (The church was demolished in 1952.) The couple honeymooned in Paris.

After her marriage, Lady Gregory's life changed dramatically. Her family home, Roxborough House, was not a literary household and contained no books. Her husband was a well-educated man, however, much involved in the social and artistic life of Europe, who had a varied and interesting career. He had a house in London where they lived when they were not travelling abroad to Ceylon, India, Italy, Spain or Egypt. Coole Park, which contained a magnificent library and fabulous *objets d'art* collected over generations, was used during the shooting season in the late summer and autumn.

George Moore gives a description of Augusta at this time in *Ave*, the first part of his trilogy: 'She divided her hair in the middle and wore it smooth on either side of a broad handsome brow. Her eyes were always full of questions, and her Protestant high-school air became her greatly, and estranged me from her. In her drawing room were to be met men of assured reputation in literature and politics, and there was always the best reading of the times upon her tables. There was nothing, however, in her conversation to suggest literary facility, and it was a surprise to me to hear one day that she had written a pamphlet in defence of Arabi Pasha, the Egyptian rebel.'

In May 1881 the Gregorys' only child, William Robert, was born. (He was later killed in the First World War.) On the death of her husband in March 1892, Lady Gregory went into mourning dress which she wore for the rest of her life. She returned to reside at Coole Park from where she edited and published her husband's autobiography in 1894.

In the 1890s she had already started to gather the legends and folktales of her native county from people in farmhouses, cottages in the wards of the workhouse and from whatever source she could. She often set off in her phaeton, a wedding present from her brother Dudley, pulled by her horse Shamrock, and travelled for miles. She drove alone across the mountains from the family's shooting lodge at Chevy Chase to Tulla to get material on Biddy Early who was accused of witchcraft. This gathering of information led to the publication of five volumes of folktales and folk history. These included *A Book of Saints and Wonders* (1906), *The Kiltartan History Book* (1909), *The Kiltartan Wonder Book* (1910) and the two-volume *Visions and Beliefs in the West of Ireland* (1920).

Lady Gregory met W.B. Yeats in 1896 at the home of her neighbour Edward Martyn of Tulira. Yeats described her as 'a plainly dressed woman . . . without obvious good looks, except the charm that comes from strength, intelligence and kindness'. At the time, Yeats was on a walking tour through Ireland with Arthur Symons, a friend and editor of the *Savoy* magazine.

Yeats and Lady Gregory became lifelong friends. He became a frequent visitor to Coole Park and for twenty years spent two or three months there each year. He loved that house more than all other houses. W.B. Yeats recalled in *Dramatis Personae* how Lady Gregory brought him from cottage to cottage collecting folklore. Every night she wrote out what they had heard in the dialect of the cottages. If his memory did not deceive him, she wrote two hundred thousand words, discovering that vivid English she was the first to use upon the stage.

Yeats' first long visit to Coole Park was in the summer of 1897, and the founding of the Irish Literary Theatre dates from around this period. Lady Gregory was visiting a friend in the neighbouring County Clare, the Count de Baserot, when Edward Martyn arrived with W.B. Yeats for lunch. The weather was wet and a discussion about the theatre ensued.

The Irish National Theatre Company was founded in 1904 from a merger with the Irish Literary Theatre Society and the National Dramatic Company owned by the Fay brothers, William and Frank. At William Fay's suggestion, Annie Horniman, an English heiress, bought the Mechanics Theatre in **Abbey Street** (which had formerly doubled up as the city morgue and a music-hall). This was was refurbished as the **Abbey Theatre** and opened with a performance of both Yeats' play *On Baile's Strand* and Lady Gregory's *Spreading the News* on 27 December 1904.

Between 1901 and 1928 Lady Gregory wrote over forty plays most of which were produced at the **Abbey** Theatre. The majority of these were written in the Kiltartan dialect, or Kiltartanese as it became known, after a village nearby her estate, and based on the language and form of expression she heard in the tenants' cottages.

She was an active director of the **Abbey** Theatre from its foundation in 1904 until 1928 when ill health forced her to retire to Coole Park, though she continued to visit Dublin regularly until 1930 to keep an eye on the Abbey. Many of the major figures of the Irish Literary Revival availed themselves of her hospitality at Coole Park and the famous copper beech tree where Lady Gregory's guests carved their initials may still be seen. It bears the initials of

W.B. Yeats, Jack B. Yeats, J.M. Synge, George Russell (Æ), George Moore, Katherine Tynan, Sean O'Casey, Violet Martin and George Bernard Shaw. Sadly the house no longer remains.

When Lady Gregory was in Dublin she stayed at various addresses. Shortly after the setting-up of the Abbey Theatre, she had her headquarters in rented rooms in the Nassau Hotel (now demolished) in **16–20 South Frederick Street**. She wrote, 'My own meals were simple enough in that occupied Dublin time, but I would have on my table in the evening some provision of cold fowl or eggs or game, for there were no eating-houses open after theatre time, and Yeats and Synge and Fay, or some other artist, would find comfort in that simple meal.' She brought heavy food parcels with her up from Gort with chicken pies and barmbracks.

She frequently used the **National Library** in nearby **Kildare Street** when she was translating the epics for *Cuchulain of Muirthemne* (1902) and *Gods and Fighting Men* (1904), followed by *Kiltartan Poetry Book Translations from the Irish* (1919).

Later she stayed at the Standard Hotel (now demolished) in **Harcourt Street**. Denis Johnston recounts that it was here she interviewed stammering dramatists in a back room and usually presented the Green Room with a hatbox full of Gort cake. She later used the Russell Hotel, **101–104 St Stephen's Green**, as her headquarters. Although this was one of the finest hotels in the city, it was closed in 1974 and demolished the following year. An office block, Russell Court, now occupies the site. The **Gresham Hotel** in **O'Connell Street** where she sometimes stayed is the only remaining one of all these hotels.

Lady Gregory, described by George Bernard Shaw as 'the greatest living Irishwoman', died aged eighty on 22 May 1932 at Coole Park. She is buried in the New Cemetery in the Bohermore area of Galway city.

Lafcadio Hearn
(Koizumi Yakumo)
1850–1904

Born in Greece of Irish-Greek parentage, Hearn spent most of his formative years in Dublin, and his writings were influenced by what he learned and heard of Irish folklore, tales and ghost stories in that time. Two of the four houses he lived in are marked with plaques.

Lafcadio Hearn had an interesting ancestry. The Hearn family had been in Ireland since the seventeenth century. His great-great-grandfather, Daniel Hearn, born in 1693, was a graduate of Trinity College. He was Rector of **St Ann's Church** in **Dawson Street**, then a new parish founded in 1707. He was also Archdeacon of Cashel and served as chaplain to the Lord-Lieutenant of Ireland, for which services he was granted property at Correagh and Moycashel in County Westmeath. His son, Robert Thomas, served with the 14th Dragoons. In turn, Robert Thomas' son, Daniel James, Lafcadio's grandfather, had a colourful career serving as a military surgeon under Wellington in the Peninsular Wars. Lafcadio's father, Charles Bush Hearn, a graduate of **Trinity College**, chose the same profession and was a military surgeon of the 76th Foot Regiment.

In the late 1840s, the regiment was garrisoned on Cerigo, one of the Ionian Islands, where Hearn fell in love with a beautiful dark-eyed local girl, Rosa Antonia Cassimatti. Her family did not approve of the match, however, so Charles Hearn took her off to the island of Lefkas (Santa Maura) where he married her according to the Greek rite. Their first child, George Robert, died in infancy and Patrick Lafcadio, so named after Lefkas, was born on 27 June 1850.

On being assigned to duty in the West Indies shortly afterwards, Charles Hearn sent his wife and son to Dublin to stay with his mother, Elizabeth Holmes Hearn, at **48 Lower Gardiner Street**, close to the city centre. Things did not work out too well, however – the Hearns were a conservative Protestant family and treated Rosa, who was of another religion and had difficulty with the language, as an alien. To ease the tension, Rosa moved with Lafcadio to the then fashionable area of **21 Leinster Square**, off Lower Rathmines Road in **Rathmines**, to stay with Mrs Sarah Brenane, a prosperous widow and younger sister of Elizabeth Holmes Hearn. Rathmines is situated two miles from the city centre and is separated from the city, at Portobello, by the Grand Canal.

In 1853, when Charles Hearn returned to Dublin, his marriage was in difficulties and Rosa departed for Greece leaving her husband and child. Her third son, Daniel James, was born in Cephalonia the following year. Lafcadio never saw his mother again. Hearn had the marriage invalidated on the technicality that Rosa had, instead of signing the marriage certificate, simply made a mark on it. He then remarried a widow, Alicia Goslin Crawford, in 1856.

Two years after their marriage, the couple left for India,

abandoning the seven-year-old Lafcadio with Mrs Brenane. Lafcadio never saw his father again and, understandably, his recollection of him is unsympathetic.

Mrs Brenane adopted Lafcadio and, being a convert to Roman Catholicism herself, decided to raise him as a Catholic. She gave him a strict upbringing but was very attached to him. In the summer she took him on holidays at Tramore in County Waterford and at Strandhill near Cong in County Mayo. During his childhood with Mrs Brenane, he lived at a couple of other addresses which included **3 Prince Arthur Terrace, Rathmines**, and **73 Upper Leeson Street**, now marked by a plaque.

Lafcadio's early education commenced in Dublin. He then went to St Cuthbert's College in Ushaw, near Durham in England, where an unfortunate accident at a school game left him blind in one eye. He remained very conscious of this for the rest of his life and, like Patrick Pearse, had most photographs of him taken in profile.

23. Lafcadio Hearn at about the time he left Ireland for Japan.

Under the misguidance of Henry Molyneux, a distant relation of Mrs Brenane, her property was mismanaged and her fortune, which was to have been Lafcadio's on her death, dwindled away. Lafcadio was removed from St Cuthbert's College and went to stay with one of Mrs Brenane's former servants in London. He then went to a Jesuit college, Yvetot near Rouen in France, but after a short time there absconded for Paris. Mrs Brenane was able to send him only small sums of money, sporadically, as she was now bankrupt. On the advice of the same Mr Molyneux, Lafcadio, now aged nineteen, was recalled from Paris and was given his boat ticket to New York where he arrived penniless. He managed to get various jobs and eventually made his way to Cincinnati where he worked as a crime reporter for the *Cincinnati Enquirer* before moving as a political reporter to New Orleans where he became the literary editor of the *Times-Democrat*. His next destination was Martinique in the West Indies, where he produced two books. In 1890 he left for Japan.

Within a year he married Setsuko Koizumi, a twenty-two-year-old Japanese girl of Samurai origin, and became a Japanese citizen, taking his wife's family name of Koizumi, and a personal name, Yakumo. Setsuko shared his interest in folklore and assisted him in collecting material. They had a very happy marriage with three sons. Yakumo earned his living by writing and teaching, and from 1896 to 1903 lectured on English language, literature, culture and folklore at the Imperial University at Tokyo. He then moved to the University of Waseda. He wrote several books on Japan, which include *Glimpses of Unfamiliar Japan* (1894), *Out of the East* (1895) and *Japan: An Attempt at Interpretation* (1904). These contain a mixture of folklore, reflections and impressions from his travels. In one of his best stories, 'The Dream of a Summer Day', he uses a theme used by Yeats in one of his early poems, 'The Wanderings of Oisín'.

This sensitive, enigmatic man, small in stature with dark eyes and sallow complexion, who loved nature, the sea and the landscape, died in Japan on 26 September 1904. He is still highly regarded for his work which is widely read and is on the school curriculum in Japan. He is commemorated in Japan with the Hearn Memorial at Matsue, and in Ireland with the Lafcadio Hearn Museum and Library at the Sundai Ireland International School, at Curragh-grange, beyond Newbridge in County Kildare.

Felicia Dorothea Hemans
1793–1835

Felicia Hemans (née Browne), the lovely and celebrated poet, was born in Liverpool on 27 September 1793. She had Irish connections as her grandfather, George Browne, was from Passage in County Cork. Her father, also George Browne, was a merchant in Liverpool. Her mother Felicity (née Wagner) was the daughter of the Imperial and Tuscan Consul at Liverpool, and was of a mixture of Italian and German descent.

24. Felicia Hemans.

Felicia spent her early childhood in Liverpool before the family moved to North Wales where she was educated by her mother, a woman of great intellect. Felicia had an excellent memory, was a good linguist and musician and was reading Shakespeare when she was six. She started writing verse at an early age and in 1808, when she was fourteen, her parents unwisely published her *Poems*. Unfortunately they were unfavourably reviewed.

Felicia had three brothers, two of whom served with the Welsh Fusiliers under Sir John Moore in the Peninsular War. This inspired her to write the poem 'England and Spain *or* Valour and Patriotism'. A remarkable feat for a fourteen-year-old, it was translated into Spanish. This work brought her to the attention of Shelley who wrote inviting her to correspond with him. When she declined, and Shelley persisted, her mother intervened by contacting friends of the poet to ask him to refrain from writing to her daughter.

The following year, she met and fell in love with Captain Hemans, an Irishman, of the 4th or King's Own Regiment. He had to leave to serve with his regiment in Spain but returned to marry her in the summer of 1812. She continued writing, publishing a fine Ode in *Blackwood's Magazine* on the death of Princess Charlotte. In 1818, when she was twenty-five and the mother of five sons, her husband left, never to return. Her own mother gave her and the family every help and support possible, even providing them with shelter. Felicia spent her time educating her boys, and during this time wrote some of her best work, winning a number of literary awards. She contributed her only prose work to *The Edinburgh Review*. In 1824–5, she was occupied writing *The Forest Sanctuary* (1829), considered her best work. This collection of poems includes 'Casablanca' which begins with the famous line, 'The boy stood on the burning deck,' and 'The Graves of a Household': 'They grew in beauty side by side.' She was exceedingly popular in America and was offered a lucrative job as editor with a Boston publisher but as she was a retiring person, now saddened by her domestic situation, she decided to stay amidst her family and literary friends in Wales.

Her mother died in 1827 and the following year Hemans moved to Wavetree in Liverpool, where she had relations, to facilitate the education of her children. The place did not particularly appeal to her but she busied herself studying music and composing airs for her lyrics. She travelled to Scotland twice where she visited Sir Walter Scott, who became a liflelong friend. She also called on William Wordsworth at Mount Rydal in Ambleside in the Lake District and stayed there with her boys in a cottage for the summer in 1830.

Hemans had been in delicate health for a number of years and early in 1831 she moved over to Dublin, to **Upper Pembroke Street**, to be near her brother, Lieutenant-General George Browne, who had been appointed Chief Commissioner of Police. Her *National Lyrics and Songs for Music and Scenes and Hymns of Life* were first published here. Among her friends were Colonel D'Aguilar, the mathematician Sir William Rowan Hamilton, Archbishop Whately, the Graves family and their relations, Dr and Mrs Percival.

In 1833 Hemans moved to **36 St Stephen's Green** (now demolished), explaining in her *Memoirs*, 'I have removed here much for the sake of having back rooms, as I suffered greatly from the noise where I lived before.'

She then moved to **21 Dawson Street** off St Stephen's Green, just a few hundred yards from her former house. Her chamber was again a back room overlooking a drab court. An unusual thing happened whilst she was living here, as recorded in her *Life*. One day a strange man called to the house to see her and 'explained in words and tones of the deepest feeling that the object of his visit was to acknowledge a debt of obligation . . . That to her he owed in the first instance that faith and those hopes which were now more precious to him than life itself; for it was by reading her poem "The Sceptic" that he had been first awaked from the miserable delusion of infidelity.'

In the summer of 1834 she contracted scarlet fever which left her very weak, and in the autumn she caught a chill from sitting too long reading in the gardens of the **Dublin Society**, then located at nearby Leinster House. Her health deteriorated rapidly and she wrote, 'I have been in a state of great nervous suffering and I am obliged to write in a reclining position, and can only accomplish it by these means without much suffering.'

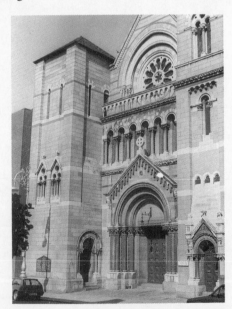

25. St Ann's Church, Dawson Street, where Felicia Hemans is buried.

Felicia Hemans died aged forty-one on 16 May 1835 in her home at **21 Dawson Street**. She is buried in a vault beneath **St Ann's Church** in the same street. The stained glass windows in this church were put in between 1859 and 1860, and one to Felicia Hemans was constructed in the chancel after an appeal made two hundred and fifty pounds. Charles Dickens did not give a donation towards the appeal because, 'I would rather read Mrs Hemans by her own light than through the colours of any painted window that ever was or will be contracted for.'

Wordsworth paid special poetic tribute to the memory of this remarkable woman and gentle poetess by commemorating her in his *Epitaphs* (number xii, stanza 10). A small tablet with some lines of her poetry marks the place where she was buried:

Calm on the bosom of thy God,
Fair spirit rest thee now!
E'en while with us they footsteps trod,
His seal was on thy brow.

Dust, to its narrow house beneath!
Soul, to its place on high,
They may have seen thy look in death
No more may fear to die.

F. R. Higgins
1896–1941

They'll miss his heavy stick and stride in Wicklow
His story-talking down Winetavern Street
Where old men sitting in the wizen daylight
Have kept an edge upon his gentle wit

Padraic O'Conaire

Frederick R. Higgins, poet, critic and theatre director, was born in Foxford, County Mayo, on 24 April 1896. He was the son of Joseph and Annie Higgins, both natives of Higginsbrook, near Trim, County Meath. They came from a strict Protestant middle-class background. Fred attended the National School in Francis Street, Ballina, County Mayo until he was aged thirteen when his father retired on pension and the family came to live in Dublin.

During his childhood, Fred spent long periods at Higginsbrook. This was a fine Queen Anne-style house which was built in 1742 by

26. F.R. Higgins by Sean O'Sullivan.

Ralph Higgins, an ancestor. At one time, it was owned by an uncle, Fred Higgins, who died in 1926.

Frederick reacted against his father's politics, and at the age of sixteen he left home and applied for a job with **Brooks Thomas**, a large building provider's office. 'I am sixteen years of age, received a good education, and have also about eighteen months' experience at office work,' he wrote on his application. He got the job. At the time he was living in lodgings at **20 North Clarence Street, North Strand** in Dublin.

In 1915, Higgins met Austin Clarke, the poet, after a lecture by St John Ervine which they had both attended and they walked part of the way home together. They remained lifelong friends. At the time, both were aged eighteen, and Clarke was awed by his companion's knowledge of 'the nineties, the Celtic Twilight, Symbolism and Maeterlinck', which he found confusing, exciting and stimulating. Higgins showed him some poems he was writing to the rhythm of Irish airs and ballad tunes. Clarke recounts in his book *A Penny in the Clouds* how Higgins told him little about his home life but how he sensed there was strain between him and his family. The truth was that Higgins had been swept into the nationalism of the literary movement and when he refused to join up and fight for King and Country, his father turned him out, so he had to live in lodgings. His poem 'Father and Son' came from a deep conflict of emotion.

In 1917 Higgins and Clarke both frequented Æ's (George Russell's) literary evenings at **17 Rathgar Avenue**. Higgins recalled meeting the poet Francis Ledwidge in 'the little painted room' in the home of Æ and that Ledwidge told him he 'earned a couple hundred pounds a year by writing stories for boys' papers'.

Soon after their meeting, Higgins founded a clerical workers' union and was sacked from his job as a result. Later he became an official in the Irish Labour Movement, and it was during this period that he started to write. He started the first women's magazine in Ireland, entitled *Welfare*, which ran for just two issues. (He later said he was sorry he had not titled the second issue *Farewell*.) His writings took the form mainly of contributions to various literary and economic reviews. In his own words, his 'contact with mechanical industry intensified a passion for primitive nature'. In 1921, after a courtship of a year and five months, he married Beatrice May, a distinguished harpist, whom he had met when he worked in Brooks Thomas. They lived for a short time in **Santry**, County Dublin, and then went to live in a cottage on the shores of Lough Conn, County Mayo, where Higgins worked, dispatching his work to Dublin by train. They remained there for three years before returning to the city.

Higgins' first book of poems, a slim pamphlet titled *Salt Air*, which was limited to five hundred copies, was published in 1923 and in 1924 another book of poems, *Island Blood*, appeared with a foreword by Æ. This was followed by *The Dark Breed* in 1927 which is dedicated to Æ, 'most generous of givers'.

Higgins was interested in folk poetry and tradition and, according to Clarke, wanted to catch the last of the disappearing traditional life. This is one of the reasons he liked living in the West of Ireland and most of his poems are concerned with legends, rural life and the natural beauty of the landscape. Brinsley MacNamara, author and playwright, who had known Higgins for over twenty years, said that in Higgins' early work it was the magic of the west that held him, but he was destined to find another magical countryside, and to make it more truly his own. This was Meath - the land of his forefathers.

After writing his poem 'The Boyne Walk', Higgins started to produce many poems about Meath. They make up a large portion of

The Gap of Brightness (1940), his last book, which contains some of his finest work. He contributed critical studies and poetry to Irish, English and American literary magazines and journals. His work attracted much attention and W.B. Yeats, George Moore, Æ (George Russell) and Padraic O'Conaire all became his friends. He wrote a very fine lament on the death of O'Conaire, the Gaelic storyteller, whom he first met in 1917.

Returning from the west in 1932, Higgins and his wife settled for a short time in a house in **Dodderdale**, in a small cul-de-sac off the main street in **Rathfarnham** village, County Dublin. They then moved to a bungalow which they named Durlas, at **39 Lower Dodder Road**. This is a narrow road bordering the banks of the river Dodder, not too far from their previous address.

It is easy to understand why Higgins chose this house. He loved water. He had lived close to the river Boyne in County Meath and in 'Father and Son' refers to 'walking alongside an old weir of my people's': this was a weir at Higginsbrook which was removed about the year 1924; Higgins had also lived on the shores of Lough Conn. **Durlas** is directly opposite a weir on the river Dodder and the sound of the cascading water could be heard from his house. (Strangely, Laithreach Cora, the Irish name for Laracor where Higgins is buried, means 'the site of the weir'.)

Many figures of the Dublin literary scene of the time lived nearby. In 1937, Austin Clarke moved to live in Bridge House in Templeogue, about a mile upstream on the banks of the Dodder, while the poet Seumas O'Sullivan lived nearby at Grange House, Whitechurch, Rathfarnham. It was to Durlas that W.B. Yeats called and inquired if it was the house where F.R. Higgins lived. Mrs Higgins brought him in and they made an appointment for F.R. to call and see Yeats at his home in **Riversdale**. This was a pleasant walk away of about a mile, through Rathfarnham village, up by the Yellow House on the corner of Willbrook Road, and on to Ballyboden Road. The two men became intimate friends and in January 1935 Higgins became joint Editor with W.B. Yeats of *Broadsides* (New Series), a collection of old and new songs. The Musical Editor was Arthur Duff and the collections were published monthly by the Cuala Press, **133 Lower Baggot Street**. The same year Higgins became a Director of the **Abbey Theatre** and his one-act comedy, *A Deuce O'Jacks*, was produced. He was a foundation member and Honorary Secretary of the Irish Academy of Letters and for his collection of poems *Arable Holdings*, he received the Casement Award. From 1928 to 1932, he was Adjudicator of Poetry in Aonach Tailteann. He won the Aonach Tailteann Award in 1924 for poetry with his book *Salt Air*, and was Professor of Literature in the Royal Hibernian Academy of Arts.

During the 1930s, one of the favourite meeting places for the literary circle was in the **Palace Bar** in **Fleet Street**. It was a convenient spot for R.M. Smyllie, Editor of the *Irish Times*, who in 1939 had started a literary page for his paper, to meet with F.R. Higgins, Brinsley MacNamara and others of the literary set. Alec Newman, who was then Assistant Editor of the *Irish Times*, wrote, 'I always think of Smyllie and Fred Higgins and Brinsley MacNamara as a sort of curious triumvirate. And what a triumvirate! Don't talk about three musketeers, these are three porthoses. I think they averaged twenty stone, conjoined they were sixty stone. And to watch those three going out for a walk up the Boyne was something wonderful!' Higgins dedicated his poem 'The Boyne Walk' to Smyllie.

In 1937 Higgins managed the Abbey Players on a tour of the United States and Canada. He gave of himself unstintingly in his efforts to make the tour a success and on his return he was appointed Managing Director of the **Abbey Theatre**. At this time he was in poor health and his final book of poetry was published shortly before his death on 8 January 1941.

The untimely death of this burly-framed and lovable man, known affectionately as F.R. to his friends in Dublin literary circles, was a great loss to Irish poetry and letters. He now rests 'under yew branches' in the graveyard of Laracor Church in County Meath, once the incumbency of Jonathan Swift:

> . . . where nothing stirs – only the shadowed
> Leaden flight of a heron upon the lean air.
>
> 'Father and Son'

Gerard Manley Hopkins
1844–89

When Gerard Manley Hopkins, SJ, died in Dublin on 8 June 1889, the short report which appeared in the *Freeman's Journal* the day after his funeral made no reference to him as a poet. It merely mentioned that his father had come from England for the obsequies, and listed the mourners who had attended the ceremony.

Hopkins' poems would probably never have been known to the general public were it not for the foresight of his friend Robert Bridges, who had a selection of his poetry published in 1918, although Hopkins' poetry remained virtually unappreciated until the publication of his *Notebooks and Papers* in 1937. These assisted enormously by interpreting and filling in the background to his work, throwing light on many of its obscurities and complexities.

The eldest of seven children, Hopkins was born on 28 July 1844 in Stratford, Essex (now Stratford St Mary). His mother, the daughter of a London surgeon, was a highly educated woman. His father, Manley Hopkins, was an Anglican missionary, and held the unlikely post of Consul-General for Hawaii in London for forty years. He was head of Manley Hopkins, Son and Cookes, a city firm of insurance adjusters. He was an amateur poet and produced books of verse as well as a history of the Sandwich Islands.

Hopkins entered Highgate School, London, when he was ten. He disliked the headmaster and in later years remarked, 'I had no love for my schooldays.' He began writing when he was still at school and was strongly influenced by Keats. Two poems, 'The Escorial' and 'A Vision of Mermaids', both of which he wrote when he was fifteen, won school prizes. He was a talented artist, and his teacher encouraged him to take up art as a career. (Two of his brothers were artists for *Punch*.) On walks he sketched wild flowers and trees; he was always interested in things of natural beauty and treated them as an extension and expression of God. He had a keen ear for birdsong, especially if it was of a persistent, repetitive nature. He liked to arrange stones and pebbles in varying patterns; this he did with infinite care.

He won a scholarship to Balliol College, Oxford, which he entered in 1863, and was later to describe Duns Scotus' Oxford as

Towery city and branchy between towers;
Cuckoo-echoing, bell-swarmed, lark-charmed, rook-racked,
river-rounded.

Hopkins did well at Oxford, being described as 'the star of Balliol'.

In 1865 he had written in his diary, 'On this day, by God's Grace, I resolved to give up all beauty until I had His leave for it,' and a year later he converted to Roman Catholicism. He regarded Cardinal Newman, who received him into the Catholic Church in 1866, as his spiritual mentor. Two years later he decided to join the Jesuits, having also considered the Benedictines. The entry dated 7 May 1868 reads, 'Warm; misty morning; then beautiful turquoise sky.

Home, after having decided to be a priest and religious but still doubtful between St Benedict and St Ignatius.' Newman wrote to him, 'Don't call the Jesuit discipline hard, it will bring you to heaven. The Benedictines would not have suited you.' Hopkins gave up writing poetry, and as an act of renunciation, he burnt all his poems except for some rough drafts contained in his notebooks. 'I saw,' he explained to his Oxford friend, Robert Bridges, 'they would interfere with my state and vocation.'

Fortunately, Bridges, later Poet Laureate, had kept copies of most of the poems. He pleaded with Hopkins to continue writing poetry, but the latter replied, 'My Society of Jesus, as you say, values and has contributed to literature and to culture but only as a means to an end. Its history and its experience show that literature proper, as poetry, has seldom been found to that end a very serviceable means.'

Hopkins kept a journal of nature from 1866 to 1875, and it was in this that his two keywords, 'instress' and 'inscape', first appear. In the journal, which illustrates his special feelings for nature, he stored away descriptions, sketches and images of nature, 'the dearest freshness, deep down things'. He was like a squirrel hoarding away things to which he would later return and use them. It was to be his poet's workshop.

The Jesuit order was hard, especially to someone of Hopkins' sensitivity, but he persevered, moving from Manresa in Roehampton, where he was a novice, to Stonyhurst and then St Buenos in North Wales. Wales was, in a sense, a turning point. Hopkins had written nothing for seven years, when his Superior requested that he write an ode to commemorate the drowning of five Franciscan nuns, exiles from Germany whose ship had gone aground near the Goodwin Sands off the Kentish coast in a snowstorm on 7 December 1875. Hopkins was moved by the event to write his masterpiece, 'The Wreck of the Deutschland'. The Jesuit magazine to which it was submitted did not accept it, and it was never published in Hopkins' lifetime.

Three of his finest sonnets, 'The Windhover', 'Pied Beauty' and 'God's Grandeur', were written in Wales in the early spring of 1877, the year he was ordained a priest. The poems Hopkins wrote in this period are essentially the poems of what he called his treasury of explored beauty, as in 'Pied Beauty'. His work contained remarkable poetic innovations. Hopkins said to Bridges that 'The Windhover' was 'the best thing I ever wrote'.

After his ordination, Hopkins was moved to different churches, including Farm Street in London and various parishes in Liverpool, Glasgow and Chesterfield. He was an ineffectual teacher and a poor preacher, often speaking for too long on subjects beyond the intellectual grasp of his audience, and sometimes losing his train of thought. He was not often called on to preach. He was never robust and suffered severely from melancholia. He was depressed by the poverty and squalor that he encountered in the industrial centres. He was given more than the usual amount of holidays, and the Jesuits tried in vain to find a place for him where he would be happy.

In 1884, he was moved from Stonyhurst to Dublin, where, except for holidays in England, he was to spend the remaining five years of his life. He was elected to the Chair of Classics in the Catholic University (later University College) then located at **86 St Stephen's Green**, and to a fellowship in classics at the Royal University. He taught Latin and Greek at the Catholic University, and was an examiner in the same subjects for the degrees at the Royal University. He said he had been warmly welcomed, 'but Dublin itself is a joyless place and I think in my heart as smoky as London is: I had fancied it quite different.'

Hopkins never really wanted to come to Dublin, and tried to decline the offer even though the assignment ranked as a promotion for him. 'I'm not at all strong enough for the requirements,' he said and, a few weeks after his arrival, he suffered a nervous collapse. He wrote to Bridges, 'I am, I believe, recovering from a deep fit of nervous prostration . . . I did not know but I was dying.'

In October the same year, Thomas Arnold, who was professor in the Department of English and a brother of the poet, Matthew Arnold, asked Hopkins if he would do a biographical sketch of his friend and fellow poet, Richard Dixon, for a forthcoming manual of English literature. This was to be one of the few tasks which Hopkins managed to complete during his Dublin years. He was to write far more prose than poetry in this period and wrote long letters to his poet friends, Bridges, Dixon and Coventry Patmore, with comments and critiques on their work. He also helped Patmore to revise his poems for a new edition.

Hopkins found his work at the university both stifling and monotonous. He agonised well into the night marking examination papers, with wet towels around his forehead. He was scrupulous and believed in marking with complete accuracy, so much so that he divided each mark into halves and quarters: 'It is killing work to examine a nation.' When holidays came, he found that he was much too tired to do the work he had planned to do. He did not appear to have much control over his students, of whom he remarked, 'I do not object to their being rude to me personally, but I do object to their being rude to their professor and priest.'

He did not socialise much outside the confines of the university. He was strict on himself, and without prior consent would hardly take a cup of tea. One day he had taken a long walk to a village some miles from Dublin and called on the curate of the place, Father Wade, who invited him to remain for dinner. He declined, saying that he hadn't permission. 'Oh! as to that,' said Father Wade, 'I will take the whole responsibility on myself.' 'That's all very well,' replied Father Hopkins. 'You may be weighed (Wade) but I should be found wanting,' and he returned home through the fields.

Being a patriotic Englishman, Hopkins differed in political opinion from his Irish colleagues: he did not understand the Irish people at all and had no sympathy with the Royal University's nationalistic objectives. In a letter to Newman he wrote, 'Politically, the times are most troubled. I live, I may say, in an air most painful to breathe and this comes home to me more, not less, with time.' At his unhappiest he wrote, 'I am in Ireland now: now I am at my third remove,' and in 1887, he wrote to Bridges to remind him that, 'Tomorrow I shall have been three years in Ireland, three hard wearying wasted years.' It was during the Dublin years that he wrote what are known as his *Sonnets of Desolation* or what he described as the *Terrible Sonnets*.

From January 1887 until March 1889, Hopkins found at least some pleasure in visiting a Miss Cassidy in Monasterevin, County Kildare, on a number of occasions. He portrays Miss Cassidy as 'an elderly lady who by often asking me down to Monasterevin and by the change and holiday her kind hospitality provides is become one of the props and struts of my existence.' The people he met there 'made no secret of liking me and want me to go down again' and he wrote that he found 'the delicious bog air of Monasterevin' a pleasing contrast to the 'joyless place' that Dublin was. Inspired by a portrait of the young niece and nephew of Miss Cassidy which hung in her house, he wrote his poem titled 'On a Portrait of two Beautiful Young People'. In this work he mentions 'the burling Barrow brown', the river which flows through Monasterevin.

In a letter to Coventry Patmore, Hopkins mentions that he had made the acquaintance of Kate Tynan, who had lately published a volume of chiefly devotional poems, highly spoken of in reviews. He gave her a copy of Bridges' poems. It was probably through her that he had met the young W.B. Yeats, 'who has written in a Trinity

College publication some striking verses and who has perhaps been unduly pushed by the late Sir Samuel Ferguson'. He visited **7 St Stephens Green**, the famous studio of John B. Yeats, artist and father of the poet, who gave him a copy of his son's poem 'Mosada'. W.B. Yeats, who met Hopkins a number of times at his father's , remembered him as 'the querulous, sensitive scholar'.

On 8 June 1889 Hopkins, who had been ailing for some months, died of typhoid fever at **86 St Stephen's Green**. He is buried in the

27. The Jesuit Plot, Glasnevin Cemetery, burial place of Gerard Manley Hopkins. His name is engraved on the Memorial Cross.

Jesuit plot in **Glasnevin Cemetery**. His name is inscribed in Latin on the Jesuit memorial cross near that of Father Conmee, SJ, Superior of Gardiner Street community, who pursues his imperturbable way through the pages of James Joyce's *Ulysses*.

Few of Hopkins' colleagues in Dublin were aware that he was a poet – he never told them – so proper care was not taken in going through his papers when he died. One of his relatives recounted the following story in an interview: 'One day not long ago I was talking to the Irish poet, W.R. Rodgers, and he told me that he had once met an old man, in Trinity College Dublin, who remembered passing the half-open door of Father Gerard Manley Hopkins' room on St Stephen's Green on the day of his death. He was surprised because a huge fire was burning in the grate and it was the height of summer. He paused, and then saw the reason. An old fellow, all in black, was heaping papers on the fire. I would give a lot to know exactly what was destroyed that day, 8 June 1889.'

Douglas Hyde
1860–1949

Douglas Hyde, poet, folklorist, bilingual scholar and first President of Ireland (1938–45), was born in the home of his maternal grandparents in Castlerea on 17 January 1860. He was the third son of Elizabeth (née Oldfield) and Arthur Hyde who was Protestant rector of Tibohine, Frenchpark, in County Roscommon. Hyde was sent to a boarding school in Dublin at the age of thirteen, but returned home shortly afterwards when he contracted the measles. From then on he received tuition at home. He spent a lot of time in the company of Seamus Hart, the bilingual gamekeeper of Fenian sentiments at Frenchpark who informed him about the local lore and traditions. Hyde accompanied him on his visits to the cottagers and listened intently to him reciting stories. It was on these visits that Hyde first picked up Irish phrases. His series of diaries, which he started when he was fourteen, were bilingual and give an insight into his great interest in the Irish language and oral tradition. He gathered fragments of stories from the local people and studied Irish with the help of an uncle, who gave him the required textbooks. During his lifetime, he was to play a leading part in efforts to preserve the Irish language.

28. Douglas Hyde in 1906 after the portrait by John B. Yeats.

In 1880, aged twenty, Hyde was admitted to **Trinity College**, where in 1883 he took rooms at house number 24 on the ground floor. He was a member of the Historical Society, the Theological Society and the Chess Club.

Like Oliver Goldsmith before him, his father wanted him to study for the ministry, but despite being awarded a first in his final divinity exam in 1885, Hyde was not interested in pursuing a career in the Church. In the same year he won the Vice-Chancellor's Prize for

English Verse; the following year he was awarded the prize for prose, and in 1887 he took the prize for both poetry and prose. He finally decided to study law and took his LL.D. in 1888.

As his successes at Trinity College indicate, Hyde's real interests were in language and literature and the names of those people who formed the nucleus of the Irish Literary Revival are recorded in his diaries of this period. They include W.B. Yeats, with whom he had many meetings and discussions, and John O'Leary, to whose house at **40 Leinster Road** in **Rathmines** he made regular visits. He records his first meeting with Maud Gonne and the subsequent lessons he gave her in Irish. She left his head spinning with her beauty. His diaries also include anecdotal information about Katherine Tynan, Rose Kavanagh and Dr George Sigerson, to whom he dedicated his *Love Songs of Connacht* (1893) which were published under the name *An Chraoibhín Aoibhinn* (*The Sweet Little Branch*). Yeats wrote that this book was the first to make the poetry of Irish country people known to non-Irish-speaking readers.

Hyde regularly attended the **Contemporary Club**, founded by Charles Oldham on 21 November 1885. Its meetings were held each Saturday in Oldham's rooms overlooking **College Green**, and the weekly debates concerned politics and literature. Those attending included John O'Leary, T.W. Rolleston, Maud Gonne, W.B. Yeats, Dr Sigerson and others connected with the Literary Revival.

Hyde was tall and handsome with dark hair and a drooping moustache. George Moore in *Hail and Farewell* gives the following description of him: 'All Hyde's head seemed at the back, like a walrus, and the drooping black moustache seemed to bear out the likeness. As nothing libels a man as much as his own profile, I resolved to reserve my opinion until I had seen his full face . . . and when he turned and I saw the full face, I was forced to admit that something of the real man appeared in it. I sat admiring the great sloping, sallow skull, the eyebrows like blackthorn bushes growing over the edge of a cliff, the black hair hanging in lank locks, a black moustache streaking the yellow-complexioned face, dropping away about the mouth and chin.'

Hyde's first collection of folktales, *Beside the Fire*, was published in 1890. This is a landmark in Irish literary history: although other collections of Irish folktales in the English language had been published in the nineteenth century, Hyde's translations were the first attempt to render Irish folklore in a true Anglo-Irish idiom. In May 1892, Hyde founded the National Literary Society in Dublin and was elected its President, and on 25 November the same year, he delivered his lecture to the members at the Leinster Hall in **Molesworth Street**, 'On the Necessity for de-Anglicising the Irish People.'

In July 1893 he founded the Gaelic League with Eoin MacNeill and Father Eugene O'Growney, and remained its President until 1915. The aim of the League was the 'de- Anglicisation of Ireland' by reviving and preserving Irish as a spoken language. The organ of the League was its newspaper, *An Claideamh Soluis (The Sword of Light)*.

In October 1893, Hyde married Lucy Cometina Kurtz. She was originally from Wurtemburg and was a graduate of Trinity College Dublin. They had two daughters, Una and Nuala.

Hyde's *Literary History of Ireland* was published in 1899. Its dedication read, 'To the members of the Gaelic League, the only body in Ireland which appears to realise the fact that Ireland has a past, has a history, has a literature, and the only body in Ireland which seeks to render the present a rational continuation of the past, I dedicate this attempt at a review of that literature which despite its present neglected position they feel and know to be a true possession of national importance.'

In 1901, his play *Casadh an tSúgáin* was staged at the **Gaiety Theatre** in **South King Street**, the first play in Irish ever to be produced at a professional theatre. It was translated by Lady Gregory as *The Twisting of the Rope*. Hyde was to write several more plays in Irish.

In 1905 he was appointed to the chair of Modern Irish at the Catholic University (which became University College Dublin in 1908) and remained there until 1932 when he retired and moved back to Ratra near Frenchpark. With the adoption of the Irish Constitution in 1938, Hyde was elected as first President of Ireland. He turned the Viceregal Lodge in the **Phoenix Park** into Aras an Uachtaráin (the House of the President). This was a mid-eighteenth-century ranger's house which had alterations done by Francis Johnston in 1808 and 1815, and which up till then had been used by the Viceroy. Hyde suffered ill health from 1940 but continued his term of office until 1945, when he retired to a residence provided by the government in the Phoenix Park. It was known as the Little Lodge and had formerly been used as the residence of the Private Secretary. Winston Churchill stayed here as a child when his father was Private Secretary to one of the Lord-Lieutenants. Hyde renamed it Ratra. The house is now the School for Civil Defence.

Douglas Hyde died there on 12 July 1949. A service was held in **St Patrick's Cathedral** before he was borne back home to his burial at the graveyard of the Protestant Church, Portahard near Frenchpark in County Roscommon.

Hyde is commemorated at **Trinity College** by the **Douglas Hyde Gallery**. This gallery of contemporary art, which opened in 1978, contains a bronze bust of Hyde by the sculptor Seamus Murphy.

John Kells Ingram
1823–1907

John Kells Ingram, poet and scholar, was born on 7 July 1823 at the rectory in Temple Carne in County Donegal. He was educated locally and at **Trinity College**, Dublin, where he had a distinguished academic career, receiving his fellowship in 1846.

Ingram spent fifty-five years associated with Trinity College, having held the positions of Professor of Oratory, Professor of Greek, Librarian, Senior Lecturer and Vice-Provost. He was Commissioner for the Publication of the Ancient Laws and Institutions of Ireland and President of both the Royal Irish Academy and the Statistical Society of Ireland. A member of the board of the **National Library of Ireland**, he was also involved in 1866 with the foundation of Alexandra College, at **6 Earlsfort Terrace**. With the redevelopment of the Terrace the school was relocated in 1972 to a site in Milltown. He lived at **38 Upper Mount Street**.

Ingram published much on the subject of sociology, economics and religion and his *History of Political Economy* (1888) was translated into eight languages. As a literary man, Ingram is remembered best for his famous lyric 'The Memory of the Dead', a martial poem which was known as the 'Irish Marseillaise'. He published it anonymously in the *Nation* when he was twenty years of age. His authorship had long been an open secret in Dublin, though he did not formally acknowledge it until he was seventy-seven years old, as he was reluctant to be associated with the sentiments he had expressed in it. Lady Gregory thought it to be 'a strange poem of liberty' for a Professor of Trinity! Other than this poem, Ingram had never displayed any nationalist sympathies. The poem, which has six stanzas of eight lines, starts:

> Who fears to speak of Ninety-Eight?
> Who blushes at the name?
> When cowards mock the patriot's fate,
> Who hangs his head for shame?
>
> He's all a knave or half a slave
> Who slights his country thus:
> But a true man, like you, man,
> Will fill your glass with us.

Ingram died on 1 May 1907 aged eighty-three. He was buried in **Mount Jerome Cemetery** in Harold's Cross, Dublin.

Thomas Caulfield Irwin
1823–92

Thomas Caulfield Irwin, poet, writer of fiction and classical scholar, was born at Warrenpoint, County Down, on 4 May 1823. The son of a wealthy physician, he was educated privately and at a young age travelled extensively in Europe and also to North Africa and Syria, accompanied by his tutor. Irwin had intended to study medicine but by 1848 the family fortune had dwindled considerably, and without the advantage of private means he had to earn his living by writing.

Irwin was on the staff of *The Irish People*, the Fenian newspaper edited by John O'Leary, whose offices were at **12 Parliament Street**. He was a prolific writer, and as well as contributing to the *Nation* (housed at **90 Middle Abbey Street**, the site of the present *Irish Independent* offices), the *Bell* and the *Dublin Magazine*, Irwin wrote one volume of prose and at least seven of poetry. A great observer of men and nature, he was strongly influenced by the English poets, Keats, Shelley and Tennyson, and was described as the 'Irish Keats' in an essay on his writings in *Tinsley's Magazine*.

> Her laugh is low, like some sweet well
> Bubbling through blossoms in a dell,
> Or pleasure's pulse, by some wild spell
> Of radiant lips made audible . . .

110

And some rare swan in sunset's calm
Sailing the lakelet's marge of balm,
Watching herself, delighted goes
Amid the shadow of her snows . . .

Irwin married and had one son who died in childhood. A natural eccentric, by all accounts he lived a desultory and rather unhappy life. In his later years he became suspicious of people and acrimonious in his manner. He was observed around the Dublin streets cutting 'a weird and uncouth but venerable figure'. Like Percy Bysshe Shelley and George Bernard Shaw, Irwin was a vegetarian and had a special affection for cats. On 16 June 1872, he issued the following advertisement: 'Robbery! One pound reward. Stolen from the back drawing room at **1 Portland Street, North Circular Road**, Dublin, between the hours of one and three o'clock of Saturday 15 June 1872, a large Dark Grey and Black Male Cat, the property of Mr Thomas C. Irwin. This poor animal, who answers to the name of Tom, and is lame in the left forepaw and weak in the left eye, can be of no value to anyone but Mr Irwin, who had him for five years before he lost him through the cruel and desperate act of a miscreant. One Pound will be given by me to whoever restores the animal uninjured, and at once, to above address, or who affords authentic information as to the party who entered Mr Irwin's room and committed the robbery.'

A further advertisement appeared nine years later for the return of 'Two grey brindled striped cats, male and female' which, he said, had been stolen from **41 St Stephen's Green**.

In a letter to Samuel Ferguson, John O'Donovan, the antiquary, wrote, 'I understand that the mad poet who is my next-door neighbour [at 41 St Stephen's Green] claims acquaintance with you. He says I am his enemy, and watch him through the thickness of the wall which divides our houses. He threatens in consequence to shoot me. One of us must leave. I have a houseful of books and children; he has an umbrella and a revolver. If, under the circumstances, you could use your influence and persuade *him* to remove to other quarters, you would confer a great favour on, yours sincerely, John O'Donovan.'

Irwin's works include *Versicles* (1856), *Irish Poems and Legends* (1869), *Songs and Romances* (1878), *Pictures and Songs* (1880), *Sonnets on the Poetry and Problem of Life* (1881) and *Poems, Sketches and Songs* (1889). He died on 20 February 1892 at his home in **36 Upper Mountpleasant Avenue, Rathmines**, and is buried in **Mount Jerome Cemetery**, in Harold's Cross, Dublin.

111

Denis Johnston
1901–84

William Denis Johnston, one of Ireland's most distinguished playwrights, theatre directors, and men of letters, was born on 18 June 1901 in Dublin. Son of the Hon. William Johnston, Judge of the Supreme Court, he lived for some time at **54 Wellington Road** and at 'Etwall', **61 Lansdowne Road, Ballsbridge**.

The novelist and playwright, Mary Manning, when she was aged eleven, recalled seeing this black-haired boy on a bicycle and thinking he looked just like Nicholas Nickleby, who was then her hero. Denis lived 'on the right side of the tracks' in Lansdowne Road and she lived on Herbert Road, across the Dodder Bridge, on what she termed the wrong side. He was educated at **St Andrew's School**, then at **21 St Stephen's Green North**, and later at Merchiston in Edinburgh, Christ Church Cambridge and Harvard Law School.

In 1925 Johnston was called to the English Bar and shortly afterwards to the Bar of Northern Ireland where he briefly practised law. In 1926 he married Shelah Richards, the well-known Abbey Theatre actress, and lived in Greenfield Manor (now demolished) in **Donnybrook**. In 1929 he wrote one of his most brilliant plays, *The Old Lady Says No!* which was produced at the **Gate Theatre** by Hilton Edwards. It had been rejected by the Abbey Theatre with the title *Shadowdance* and the new title was prompted by a note which W.B. Yeats sent Johnston informing him of Lady Gregory's rejection. The actor Micheál MacLiammóir remarked that to play the Speaker in it was as satisfying as playing Hamlet. In 1931 Johnston wrote his second play, *The Moon in the Yellow River* and became a Director of the Gate Theatre from that year until 1936. During this period he was living at **60 Fitzwilliam Square North**.

Johnston worked for the BBC in Northern Ireland and in England and served during the Second World War as the BBC Radio War Correspondent covering the Western Desert, the Italian Campaign and the Partisans in Yugoslavia. During this time he interviewed Churchill in the desert and Montgomery in Italy and later wrote *Nine Rivers to Jordan*, a complex account about his war experiences. After the war, he was for two years Director of Programmes for the BBC Television Service in London. In 1945 he was awarded the Order of the British Empire for his services, and in March the same year he married the actress Betty Chancellor. In 1947 they moved to the United States, where Johnston lectured in English Literature at Amherst, Mount Holyoke and Smith Colleges. As Head of the Drama Department at Smith, he produced plays by Shaw and Yeats.

In 1958 Johnston's play concerning the Easter Rising, *The Scythe and the Sunset*, was produced at the **Abbey Theatre**. *In Search of Swift*, a biographical study, was published the following year. In the early sixties he sold his home in Alderney in the Channel Islands where he had lived since his return from the United States. He bought **8 Sorrento Terrace** in **Killiney**, County Dublin, and commuted between there and the United States and Canada where he was much in demand as a visiting professor to various colleges. *The Brazen Horn*, a mixture of philosophy and mysticism, was published in 1977 and shortly afterwards he was awarded an Honorary Doctorate from the New University of Ulster.

Johnston's last address was **7 Adelaide Road, Glasthule**, County Dublin, where he died on 8 August 1984. He is buried in the Close of **St Patrick's Cathedral**, Dublin. Inscribed on his tombstone are the following lines from *The Old Lady Says No!*:

> Strumpet city in the sunset
> Wilful city of savage dreamers,
> So old, so sick with memories
> Old Mother;
> Some they say are damned,
> But you, I know, will walk the streets of Paradise
> Head high, and unashamed.

James Joyce
1882–1941

James Joyce was born on 2 February 1882 in a Victorian red-brick house at **41 Brighton Square, Rathgar**, and baptised in the small chapel-of-ease at Roundtown, then the only chapel in Terenure. His mother, May (née Murray), was cultured, pretty and had a musical background. His father, John Stanislaus Joyce, was a wealthy man, having inherited eleven properties in Cork, as well as a substantial sum of money, on his twenty-first birthday. He also had a well-paid job in the office of the Collector of Rates. The family were solidly middle-class, and lived in comfortable surroundings.

29. 41 Brighton Square, Rathgar, birthplace of James Joyce.

In 1884, when James was two years old, the family moved about a mile to a larger residence, **23 Castlewood Avenue**, **Rathmines**, at the corner of Cambridge Road. Three more children were born here: Margaret, known as Poppie, Stanislaus and Charles. They were all delivered by a midwife named Mrs Thornton with an address at **19a Denzille Street**, whom Bloom, in Joyce's novel *Ulysses*, summons to deliver his daughter Milly. The Joyce family remained at Castlewood Avenue for three years.

In 1887, John Joyce, attracted by the sea, moved with his family to **1 Martello Terrace, Bray**, County Wicklow, a large house with six bedrooms. This was James' third residence before he had reached the age of six. The exterior of the house, which is marked with a plaque, has remained unchanged since the Joyce family resided there. In this fashionable district, John Joyce entertained his friends, joined the local boat club, and resumed his interest in rowing. In 1888, Bray Boat Club gave a concert and the programme listed three members of the Joyce family as participants: Mr J.S. Joyce, Mrs Joyce and Master James Joyce.

Between 4 July 1887 and 26 October 1891, May Joyce gave birth to

George, Eileen, Mary (known as May) and Eva, bringing the number of children in Martello Terrace to eight, and various relations, regarded as part of the family, also stayed in the house. It was here that Joyce developed his acute facility for observation and many of the real-life characters surfaced later in his writings. Most notable were John Joyce's maternal uncle from Cork, William O'Connell, who appears as Uncle Charles in Joyce's autobiographical novel, *A Portrait of the Artist as a Young Man*; John Kelly, a colourful character from Tralee, who appears as Mr Casey; and Mrs Conway, an elderly relative known as Dante, who gave James his lessons in reading, writing, geography and arithmetic.

It was also in this house that the Christmas dinner scene in *A Portrait* took place where some of the family were for Parnell and others were against him. Dante had been accurate when she had said, 'Oh, he'll remember all this when he grows up. . . the language he heard against God and religion and priests in his own home.'

In September 1888, aged six and a half, James was sent to school with the Jesuits at Clongowes Wood College, Sallins, County Kildare, situated in a beautiful woodland setting not far from the Liffey. The college was originally a medieval castle, but it has been considerably altered over the years by new buildings and extensions. It has a formidable tree-lined drive up to the entrance, of which Joyce wrote, 'A long shiver of fear flowed over his body. He saw the dark entrance hall of the castle.'

The small, pale, thin boy with the light blue eyes remembered the tide washing against the sea wall at his home in Bray as he knelt in the College Chapel.

Shortly after the death of Parnell in 1891, the forty-two-year-old John Joyce lost his job in the office of the Collector of Rates along with the salary of five hundred pounds. He had a pension of £132 2s 4d a year which his wife had arranged with the authorities. He never held another job, and his financial state fell rapidly into decline. The rents he made on his Cork properties were taken up by the interest on mortgages. He withdrew James from Clongowes Wood College that year, with some bills left unpaid. The family's long, slow and painful descent into poverty had begun.

The Joyces moved to a large house, Leoville, at **23 Carysfort Avenue, Blackrock**. Like Bray, Blackrock is a maritime town and is situated five miles from the city centre. There is a plaque on the wall commemorating Joyce's years in the house here, which is situated at the junction of Carysfort Avenue and Frescati Road. This road formerly linked Rock Hill with Carysfort Avenue ending in a

T-junction, but it has been extended into what is now a busy road, bypassing the village of Blackrock. It is no longer the peaceful surburban road it was when the Joyces resided there.

Two more daughters were born here, Florence in 1892 and Mabel in 1893. The nine-year-old James and his great-uncle, William O'Connell, did the shopping in the main street in Blackrock and would often go to Blackrock Park where the child would practise long-distance running just as Stephen and Uncle Charles do in *A Portrait*. After their visit to the Park, Uncle Charles and Stephen would pay a visit to the church in Blackrock where Uncle Charles would pray. Stephen often wondered, was he praying that God might send him back part of his squandered Cork fortune?

All the children, with the exception of James, attended the local convent school. He stayed at home and studied on his own. According to his brother, Stanislaus, James was aged between nine and ten when his ambition to be a writer bore its first blossom. The broadside, *Et Tu Healy*, which Joyce wrote at the age of nine, was probably written here. His father had copies printed which he gave to his friends. No copy is known to exist now.

Disintegration had set in abruptly. The Joyce family left their home in Blackrock amid the clamour of dunning creditors and a threatening landlord. The move from Carysfort Avenue to the city, and subsequent moves, resulted from John Joyce's unwillingness to pay rent. He could not manage to drink as much as he did and pay the rent at the same time. Once they crossed the Liffey from the south side, they never crossed it again as a family. In *A Portrait*, it is related how Stephen and his red-eyed mother could see, from the window of their railway carriage, two great yellow caravans with their furniture lumbering heavily along the Merrion Road.

The family's next stop was at number 29 (now demolished) in **Hardwicke Street**. Joyce's story, 'The Boarding House' (which appears in *Dubliners*), is set in **Waverley House, 4 Hardwicke Street**, and Joseph Nannetti, foreman of the *Freeman's Journal*, who appears in *Ulysses*, lived at 18–19 Hardwicke Street from 1894 to 1904.

The next move, after only a few months, was to nearby 14 **Fitzgibbon Street** (now number **34**). This is a large sombre house where the Joyce family lived for over a year. At that time, it was a residential area for well-off families, and it was the last of the Joyces' good addresses. A neighbour was Mrs Sohan. In the Wandering Rocks episode in *Ulysses*, Jack Sohan was one of the three little schoolboys whom Father Conmee, SJ, met at the corner of Mountjoy Square. He gave one of them a letter to post in the red pillarbox at the corner of Fitzgibbon Street. The feelings experienced by Stephen Dedalus in *A Portrait* mirrored the experiences of the Joyce family.

As recounted in *A Portrait*, 'The sudden flight from the comfort and revery of Blackrock, the passage through the gloomy, foggy city, the thought of the bare cheerless house in which they were now to live made his heart heavy, and again an intuition, a foreknowledge of the future came to him.'

For James, like Stephen, 'Dublin was a new and complex sensation. At the beginning he contented himself with circling timidly round the neighbouring square or, at most, going halfway down one of the side streets but when he had made a skeleton map of the city in his mind he followed boldly one of its central lines until he reached the Custom House. He timidly explored the neighbourhood, and passed unchallenged along the docks and quays. The vastness and strangeness of his new bustling life amazed him . . . he was embittered and angry with himself for being young and the prey of restless foolish impulses, angry also with the change of fortune which was reshaping the world about him into a vision of squalor and insincerity.'

From 14 Fitzgibbon Street, John Joyce reluctantly sent his son to the **Christian Brothers School, North Richmond Street**. Joyce never admitted this. One day, in Mountjoy Square, John Joyce met the courtly Father Conmee, SJ, and explained the position regarding his reduced financial circumstances. Father Conmee agreed to take James and his brothers to the day school at **Belvedere College** in **Great Denmark Street** without payment.

Despite the constant moving and increasing household turmoil, Joyce took learning in his stride and did well at school, winning scholarships which briefly eased the family finances. But there was desperate poverty in the household, and in February 1894, when James was only just twelve, he accompanied his father to Cork to sell the remainder of the mortgaged properties.

No financial alleviation resulted from the Cork journey, however, as all the money was needed to pay John Joyce's heavy debts to the Dublin solicitor and moneylender, Reuben Dodd (who appears briefly in *Ulysses*). This rankled deeply with James, particularly since Dodd's son was his contemporary at Belvedere College.

The next downward step was in March 1894 when John Joyce, his wife and ten children, moved to their seventh home at **2 Millbourne Avenue** in **Drumcondra**. May Joyce gave birth to her twelfth child here, a son named Freddie. Sadly, like her first-born, he survived only a few weeks. Stanislaus Joyce described the house as 'Bleak House' and in *A Portrait* Stephen Dedalus gives a description showing the steady decline in living standards which mirrored those endured by the Joyce family since the good days in Bray: 'He pushed open the latchless door of the porch and passed through the naked hallway into the kitchen. A group of his brothers and sisters were sitting around the table. Tea was nearly over and only the last of the second watered tea remained in the bottoms of the small glass jars and jampots which did service for teacups.' This was certainly a drastic change for James, who remembered his Bray days when he wore his Eton jacket and the servants placed dishes on the table before him.

It was while living at this address that the Joyce children were beaten up by some local boys, as happens to Stephen in *A Portrait,* including one named Pisser Duffy. Duffy's father was the last man to wish them Godspeed when the family moved again. They had lived here for only a year.

Joyce won a prize of twenty pounds in the Intermediate examination in the Preparatory Grade when he was twelve and bought the family 'practical' presents with his money. A pair of boots for one, a dress for another, visits to expensive restaurants and the theatre for them all.

In 1895 the twelve Joyces moved back across the Tolka to another house with high, cold, empty, gloomy rooms, to **17 North Richmond Street**, where they remained for four years, their longest period in any house since the halcyon days in Bray: 'An uninhabited house of two storeys stood at the blind end, detached from its neighbours . . . the other houses on the street . . . gazed at one another with brown imperturbable faces.' Richard Ellmann, Joyce's biographer, said, 'It received more attention from Joyce than the others.' Certainly the Joyce children seem to have had a happy time playing in the streets on winter evenings, as described nostalgically in the story 'Araby'. The muddy lanes where they played behind the house may still be seen, and many of the decent citizens who lived in North Richmond Street appear on the pages of *Ulysses, Dubliners* and *Finnegans Wake*.

Joyce finished in Belvedere College and entered the Catholic University in 1898 when the family moved to **29 Windsor Avenue** in **Fairview**. This house was owned by a young clergyman called Love. He appears as a character in *Ulysses*, the Revd Hugh C. Love, Anglican cleric and landlord, interested in Irish history. The family remained in this house until May 1899. During their short stay in this house, May Joyce gave birth to her last child, a still-born male infant. As Stanislaus noted, brief as their stay was in each of their numerous residences, it was still long enough in most cases, to be marked by a death in the family.

It was at Windsor Avenue that James Joyce encountered the writing of Ibsen and was filled with an overmastering admiration for the Norwegian playwright. A breath of current European thought entered that unusual household.

For a short time, the Joyces shared a house with another family named Hughes in **Convent Avenue, Fairview**, and in the latter part of 1899 they had a portion of a larger house (now demolished) at **13 Richmond Avenue**, also in Fairview. In May 1900 they rented a fine house (which they couldn't afford) at **8 Royal Terrace**, Fairview, subsequently called **Inverness Road**. The rear of this house overlooks the grounds of a convent from which Joyce heard the screams of the mad nun described in *A Portrait*. It was also from this address that Joyce wrote to Ibsen to greet him on his seventy-third birthday. The Joyce family remained in Inverness Road until 1901 when John Joyce moved his entourage to **32 Glengariff Parade**, off the **North Circular Road**.

It was a depressing neighbourhood but here Joyce composed musical settings for at least six of his own poems, in addition to some by Mangan and Yeats. In this house, the youngest son, George, died of peritonitis, aged fourteen. He was a handsome gifted boy, and his mother never recovered from the blow. His death affected James deeply and he records his illness in *Stephen Hero,* with Isabel, Stephen's sister, substituted for George.

Joyce completed his arts degree and started a course at the Medical School of the Catholic University in **Cecilia Street**. He did not pursue this as his father was unable to pay.

On an impulse, Joyce left Ireland. On 1 December 1902, he departed from the North Wall for Paris, where he hoped to study medicine at the Sorbonne. He was met en route by W.B. Yeats at Euston Station in London.

John Joyce, fondly believing that his children were approaching independence, commuted half of his pension and investments into 7 St Peter's Terrace, **Phibsborough** (in 1905, it was renumbered and is now **5 St Peter's Road**). This left him with the meagre monthly sum of £5 10s 1d on which to support six daughters and three sons. He descended rapidly into financial disaster once again and this led his son Stanislaus to refer to their abode as 'The house of the bare table'. The houses in this red-brick terrace are larger inside than their exteriors would indicate. It was in a room upstairs that Mrs May Joyce died; James was still in Paris, when he received a telegram bearing the message, 'MOTHER DYING STOP COME HOME STOP FATHER STOP'. For four months May was in agony, finally dying on 13 August 1903 aged forty-four years, having given birth to thirteen children.

30. Joyce in 1904, about the time he met Nora Barnacle.

After his mother's death, Joyce dallied for a while in Dublin. He applied unsuccessfully for a post in the **National Library**. Then in January 1904, he wrote a short story entitled, 'A Portrait of the Artist', which he submitted to John Eglington, editor of the literary magazine *Dana*. When it was rejected, Joyce recast it and expanded it into *Stephen Hero*. This, in turn, was rejected by a publisher, and in a fit of despair Joyce attempted to destroy the manuscript. Later he rewrote it and in its changed, polished, and redeveloped form it was published in 1916 as *A Portrait of the Artist as a Young Man*.

Joyce wandered around the streets and made a few visits to Nighttown, Dublin's brothel area and scene of 'Circe' in *Ulysses*, with Oliver St John Gogarty. Encouraged by John McCormack, he took some singing lessons, and his name appears alongside McCormack's on a programme at the **Antient Concert Rooms**. He did well at the Feis Ceoil and just missed being awarded a gold medal because he refused to sing at sight.

In late March 1904, Joyce rented a very large room that spanned the top of a house in **60 Shelbourne Road**, where a family named McKernan lived. He paid for this with money he had borrowed from Oliver St John Gogarty, J.F. Byrne and Æ (George Russell). His lifelong passion for auburn-haired Nora Barnacle began when he was living here. He saw her walking down **Nassau Street**, and was struck by the wonder and beauty that culminated in the character of Molly Bloom. He wrote to her from Shelbourne Road for an appointment to meet.

Joyce did not remain long at 60 Shelbourne Road as he could not pay the rent and soon the symbolic cab reappeared at the front door.

He stayed with James H. Cousins at **35 Strand Road, Sandymount** for the first couple of days in September 1904, and the next night with a medical student, James O'Callaghan. The following two nights he stayed with his uncle, William Murray, at **103 North Strand Road, Fairview**, but Murray, disapproving of his nephew's unseemly hours, locked him out of the house. On 9 September 1904, Joyce ended up in the most unusual residence he was ever to occupy, the **Martello Tower** in **Sandycove**, County Dublin. His fellow tenants were with Oliver St John Gogarty and Samuel Chenevix Trench, an Oxford friend of Gogarty who had passionately embraced the Irish Revival.

Of all his Dublin addresses, Joyce spent least time here (he left on 15 September), though ironically, this is the address that has become the most famous. The sturdy granite tower with its eight-foot-thick walls was built in 1804 as a defence against possible Napoleonic invasion. The entrance was ten feet from the ground, and since there was no staircase, a rope ladder was used. A large key opened a heavy door, giving admission to the living quarters which consisted simply of a circular room with a fireplace. Two narrow openings in the wall provided some light. The lifestyle in the tower was free and easy. All undesired access was cut off by pulling up the ladder.

After a stay of only six days Joyce left the tower dramatically. He regarded himself as evicted. Chenevix Trench had a nightmare involving a black panther – he screamed, then grabbed a revolver and fired several shots into the fireplace. Joyce was understandably frightened. When Trench resumed screaming, Gogarty called out, 'Leave him to me,' and fired at a collection of pans on the shelf over Joyce's bed. Joyce dressed, and left in the rain without a word.

The scene of the first episode of *Ulysses* is set in the tower. It was

31. The Martello Tower in Sandycove, County Dublin,
now the James Joyce Museum.

formally opened as a Joyce Museum in 1962 by Sylvia Beach, the
first publisher of *Ulysses*.

Joyce and Nora left Ireland in October, 1904, penniless and
endowed with little more than his genius and her generosity. He
returned briefly to Ireland in July 1909 to bring his little son Giorgio
to meet his grandfather and aunts who were now living at **44
Fontenoy Street**. He also brought Giorgio to visit his friend J.F.
Byrne who lived at **7 Eccles Street**. This became the home of
Leopold Bloom in *Ulysses*.

The following October Joyce was back in Dublin for the opening
of the Volta Cinema in Mary Street, again staying at **44 Fontenoy
Street**.

In August 1912, Joyce returned again to Dublin for nearly a month in connection with the proposed publication of his collection of short stories, *Dubliners*. This was his last visit to his native city. He stayed at both numbers 17 and 21 **Richmond Place** (now numbers 609 and 617 **North Circular Road**).

Joyce's pattern of address-changing did not stop when he left Ireland but continued until the time of his death. He did not forget his Dublin addresses, most of which are transmuted by his Homeric humour into a couple of pages of *Finnegans Wake*, a book on which he worked for seventeen years. He died in Zurich on 13 January 1941, a few weeks short of his fifty-ninth birthday.

Of all the Dublin writers, Joyce had the most addresses and he used the moves to his advantage by the artistic use to which he puts the various houses in his works. Of all the houses he inhabited, all but one of them (the demolished Georgian house in **Hardwicke Street**), may be seen today.

Patrick Kavanagh
1904–67

If ever you go to Dublin town
In a hundred years or so,
Inquire for me in Baggot Street
And what I was like to know.
'If Ever You Go to Dublin Town'

Patrick Kavanagh, poet and novelist, was born on 21 October 1904 in Inniskeen, County Monaghan. In a family comprising seven girls and two boys, he was the fourth child and first son of James Kavanagh and Bridget (née Quinn). After finishing his formal schooling at thirteen years of age, he worked on the land and as a part-time shoemaker like his father before him. It was around this age that he started to write poetry.

In 1927 Kavanagh discovered the weekly review, the *Irish Statesman*, to which he began submitting verse. Æ (George Russell), who was Editor of the review, wrote to him and encouraged him to send more. Two years later, the year his father died, his poems 'The Intangible', 'Ploughman' and 'Dreamer' were accepted.

Kavanagh's first visit to Dublin was when he walked there to meet Æ, who greeted him warmly and introduced him to the short-story

writer Frank O'Connor, and the poet Seumas O'Sullivan, founder
and Editor of the *Dublin Magazine* which has been referred to as
'the major Irish literary periodical of its day'. Kavanagh was one of
the graveside mourners, together with Frank O'Connor and W.B.
Yeats, at Æ's funeral in 1935.

His first book of poems was published in London in 1936, the
same year as his brother Peter graduated as a teacher. In 1937,
Patrick went to London, but did not remain there long as he ran out
of money. It was here that he started writing his novel, *The Green
Fool*.

In 1938 Kavanagh left his home for Dublin, leaving behind him
'the stony grey soil' and the small fields that he loved and wrote
about so evocatively in his poems and in his novel *Tarry Flynn*. He
later said it was the greatest mistake of his life: 'The Hitler war had
started. I had my comfortable little holding of watery hills beside
the border. And yet I wasted what could have been my four glorious
years begging and scrambling around the streets of malignant
Dublin . . . I had no messianic impulse to leave. I was happy. I went
against my will. A lot of our actions are like that.'

The Irish Literary Revival was in full swing and the **Palace Bar** in
Fleet Street was crowded with coveys of poets and their admirers.
'Jerome Connor with his short wooden pipe in his gnarled fist; Pat
O'Connor, the Playboy of the Wrestling World with his great black
beard, appears in the doorway; John Betjeman next arrives, a size
eight cloth cap halfway down his forehead and a laugh on his face a
yard square.'

Most of Kavanagh's Dublin addresses were concentrated in the
same area. He was seldom far away from Baggottonia, as his friend
John Ryan called it, an area comprising **Baggot Street**, the **Grand
Canal** and **Wellington**, **Waterloo**, **Clyde**, **Raglan** and **Pembroke
Roads**:

> On Pembroke Road look out for my ghost
> Dishevelled with shoes untied.

In 1939, Kavanagh stayed for a short period in **Drumcondra**, four
miles from the city centre, before moving to **35 Haddington Road**,
which he shared with his brother Peter. It was a twelve-foot-square
bedsitter room, furnished with two beds, a table and chair, and gas
cooker, fire and lamps. On the iron gates of the house Kavanagh
would swing his nineteen-year-old girlfriend to and fro for about an
hour or so every evening, a unique form of courtship.

From 1942 to 1944, Kavanagh earned his living writing a column for the *Irish Press,* while living with Peter at **122 Morehampton Road** in **Donnybrook**. Their room was at street level and the accommodation was more spacious than before. It was at this address that Kavanagh was visited by detectives as a result of complaints about his poem 'The Great Hunger' being published in *Horizon*. (It was thought to be indecent by some Irish authorities.)

The brothers then moved for a short time to a flat in **Percy Place**, situated between Haddington Road and the Grand Canal, followed shortly afterwards by a tiny room on the sixth floor of **9 Lower O'Connell Street**. In the spring of 1943, Kavanagh left and went back to the Baggot Street/Pembroke Street area where he resided in a large apartment incorporating two levels at **62 Pembroke Road**. He remained here from 1946 to 1958, the longest period he would remain at any of his Dublin addresses.

It is autumning again over my Pembrokeshire.

This was one of Kavanagh's favourite abodes during his thirty years of peregrinations around Dublin. While living here, he was appointed as Editorial and Feature writer for the *Standard*, a position he held for three years. He was also the Film Critic monthly Diarist for *Envoy*, a short-lived literary magazine to which such writers as Brendan Behan, Brian O'Nolan, Sean O'Faoláin and Francis Stuart contributed. In 1952, he launched *Kavanagh's Weekly* with his brother Peter. Thirteen issues appeared, after which it ceased because of a lack of financial support. It was at 62 Pembroke Road that the unsold copies of the *Weekly* were disposed of 'with tongues of fire by night and smoke by day'. It tore at Kavanagh's heart to leave this place: 'It was like a death. I will confess that I walked into each room in turn and prostrated myself on the floor, concentrating the while that this would be my last look at those familiar walls and floor . . . I gazed out the window and concentrated and tried to fix in my imagination all those things. And if the truth must be told, I wept.'

In October 1958, Kavanagh moved to number **19 Raglan Road**, a wide and tree-lined street whose name is the title of one of his best-known and most popular poems. His subsequent moves were almost as numerous as those of James Joyce although, unlike him, he was faithful to one area. In 1959 he moved to **110 Baggot Lane**. In October 1960 he lived at **1 Wilton Place** and November 1963 found him in **37 Upper Mount Street**. In 1964 he was in the Halycon Hotel in **South Anne Street**, and in December 1965 he lived in **136 Upper Leeson Street**.

32. 19 Raglan Road, Ballsbridge, where Patrick Kavanagh lived in 1958. 'On Raglan Road' is the title of one of his best-loved poems.

May O'Flaherty's famous bookshop, **Parsons** on **Baggot Street Bridge**, was to Patrick Kavanagh what Sylvia Beach's bookshop in Paris, Shakespeare and Company, was to James Joyce. It was his refuge and his strength, his home from home. Here he kept his cow-stool – which he had bought in Ennistymon for five shillings from the local coffin-maker who made stools from leftover clippings – and here he read the papers, often checking the racing results, and availed himself of the books. *Kavanagh's Weekly* was sold in the shop and he often used it as his postal address.

May O'Flaherty kept a visitors book in the shop in which Kavanagh wrote, 'When someone asks me to write something in their book the temptation is to go false, to try to put down "great thoughts". One also feels too the impertinence of writing "I" this or that as if we thought ourselves important. A man has no right to talk of himself, only as a by-product of his work. It is a June day 1959. Profundity keeps coming up. Patrick Kavanagh for Miss O'Flaherty of Parsons Bookshop.' The shop remains, but has since changed hands and is no longer a bookshop.

Pubs were among the main centres of Kavanagh's social life and he frequented the **Waterloo Bar**, **Searson's**, and **Mooney's**, all in Baggot Street, as well as **Ryan's** in nearby Haddington Road. He also went to **Neary's** in Chatham Street, the **Palace Bar** in Fleet

Street, and the **Bailey** in Duke Street. He often held court in **McDaid's**, a former Moravian church, in Harry Street.

The Grand Canal runs through much of Kavanagh's poetry and prose. He regarded the banks of the canal as the place of his artistic rebirth, where he saw the beauty of water and green grass and the magic of light. He experienced the same emotion that he had known when he stood on a sharp slope in Monaghan, 'where I imaginatively stand now, looking across to Slieve Gullion and South

33. Kavanagh (*right*) with the actor Milo O'Shea, at the official unveiling of the original door of number 7 Eccles Street in the Bailey pub, Duke Street, Bloomsday 1967. The door is now at the James Joyce Cultural Centre, 35 North Great George's Street.

Armagh.' Around the canal 'the light was a surprise over roofs and around gables, and the canal water was green and stilly.' Kavanagh loved the shady leafy walks beside the water. It was while lying here, between **Baggot** and **Leeson Street Bridges**, on a hot summer's day after a long and serious illness, that he commenced his poetic Hegira and wrote the lovely sonnet:

> O Commemorate me where there is water,
> Canal water, preferably, so stilly
> Greeny at the heart of summer.

He is commemorated by a seat near the lock at **Baggot Street Bridge**, which was erected by his friends on St Patrick's Day 1968. The seat is made of ancient oak from Meath. Granite from the Dublin mountains was used for the uprights, and Liscarra slabs from the Burren in County Clare form the surrounding paving. On the opposite side of the canal, there is a life-size seated bronze statue of Kavanagh by sculptor John Coll.

Patrick Kavanagh died aged sixty-three on 30 November 1967 and his body was returned to the fields of his youth. He was buried in Inniskeen, County Monaghan, in the village churchyard situated about one and half miles from Mucker, the townland where he was born.

> And pray for him who walked apart, on the hills loving
> life's miracles.

Thomas Kettle
1880–1916

Thomas Michael Kettle, patriot, poet, essayist and politician, and regarded as one of the most brilliant men of his generation, was

34. Bust of Thomas Kettle, St Stephen's Green.

born on 9 February 1880 at **Artane** in County Dublin. He was the third son of Andrew J. Kettle, a prosperous farmer, Parnellite and one of the founders and organisers of the Land League, and Margaret (née McCourt).

Tom and his brothers and sisters had an affluent and comfortable childhood in rural surroundings. His father had land, not only in Artane but also in nearby **Swords**, **Malahide** and **St Margaret's**. Tom obviously enjoyed his rural upbringing helping his father around the farmyard with the animals, minding the sows, milking the cows and leading the horses, which were prizewinners at the annual Spring Show, held in the Royal Dublin Society at Ballsbridge in Dublin.

With his brothers, he started his education at the **Christian Brothers School** in **North Richmond Street**. Each day, they were transported by pony and trap from Artane. In 1892, Tom sat the preparatory grade examination and did extremely well. The Christian Brothers were disappointed to lose such a promising pupil when, at the age of fourteen, he was removed from North Richmond Street and sent as a boarder to the Jesuit Clongowes Wood College in Sallins, County Kildare, founded in 1814. In a lovely woodland setting, the school had fine expanses of land for sports fields and a cricket pitch.

Kettle was not long in settling in to the school. He was interested in athletics, and played rugby, soccer and cricket but never represented the school in any of these games. He was a good cyclist and was a member of the school cycling club which engaged in long tours of the surrounding countryside, to places such as Blessington, Rathmore and Hollywood Glen.

Oliver St John Gogarty, whom he had first met at the Christian Brothers School, was older than Kettle, but shared his interest in cycling and they kept up their friendship until the end of Kettle's life. At the age of sixteen, Kettle won an essay competition and was published for the first time in the school magazine, *The Clongownian*.

In the Michaelmas term of 1897, Kettle entered the Catholic University (later to become University College Dublin) which comprised numbers **85 and 86 St Stephen's Green**. With the exception of Iveagh House, these are the only stone-faced houses on St Stephen's Green. Number 85 was formerly the home of the notorious and colourful Buck Whaley and he had the adjoining number 86 built. The two houses, later known as **Newman House**, were combined in 1854 as St Patrick's House, and the Catholic University was opened there that year with Cardinal John Henry

Newman as its first Rector. A major restoration has taken place and the building is now open to the public.

The students had no proper library facilities at the university and used the **National Library** in **Kildare Street**. Here they mingled with students from the medical school of the Catholic University which was situated in Cecilia Street. Among the students at the university during Kettle's time were James Joyce, Oliver Gogarty, Francis Sheehy-Skeffington, J.F. Byrne, Felix Hackett, John Marcus O'Sullivan, James N. Meenan and others. The teaching staff included Father Joseph Darlington, SJ, Prefect of Studies; Father Tom Finlay, SJ, Professor of Metaphysics; Father George O'Neill, SJ; Thomas Arnold, a professor in the Department of English and a brother of the poet Matthew Arnold; and John Casey, described as 'a man of simple faith and subtle mathematics' who taught conics with the help of a raw potato in the old physics theatre. It was here that the Literary and Historical Society met.

In Kettle's first term, the L and H, as it was known, had been inactive for some years and was revived with Francis Sheehy-Skeffington as auditor. Kettle, who was tall, well-built and handsome and had an incisive mind, was a regular attender at these meetings and was highly regarded as an accomplished and gifted orator. He was elected auditor of the L and H for the 1898–9 session and later became editor of *St Stephen's*, the college magazine, succeeding Felix Hackett. David Sheehy, MP, who lived at **2 Belvedere Place**, adjacent to Fitzgibbon Street, held 'evenings' on Sunday, at which members of the L and H were welcome to attend. Sheehy-Skeffington, Joyce and Kettle together with other students frequented these. The Sheehy family consisted of two brothers, Richard and Eugene, and four sisters, Margaret, Hanna, Kathleen and Mary, the youngest, to whom James Joyce was attracted for a number of years.

Due to illness, Kettle failed to sit his BA degree examination in 1900. He took some time off and sat the exam in 1902, obtaining a second-class honours degree. In January 1903, he entered the **King's Inns** to study Law. At this time he was living at Tritonville Cottage, **Cranford Place, Sandymount**. He became active in politics and in 1904 was elected the first President of the Young Ireland Branch of the United Irish League, and with Francis Sheehy-Skeffington edited the *Nationalist*, which was short-lived.

In 1905 Kettle was called to the Bar but never practised. The following year he became MP for East Tyrone, a position which he retained until his resignation in 1910. He travelled in the United

States on behalf of the Nationalist Party, and also around Ireland to various political meetings. His address in Dublin at this time was **27 Northumberland Road** in **Ballsbridge** which was within walking distance of the city centre, and then for a time he rented a house a few doors away at **23 Northumberland Road**.

On a return visit to Dublin in 1909, James Joyce renewed his acquaintance with Kettle and wrote to Nora in Trieste telling her that he had had a four-hour conversation with him, the best friend he had in Ireland. Kettle was just about to marry Mary Sheehy, and Joyce invited them both to stay some days with him and Nora in Trieste during their honeymoon. He asked Nora to put the house in order for their visit. Tom and Mary were married on 8 September 1909 in St Kevin's chapel of **St Mary's Pro-Cathedral** in **Cathedral Street** and the wedding breakfast was held at **2 Belvedere Place**. Joyce did not attend the wedding but arranged to have the couple sent a specially bound copy of *Chamber Music*, of which Kettle had given a good review two years before in the *Freeman's Journal* of 1 June 1907. The couple spent their honeymoon in Austria.

The same year, Kettle was appointed the first Professor of National Economics in University College Dublin and the following year resigned as MP of East Tyrone in order to devote more time to his academic duties. His book *The Day's Burden* was published by Maunsel in 1910, followed by *Home Rule Finance* in 1911. *The Open Secret of Ireland* followed in 1912.

Kettle was Chairman of the Peace Committee for the Dublin Strike in 1913, and assisted in the founding of the National Volunteers, contingents of which later served in the British Army on the Western Front. In July 1914 he was sent to Belgium to acquire arms and, with the outbreak of the First World War, he stayed there for some months to serve as war correspondent for the *Daily News*. He was convinced that England was on the side of the small nations and the same year, on his return to Dublin, he joined the Royal Dublin Fusiliers and helped with the recruitment campaign. His *Poems and Parodies* were published that year.

The Easter Rising of 1916 came as a complete surprise to Kettle and an unanticipated blow to his whole policy. After Francis Sheehy-Skeffington was murdered on 26 April, Kettle volunteered for active service. He left Dublin on 14 July. In a letter to his wife from the Front, addressed to **119 Upper Leeson Street**, he promised that they would go and live in the country and that he would grow early potatoes. He was killed on 9 September on the muddy Western Front at Givenchy during the Battle of the Somme. He was survived by Mary and his young daughter Betty, for whom he wrote a sonnet some days before his death. His epitaph was taken from this:

> So here, while the mad guns curse overhead,
> And tired men sigh with mud for couch and floor,
> Know that we fools, now with the foolish dead,
> Died not for flag, nor King nor Emperor,
> But for a dream, born in a herdsman's shed,
> And for the secret Scripture of the poor.

Kettle is commemorated by a bust in **St Stephen's Green**. The fifty thousand Irish soldiers killed in the First World War are commemorated in the **Irish National War Memorial Park**, comprising twenty acres and designed by Sir Edwin Lutyens at **Islandbridge**. The memorial has been restored and was officially opened to the public on 10 September 1988.

Charles J. Kickham
1828–82

Charles Kickham, poet, patriot and novelist, was born at Cnoceenagow, near Mullinahone in County Tipperary. He was the son of Anne (née O'Mahoney) and John Kickham, a prosperous shopkeeper, but because he was deafened and almost blinded by a gunpowder accident in his early teens, he took no active part in his father's business. Despite his disability, he read extensively and had a keen interest in literature and poetry. He was especially influenced by the work of Thomas Davis, Charles Gavan Duffy, James Clarence Mangan and John Mitchel.

At the age of eighteen Kickham was contributing to the *Nation*, the *Irishman* and the *Celt*, with some of his best poetical works appearing in the latter. He was involved in the Young Ireland Movement and became a Fenian in 1860.

In September 1863, at the invitation of James Stephens, founder of the Irish Republican Brotherhood, he became joint editor of the *Irish People* with John O'Leary and Thomas Clarke Luby. O'Donovan Rossa was business manager. The arrangement was not a success, however, and it was agreed that O'Leary should become sole editor. Kickham's articles were generally anti-clerical, but as he remained a loyal Catholic, he always made the distinction between spiritual and political matters. Acting on information from Pierce Nagle, an informer on the staff, on 14 September 1865 the police raided the office of the *Irish People* at **12 Parliament Street** and seized the type and carried off documentation and papers. O'Donovan Rossa, Luby and O'Leary were all captured. Kickham was with a friend in Kingstown (now Dun Laoghaire), and on hearing the news of the arrests went directly to **Fairfield House** in **Sandymount**, where he stayed with James Stephens. The house is situated at the junction of Herbert Road and Newbridge Avenue. Stephens had rented it for a few months beforehand in case of such an emergency and was directing business from it. A few weeks later they were both arrested when police surrounded the house.

On 6 January 1866, Kickham was tried for treason–felony in **Green Street Courthouse** which is situated due west of Parnell Street. When Stephens had left Dublin for America on one occasion, he had left behind him a document, which was found by the police, constituting Messrs Luby, O'Leary and Kickham as an Executive to control the IRB (Irish Republican Brotherhood) during his absence. Kickham was sentenced to fourteen years' penal servitude by Justice Keogh, who first achieved notoriety through his association with the politician and swindler, John Sadleir. Kickham served his sentence at **Mountjoy Gaol** in Dublin and at Pentonville, Portland and Woking Prisons in England, and was released after three and a half years with his hearing and sight seriously impaired. It was while he was in prison that he wrote his novel *Sally Cavanagh or The Untenanted Graves* which he dedicated to John O'Leary. A sentimental love story of a small farmer's daughter, it ends sadly as a result of the evils of landlordism. In Woking Prison he wrote his poem 'St John's Eve', which concerns the lighting of the bonfires on the Eve of the Feast of St John the Baptist.

After his release from prison in 1869, Kickham returned to Mullinahone. Following the death of the sitting Member for Tipperary there was a by-election to the House of Commons. O'Donovan Rossa was elected but disqualified as an unpardoned felon. Kickham was then nominated but took no part in the election campaign and was defeated by thirteen votes. This was more or less the end of Kickham's public political career and he devoted much of the remainder of his life to writing. He moved to Dublin where he stayed with his brother Alexander, and resumed his work with the IRB. In 1872, he became a member of the Supreme Council, shortly afterwards becoming Chairman, a position he held until his death. In 1873, *Knocknagow or The Homes of Tipperary*, the novel for which he is best remembered, was published, and in 1886 *For the Old Land* appeared.

In November 1879, he moved to lodgings with the O'Connor family at **2 Montpelier Place**, Stradbrook Road, **Blackrock**, County Dublin. This was an interesting residence for Kickham. It was close

35. Plaque on the wall of Kickham's last home,
2 Montpelier Place, Stradbrook Road, Blackrock.

to the sea, reminding him of his childhood summer holidays spent at Tramore in County Waterford. O'Connor worked for the *Irish Peasant*, and more or less kept open house for his literary friends, including Katherine Tynan and George Sigerson (who was Kickham's doctor). His two daughters, Dora and Hester, who later became literary figures, enjoyed Kickham's company. It was here, too, that Kickham met Rose Kavanagh. She was the inspiration for his poem 'The Rose of Knockmanny', and the last poem which he wrote (in August 1882) was dedicated to her.

Already imprisoned by his deafness, Kickham was by now almost totally blind. All his mail was read to him by means of the finger alphabet. He said to Rose Kavanagh that he longed to hear 'the patter of the summer rain among the leaves'.

Kickham's novels and poems depict rural life in nineteenth-century Tipperary, and O'Leary said of him, 'A man endowed with his gifts of observation, humour, and romantic feeling, and with his humane, sincere and lovable character, might in happier circumstances have rivalled Carleton as a delineator of Irish peasant life.'

In late 1880, Kickham was knocked down by a jaunting car in **College Green** and broke his leg, which confined him to bed for a few months. On 19 August 1882, he suffered a stroke and died on 22 August, aged fifty-four. His remains were brought to Kingsbridge Station (now **Heuston**) for burial in the graveyard of St Michael's Church in Mullinahone.

Archbishop Croke wrote, 'I take him to be of all men that I have ever met about the gentlest, the most amiable, the most truthful . . .'

Rudyard Kipling
1865–1936

Rudyard Kipling, novelist, short-story writer and poet, the son of John Lockwood Kipling and Alice (née Macdonald) was born on 30 December 1865 in Bombay. His father was a sculptor and the author and illustrator of *Beast and Man in India*. He was principal of the Mayo School of Art and Curator of the Museum, both in Lahore.

When Rudyard was aged six, he and his younger sister Trix were brought to England. As was customary at the time, many British settlers in India sent their young children back to England to immerse them in their own culture. This also protected the children from contracting infectious diseases which often proved fatal. Rudyard and Trix were boarded with an adoptive family in Southsea who turned out to be most unpleasant. In his short story 'Baa, Baa, Black Sheep' (1888) and his novel *The Light that Failed* (1890), Rudyard recalls this unhappy period in his childhood. In 1878 he entered the United Services College, Westward Ho!. His friendships and events at the school are described in his schoolboy tales, *Stalky & Co.* (1899).

In 1882 Kipling returned to India as a journalist (where he remained until 1889). He joined the staff of the *Civil and Military Gazette* in Lahore and with his ability for recollection he turned out to be a first-class reporter. Works from this period include *Departmental Ditties* (1886), *Plain Tales from the Hills*, *Soldiers Three* (privates Learoyd, Mulvaney and Ortheris), *The Story of the Gadsbys*, *In Black and White*, *Under the Deodars*, *The Phantom Rickshaw* and *Wee Willie Winkie* (all 1888). These works comprise over seventy stories, the background for many of which was provided by British India.

It was during this time that Kipling first met Lord Roberts (from the well-known Waterford family) who was Commander-in-Chief in India from 1885 to 1893. Kipling later recalled, 'The proudest moment of my young life was when I rode up Simla Mall beside him on his usual explosive Arab, while he asked me what the men thought about their accommodation, entertainment-rooms and the like. I told him, and he thanked me as gravely as though I had been a full Colonel.' Roberts was later to serve as Master of the **Royal Hospital** at **Kilmainham** in Dublin where he was based from 1895 to 1900. Kipling paid tribute to his friend, known affectionately as 'Bobs', in his poem entitled 'Lord Roberts':

> Clean, simple, valiant, well-beloved,
> Flawless in faith and fame,
> Whom neither ease nor honours moved
> An hair's breadth from his aim.

In 1889 Kipling returned to England and three years later married Caroline Balestier, his agent's sister. For their honeymoon they took a world tour and settled in Vermont in the United States near to some of Carrie's relations. They remained here for four years and it was during this period that Kipling wrote some of his finest works including *The Jungle Books*. On account of a family conflict, they returned in 1896 to England where they lived for a brief time at Torquay and then at Rottingdean, a coastal village near Brighton. By this time they had three children, named Josephine, John and Elsie. During the harsh winter of 1898–9, the family went to America to visit Carrie's parents despite being forewarned of the extreme weather conditons. During the visit Kipling suffered a severe bout of pneumonia in both lungs, which made front-page news – the Kaiser even sent him a Get Well message. The children contracted a fever and sadly Josephine died. Kipling wrote, 'People say that kind of wound heals. It doesn't.' He never recovered from this tragedy, nor did he ever go back to the United States. The family returned to their home at Rottingdean and in 1902 they put roots firmly down in English soil when they bought the Jacobean mansion Bateman's, at Burwash in Sussex. Kipling continued to travel widely and went to South Africa to cover the Boer War.

In 1901 *Kim*, generally considered Kipling's masterpiece, was published. Described as a 'naked picaresque novel' by its author, it recounts the exotic adventures of Kim O'Hara, the young orphaned son of an Irish soldier who travels through India with a *lama* or holy man from Tibet.

In 1902 Kipling's *Just So Stories* were published. These contain some wonderful fables, perhaps the best-known being 'The Cat that Walked by Himself'.

In 1907 Kipling was awarded the Nobel prize for literature. In mid October 1911, Kipling and Carrie visited Dublin. (This was not Kipling's first visit to Ireland though it was his first time in Dublin – he had been to Ireland in 1897 and 1898.) They stayed at the **Shelbourne Hotel** in **St Stephen's Green** where he found the food was good and *recherché*, and most of the waiters German. In a letter to his children which he wrote from the Shelbourne, he said that he could hear from his bed the pat-pat of horses' feet and very rarely heard the hoot of a motor. He and Carrie visited **Trinity College** to see the Book of Kells. Kipling described Trinity as 'great blocks of grey stone houses and chapels and libraries, set in gardens and sheets of turf greener than emerald'. They shopped in **Grafton Street** which Kipling compared favourably to Bond Street and

36. Grafton Street at about the time of Kipling's visit to Dublin.

Carrie bought quite an amount at the Royal Irish Industries at number **76**, which stocked Irish tweeds, linens, poplins and Irish point lace. They drove along the banks of the river Liffey, the colour of which Kipling likened to Dublin porter. Like Charles

Dickens before them, they took a tour of the **Phoenix Park** in a jaunting car, visiting the **Viceregal Residence** (now **Aras an Uachtaráin**) where they signed their names in the Viceroy's visitors' book. They also visited the **Royal Hospital** at **Kilmainham**, founded in 1680 by James Butler, the Duke of Ormonde, as a home for pensioner soldiers. (It now houses the Irish Museum of Modern Art.) Here they signed the visitors' book of Sir Neville Lyttleton, Master of the Hospital at that time.

Kipling would have known some of the Irish soldiers at the Royal Hospital who had served in India when served in India when he was there, and he would of course have remembered Vonolel (named after a Lushai chief) from his ride with Lord Roberts down Simla Mall. This famous Arab charger, little bigger than a pony, carried Lord Roberts throughout the Afghan War and on the march from Kabul to Kandahar, a distance of over three hundred miles. On leaving India, Lord Roberts had brought Vonolel back from Bombay with him to England and then to Ireland when he became Comander-in-Chief and Master of the Royal Hospital. This courageous little horse died at Kilmainham aged twenty-seven years in June 1899. Vonolel was decorated by Queen Victoria with the Afghan Medal with Four Clasps, the Kandahar Star and the Jubilee Medal. He is buried in the Master's Garden at the Royal Hospital where he is commemorated with a marble slab bearing an inscription written by Lord Roberts. He ranks with Bucephalus, Copenhagen and Marengo amongst the famous war chargers.

Another place with a Kipling connection is **Ellis Street** which runs from Benburb Street to Rory O'More Bridge. Formerly named Silver Street, it has achieved a certain fame through one of Kipling's *Barrack Room Ballads* (1892) entitled 'Belts'. It relates how soldiers from a neighbourhood barracks were engrossed in a fierce fight:

> There was a row in Silver Street that's near to
>   Dublin Quay,
> Between an Irish regiment an' English cavalree;
> It started at Revelly an' it lasted on till dark:
> The first man dropped at Harrison's, the last
>   forninst the Park.

The Barracks in question was the Royal Barracks (now **Collins Barracks**) in **Benburb Street**. It overlooks the Croppies Acre alongside Wolfe Tone Quay. Designed by Thomas Burgh and built in 1701 it was the oldest inhabited barracks in Europe. Its long association with the military ended in April 1997 when the Army officially vacated it. It has been taken over by the National Museum of Ireland.

Kipling's only son, John, enlisted when he was eighteen with the 2nd Battalion of the Irish Guards. Six weeks after he left home he was reported missing, believed killed, at the Battle of Loos in October 1915. This was a tragic and devastating blow for Kipling which was reflected in his writings. In 1917 he became one of the War Graves Commissioners and worked at this for the rest of his life. He wrote the history of his son's regiment entitled *The Irish Guards in the Great War* (two volumes, 1923). He was awarded the gold medal of the Royal Society of Literature in 1926, which only Walter Scott, George Meredith and Thomas Hardy had received before him.

In 1934 Kipling began his autobiography *Something of Myself.* It was never finished and was published posthumously in 1937.

Rudyard Kipling died on 18 January 1936 and his ashes are in Poets' Corner, Westminster Abbey in London.

Maura Laverty
1907–66

Maura Laverty, novelist and playwright, was born in Rathangan in County Kildare in 1907. She was educated at the Brigadine Convent in Tullow, County Carlow. At the age of eighteen she went to Madrid where she worked as governess, secretary and journalist for the paper *El Debate*, and then returned to live in Dublin in 1928 where she worked as a journalist anad broadcaster.

Laverty's first novel, *Never No More* (1942), makes use of her early environment in Rathangan. Her novel *Touched by Thorns* (1943) received the Irish Women Writers Award, but was banned in Ireland. Her best-known novel, *Lift up your Gates* (1946) concerned a Dublin family in the 1920s who lived in the **Westland Row** area. It is an interesting social record of that time as it portrays the day-to-day life of a poor family living in extreme hardship and squalor in a tenement room. The novel was dramatised as *Liffey Lane*, and RTE's long-running soap opera *Tolka Row* was based on it. *A Tree in the Crescent* was published in 1952.

Laverty wrote several children's books, and also some books on cookery. She died in 1966 and is buried in **Glasnevin Cemetery**.

Emily Lawless
1845–1913

Among the strange, legendary women of Anglo-Irish forebears whose beauty streams like a wraith through Irish history, Emily Lawless, 'the girl with the corn-coloured hair', takes an honoured place by virtue of her poetry.

37. Emily Lawless.

Her father, the 3rd Lord Cloncurry, was a member of the United Irishmen, and her grandfather, Valentine Browne Lawless, was twice confined to the Tower of London. Her family had affiliations with the Wild Geese and some of them vanished into Continental armies with Patrick Sarsfield after Limerick in 1691. In 1776 her great-grandfather returned to Ireland and was created a Baron. A General Lawless, another member of the family, interviewed Napoleon a few years later with plans for an Irish invasion. His companion was Wolfe Tone.

Castle Lyons, where Emily was born on 17 June 1845, one of eight children of Lord Cloncurry, was always filled with freedoom-loving men of European stature, and their influence and tradition. Henry Grattan and John Philpot Curran were frequent visitors to the house. There Daniel O'Connell discussed Repeal, Land Tenure and Emancipation. In fact, Lyons Hill is one of the places claimed as the scene of O'Connell's celebrated duel with d'Esterre in 1815.

Castle Lyons is a large, stone, Georgian mansion situated three miles south of Dublin on the east side of the river Liffey in **Celbridge**. It was Nicholas Lawless, the 1st Lord Cloncurry, who initiated its construction in 1797. The architect was Oliver Grace, and it followed the style of Richard Cassels. The mansion, which had as its surrounds acres of parkland and gardens with lawn and lake artistically landscaped, was full of the finest works of art which included frescoes, stucco ceilings and sculptures brought from abroad. Ornaments from as far as Herculaneum adorned it, and three of the columns in its portico originated from the Golden House of Nero in Rome.

Lord Cloncurry also had a large summer residence with extensive grounds leading down to the sea, named **Maretimo**, in the Dublin suburb of **Blackrock**, where Emily would have spent some of her summer holidays. Her father inherited it in 1853 on the death of his father, Valentine Lawless, who died in the house. George IV was entertained at Maretimo and many parties were held in the house. One description says of an entertainment, 'It lasted for the round of a clock, and truly was deserving of the name of a rout. It was summer, and tables were spread in large tents on the lawn, and many who were unable to find room at the tables outside were reduced to dining in the house.' Blackrock was a fashionable watering place at the time where many of the gentry owned houses. Maretimo has been demolished and replaced with apartments but the original stone bearing the name Maretimo is preserved in the wall.

With this magnificent background, the inquisitive-minded little Emily had great scope for education and recreation in her formative years. In the grounds of Castle Lyons was a ruined castle which had been occupied by the Aylmers for five hundred years. It was blown up in 1642 by Ormonde because the Aylmers were hiding enemies of the Cromwellians. This interested Emily very much and gave her a theme for many a question. Lyons Hill, one of the early royal seats of the kingdom of Leinster, is also situated in the demesne.

Emily Lawless loved nature and collected a wide variety of wild flowers, birds and animals which she brought home to her nursery and even into her dining room to study. Like Countess Markievicz,

Emily was a fearless horsewoman, and was questing enough to explore and write about little-known Connemara and the Aran Islands before John Millington Synge ever went there. She, like James Joyce, loved the river Liffey which passed near her home.

Emily's mother was an O Cuardubhán, 'the jet-black folk' of County Galway, her Scots grandmother the daughter of Lord Archibald Douglas. She spent much of her early life in Galway with her mother's people at Castlehacket, and was exceptionally fond of Clare, Connemara and Aran. The ruggedness and wild features of the Connaught area had a profound influence on her and in some way reminded her of the nostalgic spirit of the O'Briens and other young Irish fighting men. She includes in her work poems about the young soldiers reminiscing in their tents before the Battle of Cremona in 1702 and portrays the joy of the Irish coming home after the battle of Fontenoy in the year 1745 in her poem of that name.

Her time in Connaught gave her themes in verse and prose for her novel *Hurrish* (1886) and also for *Grania: The Story of an Island*, which appeared six years later. Her *History of Ireland* was well received and in the year 1890 *With Essex in Ireland* was published. She considered this 'the only of my books that gives me personal satisfaction'. She wrote ten novels, short stories and historical essays and four books of verse.

Gladstone called on Emily Lawless while holidaying in Cannes to congratulate her on her work, and her other admirers included Algernon Swinburne, William Lecky, Aubrey de Vere and Cardinal Manning. The **University of Dublin (Trinity College)** awarded her an Honorary D.Litt. in 1905, which she cherished.

She travelled abroad frequently and decided to leave Kildare for the gentler climate of the South of England when she was in her sixties, under her doctor's orders, missing very much the nearby Liffey, the woods, the lawns and the lakes of Lyons. The remaining years of her life were spent with her good friend Lady Sarah Spencer, in a little house at Gomshall. It was called Hazlehatch after the station on the Grand Canal that served Lyons Estate. The name was originally Hazlehurst, meaning a hurst, or wood, of hazel trees.

Emily Lawless died on 19 October 1913, and is buried in Surrey under a Celtic cross similar to the ones existing in the Lyons burial ground. The chancel of the little church of the Blessed Virgin Mary in the Lyons Estate has been converted into a Mausoleum.

> Who am I, Lord lead me on,
> the night is dark, no stars are in the sky.

Joseph Sheridan le Fanu
1814–73

Joseph Sheridan Le Fanu, the novelist and short-story writer who, along with Charles Maturin and Bram Stoker, forms a Dublin triumvirate of famous writers about the supernatural, was born on 28 August 1814 at 45 **Lower Dominick Street** (the house has been demolished). He was the son of Dean Thomas Philip Le Fanu, and Emma (née Dobbyn) and great – nephew of the dramatist and statesman Richard Brinsley Sheridan.

38. Joseph Sheridan Le Fanu from the portrait by Brinsley Le Fanu.

The name Le Fanu, like that of Maturin and Boucicault, was of Huguenot origin. At the time of the revocation of the Edict of Nantes in 1685, the Le Fanu estates of Mandeville, Cresseron and Sequeville in France were seized; many Huguenots settled in Ireland.

When Joseph Le Fanu was born, his father Philip Le Fanu was the curate of St Mary's Church (which no longer functions as a church), situated between Stafford Street (now **Wolfe Tone Street**) and

Jervis Street. In 1815, Dean Le Fanu was appointed by the Lord Lieutenant to be Chaplain to the Royal Irish Artillery and Superintendent of Morals at the **Royal Hibernian Military School** in the **Phoenix Park**.

As you enter the Park from the Chapelizod Gate, the old Hibernian Military School is the focal point, though most of the view of it is now obliterated by trees. The foundation stone of the military school was laid in 1766 with ceremonial pomp, in the presence of the Lords Justice. It was established by Lord Townsend in 1767 for the education of orphans and soldiers' children and had accommodation for six hundred children, both boys and girls. The school was closed in 1922, and became **St Mary's Hospital**, which is now run by the Eastern Health Board.

Although his father presided here, Joseph did not attend this school but was educated privately by Dean Le Fanu who taught him English and French. He was later taught classics and science by an elderly and eccentric tutor named Stinson, who was a keen fisherman and spent the greater part of his time tying flies for fishing trout and salmon.

At an early age, Joseph showed a talent for writing and availed himself of his father's extensive library; unlike his brother, he did not participate in sports. He had a great sense of fun, as was related by his brother. Much to the annoyance of his father, Joseph was continually late for his morning prayers. One morning he appeared just as breakfast was over, and the Very Revd Le Fanu, with his watch in his hand, said in his severest tones, 'I ask you, Joseph, I ask you seriously, Is this right?' 'No, sir,' said Joseph, glancing at the watch, 'I am sure it must be fast.'

In their free time, Joseph and his brother explored the grounds of the magnificent **Phoenix Park**, which is the largest urban park in Europe, encompassing 1,670 acres. The land stretching between the school and the Royal Infirmary (now the Army Headquarters) in Parkgate Street was used regularly for the practise of military manoeuvres; a large single stretch of land, it was eminently suitable for both artillery and cavalry. Here the glamorous cavalry units from Marlborough and Islandbridge Barracks carried out their entire manoeuvre from the stand to the charge. To witness such scenes was thrilling for the Le Fanu boys.

The boys also frequented the nearby Liffeyside village of **Chapelizod**, where the Royal Artillery were stationed. The officers' headquarters was in the King's House. Chapelizod was later deemed unsuitable for the unit as the men were exposed to 'too much contact with the villagers'. Le Fanu, taking the pseudonym of his famous ancestor Charles de Cresseron, describes Chapelizod in the prologue of his novel *The House by the Churchyard* as 'about the gayest and prettiest of the outpost villages in which old Dublin took a complacent pride. The poplars which stood, in military rows, here and there, just showed a glimpse of formality among the orchards and old timber that lined the banks of the river and the valley of the Liffey, with a lively sort of richness. The broad old street looked hospitable and merry, with steep roofs and many coloured hall-doors.' He also gives descriptions of the village church and the

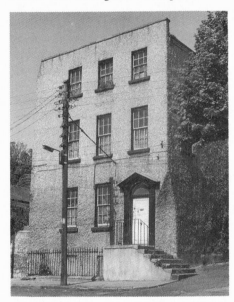

39. The House by the Churchyard in Chapelizod.

barrack of the Royal Irish Artillery with 'the great gate leading into the parade ground, by the river side'. This was close to the school and it was an exciting event for Joseph and his brother to watch the military reviews with veteran soldiers marching, wearing the uniforms they had worn at the Battle of Waterloo in 1815, only a short while before. They loved the excitement when the Lord-Lieutenant 'stepped forth between the files of the guard of honour of the Royal Irish Artillery, in their courtly uniform, white, scarlet, and blue, cocked hats, and cues, and ruffles, presenting arms – into his emblazoned coach and six, with hanging footmen, as wonderful as Cinderella's, and outriders out-blazing the liveries of the troops, and rolling grandly away in sunshine and dust.'

In 1823, the Very Revd Philip Le Fanu was appointed to the rectory of Abington, a small village in County Limerick. Three years later he was appointed Dean of Emily, and it was then, when Joseph was aged twelve, that the family left the Hibernian Military School to live in Abington. They were to remain here for seven years, during which time the young Le Fanu gathered material for his stories. As he wrote later of this period, 'I heard a great many Irish traditions more or less of a supernatural character, some of them very peculiar, and all, to a child at least, highly interesting.'

In October 1832, Joseph returned to Dublin and entered **Trinity College** to study law. He was a member of the Historical Society and was elected President the same night as Thomas Davis was elected Auditor. A brilliant debater, he took the top place in the Historical Society and was awarded a medal for oratory. One of his contemporaries at Trinity was William Wilde, who was studying medicine at **Dr Steevens' Hospital**. While at college, Le Fanu contributed a story, the first of a series, entitled 'The Ghost and the Bonesetter' to the *Dublin University Magazine*, a monthly literary magazine founded by Isaac Butt in 1833. Butt's idea was that the magazine should be a 'monthly advocate of the Protestantism, the intelligence, and the respectability of Dublin'.

In 1837, Le Fanu graduated with his BA degree in law. Two years later he was called to the Bar but never practised, preferring to devote himself to literature and to work first as a journalist, then editor and finally a newspaper owner. He purchased a number of newspapers, later amalgamating three of them, the *Warder*, the *Dublin Evening Packet* and the *Evening Mail* into the *Dublin Evening Mail*, the paper for which Bram Stoker later wrote his theatre reviews. Le Fanu edited the newspaper for the next two decades and continued to write short stories and verse. One of his stories, 'A Chapter in the History of a Tyrone Family', is said to have been a possible influence on Charlotte Brontë for the plot in her novel *Jane Eyre*.

In 1844, Le Fanu married Susan Bennett, the daughter of George Bennett, QC, a leading Dublin lawyer. They settled at **2 Nelson Street**, on the then fashionable north side, which links Berkeley Street and Eccles Street. The following year, they crossed the Liffey to **1 Warrington Place**, alongside the Grand Canal between Upper and Lower Mount Streets, and a year later moved to number **15** on the same street.

Although Le Fanu was not involved with politics he wrote some well-known ballads about the state of the nation. He was influenced by his mother, a talented and gifted woman, who instilled in him details about the troubles of 1798 and about the brothers Sheares, whose remains are in St Michan's Church in Church Street. In her day, she had acquired some objects of historical importance: one was a letter written to her father, Dr Dobbyn, by John Sheares before his execution, and the other was a dagger belonging to Lord Edward Fitzgerald which she had procured on a visit to Major Swan's house in **North Great George's Street**.

In 1845, Le Fanu's first book, *The Cock and the Anchor*, was published. It gives a colourful picture of eighteenth-century Dublin, with its duels and alehouses, such as the **Bleeding Horse** in **Camden Street**, which James Clarence Mangan frequented.

In 1850 his best-known ballad, 'Shamus O'Brien', which he had written in 1837, was published. Over a decade later it was recited by Samuel Lover on his American tour.

In 1851, on the death of Dr Dobbyn, the Le Fanu family moved from Warrington Place to his house at 18 **Merrion Square** (now number **70**) which Dr Dobbyn left to his daughter. This was one of the best addresses in Dublin. There were now four children in the family, two daughters and two sons. The house had a rear garden which was an ideal place for the children to play. Most of the houses on Merrion Square are no longer private homes but are used as offices and 18 Merrion Square is no exception: it now houses the Arts Council.

In 1858, after fourteen years of marriage, Mrs Le Fanu died following a short illness. Le Fanu was devastated with grief. Formerly somewhat of a socialite, he now turned into a recluse and became known as 'the invisible prince'. He was rarely seen, as most of his wanderings around the Georgian squares and streets were nocturnal. His close friend Charles Lever was not admitted when he returned on one of his visits to Dublin and on what was to be his last visit to Le Fanu. A description of his working pattern at 18 Merrion Square was given by his son Brinsley in a conversation with Mr S.M. Ellis. He said that most of his writing was done in bed at night by candlelight in copy-books and scraps of paper, and he kept himself going by drinking strong cups of tea. He always had his breakfast in bed and at twelve noon would retreat to the dining room at the rear of the house where he would resume writing on the little table which had belonged to his great-uncle, Richard Brinsley Sheridan. If the weather was fine, he would exercise in the back garden by walking up and down with a pencil and a copy-book in his hand, revising the work he had done the previous night. He rarely went to town, and if he did it was usually to visit a bookshop to browse in some work on demonology or ghosts.

In the years following his wife's death, Le Fanu published twelve novels. *The House by the Churchyard* (1863) was a macabre story about a haunted house. Le Fanu drew in the topography of **Chapelizod** he had known as a child, and there are interesting theatrical and other references to Dublin life of the time. Many of the eighteenth-century landmarks still remain in Chapelizod today, including the actual house by the churchyard of the Protestant Church, just south of **Anna Livia Bridge**. Le Fanu's book was used by James Joyce as a source for his novel *Finnegans Wake*.

Uncle Silas (1864) was adapted for stage and produced at the Shaftesbury Theatre in London. Two of his stories, 'Carmilla', a vampire story which could possibly have been the inspiration for Stoker's *Dracula*, and 'The Watcher', were also adapted for the stage and were produced in the **Gate Theatre** in Dublin in the 1940s.

On 7 February 1873, Le Fanu died in his fifty-ninth year at **18 Merrion Square**. His obituary in the *Dublin University Magazine*, of which he had been Editor from 1861 to 1869, read, 'He was a man who thought deeply, especially on religious subjects. To those who knew him he was very dear. They admired him for his learning, his sparkling wit and [his] pleasant conversation, and loved him for his manly virtues, his noble and generous qualities, his gentleness, and his loving, affectionate nature.'

Le Fanu is buried in **Mount Jerome Cemetery** in Harold's Cross, Dublin.

Charles Lever
1806–72

Charles Lever, novelist and doctor, was born at Sunnybank, **34 Amiens Street**. This comfortable house, with outhouses, a yard and a garden, no longer exists. From 1728, the thoroughfare was called The Strand, but on a map dated 1829 it appears as Amiens Street. It was renamed after Viscount Amiens, created Earl of Aldborough in 1777, who was responsible for building the nearby Aldborough House, one of the last great mansions to go up before the Act of Union of 1800. It was subsequently used as a boarding school, and during Lever's youth, at the time of the Crimean War, it was used as a barracks, Dublin being then a garrison town. The once beautiful gardens are now covered with corporation flats and Aldborough House is used as a store for Telecom Eireann. Lever's home, Sunnybank, was in the vicinity of 'Beresford's Riding-School', used for drilling yeomanry. The grotesque-looking yeomanry were known as 'Caesars', from their habit of seizing persons who they then tortured at the 'Riding School', and taking their property.

40. Charles Lever from the miniature by Samuel Lover, 1841.

Charles Lever was the second son of James Lever, architect and builder, and Julia (née Candler), described as a little woman of coquettish manners. Both were from Cromwellian families who had received grants of land. James Lever left his mark on Dublin having built 'the Round Church', designed by Francis Johnston; he was also connected with the building of St George's Church in Hardwicke Place and the General Post Office in Sackville Street (now O'Connell Street).

Lever received a somewhat scattered education, having been sent to a number of different schools. He was aged four when he attended the first one, in the adjoining house to his own in **Amiens Street**, run by a Mr Ford who was known to be severe on his forty pupils. The next school he attended had eighty pupils and was at **56 South William Street** within a door or two of Powerscourt House. It was run by an accomplished man named Florence McCarthy. This was followed by a school at **113 Abbey Street** run by a William

O'Callaghan, described as 'a mathematician'. Dramas were performed periodically at this school. When Lever was aged eleven, he spent some time attending school in Inistioge in County Kilkenny. He was described at this time as being remarkably handsome, somewhat vain, ready of speech with a laughing manner, and wonderfully self-possessed for a youth of his standing.

The Dublin Directory for 1819 records 'Revd G.N. Wright, Principle of the Proprietary School, Great Denmark Street' and this was the school Lever attended on his return from Inistioge. Situated at **2 Great Denmark Street**, it was formerly the home of Lord Ashtown. Here Lever was taught fencing and was the pride of Mr Montague, the professor of dancing. Mr Wright, who wrote a life of the Duke of Wellington and with Petrie compiled *An Historical Guide to Dublin*, had literary tastes, and the silver-end of Lever's tongue pleased him. In 1821, on the occasion of King George IV's visit to Dublin, the pupils trooped off to see him. Lever wrote, 'Certainly that autumn eve when he went away, it presented a glorious and most spirit-stirring sight, as the gorgeous western sun beamed down on the hundreds of thousands of loyal lusty-voiced mortals. After all, there is an indescribable magic in the loud huzza of a million reasoning bipeds, whether rushing to battle or hailing a king.' Lever became one of Mr Wright's favourite pupils and years later, when he was famous and met his old master, who congratulated him on his work, Lever replied, 'The work is yours. What you see is but the stucco upon the building of which you laid the foundation.'

Mr Wright moved the school to Rutland Square (now **Parnell Square**) to the house adjoining that of Lord Chief Justice Norbury. Lever used to amuse the other pupils by telling them stories based on actual happenings from day to day. Most of the boys at Mr Wright's school came from well-off families and were often subjected to attacks from the pupils at a neighbouring and more lowly school in **Grenville Street**. Skirmishes took place regularly, and an actual battle once occurred between both factions in Mountjoy Fields, then a piece of wasteground on which **Gardiner Street Church** now stands. Lever helped to organise the troops from his side, and a fellow pupil, later an eminent engineer, laid a small mine which inflicted scorches and scratches on the troops' faces from both sides. The police from nearby **Marlborough Street** intervened. Finally Lever, a master of eloquent speech, managed to talk his way out, while his comrades received minor fines.

In his spare time, Lever, a fair-haired youth with ringlets, wandered around the old bookstalls browsing in the likes of *The Mysteries of Udolpho* or *The Adventures of Count Fathom*. While still at school, he fell in love with Kate Baker, a young girl who lived at **89 Sir John Rogerson's Quay**, and frequently threw flowers in through the iron gate of the courtyard of her house. The couple married many years later against her father's wishes.

In Dublin, Lever lived for some time at **Moatfield, Clontarf**, a house which had been built by his father. In his book *The O'Donoghue*, a romance of Killarney, he devotes a chapter to Clontarf, describing it as 'the then fashionable watering-place', and its 'Green Lanes' are mentioned in *That Boy of Norcott's*. He lived for a time at **74 Talbot Street** when his parents moved from Clontarf.

In 1822 he entered **Trinity College** where he was undistinguished as a student, but was remembered for his sense of fun and storytelling. His rooms in college were in house number **2, Botany Bay**. He also stayed for a period at Lisle House, **33 Molesworth Street**, a fashionable boarding house at that time. He did not graduate until 1827 – a delay which may be accounted for by the fact that he went to Quebec in charge of an emigrant ship for some of this time. By 1828, he had already travelled in Holland and Germany, spending some time at Göttingen, where he studied medicine.

On his return to Dublin in 1830, Lever continued his medical studies at **Sir Patrick Dun's Hospital**, a building designed by Sir Richard Morrison at **Lower Grand Canal Street**. It ceased to be used as a hospital in 1986. He then studied at **Dr Steevens' Hospital** in **Steevens' Lane**, on the south bank of the Liffey at the western periphery of the city. William Wilde was a fellow student. Designed by Thomas Burgh, Steevens' is Dublin's second oldest hospital, of which Dean Swift was one of the original trustees. The hospital was built with money left by Dr Richard Steevens to his twin sister Grizel for her life, and after her death 'to provide one proper place or building within the City of Dublin for an hospital for maintaining and curing from time to time such sick and wounded persons whose distempers and wounds are curable.' The first patients were admitted in July 1733 and it remained a hospital until 1987 when it was taken over by the Eastern Health Board.

Through its history many famous doctors were associated with it, such as William Wilde, Abraham Colles, Robert Graves, and William Stokes. Lever obtained the degree of Bachelor of Medicine in the summer of 1831, after which he held appointments at Kilkee and Kilrush in County Clare and Portstewart, County Derry, where he wrote part of his novel *The Confessions of Harry Lorrequer*. The following year, he was back working in Dublin during an outbreak of cholera in which a great number of people perished. That year both his parents died. Around this time he married Kate Baker and although he inherited half of his father's considerable property, his heavy gambling brought him into debt. He started to write as a resource to pay off his debts. In 1839, *The Confessions of Harry Lorrequer*, which is considered his best novel, was published in serial form by the *Dublin University Magazine. Charles O'Malley, the Irish Dragoon* followed and proved to be the most popular of his works. In 1840 he moved to Brussels, to work as secretary to the British Ambassador in Belgium. Three years later *Jack Hinton, the Guardsman* was published, in which his former dance teacher, Professor Montague, appears.

Abandoning medicine for good, Lever returned to Dublin and became Editor of the *Dublin University Magazine*, contributing his own stories which added to its success. He increased the number of contributors to the magazine, but never felt comfortable as Editor. He no longer had the time to spend observing people and collecting stories and anecdotes.

During this time the Levers lived briefly in **Stillorgan** and Kingstown (now **Dun Laoghaire**). Kingstown was an exciting place, as the first railway in Ireland, which had just been constructed by William Dargan, ran from **Westland Row** station, just east of Trinity College, to the West Pier in Kingstown, serving the Mail Boat. Lever regularly travelled into the city centre by train and derived great amusement from other passengers. He found the 8.30 train filled with attorneys: 'The ways of Providence are inscrutable: it arrives safely in Dublin . . . A different set of travellers are on the 9.00 train. They comprise a fresh, jovial set of fellows, with bushy whiskers, and geraniums in buttonholes. These are traders who have half an acre divided into meadow and tillage near Kingstown. The housekeepers' train is at 9.30 a.m. followed at 10.00 a.m. by the barristers' train. Fierce faces look out at the weather with the stern glance they are accustomed to; and stare at the sun in the face as though to say, "None of your prevarication with me. Answer me, on your oath, is it to rain or not?" '

Lever then moved to **Templeogue House**, now situated on **Cypress Grove Road, Templeogue**, on the outskirts of Dublin. Formerly a resort of the Knights Templar, it is included in the number of mansions in which King James II is said to have slept after his defeat at the Battle of the Boyne in 1690. The house had gracious surroundings, expansive gardens with terraced walks, an old Dutch waterfall, grottoes and a subterranean passage passing beneath the road. Together with his children's ponies, Lever kept a dozen horses, all named after characters from his books. Many discussions took place here concerning the contents of the next issue of the *Dublin University Magazine*. Visitors included Isaac Butt, Petrie, Mortimer O'Sullivan and, of course, William Thackeray, who dedicated his *Irish Sketch Book* to his friend Lever, 'from whom I have received a hundred acts of kindness and cordial hospitality'.

When Thackeray visited Lever during his Irish tour in 1842–3, he advised him in vain to quit Dublin for London. Before he resigned in 1845 as Editor, Lever lived for a brief spell at a house called **Oatlands** in **Stillorgan**. He then went to live on the continent, in Belgium, then Germany; finally in 1847 he settled in Florence. Here he wrote essays for *Blackwood's Magazine*, the famous literary periodical. In 1867, he was appointed British Consul at Trieste. He visited Ireland in 1871 and the following year died in Trieste on 1 June. He is buried in the British cemetery.

In his *Autobiography*, Anthony Trollope wrote that Lever's novels were just like his conversation: 'Of all the men I have encountered, he was the surest fund of drollery . . . Rouse him in the middle of the night, and wit would come from him before he was half awake.'

Lord Longford
1902–61

Edward Pakenham, 6th Earl of Longford, playwright and producer, was born on 29 December 1902 into a family who had been in Ireland since the middle of the seventeenth century. He was sent away to be educated at Eton and at Oxford. It was while he was at university that his interest in the theatre developed, and here that he met his wife Christine (née Trew), a playwright and woman of letters, whom he married in 1925.

In 1931, Longford became a director of the **Gate Theatre** which had been founded three years before by Hilton Edwards and Micheál MacLiammóir. In 1936 he founded his own company, *Longford Productions*, and rented the Gate for six months each year, from April to September, to produce a wide range of plays.

41. The Gate Theatre, Cavendish Row.

Longford's company brought theatre to the provinces by touring the country with its classic repertory from 1937 until 1961. Many of his own plays and translations were produced in the theatre, including *Yahoo*, which concerned Dean Swift and was one of the successes of the 1933–4 season. Longford was a scholar of Greek and Gaelic and he translated quite an amount from the Irish language including Brian Merriman's *Midnight Court*, as well as plays by Euripides and Sophocles. He also translated Molière, Beaumarchais and Calderón, and dramatised Le Fanu's *Carmilla*.

The Gate Theatre did not receive any state assistance until 1970 and depended upon its ticket sales and subscriptions to keep it going. On more than one occasion it was rescued from financial ruin by Longford who offset the theatre's deficit from his own personal funds and paid for its maintenance.

Longford served in the Irish Senate from 1946 to 1948, and was a member of the Irish Academy of Letters. In 1954 he was awarded a D.Litt. from the **University of Dublin (Trinity College)**. The Longfords lived at **Grosvenor Park**, 123 Leinster Road, **Rathmines**. Longford died on 4 February 1961 and his widow Christine, who had collaborated with him at the Gate Theatre, continued as Managing Director from 1961 to 1964.

Samuel Lover
1797–1868

Samuel Lover, novelist, songwriter and painter, was born on 24 February 1797 at **60 Grafton Street**, Dublin. The earliest reference to the street occurs in a statute dated 1708 although it was in existence before the end of the seventeenth century.

Before the Act of Union in 1800, Grafton Street was a popular address with publishers and booksellers and many of them lived here. One of these was Alderman John Exshaw, publisher of *Exshaw's Magazine*, who lived at number **98**. On St Patrick's Day 1797, just a few weeks after Lover's birth, the 1st Regiment of Royal Dublin Volunteers, commanded by John Exshaw, was presented by his daughter Miss Exshaw with elegant stands of colours richly embroidered by her, accompanied by an address.

Lover was the eldest son of a prosperous Protestant stockbroker. He was a delicate child cosseted by his mother, lucky to have survived as all his brothers and sisters had died in their infancy. He was born at a politically stirring time; it was the year before the Insurrection of 1798, which was followed by Robert Emmet's rising in Dublin in July 1803, and his subsequent trial and horrific execution outside the grey, granite-stoned front of **St Catherine's Church** in **Thomas Street**. For young Samuel, who often heard the drums beating in the street and the tramp of soldiers summoned to

155

search for arms in all directions, it was a terrifying time: 'What tales were then current of hangings, floggings, imprisonment of victims who were subjected to the horrible torture of the pitch-cap, of citizens and others who were grossly insulted and assaulted by soldiery, and domiciliary visits made in the most savage and repugnant manner . . . This I witnessed as a child.'

42. Samuel Lover from the portrait by James Harwood.

The horror did not end there. As seen on John Rocque's map of 1756, *Exact Survey of the city and suburbs of Dublin*, **Grafton Street** was just across the river from Marlborough Bowling Green, a spacious tree-filled park. This was located east of **Marlborough Street**, in the space between the present Talbot and Lower Abbey Streets. It was near this spot that John Beresford, MP, one of the government agents most involved in the suppression of the 1798 Insurrection, tortured many a suspected rebel, whose chilling screams could be heard in the neighbourhood. Sir Jonah Barrington recalls that a washerwoman's signboard was placed over Beresford's Gate by some satirists, which aptly read, 'Mangling done here'. Lover passed this way to school each day. The English soldiers did not discriminate between Protestant and Catholic and Lover recalls the day an abusive drummer boy called and tried to force his way into their home. On his return from business, Mr

156

Lover found his wife in a state of shock, and tackled the soldier, who drew his bayonet. A struggle ensued before an officer from the Billet Office arrived and removed the offender amid the screams of young Samuel Lover who remarked later, 'What a scene was this for a delicate child to witness, one who was more than usually susceptible of terrifying impressions. Here was an English soldier outraging in an Irish Protestant home.' From then until his sixteenth year, when he became a staunch asserter of national rights, he eagerly remembered every word he heard of English oppression and Irish wrong. He loved Irish songs, which he had learnt from his mother who sang to him nightly.

As a boy, Samuel showed a great aptitude for drawing and also for music. Someone once heard him play the piano and, just as was the case with Handel, persuaded his father to buy him one. He studied so hard at his music and schoolwork that in 1809, when he was only eleven, his doctor recommended that he have a complete rest cure from books and go and live in the country. He went to a farmhouse in County Wicklow. Within a short time of his being there, however, his mother died, to his inconsolable grief. This later prompted his song entitled 'My Mother Dear'. Aged thirteen, he returned home and displayed such ability at school that his teachers recommended he attend **Trinity College**, but his father thought otherwise, and had him work in his office. Samuel was uninterested in a business career and continued his studies in the evening, which caused frequent quarrels between them. When he was seventeen he left home determined to earn his living by giving drawing lessons. By the time he reached twenty, he had exhibited drawings at the Dublin Society's house in **Hawkins Street** and four years later he was included in the Society's watercolour exhibition. Initially he concentrated on landscapes and marine topics, and then, with encouragement from a fellow artist, John Comerford, he began doing miniature painting at which he was moderately successful, his best-known work being a study of Paganini.

Lover became a member of the **Royal Hibernian Academy** to which he contributed almost a hundred landscapes, miniatures and drawings between 1826 and 1835. The Academy, which was founded in 1823 for the purpose of encouraging Irish artists by offering them an annual opportunity of exhibiting their works, is now situated at **15 Ely Place** (on the site where Oliver St John Gogarty's house once stood).

Lover also became known as a songwriter, when he composed a lively eulogy on Thomas Moore for the special banquet held in honour of the poet in 1818. Moore was impressed with the song and requested an introduction to the twenty-one-year-old composer. They became good friends and this friendship gained access for Lover into a privileged social circle and to clubs such as Charles Lever's Burschenshaft and the Glee Club of Dublin. He continued writing, contributing to the *Dublin Literary Gazette*, followed by the publication of what is his best known ballad, 'Rory O'More', which was later a novel, then a play. A founder member of the *Dublin University Magazine*, he contributed many of his Irish tales to it. In 1827, Lover married Miss Berrel, a Catholic and the daughter of a Dublin architect. In the early 1830s, they lived at **9 D'Olier Street**, not far from his birthplace in Grafton Street. Here, with his bright happy disposition he acted as host to his friends. The couple did not, however, remain at this address for long.

In 1835, they moved to London, where Lover worked as a portrait painter. He mixed with other artists and attended Lady Blessington's receptions. He also met various writers, including Dickens with whom he organised the founding of *Bentley's Miscellany*. His first novel, *Rory O'More*, based on his earlier ballad, was published in 1837. William Maginn, another Irishman who was an important and prolific contributor to *Blackwood's Magazine*, described him as 'at once a musician, a painter, a novelist, and a poet'.

In 1844, because of failing eyesight, he abandoned painting and gave public recitals of his work which he termed his *Irish Evenings*. He brought his performance on tour in the United States for two years, where it was a great success. In 1847, while he was still in the United States, his wife died. In 1852, he married the daughter of a Cambridgeshire squire named Wanby. Four years later he received a Civil List pension.

Samuel Lover's songs have been praised as having 'much of the rich caprice and not a little of the force of passion' but he is best remembered for his literature and in particular for his *Legends and Stories of Ireland*, *Rory O'More*, and *Handy Andy*, his most famous novel.

He died on 6 July 1868 aged seventy-one, at St Helier in Jersey, and his body was later interred at Kensal Green, London. In his native city he is commemorated by a plaque in **St Patrick's Cathedral**, which reads:

In memory of Samuel Lover, Poet, Painter, Novelist, and Composer, who in the exercise of a genius as distinguished in its versatility as in its power, by the pen and pencil illustrated so happily the characteristics of the Peasantry of his country that his name will ever be honourably identified with Ireland.

Denis Florence MacCarthy
1817–82

Long have I loved the beauty of the streets,
Fair Dublin; long, with unavailing vows . . .

Denis Florence MacCarthy, poet, scholar and translator, was born in a house on Sackville Street (now **O'Connell Street**) which became the Imperial Hotel. It was from one of its balconies that James Larkin gave his famous address during the 1913 lock-out that ended with his arrest and the police's baton-charge of the crowd. The hotel was destroyed in the Rebellion and Clery's Store now stands on the site.

MacCarthy was educated locally and also at Maynooth College, County Kildare, where he studied for the priesthood for a time before changing to law. He was nearly fifty when he was called to the Bar and never practised.

He lived at various addresses in the city which included 74 **Upper Gardiner Street** (now number **53**). Now divided into flats, it stood on the corner of Sherrard Street, which dates from 1795 and is named after Mr Thomas Sherrard, Secretary of the Commissioners of Wide Streets. It was from his home at **38 Upper Baggot Street** that he wrote to William Carleton.

In 1834, he started to contribute prose and poetry to the *Nation*. He wrote also for the *Dublin Magazine* and other periodicals.

He was appointed Professor of English Literature in the Catholic University in 1854. This was situated at numbers **85** and **86 St Stephen's Green**; the two houses were then combined and known as St Patrick's House (later known as Newman House). Cardinal John Henry Newman was its first Rector. Other staff members at Mac Carthy's time included Aubrey de Vere, the poet, and Eugene O'Curry, Professor of Archaeology and Irish History and an expert on Irish manuscript material.

MacCarthy had nine children and named one of his daughters

Mary Stanislaus, maybe to settle an old score with his own naming as Denis Florence. He and his family lived for a time at **Summerfield** at the corner of **Dalkey Avenue** and **Old Quarry**. This was a large house standing in its own grounds, and as the family grew in size, more extensions were added to the building. The house, now a private residence, has interesting connections. In 1904, a portion of it was used by Clifton School, the founder of which was Francis Irwin, an Ulster Scot and graduate of Trinity College. The school is depicted as Mr Deasy's establishment in the Nestor episode in James Joyce's *Ulysses*, where the headmaster is modelled on Francis Irwin. Joyce taught for a short while at this school and uses the names of students he taught there as models for the pupils in *Ulysses*. Interestingly, MacCarthy's *Poetical Works* are among the volumes on Bloom's bookshelf in *Ulysses*:

> Catalogue these books.
> Thom's Dublin Post Office Directory, 1886
> Denis Florence MacCarthy's *Poetical Works* (Copper beechleaf bookmark at p. 5) . . .

As well as writing his own works, MacCarthy published translations from the Spanish of thirteen plays of Pedro Calderón de la Barca, the great Spanish dramatist (1600–81). One of these included *The Purgatory of St Patrick* and some of them were assembled into a *MacCarthy Memorial Volume* (1887).

The Revd Father Meehan, antiquarian and scholar, who lived on the Quays, was a friend of MacCarthy – that is until MacCarthy sent him one of his Calderón translations. The translation was immediately returned by Father Meehan accompanied by a note which said, 'The Revd C.P. Meehan thinks very little of Mr Mac Carthy or Mr Calderón, and he has found in the *Penny Warbler* better poetry than produced by either.' Not to be outdone, Mac Carthy read through some copies of the *Penny Warbler* until he came upon the line, 'A queer little man, with a very red nose,' a description which aptly fitted the Revd Meehan. He sent this to the priest with the page well marked.

Denis Florence MacCarthy died on Good Friday 1882, aged sixty-five, at **28 Mount Merrion Avenue, Blackrock**, the house where he had lived during his final years.

Donagh MacDonagh
1912–68

> The Dublin of old statues, this arrogant city,
> stirs proudly and secretly in my blood.

Donagh MacDonagh, poet, playwright and short-story writer, and son of the poet and patriot Thomas MacDonagh (see below), was born in Dublin on 22 November 1912. He was orphaned at an early age, as shortly after his father was executed for his part as a leader of the 1916 Easter Rising, his mother tragically drowned in a swimming accident.

MacDonagh was educated at **Belvedere College** and at **University College**, Dublin, where he had as contemporaries his fellow writers Brian O'Nolan, Mervyn Wall and Niall Sheridan. He then lived at **Dartmouth Square** and after his marriage to Maura (née Smith), moved to **33 Farney Park, Sandymount**. The couple had a son and a daughter. On the death of his wife, he married Nuala Smith with whom he had two children. In 1935 he was called to the Bar and practised on the Western Circuit and in 1941 became a District Justice. In 1944 the family moved to **141 Strand Road, Sandymount**. He was Justice for the Dublin Metropolitan Courts at the time of his death on 1 January 1968. He is buried in Deansgrange Cemetery, in Deansgrange, County Dublin.

A versatile man, he had a diverse literary career. He edited the *Oxford Book of Irish Verse* with Lennox Robinson (1958) and wrote a ballad opera, *God's Gentry* (unpublished). His poetry appeared in two volumes, *The Hungry Grass* (1947) and *A Warning to Conquerors* (1968). His most successful play, *Happy as Larry*, has been translated into a number of languages. He also wrote *Lady Spider*, a verse treatment of the Deirdre story, and *Step-in-the-Hollow*, a comedy of intrigue.

Thomas MacDonagh
1878–1916

One of the three literary signatories to the Proclamation of the 1916 Rising along with Patrick Pearse and Joseph Plunkett, Thomas MacDonagh, poet and patriot, was born on 1 February 1878 in Cloughjordan, County Tipperary.

Both MacDonagh's parents were teachers. Educated at Rockwell College in Tipperary, he studied for the priesthood for a time, but left and after a sojourn in France became a teacher. His first post was at St Kieran's College in Kilkenny, followed by a position at St Colman's College in Fermoy, County Cork. He joined the Gaelic League and became a fluent Irish speaker.

Just as Patrick Pearse had done, MacDonagh studied the Irish language among native speakers on the Aran Islands. On Aran, he was known as 'Fear an Rothar' (the man with the bicycle) as his bicycle was the first ever seen on the island. It was on Aran that MacDonagh met Pearse and in 1908 he was the first teacher to join Pearse's staff when **St Enda's School** was opened at Cullenswood House, **Ranelagh** in Dublin. His circle of literary acquaintances expanded to include W.B. Yeats, J.M. Synge, Douglas Hyde and Edward Martyn. The same year, his play *When the Dawn is Come* was produced at the **Abbey Theatre**. MacDonagh lived for a time at **29 Oakley Road, Ranelagh**.

When Pearse relocated **St Enda's School** in **Rathfarnham**, MacDonagh moved to live in a gate lodge in the grounds of Grange Lodge, **Whitechurch**, which belonged to a friend, Professor David Houston. The Whitechurch area was quite close to St Enda's. Here MacDonagh generously kept open house for all his literary friends and Irish revivalists who frequently called to the Dublin foothills. They included Padraic Colum, a fellow teacher at the school, James Stephens, Joseph Plunkett, Seumas O'Sullivan, W.B. Yeats and Æ (George Russell). MacDonagh relished having his friends around him and good conversation flowed. His father had instilled in him a great love for the Irish countryside, its traditions and folk songs.

While teaching at St Enda's School, MacDonagh studied for his BA degree, which he was awarded in 1910. The following year he got his MA degree after which he became a lecturer in the English

Department at University College Dublin, then situated in **Newman House, St Stephen's Green**. The literary magazine, the *Irish Review*, was founded the same year. Thomas MacDonagh was one of the co-founders, as were his friends David Houston, Padraic Colum, Joseph Plunkett and Mary Maguire, one-time girlfriend of Mac-Donagh. MacDonagh was a regular contributor to the magazine.

MacDonagh married Muriel Gifford, one of the five Gifford sisters, in January 1912. They were to have two children, a daughter Barbara, and a son Donagh, who became a writer like his father (see above).

In 1914, MacDonagh, together with Edward Martyn and Joseph Plunkett, founded the Irish Theatre in **Hardwicke Street** which produced his play *Pagans* in 1915. He had already published his *Lyrical Poems* and was engaged in his work on *Literature in Ireland: Studies in Irish and Anglo-Irish* which was his Ph.D. dissertation published posthumously (1916).

He was a founder member of the Irish Volunteers and was in charge of the marshalling arrangements of the funeral of O'Donovan Rossa in 1915 where he displayed great organisational ability. On Easter Sunday 1916, he commanded the garrison which occupied Jacob's biscuit factory. His area of authority extended to

43. Kilmainham Gaol, where Thomas MacDonagh was executed for his part in the 1916 Rising.

the forces in **St Stephen's Green**, the **College of Surgeons** and **Harcourt Street Station**. Like all those who signed the Proclamation, MacDonagh was sentenced to death, executed in **Kilmainham Gaol** and buried in quicklime at **Arbour Hill**.

He was commemorated by the Meath poet, Francis Ledwidge, in his beautiful poem entitled 'Thomas MacDonagh', the first verse of which is:

> He shall not hear the bittern cry
> In the wild sky, where he is lain,
> Nor voices of the sweeter birds
> Above the wailing of the rain.

Micheál MacLiammóir
1899–1978

Micheál MacLiammóir, playwright and actor, was born Alfred Willmore in Cork on 25 October 1899. He later changed this to the more poetic Gaelic name. He was brought to London by his parents in 1907 and a couple of years later was performing as a successful child actor in Beerbohm Tree productions of *Macbeth*, *Peter Pan* and *Oliver Twist*. He spent a year in Spain and returned to London to study art at the Slade while at the same time learning Irish at the London branch of the Gaelic League.

MacLiammóir then returned to Ireland to work with Andrew McMaster, the actor–producer who toured the country with his Shakespearean productions and gladdened the heart of many a country person who had little else in the way of entertainment. It was through McMaster that MacLiammóir met Hilton Edwards, the actor–producer–director and in 1928 they formed a partnership which became the most celebrated in the history of the Irish theatre. Together they founded Taibhdhearc na Gaillimhe in Galway city, a theatre for works in the Irish language, whose first production was MacLiammóir's *Diarmuid agus Gráinne*, and in the same year they also founded the **Gate Theatre** in Dublin.

Initially, the Gate was housed in the old Peacock Theatre in **Abbey Street** before moving in 1930 to the Concert Rooms of the **Rotunda** which became its permanent home. The policy of the Gate was to produce international drama as well as non-peasant drama by Irish writers. The theatre's first production was Ibsen's *Peer Gynt* on 14 October 1928. Other early productions included works by Gertrude Stein, Henrik Ibsen, Jean Cocteau, August Strindberg, Anton Chekhov, Elmer Rice, Aeschylus, G.B. Shaw, W.B. Yeats and MacLiammóir himself.

For the next fifty years, Edwards directed most of the plays at the Gate while MacLiammóir designed nearly three hundred productions. Both performed whenever time permitted and MacLiammóir acted in a number of his own works and in international classics as well as in plays by Irish playwrights. His performance as Robert Emmet in Denis Johnston's *The Old Lady Says No!* is considered an Irish classic. His own plays included *Where Stars Walk* and *Ill Met By Moonlight.*

MacLiammóir achieved his greatest success with his one-man entertainment, *The Importance of Being Oscar*, in which he chronicled the work and correspondence of Oscar Wilde. First produced in September 1960, it won him international fame. His last stage appearance was on 13 December 1975 with a performance of *Oscar* at which he received a standing ovation. He was then aged seventy-six and partially blind.

MacLiammóir received many awards, including a doctorate from **Trinity College**. With Hilton Edwards he was made a Freeman of

44. 4 Harcourt Terrace, which Micheál MacLiammóir shared with fellow actor and theatre impresario Hilton Edwards for thirty-four years.

165

the City of Dublin and from France he received the Chevalier of the Légion d'Honneur.

From 1944 to 1978, MacLiammóir shared a house with Hilton Edwards at **4 Harcourt Terrace** which runs from Adelaide Road to the Grand Canal. An interesting terrace architecturally, it was once enclosed by railings and a gate which were removed when the police station was built on the far side of the road. Some of the houses in the terrace have been restored, including numbers 6 and 7 which have four splendid Ionic columns surmounted by a Greek-style frieze. The MacLiammóir house still retains its own private back garden, while some of the gardens from the rest of the terrace have unfortunately been taken over for building development.

A plaque commemorates MacLiammóir's thirty-four years at 4 Harcourt Terrace. He died here on 6 March 1978 and is buried in **St Fintan's Cemetery**, in **Sutton**, County Dublin.

James Clarence Mangan
1803–49

James Clarence Mangan, poet, was born at 3 **Fishamble Street**, one of the city's oldest streets. It appears on Speed's map of Dublin which was published in 1611. As the name, which is an elision of Fish Shambles, implies, it was originally a place where fish was sold. Over the years, many notable people resided there. Mangan's birthplace was demolished in 1944, and has been replaced by the Castle Inn at what is now **5 Lord Edward Street**.

Mangan had a miserable childhood. He was the son of a quick-tempered, improvident grocer, who treated his four children 'as a huntsman would treat refractory hounds'. He thought that all feelings with regard to his family, and the obligations imposed by them, were totally beneath his notice. Mangan blamed all his misfortunes on his father. He sought refuge in books and solitude, and days would pass during which his father seemed neither to know nor care whether his son was living or dead.

Mangan was educated at Mr Courtney's Academy, in Darby Square, where he got a good grounding in languages. Darby Square, now demolished, was situated in **Werburgh Street**. It was originally surrounded by twelve houses built by John Darby, 'Butterer', who is mentioned in an official inquiry of 1690 as holding property in the vicinity. In the early part of the eighteenth century, many eminent lawyers resided in the square, in which were housed the Examiner's Office of the Court of Chancery, and the office of the Master of Chancery, 1738–43. Some years ago, when a portion of the square was excavated to locate a fault in the water supply, a number of skeletons were found, confirming that it was probably the site of the old St Martin's graveyard.

Mangan was an excellent student. A visiting Roman Catholic clergyman to the Academy who heard Mangan read 'Blair on the Death of Christ' from *Scott's Lessons* exclaimed, 'You will be a rattling fellow, my boy – but see and take care of yourself.'

While Mangan was still at school, his father's business ventures went into rapid decline, plunging the family into dire poverty. He was removed from school aged fifteen and apprenticed to a scrivener for whom, over a period of seven years, he worked long hours for miserly wages.

The family moved a short distance from Fishamble Street to dismal accommodation, consisting of two wretched rooms at the back of an old house in **Chancery Lane**. According to Mangan's autobiography, the upper room which served as sleeping quarters was occupied by insects, and the rain and winds blew in from all directions, but he scarcely thought about his own feelings when he saw the plight of his unfortunate mother.

It was to this dreary abode that the young Mangan returned from work between eleven p.m. and midnight. His poem 'Genius', which he wrote at this time, reflects his feelings of gloom.

Because of his poor living conditions, Mangan contacted a fever and was hospitalised. Owing to a shortage of beds, he shared one with a youth suffering from leprosy, which he said gave him an incurable hypochondriasis, that seems to have remained with him for the rest of his life. After this experience, Mangan's apprenticeship as a scrivener ended, but he still had the responsibility of his entire family, 'and the down-dragging weight on my spirit grew heavier from day to day.'

Through the kindness of Dr George Petrie, he was employed for a time as a copyist in the topographical section of the Ordnance Survey Office at **21 Great Charles Street**, and then in the library at **Trinity College**. John Mitchel, the Young Irelander and journalist, described Mangan as 'an unearthly figure, in a brown garment – the same garment (to all appearance) which lasted till the day of his death. The blanched hair was totally unkempt; the corpse-like features still as marble; a large book was in his arms, and all his soul was in the book.'

Mangan had lodgings at **6 York Street**, off St Stephen's Green. This street appears in *Brooking's Map* of 1728 and the houses built subsequently have been demolished and replaced. When Mangan lived here, his neighbour in number 37 was Charles Maturin, one of the most important writers of the Gothic novel. Mangan copied Maturin's peculiar form of dress and one of his colleagues remarked, 'There was poor Clarence Mangan with his queer puns and jokes, and odd little cloak and wonderful hat.'

His work appeared in various journals and magazines such as the *Dublin University Magazine*, the *Nation* and the *Dublin Penny Journal*, and his *Anthologia Germanica* was published in 1845, but Mangan is probably best remembered for his powerful songs and ballads such as 'Dark Rosaleen', 'The Nameless One' and 'Lament for Kincora'.

Mangan's last address was a dismal lodgings in **Bride Street**, near to the area with which he was most familiar. He became ill here during the cholera epidemic which swept through Dublin and died nearby in the **Meath Hospital** in **Heytesbury Street** at the age of forty-six. An account of his death is given in the biography of the eminent physician William Stokes, written by his son Sir William Stokes in 1898: 'Mangan had been lost sight of by everybody for a very long time, when one morning, as Stokes was going his rounds in the Meath Hospital, the porter told him that admission was asked for a miserable-looking man at the door. Stokes was shocked to find that this was Mangan, who said to him, "You are the first who has spoken one kind word to me for many years." . . . Stokes got him a private room, and had everything possible done for him; but not many days after he died. Immediately after death, such a wonderful change came over the face that Stokes hurried away to Sir Frederic Burton, the artist, and said to him, "Clarence Mangan is lying dead at the hospital. I want you to come and look at him, for you never saw anything so beautiful in your life!" So Sir Frederic came, and made the sketch which is now in the National Gallery. Only three persons are said to have followed his body to the grave.'

An addendum letter in the book from Thomas O'Reilly, MD, states, 'My Dear Sir William, The note in your memoir in reference to the death of Clarence Mangan in the Meath Hospital is mainly correct, except that it was I (not the porter) who drew your father's attention to him. He was shivering and almost naked when he presented himself for admission, but I had him cleaned and put in the public ward as I would have done with the ordinary patients. His miserable condition did not impress me, as the applicants for hospital admission at that time were almost all destitute, but what did impress me was the amazement of your father on seeing him. For a moment he seemed bewildered, as if he did not recognise Mangan, but it was only for a moment, as he told the class the patient before them was Clarence Mangan the poet. Your father, with his characteristic humanity and sympathy, turned to me and directed that Mangan should be placed in a private room, clothed with flannels, and supplied with every necessary comfort at his expense. I think the poor fellow lived only eight or nine days after his admission, and I am almost certain your father paid the funeral expenses through Mr Parker, the hospital steward. The account of the artist is also correct except an omission. The head was shaved and a plaster cast of the head and neck was taken. I saw it a few days after in the home now occupied by you.'

Mangan was buried in **Glasnevin Cemetery** and is commemorated amongst the statuary in **St Stephen's Green** with a bronze bust.

45. Bust of James Clarence Mangan by Oliver Sheppard in St Stephen's Green. The marble inset of Róisín Dubh, or Dark Rosaleen, heroine of one of his most famous poems, is by James H. Pearse, father of Patrick. It was unveiled in 1909 by Sir George Sigerson.

Edward Martyn
1859–1924

Edward Martyn, playwright, was born on 30 January 1859, at Tulira, Ardrahna in County Galway. His home, Tulira Castle, was one of three tower houses owned by writers who were friends of Lady Gregory of Coole Park, near Gort. These included W.B. Yeats of Thoor Ballylee and Oliver St John Gogarty of Dunguaire Castle.

46. Edward Martyn from the portrait by Norman McLachlan.

Martyn was a descendent of Oliver Martyn who came to Ireland with Strongbow in the twelfth century. His parents were wealthy landowners with extensive estates in two counties as well as property in Galway city. By a special Act of Queen Anne, the Martyn family, who were Roman Catholic, were exempted from the Penal Laws in 1709 because they had been kind to Protestants during the Jacobite Wars.

Edward Martyn was eight years old when his father died leaving him a considerable fortune. George Moore, from Moore Hall, in the adjoining County Mayo, was his cousin, and as boys they were close friends.

Martyn was educated at Beaumont College and Christchurch, Oxford and after an undistinguished academic performance at university returned to Tulira. Here, under the influence of a domineering mother, he restored the Queen Anne-style Castle and its fifteenth-century tower. His mother wrongly thought that, once the restoration had been done, her son would get married. But Martyn decided he would never marry as he did not wish to be dominated by the opposite sex, 'walking after her and carrying her parasol and shade'.

At this magnificent castle, Martyn, who was known to be slightly eccentric, decided to live in spartan conditions in a cell-like room with a bare bed in the Norman keep. He used the castle to entertain his friends. He had an excellent library and a passionate interest in traditional church music. He later founded the Palestrina Choir at **St Mary's Pro-Cathedral** in **Marlborough Street** in Dublin and the Feis Ceoil, an annual festival of music. In 1896, Martyn introduced W.B. Yeats to his neighbour, Lady Gregory, then a middle-aged widow, and with them he became a co-founder of the Irish Literary Theatre in 1899. Martyn's play *The Heather Field*, written in the Ibsen manner, and Yeats' *The Countess Cathleen*, were the first productions.

During the theatre's short lifetime, financial debt was incurred, all of which was paid off by Martyn. From the Irish Literary Theatre developed the **Abbey Theatre** of which Martyn was a member, but he severed his connections with it in 1914, having become disenchanted with its policy. Following this, he became co-founder with Thomas MacDonagh and others of the Irish Theatre which lasted for a brief period in **Hardwicke Street**.

Martyn was a member of the **Kildare Street Club**, which had been formed in 1782. Its members were mainly from the landed classes. In the nationalist developments of the time, Martyn supported Sinn Fein and the National Council. The National Council, of which Martyn was Chairman, was formed by members of the Cumann na nGaedheal Executive to protest against the proposed visit of Edward VII to Ireland in 1903.

With Martyn's involvement in the denouncement of the King's visit, the Kildare Street Club began to scrutinise his activities carefully. In 1904, Arthur Griffith outlined the policy of the Sinn Fein at the National Councils Convention at the **Rotunda**, at which

Martyn presided. Following this, Martyn was promptly expelled from the Club. He took the members of the committee to court, won his case and continued to attend the Club that had no time for him or his ideals. When one member asked him why he returned to a club which had expelled him, Martyn replied, 'It is the only place in Dublin I can get caviar.' To infuriate the members further, each evening he would kneel down at a window in the Club overlooking **Nassau Street** where he was quite visible to the public. When the Angelus struck at six o'clock, Martyn, with his rosary beads displayed prominently in his hands, would commence saying the rosary while a gathering of people outside would stand and answer the responses.

George Moore used to visit Martyn in his rooms in **Lincoln Place** where Martyn would be reading by candlelight, 'and I fell to admiring his appearance more carefully than perhaps I had ever done before, so monumental did he seem lying on the little sofa sheltered from draughts by a screen, a shawl about his shoulders. His churchwarden was drawing famously, and I noticed his great square hands with strong fingers and square nails pared closely away, and as heretofore I admired the curve of the great belly, the thickness of the thighs, the length and breadth and width of his foot hanging over the edge of the sofa, the apoplectic neck falling into great rolls of flesh, the humid eyes, the skull covered with short stubby hair. I looked round the rooms and they seemed part of himself; the old green wallpaper on which he pins reproductions of the Italian masters. And I longed to peep once more into the bare bedroom into which he goes to fetch a bottle of Apollinaris . . . Is there another man in this world whose income is two thousand a year, and who sleeps in a bare bedroom, without dressing-room, or bathroom, or a servant in the house to brush his clothes, and who has to go to the baker's for breakfast?'

Martyn's health deteriorated and he spent his final years living as a recluse on his estate in Tulira. He died in 1924 and, as directed in his will, his body was taken to **Cecilia Street** Medical School in Dublin for research. On 19 December, his remains were taken to **Glasnevin Cemetery** in the workhouse van with six other bodies. A Mass was celebrated in the cemetery chapel for him and the nameless six who were to share his grave. Members of the Palestrina Choir, which Martyn had established in 1899, sang the Benedictus as they were lowered into the earth in an unmarked grave in an area known as the Poor Ground.

Charles Robert Maturin
1782–1824

Charles Maturin, one of the most important writers of the Gothic novel, was born in Dublin on 25 September 1782. His ancestry is as intriguing as his work. His name is derived from the Rue des Mathurins in Paris where the first Maturin, Peter, a French Huguenot priest, had been found as a baby by a French noblewoman. After the revocation of the Edict of Nantes, Peter suffered religious persecution, and was imprisoned for a time in the Bastille.

47. Charles Robert Maturin from the engraving by Brocas and Meyer.

Like many fellow Huguenots, he came to Ireland, and was Dean of Killala, County Mayo, from 1724 to 1741. His son, Gabriel James Maturin, became Archdeacon of Tuam in 1733 and succeeded Swift as the Dean of St Patrick's Cathedral in 1745. Gabriel James died a year later and was buried in the cathedral. His son, William, held an important government post.

Charles Maturin, the son and only surviving child of six children born to William and Fidelia Maturin, was born into this well-off ecclesiastical family. As a child he was interested in theatricals and dress, an interest he held for the rest of his life.

In 1798, Maturin obtained a scholarship to **Trinity College** where he graduated with an honours degree in Classics. Three years later he was ordained into the Anglican Church and obtained a curacy in Loughrea in County Galway. He married Henrietta Kingsbury, the daughter of Thomas Kingsbury, afterwards Archdeacon of Killala.

In 1805 the Maturins returned to Dublin where, through the influence of his family, Charles obtained a curacy at **St Peter's Parish**, a fashionable parish at that time. He remained there for the rest of his life.

St Peter's Church (now demolished) was built on the site of an old chuch, situated in **Aungier Street** just opposite York Street. The site has now been redeveloped. It was the largest parish in Dublin with a population of 16,292 and 1,650 houses. The Archdeacon of Dublin was always vicar of this parish and on account of the amount of work employed three curates and required the assistance of several chapels around the neighbourhood.

Maturin's wages for his curacy were slender, being only seventy-five pounds per annum. Until 1817 the three curates were each paid an extra fifty pounds for performing Sunday services. For economic reasons, Maturin moved with his family to his father's house. His father supplemented his son's low income until suddenly dismissed from his job. He was later found innocent of the charge for which he had been dismissed, but in the interim the family suffered great embarrassment and Maturin was responsible for supporting the extended family.

Although Maturin carried out his parish work diligently, he never advanced his career beyond Curate, due to his eccentricities and unconformity. By all accounts, he was quite eccentric both in his manner and dress. He was a tall, slender, handsome man with large almond-shaped melancholy eyes. He was fond of society, and was well known for the late-night dancing for which he had a passion. During the day, he blackened his drawing-room windows, turning day into night, so that he could indulge incessantly in dancing! He alternated his dress according to his mood and sometimes his income. One day he would dress slovenly as described by Mangan and Carleton who visited him in York Street, and the next day he would be clad like a dandy wearing pantaloons and tight black clothes showing off his slender figure. He always insisted that his wife wear rouge, even though she had a naturally high colour.

At times, he liked to write his stories when the room was filled with people and conversation. He would cover his mouth with a sticky paste made from flour and water to prevent it from opening so that he could not enter into conversation. Other times, when writing, he would sit in his study with a red wafer stuck on his forehead as a signal that he was in the middle of composition and was not to be disturbed by members of his family. If the weather was favourable, he would take the air and compose during the course of a long walk, 'But the day must neither be too hot, nor cold; it must be reduced to that medium from which you feel no inconvenience one way or the other.' He was forgetful and would often make a call in his dressing-gown and slippers. He often got the dates of parties wrong and would turn up the day after they had taken place.

As well as carrying out his duties in the parish, Maturin wrote his novels. He frequented **Marsh's Library** in **St Patrick's Close** and, according to William Carleton, wrote the greater portion of several of his novels there on a small plain deal desk, which he removed from place to place according as it suited his privacy and convenience. (Coincidentally, his son William Maturin was librarian here around 1860.)

In 1807, Maturin published, under the pseudonym of Dennis Jaspar Murphy, and at his own expense, *The Family of Montorio or The Fatal Revenge*, a Gothic novel set in Italy. On learning that Walter Scott was the author of a favourable review of his book, Maturin wrote to him and Scott proved to be a great literary adviser to him over the next twelve years. He also gave money to Maturin which at times actually staved off starvation. *The Family of Montorio* was followed a year later by the publication of *The Wild Irish Boy*, again published at his own expense. Sydney Owenson (Lady Morgan) had published *The Wild Irish Girl* to great acclaim the previous year, and Maturin wished to cash in on the interest which her book had generated.

With the help of his wife's money, Maturin purchased a big house at **37 York Street**, situated on the left-hand side on the approach from Aungier Street to St Stephen's Green, where James Clarence Mangan, who had lodgings in number 6, was a neighbour. (The houses in this street have since been demolished and replaced.) The extra room in the house enabled Maturin to board students, to help supplement his meagre stipend from his curacy at St Peter's Church. He also tried to start a school here, but it was not a financial success. The first year he made one thousand pounds, the next year five hundred pounds and the third year nothing. He wrote to Scott that he had great difficulty in getting the students, and that it was also difficult trying to keep them, given 'the Caprice of parents, the dullness of children, the expectation that I am to make a genius of him whom his Maker has made a dunce'.

In 1812, *The Milesian Chief*, a novel set in Ireland, was published. In the preface he states, 'I have chosen my own country for the scene, because I believe it the only country on earth where, from the strange existing opposition of religion, politics, and manners, the extremes of refinement and barbarism are united, and the most wild and incredible situations of romantic story are hourly passing before modern eyes.'

On the advice of Scott, Maturin's play *Bertram* was submitted to Byron who at the time was on the board of London's Drury Lane Theatre. Byron made suggestions for its stage production and the play was performed and proved to be a great success. Unfortunately the profits resulting from this were largely taken up by paying off the debts of a friend for whom Maturin had acted as guarantor, and who had declared bankruptcy immediately afterwards. The nature and extent of this debt is the major biographical issue of Maturin's life and an excuse for his poverty. In May 1819, he wrote to Constable, his publisher, asking for an advance of two hundred and fifty pounds for his novel *Melmoth the Wanderer*, referring to 'the cruel and oppressive extravagance' of the person in question. This masterpiece, published in 1820 when Maturin was thirty-eight, is responsible for his fame as a writer. It is a classic Gothic novel on the theme of a wandering Jew which had a great influence on contemporary European literature. He made a profit of five hundred pounds. The hero was named Sebastian Melmoth, and this name was assumed by Oscar Wilde, Maturin's great-nephew, on his arrival in France. Wilde used the name when he took rooms at the Hôtel Sandwich in Dieppe.

A friend of Maturin's left an interesting description of him during the time when he was writing the novel. He recalls that, 'His mind travelling in the dark regions of Romance seemed to have deserted his body and left behind a mere physical organism. His long pale face acquired the appearance of a cast taken from the face of a dead body, and his large prominent eyes took a glassy look so that when at that witching hour he suddenly, without speaking, raised himself and extended a thin and bony hand to grasp the silver branch with which he lighted me downstairs, I have often stared and gazed on him as a spectral illusion of his own creation.'

Scott had planned to visit Maturin in the summer of 1825, but the meeting never took place. Maturin died on 30 October 1824, leaving a wife and four children. He was buried on 2 November in **St Peter's Church**, where he had been Curate. During his last years, he was dogged by ill health and his death, it is alleged, was hastened by his taking incorrect medicine. During his lifetime, he wrote four plays, six novels, and numerous short stories, essays and sermons. His final book, *The Albigenses*, was written the year he died.

Of his literary talent, Maturin said, 'If I possess any talent, it is that of darkening the gloomy, and of deepening the sad; of painting life in extremes, and representing those struggles of passion when the soul trembles on the verge of the unlawful and the unhallowed.'

George Moore
1852–1933

George Moore, the novelist, was the product of an intriguing family background. His great-grandfather, also called George Moore, who made the family fortune as a wine merchant in Alicante, Spain, built the family home, Moore Hall, on the shore of Lough Cara in County Mayo. Three flights of stone steps led up to the massive door above which was the motto *Fortis cadere, cedere non potest* (the brave man may fall, but he will not yield) which Moore translated as *Scratch a Moore and you yourself will bleed.* One of his sons, John, became a United Irishman and president of the Republic of Connaught for three weeks, under General Humbert. He died later of a fever in a Waterford prison. The novelist's grandfather, another George Moore (1770–1840) spent his declining years writing *An Historical memoir of the French Revolution*. He was a friend of Maria Edgeworth, who found him over-pertinacious in his questions, a trait which, according to Joseph Hone, descended to his grandson.

The novelist's father, George Henry, (1811–70) was elected MP for Mayo in 1847. As well as being a good landlord and supporting the Tenant Right, he was a founder of the Catholic Defence Association and was a leader of the Irish Brigade.

George Augustus, the novelist, was born in Moore Hall on 24 February 1852. As a young child he liked to listen to his mother reading to him from Scott's novels while his father recounted tales of his youthful adventures in the East, no doubt kindling the child's imagination with a spirit of adventure and paving the way for things to come. As a boy, George spent much of fhis time outdoors. His closest friend was his brother Maurice; he also played with Oscar and Willie Wilde who spent their summer holidays nearby. He had no formal education except for two years which he spent at St Mary's College, Oscott, near Birmingham, which he disliked intensely.

The President of the College wrote to his father saying, 'There is nothing singular or outstanding in Maurice's backwardness . . . George however is deplorably deficient.' In George's own words, 'I was a boy that no schoolmaster wants, and the natural end to so wayward a temperament was expulsion. I was expelled when I was sixteen, for idleness and general worthlessness, and returned to a wild country home.' Oscar Wilde was later to say of Moore that he conducted his education in public.

Moore inherited his father's estate, which he left to his brother Maurice to manage and went to Paris to study painting. Here he met many contemporary writers and painters such as Renoir, Pissarro, Degas, Daudet, Turgenev, Monet and Mallarmé. He met Zola also, the French master of Naturalist writing, who influenced his early works. W.B. Yeats' description of Moore at this time reads, 'He sat among art students, young writers about to become famous, in some café; a man carved out of a turnip, looking out of astonished eyes.'

A turning point came in Moore's career when, in order to attend to family business, he was forced to leave Paris in 1880 and return to Ireland. He decided that as he was not destined to become a painter he would become a professional writer. When he had sorted out his family affairs, he settled in London. During the next fifteen years he wrote his naturalist–realist novels much influenced by Zola. These included *A Mummer's Wife*, *A Drama in Muslin* and *Esther Waters*, much of the background for which was provided by his boyhood racing pursuits. Of *Sister Teresa*, a story about a convent, Yeats wrote, 'Everything is there of the convent, a priest said to me, except the religious life.'

Moore paid frequent visits home to Ireland and in the winter of 1883–4 he lived in the **Shelbourne Hotel** on **St Stephen's Green**, Dublin, from where he attended the Levee (the State Ball at Dublin Castle) and a Calico Ball at the Rotunda. He gives a vivid description of the various activities in the hotel when the suites and rooms were filled with people at the height of the social season. Much of his novel *A Drama in Muslin* is set in the Shelbourne, and the hotel appears numerous times in his trilogy *Hail and Farewell*. He used the Shelbourne for writing and had a bedroom high up in

48. The Shelbourne Hotel, St Stephen's Green,
where George Moore lived during the winter of 1883–4.

the front of the building overlooking St Stephen's Green: 'All about
the square the old brick houses stood sunning themselves, and I
could see a chimney-stack steeped in rich shadow, touched with
light, and beyond it, and under it, upon an illuminated wall, the
direct outline of a gable; and at the end of the street the mountains

appeared, veiled in haze, delicate and refined as [W.B. Yeats'] *The Countess Cathleen.*'

It is due to the generosity of Sir Arthur Guinness, later Lord Ardilaun, that **St Stephen's Green** is a public park today. He once said, 'It was a dream of my early youth. I remember when a lad walking in St Stephen's Green with a relative. I told her of my determination that should it ever be in my power I would do my best to effect the opening of that enclosure to the public.' Lord Ardilaun obtained an Act of Parliament in 1870 whereby the Green was thrown open to the public and put in the care of the Commissioners of Public Works. He had the swampy waste transformed into a magnificent park with lakes, lawns, a variety of trees, paths and wildfowl, though the snipe seem to have vanished nowadays. So it was open just a few years before Moore lived in the Shelbourne. Moore recounts one of his walks over to the park from the hotel: 'The clocks had not yet struck seven and, as I did not dine till half-past, I turned into Stephen's Green and followed the sleek borders of the brimming lake, admiring the willow trees in their first greenness and their reflections in the tranquil water. The old eighteenth-century brick was beautiful in the warm glow of the sunset.'

In 1901 Moore returned to Dublin in response to a telegram from his cousin, Edward Martyn: 'The sceptre of intelligence has passed from London to Dublin.' He left his flat in London's Victoria Street and took a house at **4 Upper Ely Place**, which he remained in for the next ten years. He had terrible difficulty in finding the right house. He went to an estate agent in Grafton Street and described to him what he wanted. Moore found that the houses in Merrion Square were too large for a single man of limited income. Stephen's Green did not tempt him either, his imagination 'turning rather to a quiet, old-fashioned house with a garden situated in some sequestered half-forgotten street in which old ladies live – pious women who would pass my window every Sunday morning along the pavement on their way to church.'

The helpful estate agent suggested a house in Mount Street. Moore recalled that a 'bucolic relation had taken a house in **Upper Mount Street** and had given parties in the eighties with a view of ridding himself of two uninteresting sisters-in-law, but the experiment failed' so that more or less put him off that particular street. He then viewed a house in **Baggot Street**, which 'lives in my memory not by marble chimney-pieces nor Adam ceilings, but by the bite of the most ferocious flea that I ever met, caught from the caretaker, no doubt, at the last moment, for I was on the car before he nipped me in the middle of the back, exactly where I can't scratch, and from there he jumped down upon my loins and nipped again and again, until I arrived at the Shelbourne, where I had to strip naked to discover him.' That episode did not entice him to Baggot Street.

His peregrinations in search of a house then took the jarvey and his horse to Fitzwilliam Square, Harcourt Street, Waterloo Road, Pembroke Road, Upper Leeson Street, Castlewood Avenue, Clonskeagh, and out as far as Terenure and Clondalkin, without success. Finally, Moore called on his friend Æ (George Russell): 'He settles everybody's difficulties and consoles the afflicted.' Within three days, Æ had found him the house at **4 Upper Ely Place**. Æ had lived in number 3 when it was the headquarters of the Dublin Theosophical Society. There was an iron gateway on the street, behind which there were five eighteenth-century houses. They overlooked cottages to the rear. The garden of the Loreto Convent was close by. Moore commented to the caretaker about the great many nightshirts out drying, but it turned out to be the nuns' underwear.

Situated in a quiet cul-de-sac, **Ely Place** was an idyllic place to live. Many famous names in the legal and medical professions were associated with the area during the late eighteenth and early nineteenth centuries, such as John Philpot Curran, whose speeches were edited by Thomas Davis; Barry Yelverton, Lord Avonmore; John Wilson Croker, politician and man of letters who was editor of *Boswell's Life of Johnson*; Oliver St John Gogarty; and Sir Thornley Stoker, surgeon to the Richmond Hospital, who treated Moore when he met with a severe accident with his bicycle which 'he now considers a more vicious and dangerous steed than a horse'.

Moore's orchard garden was a botanical paradise, filled with flowering trees and shrubs. He liked to sit here in the summer and entertain his friends such as Æ and Oliver St John Gogarty who lived close by.

All the houses in the immediate vicinity had their hall doors painted white; Moore decided to paint his green, which caused so much consternation amongst his neighbours that a lawsuit was threatened. In retaliation, Moore used to walk out at night, and bang the railings with his walking cane to rouse the neighbours' dogs. The neighbours in turn hired an organ-grinder to play under Moore's window when he was settling down to write. It was in this house that he wrote *The Lake*, *The Untilled Field* and a portion of *Hail and Farewell*. This latter is a three-part account of the fictionalised history of the Irish Literary Revival, fused with what Moore is pleased to claim as his autobiography. This book is a tapestry in which are woven most of the famous literary and artistic names of Ireland in the opening years of the century. Many of Moore's friends appear as characters and form the framework of the book. Their personal appearance is described with infinite detail. Moore had an unerring eye for the physical eccentricities of himself and his friends. He speaks of his own 'sloping shoulders and long female hands'. In a letter to John Eglington, he writes, 'Your suggestion has fairly puzzled me, that Rolleston will be offended with me because I say he has not enough back to his head, and that Hyde will be offended because I say he has too much.' Moore also describes Yeats sitting with his head drooping on his shirt front, like a crane, uncertain whether he should fold himself up for the night. Moore's cousin, Edward Martyn, refused to read the trilogy, saying, 'George is a pleasant fellow to meet, and if I read the book, I might not be able to meet him again.'

Moore's brother Maurice did not escape either. He took great exception to what was said about him in the second part of the trilogy: 'To what business is he going I often wonder, as I stand by the windows watching him, remembering all the while how he had lain back in his armchair after breakfast, reading a book, his subconsciousness suggesting to him many indifferent errands. As soon as I discovered my mistake I retraced my steps. Not so the Colonel. He knows at the bottom of his heart that the Irish language cannot be revived, and it was irritating to be asked to change the hour of dinner for the sake of so futile a thing as the Coisde Gnotha. If he loves Ireland as well as he professes to, why did he go into the British Army? . . . Was there behind his mind, far back in it, some little flickering thought that if Ireland rose against English dominion he would be able to bring to the service of his country some tactics he had learnt in the enemy's ranks? A sentiment of that kind would be very like him.'

Moore's closest associates in Dublin were Æ, Edward Martyn and W.B. Yeats. Of Dublin, he remarked, 'Its acoustic properties are perfect.' At the time, there were a number of literary and artistic characters in Dublin such as John Butler Yeats, who had his studio on **St Stephen's Green**, Nathaniel Hone, Walter Osborne, John Hughes, the sculptor, Mahaffy, John Eglington, Douglas Hyde, Lady Gregory, W. B. Yeats and many others. Moore became very much involved with the Irish Literary Revival and the founding of the Irish National Theatre, a work which, in the words of Yeats, 'could not have been done at all without Moore's knowledge of the stage'. He also engaged himself in numerous quarrels with various people.

One of these was with Yeats, with whom he fought bitterly over a drama which they wrote together for the Irish Literary Theatre. Together they wrote a play entitled *Diarmuid and Grania*. It was arranged that Moore write the original play in French; this was to be translated into Irish by Tadgh O'Donoghue, an Irish poet, then retranslated into Kiltartanese by Lady Gregory, and Yeats was to put the finishing touches to it. According to Yeats, their worst quarrels were when Moore tried to be poetical, or to write in what he considered was Yeats' style. He made the dying Diarmuid say to Fionn, 'I will kick you down the stairway of the stars.' The play was produced in October 1900 at the **Gaiety Theatre** in **South King Street**.

Inspired by Turgenev's *Sportman's Sketchbook*, Moore gathered his thirteen short stories together and published them as *The Untilled Field* (1903). This was the birth of the modern Irish short story.

Susan Mitchell, the poet and assistant editor for Æ on the *Irish Homestead*, gives a description of Moore around this time: 'Moore seemed to me then to be a man of middle height with an egg-shaped face and head, light yellow hair in perpetual revolt against the brush, a mouth inclined to pettishness, lips thick in the middle as if a bee had stung them. He had champagne shoulders and a somewhat thick, ungainly figure, but he moved about a room with a grace which is not of Dublin drawing-rooms . . . I found that he was the only man in Dublin who walked fashionably. . . he wore an opera hat . . . and when Moore put it like a crown upon his yellow head or crushed it fashionably under his arm, it acted on Dublin like an incantation.'

After the appearance of his first volume of memoirs, Moore thought it best to leave Dublin, and he moved to London where he remained for the rest of his life apart from frequent visits to France.

In February 1923, Moore Hall was burned down. George wrote to a friend, 'Since the burning down of my house, I don't think I shall ever be able to set a foot in Ireland again.' He died at his London home in Ebury Street on 21 January 1933. He left eighty thousand pounds, none of which went to his brother Maurice who was once his best friend. Moore had said to his steward, 'Get my ashes when I die, take them out on the lake and scatter them, but make sure that the wind is blowing in the right direction.' He was cremated in London on 27 May, and an urn containing his ashes was placed in a hollow on an island in Lough Cara.

> Life should continue to unfold for each one of us, and it
>   is time enough for
> Death to lower the banner when the last stitch of canvas
>   is reached.

Thomas Moore
1779–1852

Number **12 Aungier Street** occupies the site of the house where Thomas Moore, the poet, was born on 28 May 1779. The house, which is situated on the corner of Little Longford Street and Aungier Street, has practically been rebuilt, the front of it having been remodelled in 1965. The 'little gable windows' under whose light Moore's earliest poems were written, had disappeared by 1890.

49. Thomas Moore in 1832, from the engraving by Lawrence and Findon.

Here Tom Moore's father, John Moore, who was tall and handsome, carried on his trade as a wine merchant and grocer. His mother Anastasia (née Codd) came from the Cornmarket in Wexford. Moore described her as 'one of the noblest minded as well as the most warm-hearted of all God's creatures' and recalled that his was a house of gay entertainment given 'by my joyous and social mother. Our small front and back drawing-rooms, as well as a little closet attached to the latter, were on such occasions distended to their utmost capacity, and the supper table in the small closet, where people had least room, was accordingly always the most merry.'

The first school Moore attended was a few doors from his home in **Aungier Street**. Mr Malone, his schoolmaster, was a slightly erratic man who drank till the early hours, and consequently was in no fit condition to take classes the following day. Moore, being bright, was one of his favourite pupils and so escaped the brunt of his humours.

At an early age, Moore showed a talent for reciting. His mother encouraged him and taught him a number of poems. Aged six, he was awarded a silver medal for 'Reading History at a publick examination'.

In 1786 Moore was sent to **Samuel Whyte's Academy**, which was then highly thought of in Dublin. It had many notable pupils such as Richard Brinsley Sheridan, George Petrie, Arthur Wellesley and Robert Emmet. It was situated at **79 Grafton Street**, where Bewley's Café now stands. A plaque on the wall commemorates some of the famous pupils. The headmaster, Samuel Whyte, was a Classical scholar and poet, and somewhat of a celebrity himself. He was born at sea, did not take to it, and at the age of twenty-five opened this school for 'young gentlemen'. Moore wrote an Ode to Samuel Whyte when he was aged fourteen, which Whyte, vain as he was, added as an ornament to his own *Poems on Various Subjects*.

It was during these early years at Whyte's Academy that Tom Moore and Robert Emmet formed a friendship which lasted until Emmet was hanged outside St Catherine's Church in **Thomas Street** at noon on 20 September 1803. Moore was later to write the famous lyric commemorating Emmet's speech from the dock before his execution.

Moore's parents were interested in politics and their home was frequented by members of the United Irishmen. As a child, Moore was caught up in the buzz of excitement which surrounded these visits.

When Henry Grattan and Lord Edward FitzGerald were returned in the general election in 1790, they were paraded through the streets of Dublin. The route included **Aungier Street**. Young Thomas sat at the window and waved a laurel, and he waved it with such enthusiasm that he said he caught Grattan's eye and was 'prodigiously proud in consequence'.

Moore published his first lines of verse in a literary magazine, *Anthologia Hibernica*, published in **Anglesea Street** by the university bookseller, Mercier and Company. He sent a letter to the editor with the verse which read, 'Sir, If the following attempts of a youthful muse seem worthy of a place in your Magazine, by inserting them you will much oblige a constant reader.'

Moore entered **Trinity College** in 1795, the year after the partial repeal of the Penal Laws permitted a Roman Catholic to do so. It was during this period that he spent his holidays with the Burstons in **Blackrock**, County Dublin, a period referred to in his memoirs: 'If I were to single out the part of my life the most happy and the most poetical, it would be that interval of holidays'.

Moore graduated with his BA degree in 1798 and went to London, and under the patronage of Lord Moira, published his translation of the *Odes of Anacreon*, the first copy of which he sent to his mother. On account of his great talent and pleasing personality he was soon in great demand on the London social scene.

In 1803 he was appointed Admiralty Registrar in Bermuda and later toured the United States where he met President Thomas Jefferson, the man who had been responsible for drawing up the American Declaration of Independence of 1776.

Moore married Bessy Dyke, a sixteen-year-old actress, in 1811, and was absolutely devoted to her for the rest of his life. His *National Airs* were published in 1815, followed by his *Sacred Songs*. One of his most popular works, *Lalla Rookh*, followed in 1817.

In 1819, Moore met Lord Byron in Venice, who presented him with his memoirs. Byron said Moore was one of the two men he loved best in the world. Byron died in 1824, and his relatives were opposed to the publication of his memoirs. Moore burnt them and in 1830 published *The Life of Byron* in two quarto volumes which Lord Macaulay characterised as 'deserving to be classed amongst the best specimens of English prose which anyone has produced. The style is agreeable, clear and manly, and when it rises into eloquence, rises without effort or ostentation.'

During his time abroad Moore returned home on visits from time to time. On one of these he visited his former home in **Aungier Street**. The then owner of the house did not realise who he was, 'but the moment I mentioned who I was, adding that it was the house I was born in, his countenance brightened up with the most cordial feeling and, seizing me by the hand, he pulled me along to the small room behind the shop exclaiming to his wife , 'Here's *Sir* Thomas Moore, who was born in this house, come to ask us to let him see the rooms; and it's proud I am to have him under the old roof.'

In his later years, Moore's life was marred by domestic tragedy as all his five children predeceased him. His father, mother and sister are all buried in **St Kevin's Churchyard, Camden Row**, off Camden Street, within walking distance of his birthplace. The final entry on their tombstone reads, 'To the great grief of her brother, Thomas Moore, the bard of his beloved country, Ireland.' The spirit of the Irish rebel never left Moore, despite the fact that he had spent nearly all his life in England, mixing with English aristocrats.

On Moore's last visit to Dublin, when he was driving to Dublin Castle, accompanied by George Petrie, whom he had first met at Mr Whyte's Academy, he asked the driver to go by **Aungier Street**. 'Upon arriving opposite No. 12,' Petrie recalled, 'he desired the car to be stopped and, gazing at the well-remembered domicile, his eyes became suffused with tears. "I am looking, Petrie," he explained, "for the little gable window by which I penned my earliest verses, the *Melodies*." '

Moore, whom Lord Jeffrey described as 'the sweetest-blooded, warmest-hearted, happiest, hopefullest creature that ever set fortune at defiance', died at Sloperton Cottage, near Devizes, Wiltshire, in February 1852. He was aged seventy-two. He was buried in Bromham Churchyard, in a vault on the north side of the church.

Lady Morgan
1776–1859

Lady Morgan (née Sydney Owenson), the celebrated nineteenth-century novelist and hostess was, according to one account, born at sea on board the Dublin packet. Her father, Robert Owenson, an Irish actor from Mayo, who was related to Goldsmith, had come to Dublin from Covent Garden to appear in a comedy, *The West Indian*, at the Theatre Royal in **Crow Street**. He then decided to stay and sent for his wife to join him and on the cold winter journey his daughter was born. Sydney always lied about her age, but there is evidence to suggest it was 1776. Another account states that she was born one Christmas Day; her mother withdrew and some hours later Mr Owenson informed his guests, who were still at the table, 'We have a lovely little Irish daughter, just what I've always wanted.'

50. Lady Morgan (Sydney Owenson) at her writing table, from the portrait by René Berthon.

When Mr Owenson decided to set up his own theatrical company, he moved his family into the old Musick Hall in **Fishamble Street**, which he leased. This is the hall, opened in 1741, where Handel's *Messiah* had had its first performance in 1742. It was close to **Crow Street Theatre**. Most of the houses in the street were built of timber or 'cage-work' and were occupied by writers, merchants, printers, academics, a baronet and other decent, orderly people. The Owensons also had a house in **Drumcondra**. Mrs Owenson was in poor health and, following her death, Sydney and her sister Olivia were sent to a boarding school in **Clontarf**, the headmistress of which was a Huguenot named Madame Terson. On her retirement in 1792, the girls were sent to a finishing school in **Earl Street**. They also received training in ballet from Fontaine and music lessons from Giordani.

Sydney spent much time in Longford House, Beltra, County Sligo with the Crofton family who were related to her father. She was later to write part of her novel *The Wild Irish Girl* here.

When Sydney finished school she occasionally accompanied her father around the countryside with his theatrical productions. His theatrical business was not successful and in 1798 he was declared bankrupt. The same year, to help out, Sydney worked as a governess with the Featherstonehaugh family of Braklin Castle, Killucan in County Westmeath. They also had a town house in **Dominick Street**, where Sydney came across some letters of Pope and Swift which she was allowed to keep. She remained with this family until 1800, when she moved to the Crawford family of Fort William in County Tipperary. Between 1802 and 1803 her two novels, *Saint Clair or The Heiress of Desmond* and *The Novice of St Dominick*, were published.

While working as a governess, Sydney Owenson saw different parts of the country and came in contact with the aristocratic way of life. *The Wild Irish Girl*, which made her name, was published in 1806. Her fame spread, and she was invited to became a lady's companion to the Marchioness of Abercorn at Baronscourt, Newtownstewart in County Tyrone. It was here she met the family surgeon, Sir Charles Morgan, whom she married in 1812. The same year, George Owenson died aged sixty-four, in the house of Sir Arthur Clarke, his son-in-law, at **44 North Great George's Street**.

Sydney Lady Morgan, as she liked to be called, and her husband moved to 35 **Kildare Street** in Dublin where they remained for almost eighteen years. Number 35 was changed to number **39** which has now, along with other buildings, been replaced by an office block named Setanta House. Lady Morgan wrote in May 1813, 'We have at last got into a house of our own. We found an old dirty dismantled house and we have turned our piggery into a decent sort of house enough; we have made it clean and comfortable, which is all our moderate circumstances will admit of, save one little bit of a room, which is a real bijou, and is about four inches by three, and, therefore, we could afford to ornament it: it is fitted up in the Gothic.'

This house was to become one of Dublin's liveliest literary salons in the 1820s and 1830s. It became a focal point of social and literary life in the city. Lady Morgan's visitors included Mrs Felicia Hemans, from nearby **Dawson Street**; the eccentric Charles Maturin from **York Street**, the young Samuel Lover whom she influenced to write *Rory O'More*, and Thomas Moore. She wrote, 'I had a little dinner got up in a hurry for Moore yesterday; it was got up thus: I threw up my window and asked the inmates of the cabs and carriages of my friends as they passed the windows, and sent out some penny porters and lighted up my rooms. Moore was absolutely astounded when he saw my party. He sang some of his most beautiful songs then in his most delightful manner without stopping, some of them twice over, and all of them as if every word was applicable to the people around him.' Besides entertaining various prima donnas, she entertained Nicolo Paganini, the great violinist and one of the most celebrated of all nineteenth-century Italian musicians. She even organised special Italian dishes for him, by which he was quite overwhelmed. The German Prince von Puckler-Muskau, friend of Goethe, was also a visitor. On 14 August 1835, she wrote, 'My soirée was very fine, learned, scientific, and tiresome. Fifty philosophers passed through my rooms last night.'

Lady Morgan was house-proud and interested in plants, and wanted to erect a greenhouse on the open space at the back of her stairs. 'Morgan vows I shall never have it, and is gone out in a passion, but I don't despair. Upon this occasion I am a bore and he is – a bear.' Sir Charles Morgan was rather shy and timid but Lady Morgan did manage to persuade him to drive a very high and springy carriage with huge wheels which she had brought over from London. Their horse, which was placid, was much too small for the vehicle. Sir Charles, who was short-sighted, wore large green spectacles when out of doors and was accompanied by James Grant, their 'tall Irish footman', whose job it was to jump down off the carriage whenever anybody was knocked down or run over.

One of the causes espoused by Lady Morgan was the Emancipation of Ireland. She and her husband were both involved in the movement for Catholic Emancipation and many young men met in her home and recognised her as an effective ally. In some of her work she portrayed the Irish troubles in great detail.

In 1837 the Morgans moved to London. Sir Charles died in 1843 and Lady Morgan died on 13 April 1859 and was buried in Brompton Cemetery. She left a large fortune as her books were extremely popular. Among the most popular were *O'Donnell*, *Florence Macarthy*, *The O'Briens and the O'Flahertys* and *Dramatic Scenes from Real Life*.

T.C. Murray
1873–1959

Thomas Cornelius Murray, one of the great Abbey Theatre playwrights, was born in Macroom in County Cork on 17 January 1873. Educated locally, he came to Dublin and entered **St Patrick's Training College, Drumcondra**, in 1891. Surrounded by wooded grounds, Belvedere House, which once formed part of the college, was formerly the seat of the Coghill family, who for many years were associated with the locality.

Murray qualified as a teacher in 1893 and taught in Cork before taking up the post of headmaster of the **Inchicore Model Schools** where he remained until his retirement in 1932.

Murray was one of the co-founders of the Little Theatre in Cork with Daniel Corkery, Con O'Leary and Terence McSwiney, and his first play, *Wheel of Fortune*, was produced there in 1909. The following year, his play *Birthright* was staged at the **Abbey Theatre** and this launched his career as a playwright. Murray wrote fifteen plays, the majority of which are set in the Cork region. He used local dialect in these plays, which concern the feelings of entrapment, hopelessness and frustration that individuals encounter resulting from situations and conflicts in rural family life. His plays, *Maurice Harte* (1912) and *Autumn Fire* (1924) are regarded as masterpieces.

Murray lived at **11 Sandymount Avenue, Ballsbridge**, a few doors away from W.B. Yeats' birthplace, and his house is marked with a plaque. He was conferred with a D.Litt. by the National University of Ireland in 1949.

Cardinal John Henry Newman
1801–90

John Henry Newman, the most brilliant preacher and scholar of his generation, was born an Anglican, educated at Trinity College, Oxford, and ordained in 1824. Twenty-one years later, he joined the Roman Catholic Church and was ordained in Rome in 1847.

In 1851, when Cardinal Paul Cullen, Archbishop of Dublin,

wished to establish a Catholic University, he invited Dr Newman to become its first Rector. At the time, Newman was superior of the Birmingham Oratory. He accepted the post and for the next seven years spent a lot of time travelling the wearisome journey between Dublin and Birmingham.

When he came to Dublin, Newman gave a series of lectures on 'The Idea of a University' in the Assembly Rooms at the **Rotunda**. These were held between 10 May and 7 June 1852 and attended by the hierarchy: Jesuits, Trinity Fellows and, according to James Duffy, his publisher, 'all the intellect, almost, of Dublin'. The series was later published.

Newman did not have the degree of autonomy which he had expected. He had a hard task as his job was fraught with difficulties, especially in relation to the differences that arose with John MacHale, Archbishop of Tuam, and the resistance he encountered over a period from other nationalistic bishops.

For May and June 1852, Newman took lodgings in **Dorset Street**, his only request being that he should have 'a low bed with a single hard mattress'. Dorset Street was convenient to the Jesuit Church, St Francis Xavier's, in **Upper Gardiner Street** where he celebrated Mass and also had his breakfast. Dublin had not got a great selection of places which Newman deemed suitable for eating in and he considered joining the Stephen's Green Club, where as a member he would be provided with his dinner. The Club, at number **9**, was situated on the same side of **St Stephen's Green** as the Palace of the Protestant Archbishop of Dublin, Dr Richard Whately, which was at number 16. Whately, a burly-framed man of simple taste who hated pomp and ceremony, had been a patron of Newman in Oxford before they had their differences. Newman remembered him in Oxford walking his dogs in Christchurch Meadows. Whately continued this practice in Dublin and was seen daily about the Green, where he played 'tig' and 'hide-and-seek' with his three dogs. He was often observed swinging on the chains in front of the Green, smoking his long clay pipe. Whenever he met Newman – and this was often – he cut him dead. It was hard for Newman to avoid him as he dined daily in the Stephen's Green Club.

Fortunately, a friend whom Newman had met in Rome, Dr James Quinn, ran a boarding school at **16** and **17 Harcourt Street** and rented him a nice bright room containing a large bay window. This was an ideal base for Newman when he was staying in Dublin, where he could leave his books, papers and other effects while he was away.

On 4 June 1854, at **St Mary's Pro-Cathedral** in **Marlborough Street**, Newman was officially installed as the first Rector of the Catholic University of Ireland. Newman wrote, 'A University is not founded every day . . . This great institution is to take its place among us without antecedent or precedent.'

On 5 September 1854, Newman joined his assistant and friend, Father Ambrose St John, at the house of Henry Wilberforce, at **2 Croswaithe Terrace**, Kingstown (now **Dun Laoghaire**). From here they went in search of a house and on 9 September moved for two months into **2 Mount Salus**, Knocknaree Road in **Dalkey**, County Dublin. One room was converted into a chapel where the visiting priests could say Mass. Newman enjoyed the sea air and the magnificent view from the house. He wrote that had never seen a place out of Italy or Sicily like it, for beauty of rock and sea. The weather remained good and the spectacular view from the house was appreciated by all the visitors.

Charles Bianconi, acting on behalf of the Catholic University Committee, purchased **86 St Stephen's Green**, now known as **Newman House**, for use as the main university building. The Medical School was situated in **Cecilia Street**. From November 1854, Newman lived at **6 Harcourt Street**, which he named St Mary's House. Dr Quinn's house at **16 Harcourt Street** also became a house of the university.

A church was essential to Newman's idea of a university and despite getting no encouragement from Dr Cullen, he went about the task by himself. He acquired some ground which lay between numbers 86 and 87 **St Stephen's Green**. 'My idea was to build a large barn and decorate it in the style of a basilica, with Irish marbles and copies of standard pictures.' The architect he chose was John Hungerford Pollen, the English artist whom he had appointed to the professorship of Fine Art at the Catholic University. The **University Church**, a Byzantine basilica, measured one hundred feet in length, thirty-six feet in breadth and forty feet in height. The porch was completed a few years later. The interior is elaborate with marble walls and reproductions of Raphael cartoons. Above the altar is a large semi-dome depicting Our Lady, Seat of Wisdom, the design of which is based on the apse of the church of San Clemente in Rome. Hungerford later described the church as something in the manner of the earlier Roman basilicas. Newman, he said, 'felt a strong attachment to these ancient churches with rude exteriors but solemn and impressive within, recalling the earlier history of the Church as it gradually felt its way in the converted Empire and to possession.' The success of such an unusual design had some influence on the choice of the Byzantine style for Wesminster Cathedral.

51. Newman House, 86 St Stephen's Green.

The University Church of SS Peter and Paul, next door to the University building, was solemnly opened on 1 May 1856. It was made a parish church in 1974. The original bell, known as the Newman Bell, is now mounted on a simple black pedestal and housed in the entrance hall of the Administration Building at University College in Belfield Campus, Stillorgan.

Newman resigned his position and left Ireland on 4 October 1858 leaving, as a legacy, the Catholic University, a medical school for the Catholic University at **Cecilia Street** and a church. He was created a cardinal in 1879. The Cause for the beatification of Cardinal Newman was opened in 1958. Pope John Paul II signed the declaration of his heroic virtues in January 1991 and he is now entitled to be called the Venerable John Henry Newman.

Sean O'Casey
1880–1964

'The whole world is in a terrible state of chassis.'
Juno and the Paycock

Sean O'Casey was born on 30 March 1880 at **85 Upper Dorset Stree**t, where one of the four great roads of ancient Ireland, the Slighe Mhidhluachcra, passed through from the north on its route to Dublin.

The Bank of Ireland (marked with a plaque) occupies the site where the four-storeyed brick house with a basement once stood. A banker, Luke Gardiner, and at a later date the Wide Street Commissioners (a body first appointed in 1757), are responsible for the wide, airy and 'drowsy' Dorset Street.

O'Casey's birthplace was not, as is sometimes thought, a tenement house. The background for some of his work came from the Dublin which he knew, some of which were the poorer parts of the city, which at the time were poor, unkempt, decayed and overcrowded. This overcrowding led to disease, resulting in the death rate among the Dublin labouring classes being the highest in Britain and Ireland. O'Casey came from a class known as the 'shabby genteel'. A street directory for 1880 shows that the inhabitants of Dorset Street included a civil engineer in number 92 and a surgeon and physician in number 93. Various other trades, crafts and professions were also represented.

O'Casey was born into an impoverished Protestant family. His mother Susan (née Archer) was originally from Wicklow and his father, Michael Casey, was a well-educated Wicklow man, who acted as caretaker in the house and got accommodation rent-free in return. Sean was the youngest of thirteen children, of whom only three sons and one daughter survived infancy, the rest having fallen victim to croup, a disease which was prevalent at the time. He was baptised John at St Mary's Church in **Wolfe Tone Street** (no longer a place of worship), where Brinsley Sheridan, one of his favourite playwrights, had been baptised many years before. He later changed his name from John Casey to Sean O'Casey.

Within a couple of years, Mr Casey suffered a spinal injury when he fell from a ladder and his back struck a chair. To make life easier for him, he and his wife and their five children, Bella, Tom, Michael, Archie and Sean, moved to a house with no stairs in it, **9 Innisfallen Parade**, a peaceful area off Lower Dorset Street. There are eighty-nine neat cottage-style houses in the Parade, with a view of part of Mountjoy Gaol at one end of it. Again, this was a good address where the neighbours included a law clerk and an insurance agent.

From an early age, Sean suffered badly with his eyes as is portrayed in his autobiography, the first four volumes of which are a rich record of four decades of Dublin life. It was from Innisfallen Parade that he first attended Mr J.B. Story, the surgeon at **St Mark's Opthalmic and Aural Hospital** at **32 Lincoln Place**, founded by Sir William Wilde. This was a branch of the Royal Victoria Eye and Ear Hospital and the building, which was beside the back entrance to Trinity College has now been replaced by another structure. He recalls these visits in Volume One of his autobiography, *I Knock at the Door*, when his mother brought him in the tram drawn by the 'patient muscle-wrenched horses' operated by the Dublin United Tramways Company. They got out at Westland Row and walked up to Lincoln Place. The surgeon recommended a complete rest for is eyes and no school. Mrs Casey and Bella both encouraged and helped Sean and taught him long passages from the Bible and other works. His father thought, however, that because Sean had bad eyes he would grow up to be a dunce, and Sean felt rejected by him.

On 9 September 1886, Mr Casey died in **Innisfallen Parade**, aged forty-six. Sean remembered seeing the funeral cab drivers dismount from their seats and lean 'against the walls of the houses in twos and threes, forming a grotesque, shaggy lurching frieze on the face of the sun-mellowed, rain-stained bricks of the houses.' He watched the hearse, drawn by four black horses, each with a black plume on its head, come slowly up the street. He shuddered deeply when he felt the tip of his finger touching the shiny cold side of the coffin.

In 1887 Mrs Casey took Sean to live with Bella in the caretaker's two-roomed attic flat at **20 Lower Dominick Street**. It was from this house that Bella heard the bells of St George's Church chime the hours, one after the other, the night before she got married. It was in the same building that Sean O'Casey attended St Mary's Infants School where his sister was the principal teacher. It bears no resemblance whatsoever to the dreary place described by O'Casey. The house is quite remarkable in that Robert West, the master-builder and one of the most distinguished of Irish stuccoers, built it for himself in 1775. It has a magnificent entrance hall and interior which includes a Venus room. It is now the headquarters of the National Youth Federation. Sean then went to St Mary's National School in Lower Dominick Street, where he suffered some bad experiences which are harrowingly described in his autobiography.

The family moved in the early 1890s to **25 Hawthorne Terrace**, one in a terrace of thirty-two single-storeyed houses, in the East Wall. Sean enrolled at St Barnabas' National School. It was at Hawthorne Terrace that drama, and Shakespeare in particular, was introduced to the house by Archie, Sean's artistically inclined older brother. A makeshift stage was made and the boys put on plays of Boucicault or Shakespeare, Sean wearing black silk shoes, bossed with the red rose of Lancaster, which were stuffed with paper to make them stay on. When Sean was in his early teens, quite by chance he got the part of Father Dolan in Boucicault's play *The Shaughraun*, staged in the old Mechanics Theatre in **Abbey Street**. Twenty-eight years later his own play, *The Shadow of a Gunman*, was performed on the same site, in the **Abbey Theatre**.

When Sean was fourteen he left school and went to his first job as a stock boy with Leedom, Hampton and Company of **50 Henry Street**. Apart from this, he worked at various other jobs and spent nine years working on the railroad.

In 1897 the family moved to **18 Abercorn Road**, a two-storeyed house. It is just a few streets away from Hawthorne Terrace. The area is of particular topographical interest. Both houses are situated in a place which consists of a myriad of little streets enclosed by the railway line, the Royal Canal, the North Wall Quay and the East Wall Road. O'Casey spent twenty-one years of his life, the years from 1889 to 1920, in the East Wall area, which were the formative years in the moulding of him as playwright.

Sean had many interests and in 1906 he joined the Gaelic League in **Drumcondra** and learned Irish. Like his sister and brother, he had an interest in music and was a founder member and Secretary of the St Laurence O'Toole Pipers' Band. He wore the uniform and learned to play the Irish pipes. He later became involved with the Irish Republican Brotherhood and then, because he was very aware of the appalling conditions in which many Dublin people lived, he became involved with Jim Larkin's union for unskilled labourers, the Irish Transport and General Workers' Union. He was also busy building up his own library and would wander around the city bookstalls buying up his favourite authors. In 1914, the year his brother Tom died, he became Secretary of the Irish Citizen Army formed by Larkin after the General Strike of the previous year, and his *Story of the Irish Citizen Army* was published a few years later.

O'Casey's mother died in **Abercorn Road** in 1918. Sean went to live with an Irish-speaking friend in 35 **Mountjoy Square** (the house has been demolished) where he was later to set his play *The Shadow of a Gunman*. He remained here for five months before his final move in Dublin to **422 North Circular Road**, quite near his former residence at Innisfallen Parade. It was at this address that his greatest plays were written.

52. 422 North Circular Road, where Sean O'Casey wrote his early plays.

Aged forty-four he gave up his job as a labourer and decided to make his living by writing. On 8 February 1926, *The Plough and the Stars* opened at the **Abbey Theatre**. Two days later, riots broke out and some Irish Nationalist members in the audience threw chairs at the stage. It was the biggest dramatic row since Synge's *Playboy of the Western World* had caused riots in 1907. The curtain was hastily dropped and the police called in to restore order. Before the crowd dispersed, W. B. Yeats, a Director of the Abbey, addressed the irate audience: 'You have disgraced yourselves again. Is this to be an ever-recurring celebration of the arrival of Irish genius? Synge first and then O'Casey. The news of the happenings of the past few minutes will go from country to country. Dublin has once more rocked the cradle of genius. From such a scene in this theatre went forth the fame of Synge. Equally the fame of O'Casey is born here tonight. This is his apotheosis.'

Six weeks later O'Casey left Ireland for London to receive the Hawthornden Prize for *Juno and the Paycock*. In May, he met Eileen Reynolds Carey, the beautiful Irish-born actress whom he married the following year. He returned periodically to Dublin for short visits but his departure on that March day in 1926 was perhaps his Farewell to Innisfallen. He died at his home in Totnes, Devon, on 18 September 1964 aged eighty-four.

It was time for Sean to go. He had had enough of it. He would be no more of an exile in another land than he was in his own.

Autobiography

Frank O'Connor
1903–66

Michael O'Donovan, who wrote under the name Frank O'Connor, and was compared by Yeats to Chekhov as a short-story writer, was born in Douglas Street, Cork, on 17 September 1903. He was the son of Michael O'Donovan who served in the Munster Fusiliers, and Minnie (née O'Connor), from whom he derived his pseudonym.

When Frank was a year old, his family moved to a cottage at 251 Blarney Lane in Cork. He was never a robust child and was brought up in poor conditions due to his father's habitual drinking. He was educated locally at Strawberry Hill School near Blarney Lane and St Patrick's National School, where Daniel Corkery was one of his teachers. He encouraged O'Connor and introduced him to the Irish language. O'Connor then attended the Christian Brothers School at Our Lady's Mount.

In the spring of 1910, the family moved to 10 Harrington Square in the Barrack Stream area in Cork. Harrington Square was not a square as such; it was two rows of small houses in a deserted lot. It was to become the location of much of Frank's later fiction. His childhood is recounted in his biography, *An Only Child*.

Frank finished his formal schooling when he was fourteen, then educated himself in the local library and attended the Technical School at night to learn arithmetic, book-keeping and typewriting.

He worked briefly in a drapery shop, in a printer's office and as a clerk in the Great Southern Railway Office in Cork. While still in his teens he supported the Republicans during the War of Independence and was imprisoned at Gormanstown. On his release, he worked as a librarian for the public library in Sligo and a short time later was transferred to the library in **Wicklow**. His superior introduced him to Æ (George Russell) and he soon became a regular guest at Æ's Sunday 'evenings'. Æ looked after him and gave him literary guidance. He contributed a number of poems, reviews and stories to the *Irish Statesman*, a weekly review edited by Æ.

In December 1925, O'Connor was appointed librarian of County Cork where he worked for three years before returning to Dublin in 1928 as librarian for Pembroke District Library in **Anglesea Road** in **Ballsbridge**. Initially he had lodgings at **Sandymount Green** close to the Library, then moved to lodgings with Mrs Molly Alexander at **34 Chelmsford Road** in **Ranelagh**, where he remained for almost two years. It was in this house that he wrote his first volume of short stories entitled *Guests of the Nation* (1931). In October 1930 he moved to **Anglesea Road** which was closer to the Pembroke Library. His mother often came and stayed with him for lengthy periods. Here he wrote his novel *The Saint and Mary Kate*.

In December 1931, he shared a flat with a friend, Paddy Corr, in a large house named Trenton at **30 Merrion Road**, opposite the Royal Dublin Society. He moved out for a period in 1933 to a small basement flat in **Raglan Road**, returning to Trenton on his own in 1935. From this time until 1939 he was a Director of the **Abbey Theatre** at which two of his plays, *In the Train* (1937) and *Moses' Rock* (1938), were produced. In 1939 he left the Abbey after a bitter quarrel.

In 1938 O'Connor quit his post in the library service to write full-time. He left Dublin and moved to a farmhouse named Lynduff, in **Woodenbridge**, County Wicklow, with Evelyn Bowen, the young Welsh actress whom he had married. In the late summer of 1941, he moved back to Dublin for financial reasons and rented a house at **57 Strand Road, Sandymount**. He chose for his study a room overlooking the strand. One of the things he loved most about Dublin was to walk along **Sandymount Strand**. During the time he lived here, he did some work in London and travelled there frequently. He was also the poetry editor of the *Bell* which had been founded in 1940 by Sean O'Faoláin.

O'Connor remained at his home in Strand Road until August 1949 when he left due to family circumstances. Over the next three years, O'Connor would use twelve different addresses of friends in London and Dublin. Eventually he moved to **Seafield Crescent** off the Stillorgan Road. In March 1952 he left from the port of Cobh in County Cork, bound for America. He was no longer able to support himself in Dublin and accepted an invitation to teach for a summer term at Harvard. He proved to be popular and from then on he lectured in various universities in the United States. He contributed to the *New Yorker* and his stories and autobiographical sketches appeared frequently in American magazines.

O'Connor married Harriet Rich on 5 December 1953 and visited Ireland frequently after 1956. They spent the winter of 1958–9 living in **Mespil Flats, Sussex Road**, and in 1960 returned to live permanently in Dublin, where he lectured in English at **Trinity College**, and occupied a third-floor flat in **Court Flats, Wilton Place**, overlooking the Grand Canal.

O'Connor died in Dublin on 10 March 1966 in Court Flats and was buried in **Deansgrange Cemetery**, Deansgrange, in County Dublin.

Sean O'Faoláin
1900–91

Sean O'Faoláin, one of the most accomplished of the Irish short-story writers, was born John Francis Whelan on 22 February 1900 in Cork. He was the youngest of three sons of Denis Whelan, a constable in the Royal Irish Constabulary, and Bridget (née Murphy). The family home was at 5 Half Moon Street in Cork, where his mother took lodgers to help supplement the income. In his autobiography *Vive Moi* (1964) O'Faoláin describes his family as being 'shabby genteels at the lowest possible social level'.

He received his early education in Cork at the Lancastrian National School and the Presentation Brothers' College. During the summer each year, he stayed with relations who lived on farms in Counties Limerick, Donegal and Kildare. Here he enjoyed the peace and quiet of nature and observed the rural people and their customs. This impressed him and later provided background for his short stories and novels.

Aged fifteen, he attended Lennox Robinson's Abbey production, *The Patriots*, at the Opera House in Cork. Here he witnessed the reality of what was taking place around him and became interested in Gaelic and the rebel cause. In 1916, he became active in the Irish Volunteers, taking the Republican side in the Civil War. He served for a time with the Irish Republican Army, becoming a publicity director, and was editor of the shortlived political literary journal, *An Long* (*The Ship*).

He entered University College, Cork, in 1918 on a scholarship, and changed his name to the Irish form. He received MA degrees both in English and in Irish and in 1926 an MA from Harvard University. On 3 June 1928, he married his Irish girlfriend, Eileen Gould, in Boston. They left Boston for England in 1929 and he taught at Strawberry Hill, Richmond. At that time, he was friendly with Edward Garnett, who advised and encouraged many of the most important writers of the time.

In 1932, O'Faoláin's first collection, *Midsummer Madness and Other Stories*, was published. All seven stories were set in the time of the Troubles (1916–22). He returned to Ireland in 1933 to devote his time to writing and became a member of the Irish Academy of Letters. During the 1930s, the O'Faoláins lived in a cottage in the Wicklow hills beyond **Enniskerry**. There was no running water in the house and he had to go to the well. He also chopped his own firewood. He later recalled that these were some of the happiest years in his life. His next home was Knockaderry in **Killiney**, quite near to Lennox Robinson's home near the Vico Road where the family lived in the 1940s and 1950s. He always kept open house.

In 1940, O'Faoláin founded the *Bell*, a literary monthly magazine with offices at **14 Lower O'Connell Street** which lasted, with one interruption, until 1955. He was editor from 1940 to 1946. Originally, the *Bell* was subtitled *A Survey of Irish Life*. This subtitle was later dropped but it gives the essence of what the magazine was about. Its aim was to encourage young writers to describe their impressions and experiences of the country to 'encourage Life to speak'. It invited contributions from non-Irish authors to which some editions are devoted.

O'Faoláin had extraordinary versatility as a writer. With a high literary output, he wrote ten volumes of short stories, a play, three novels, five biographies, an autobiography, various travel books and critical works and a number of prose works and editions of the works of Irish authors.

Sean O'Faoláin, who lived for the last years of his life at **17 Rosmeen Park, Dun Laoghaire**, County Dublin, died aged ninety-one on 20 April 1991.

Liam O'Flaherty
1896–1984

Liam O'Flaherty, novelist and short-story writer, who caught the attention of Hollywood with his famous novel *The Informer*, was born in Gort na gCapall, in Inishmore, the largest of the Aran Islands off the west coast of Galway. He was the second son of Michael O'Flaherty and Margaret (née Ganly), whose people were originally from County Antrim. Although brought up in an Irish-speaking community, he was educated in English at the Oatquarter School on the Island and later at Rockwell College, Tipperary and **Blackrock College**, Dublin. With a scholarship he completed one year at **University College**, the first two months of which he was a seminarian. Not suited to the religious life, he left the university with a dislike for the clergy, an animosity which sometimes comes through in his works.

Under his mother's maiden name, Ganly, he joined the Irish Guards in 1915. He served on the Western Front, was shell-shocked and invalided out in the final months of the First World War. He returned to Dublin. It was during that period that he first came in contact with Communist and Socialist ideas.

In 1921, he was back in Ireland and was a founder member of the Communist Party in Ireland. The same year, O'Flaherty and some unemployed dockers took over the **Rotunda Concert Rooms** and hoisted the red flag over the building in protest against the unemployment endured by 30,000 Irish citizens. After four days, he surrendered the building. In the Civil War he took the Republican side against the Free State Government and at this time contributed to Republican papers.

He soon gave up politics and left the Free State for London, where he started to write seriously. His novel *Thy Neighbour's Wife*, which is set in Aran, was published in 1923 with the encouragement of Edward Garnett. This was followed by others, *The Black Soul* (1923) and his most acclaimed novel, *The Informer* (1925).

O'Flaherty married Margaret Barrington, the novelist, in 1926. Their marriage lasted only until 1932. During the late 1920s and early 1930s, he was quite prolific, although in the latter period much of his work was banned in Ireland. In 1932, with Yeats, Shaw and F.R. Higgins, he was a founder member of the Irish Academy of Letters. During the Second World War he went to the Caribbean, then South America, and settled for a while in Connecticut. Most of his later life was spent in Dublin at **Court Flats** in **Wilton Place**.

Four of O'Flaherty's novels are set in Dublin, *The Insurrection*, *The Informer*, *The Assassin* and *The Puritan*. All are set in the early 1920s and vividly portray the poverty, wretchedness and squalor of the poor in the slum areas of the city during that time.

O'Flaherty wrote one hundred and fifty short stories and was dominant in that field. Some of his most brilliant work is contained in these and it is probably for the ones about animals and rural people that he will best be remembered. He published three volumes of memoirs, *Two Years* (1930), *I Went to Russia* (1931) and *Shame the Devil* (1934).

John O'Leary
1830–1907

John O'Leary, Fenian and journalist, was born in Tipperary on 23 July 1830. From a propertied background, he was educated locally at the Erasmus Smith School and later studied law at **Trinity College**, Dublin, but refused to complete the course when he discovered that barristers were required to take an oath of allegiance to the British Crown. He then studied medicine, attending for a time the Queen's Colleges in Cork and Galway and later, medical schools in Dublin, London and Paris, but never graduated.

O'Leary, a striking man with a falcon nose and great burning eyes, joined the Young Ireland Movement and was arrested in 1865 after the Fenian uprising. He was imprisoned for five years and exiled from Ireland for a further fifteen, during which time he lived in Paris.

On his return in 1885, he lived with his sister Ellen at **40 Leinster Road, Rathmines**, which became a meeting place for the young Irish nationalists, poets and writers. Among the callers were Douglas Hyde, T.W. Rolleston, Katherine Tynan and the young W. B. Yeats. O'Leary became the friend and mentor of Yeats, who sought his advice when editing *Folk Tales of the Irish Peasantry* (1888), *Stories from Carleton* (1889) and *Representative Irish Tales* (1890).

John O'Leary

53. John O'Leary in 1904 from the portrait by John B. Yeats.

In October 1889, Ellen died and O'Leary then moved to **134 Rathgar Road** and the following year to **30 Grosvenor Road, Rathmines**. He later lived at **53 Mountjoy Square** and **17 Temple Street** close by.

When the Yeats family moved to London in 1887, W.B. Yeats, when he visited in Dublin, used to stay with O'Leary at Lonsdale House, on **St Laurence Road, Clontarf**. O'Leary's last address was at **11 Warrington Place**, near Mount Street Bridge at the Grand Canal.

O'Leary's main work is *Recollections of Fenians and Fenianism* (two volumes, 1896). He died on 16 March 1907 and is buried under a Celtic cross in **Glasnevin Cemetery**. In his poem entitled 'September, 1913,' W. B. Yeats wrote:

> Romantic Ireland's dead and gone,
> It's with O'Leary in the grave.

Brian O'Nolan
(Flann O'Brien, Myles na gCopaleen)
1911–66

Brian O'Nolan, Ireland's greatest modern satirist, always considered himself to be a Dubliner, although he was actually born in Strabane in County Tyrone on 5 October 1911. The third of twelve children, he was the son of Michael Nolan (or Ó Nualláin), an Irish enthusiast who worked as a customs and excise officer.

Not long after Brian's birth, Michael Nolan was transferred to Glasgow and shortly after this was moved to Dublin where he lived at **St Michael's Terrace, Inchicore**, on the western fringe of the city. The terrace is not a street terrace as such, but is situated on its own private grounds at the end of a driveway which has gateposts at the entrance bearing the name St Michael's. It is opposite the junction of Sarsfield Road and St Laurence Road, just above Chapelizod. It was convenient to a number of distilleries where Mr Nolan carried out his work overseeing the payment of excise duties. Compared to their neighbours, many of whom were employees of the Great Southern and Western Railway, the Nolan children, Ciarán, Gearóid, Brian and Roisín, had a privileged background with two uniformed maids bringing them out for walks.

The Nolan children kept to themselves and did not mix with the neighbouring children, nor did they attend school. Michael Nolan wanted them educated at an Irish-speaking school and as there was none in the vicinity, he himself taught them to read.

In 1917, a year after the Easter Rising, Michael Nolan was promoted and worked in Strabane and then Tullamore. With the establishment of the Irish Free State in 1921, and the setting up of the Board of Revenue Commissioners, he returned to settle finally in Dublin and was employed with the Commissioners as an Inspector, quickly rising to the rank of Commissioner himself.

The family then lived in a fine Georgian house at **25 Herbert Place**, a pleasant location overlooking the Grand Canal and close to the more fashionable Dublin squares. Michael Nolan had an excellent library and purchased many books, which resulted in the children being well read and knowledgeable on a variety of subjects. Being interested in the theatre as well, he frequently took his wife and three eldest sons to the **Abbey Theatre** to see the latest productions.

The first school which Brian attended was the **Christian Brothers School** in **Synge Street**, situated within walking distance from Herbert Place. He disliked the school and found it difficult to settle in having been used to so much freedom; it was quite an adjustment for him to make. Later in his novel *The Hard Life*, writing under one of his pseudonyms, Flann O'Brien, he refers to the protagonist entering 'the sinister portals of Synge Street School'.

In 1927, when Brian was sixteen, the family moved to a large house at **4 Avoca Terrace, Blackrock**, County Dublin, which is six miles from the city centre. Again, the family had two maids. It was at this address that Brian started to write his first book, *At Swim-Two-Birds* (1939), later praised by James Joyce and Graham Greene.

Much to the relief of Brian and his brothers, they did not return to school at Synge Street but resumed their education with the Holy Ghost Fathers at **Blackrock College**. During the summer holidays they sometimes went camping to the Gaeltacht in Donegal and attended the local dances or *ceilidhes*.

Brian finished school in June 1929, doing well in his final examination without much effort. The following autumn he enrolled at University College in **Earlsfort Terrace**, off St Stephen's Green, where he took his BA degree in 1932 in Irish, English and German and was awarded a Master of Arts for his thesis on Nature in Irish Poetry. During his college years he achieved fame as a brilliant debater in the College Literary and Historical Debating Society, which held the meetings in **86 St Stephen's Green**, the original site of the Catholic University, founded by Cardinal Newman.

O'Nolan contributed to a student magazine, *Comhthrom Féinne*, under various pseudonyms, including Brother Barnabas. He also had his own magazine, *Blather*, which lasted for six issues. His time at university provided much material and background for his book *At Swim-Two-Birds*. He and his group of literary friends from Earlsfort Terrace discussed literature in **Grogan's Pub**, now **O'Dwyers**, of Lower Leeson Street.

In January 1935, O'Nolan joined the civil service and in 1937 was made Private Secretary to the Minister for the Department of Local Government. He remained for eighteen years working at this office, which is located in the **Custom House**, James Gandon's masterpiece, which was completed in 1791. It is situated on Custom House

Quay overlooking the Liffey. During these years he liked to drink in **McDaid's**, the Pearl Bar and the **Palace Bar** and also in the Scotch House, some of which which were relatively near his office.

In July 1937, tragedy struck the family with the death of his father, without a pension, leaving Brian with the heavy responsibility of supporting the family of twelve. He was the only member of the family earning at the time.

In 1940, he started writing his satirical column for the *Irish Times*, 'Cruiskeen Lawn'. This was written both in Irish and in English and appeared at least three times a week for twenty-five years. He used the pseudonym Myles na gCopaleen which was the name of a character in a play by Dion Boucicault. He typed out his column with two fingers on his Underwood typewriter on Sunday afternoons in the dining room of **Avoca Terrace**. His second book, *An Béal Bocht* (1941), a satire of the Irish language, was an immediate success. It was later translated into English as *The Poor Mouth*. Two years later, he produced three plays, *Faustus Kelly*, *The Insect Play* and *Thirst*.

On 2 December 1948, Brian O'Nolan married Evelyn McDonnell in the Church of Our Lady of Refuge in **Rathmines**, the church in which James Joyce's parents had been married on 5 May 1880. He leased a house, which he later bought, at **81 Mount Merrion Avenue, Blackrock**, which was close to his previous address at Avoca Terrace. It was at this period that O'Nolan wrote detective stories under the name Stephen Blakesley. The O'Nolans remained in this house until they moved to **10 Belmont Avenue** in Donnybrook in the early 1950s. In 1953 O'Nolan retired from the civil service due to ill health.

At Swim-Two-Birds was reissued in 1960. That same year the O'Nolans moved again, this time to a modern bungalow in Waltersland in **Stillorgan**, a suburb of Dublin, which was ideal because it had no stairs in it. *The Hard Life* was published in 1961 and this was followed by *The Dalkey Archive* in 1964 which the playwright Hugh Leonard dramatised as *The Saints Go Cycling In* for the Dublin Theatre Festival in 1965.

Brian O'Nolan died on 1 April 1966. His masterpiece, *The Third Policeman*, was posthumously published in 1967, followed in 1973 by *The Poor Mouth*, a translation of *An Béal Bocht*. His first three books have similarities with the works of Joyce.

Patrick Pearse
1879–1916

Patrick Pearse, poet, writer and patriot, was born on 10 November 1879 at **27** Great Brunswick Street (now **Pearse Street**) . His father, James Pearse, was an English monumental sculptor who came to Dublin to put his artistic skills to use. The opportunity existed with the boom in church building following Catholic Emancipation. James Pearse joined the firm of Harrison in Great Brunswick Street as a journeyman before setting up, with a partner, the firm of Neill and Pearse in the early 1870s.

The year after the death of his first wife in 1876, James Pearse married Margaret Brady from County Meath, who came from a family of small tenant famers. He separated from his business partner and leased premises at **27 Great Brunswick Street** where the family lived in three rooms above the workshop. In the first six years of their marriage, their four children, Margaret (1878), Patrick (1879), William (1881) and Mary Bridget (1884) were born.

Patrick had a vivid imagination and was intelligent and industrious. His mother's Aunt Margaret was a popular visitor to the Pearse home and had a very definite influence on him, relating stories about Wolfe Tone, Robert Emmet and the Fenians. Later he wrote of these visits, 'I remember as a child sitting by a turf fire and listening to a grey-haired woman telling Irish folktales. From that gentle *seanchaí* [storyteller] I first learned how gracious and noble is Mother Eire. . . . I realised that Eire had a voice and a speech of her own; from her I first learned the names of Cuchulainn and Fergus and Fionn.'

In 1884, when Patrick was five, the family moved to a house in **Newbridge Avenue** in **Sandymount**, with his father retaining the original premises and thriving stone-carving business in Great Brunswick Street.

Sandymount, three miles from the city centre, was a fashionable area with many small roads containing a range of different types of houses and some detached villas. Patrick attended a private school for four years, which was run by a Mrs Murphy. In 1891, he and his brother Willie, with whom he was very close, continued their education at the **Christian Brothers School** situated in **Cumberland**

Street South (though actually known as the CBS in Westland Row), adjacent to Pearse Street. At this time, the family moved back to their former address as it was more convenient. Patrick was diligent at school and was not particularly interested in sport, preferring to devote his time to his studies. Between 1893 and 1896 he sat the four grades of the Intermediate and managed to win an exhibition each year.

The Irish language was rarely taught in schools at that time, but it was included in the curriculum of the Christian Brothers in Westland Row. From the age of twelve, Patrick displayed a great interest and love for the Irish language and for Gaelic literature. He could now read about Oisín and Gráinne and other tales he heard from his great aunt. He went to the **National Library** to do research and here he read Douglas Hyde's folk tales. Coincidentally, his introduction to the Irish language happened around the time when the Gaelic League, a movement dedicated to its revival, was founded by Douglas Hyde and Eoin MacNeill in 1893. Patrick joined the Gaelic League three years later.

In June 1898 he sat the Matriculation Examination for the Royal University and the same year was co-opted on to the executive committee of the Gaelic League. In the summer of that year he made his first visit to the Aran Islands which left him with a love of the Irish-speaking areas and from then on he tried to get to the West three or four times each year and later bought a cottage in Rosmuc in County Galway.

With the business prospering, the family moved to **George's Ville, 5 Sandymount Avenue**, a few doors away from W.B. Yeats' birthplace.

James Pearse died in September 1900, when Patrick was at the university studying law. Willie, who was to take over the firm, had just completed his third year at the **Metropolitan School of Art** in **Kildare Street**. The following spring, the family moved to a smaller house at **Lisreaghan Terrace, Sandymount**.

Patrick graduated from the university and received his BL from the **King's Inns** in 1901. He had no interest in practising law and in 1903 became editor of *An Claidheamh Soluis* (the Sword of Light), the weekly organ of the Gaelic League which did much to promote the Irish language. During his years as editor and journalist, he developed his creative side as a writer and produced a number of short stories, poems and essays.

In 1904 the family moved to **39 Marlborough Road** in **Donny-brook**, a large Victorian red-bricked terraced house with granite steps to the front door, where they remained for three years before moving in 1907 to Brookville in **Sallymount Avenue**. Now numbered **17**, it was a large, grey stone, three-storey house over a basement in its own grounds, situated at the intersection of Chelmsford Lane. It has now been replaced with apartments. When the Pearses resided there, the family renamed the house Cuil Chrannach, Leeson Park, to make it sound slightly more upmarket.

Pearse was interested in the intellectual development of young people and in the educational system in Ireland as compared to other European counterparts. He had travelled to Belgium to study these and had read widely about them. As there was no Irish High School in the country, Pearse founded **St Enda's School** in 1908 in Cullenswood House, **Oakley Road, Ranelagh**. This is a short distance from his two former homes in Marlborough Road and Sallymount Avenue. Cullenswood House, set in mature gardens, was built in the early 1700s. Bartholomew Mosse, the founder of the Rotunda Hospital, stayed here for a time, and in the 1800s, it was the home of William Lecky, the historian and politician. It is being restored as a museum and local centre for culture and the arts.

Pearse's school was one of the most exciting developments in Irish education in this century. His aim was that the pupils should not be crammed for success at examinations, but rather that education should strive for 'the eliciting of the individual bents and traits of each'. There would be maximum freedom given to both teacher and pupil within the curriculum and the classroom. The school was bilingual, Irish was taught by the direct method and particular regard was given to science, while not overlooking the classical side. The children were taught to respect and love nature and animals and the only child ever expelled was sent home because of cruelty to a cat. The works of artists such as Jack B. Yeats, Æ (George Russell), Sarah Purser and Beatrice Elvery enhanced the school walls, while the friezes were the work of the stage designers, Edwin and Jack Morrow. Poets and writers such as W.B. Yeats, Standish O'Grady, Edward Martyn, Douglas Hyde and Padraic Colum and Alice Stopford Green, the historian, gave occasional lectures to the pupils.

Together with running St Enda's and his activities with the Gaelic League, Pearse found time to write poems, short stories and plays, some of which he wrote for the school. Three of his plays were produced in the **Abbey Theatre**.

Pearse realised that his plans for his pupils could not be carried out at **Cullenswood House** and decided to find other premises for his school. St Enda's had the 'highest aim in education of any school in Ireland; it must have the worthiest home'.

54. St Enda's, Rathfarnham, now the Pearse Museum.

In 1910, St Enda's moved to the **Hermitage** in **Rathfarnham**. Standing in its own wooded grounds comprising fifty acres, complete with weir, lake and stream, it was an ideal setting for the school. It was opposite the **Priory** (now demolished) where John Philpot Curran, the well-known lawyer and orator, and father of Sarah, the sweetheart of Robert Emmet, lived. Sarah and Emmet often met secretly and walked in the grounds of the Hermitage; the tree-lined avenue to the left of the house is now known as Emmet's Walk. The grounds contain some interesting monuments, such as Emmet's Fort and a monument erected by a former owner, Major Doyne, to his horse which carried him through the Battle of Waterloo in 1815.

Between 1914 and 1916 the school ran into financial problems and Pearse, who was now a political figure of some stature, went to the United States where he raised money from republican sources. In 1915, he was elected to the executive council and military council of the Irish Republican Brotherhood (IRB). Some of the preparations for the Easter Rising of 1916 took place in the basement of the **Hermitage**. It was from this address that Patrick and his brother

William cycled into the city for the Easter Rising. Patrick was the Commander-in-Chief of the Republican Army and was President of the Provisional Government. Both were executed in **Kilmainham Gaol**, Patrick on 3 May and Willie on 4 May, 1916.

Kilmainhan Gaol is now a Museum as is St Enda's at **Pearse Park** which is dedicated to Patrick Pearse and the Pearse family and contains letters, speeches and other memorabilia. It is in the care of the Office of Public Works and is open daily.

> The beauty of the world hath made me sad,
> This beauty that will pass;
> Sometimes my heart hath shaken with great joy
> To see a leaping squirrel in a tree,
> Or a red ladybird upon a stalk,
> Or little rabbits in a field at evening,
> Lit by the slanting sun. . .
>
> 'The Wayfarer'

Joseph Plunkett
1887–1916

Joseph Plunkett, poet and patriot, was born in Dublin in November 1887. He was the son of George Noble, Count Plunkett. He was descended from an Anglo-Norman family, one member of which was the seventeenth-century martyr, Oliver Plunkett.

Described as having delicately-cut features and hands like an artist, Plunkett attended **Belvedere College** in **Great Denmark Street**, Dublin, and at the age of fifteen went to the Jesuit Stonyhurst College in England. He was proficient in several languages, read widely, his chosen authors ranging from Euripides to Chesterton, and was strongly influenced by the mystic poet, Francis Thompson.

On his return to Dublin, Plunkett studied for his matriculation to the **National University**. He was tutored in the Irish language by Thomas MacDonagh, who was teaching at St Enda's in Rathfarnham. Although MacDonagh was nine years older than Plunkett, they became good friends, both being poets and having many interests in common. On completion of his degree, Plunkett travelled to Europe and then on to Egypt, where he studied the ancient Egyptian civilisation.

In 1911, he returned to Dublin to the family home at **Larkfield, Kimmage**, then in County Dublin. The same year his first volume of verse, *The Circle*, was published. It was the only volume of verse he published during his lifetime. A further volume was published posthumously in 1916 which contained the best of these poems and also a collection from his later work.

Plunkett helped Padraic Colum when he was founding the *Irish Review*. In 1913 he became joint Editor with Thomas MacDonagh and James Stephens. The publication of some of his own articles, however, brought about its suppression in November 1914. Although shortlived, the *Irish Review* produced poems, plays, criticisms and reviews by some of the best writers of the time.

Plunkett was a regular contributor to the newspaper *Irish Freedom* which was managed by Sean MacDiarmada and was published between 1910 and 1914 by members of the Irish Republican Brotherhood. In 1914 Plunkett was co-founder of the Irish National Theatre with Edward Martyn and Thomas MacDonagh in the eighteenth-century house in **Hardwicke Street** which had been bought by the Plunkett family as a workshop for the Dun Emer Guild of female artisans and as a venue for dramatic performances. The purpose of the Irish National Theatre was to provide an alternative to the other commercial theatres in Dublin and to the 'peasant drama' of the Abbey Theatre. It was during this time that he met Grace Gifford, the artist, whom he married in **Kilmainham Gaol** the night before his execution.

As a member of the Irish Republican Brotherhood, Plunkett joined the Irish Volunteers. He was director of military operations, and was to draw up detailed plans for the 1916 Rising with Thomas MacDonagh and Patrick Pearse. On Easter Monday, shortly after he had been in hospital, he marched with Pearse and Connolly from **Liberty Hall** at the head of the contingent of the Irish Volunteers and the Irish Citizen Army which took over the **General Post Office** in **O'Connell Street**, making it their headquarters. At about 1 p.m., a Proclamation declaring an Irish Republic was read by Pearse.

Like all the signatories of the Proclamation, Plunkett was sentenced to death. He was executed in **Kilmainham Gaol** on 4 May 1916. His remains were brought to **Arbour Hill** where he was buried in the outer yard.

> I see his blood upon the rose
> And in the stars the glory of his eyes,
> His body gleams amid eternal snows,
> His tears fall from the skies.
>
> 'I See His Blood Upon the Rose'

Lennox Robinson
1886–1958

Esme Stuart Lennox Robinson, playwright, writer, producer and director, described by Micheál MacLiammóir, as 'long and bony as Don Quixote', was born on 4 October 1886 in Westgrove, a large country house near Douglas, three miles south of Cork city. He was the youngest of seven children of Andrew Craig and Emily (née Jones Robinson).

55. Lennox Robinson with his long-haired tabby cat
from the portrait by Dermod O'Brien.

When Lennox was aged six, his father, a stockbroker in Cork, abandoned his career to become a Church of Ireland curate. The family moved to his parish in Kinsale in County Cork and then, after seven years, to Ballymoney, a small parish ten miles west of Bandon. Due to his delicate health, Lennox's education consisted of private tuition for many years, followed by a short time at

Bandon Grammar School. He studied music and played the organ and the violin. He was a voracious reader.

In August 1907, he became interested in the stage after a visit to the Cork Opera House to see the Abbey Players who were on tour. They were performing in Yeats' *Cathleen ni Houlihan* and Lady Gregory's *The Rising of the Moon* with the Fay brothers, Sara Allgood and Maire O'Neill. He describes the effect this had on him in his autobiography entitled *Curtain Up*: 'Certain national emotions and stirrings hidden from my good Unionist parents were crystallised for ever by *Cathleen ni Houlihan*.' The same year, his first work, a poem, was published in the *Royal Magazine*, and the following year, the first of his twenty-two plays, *The Clancy Name*, was produced in the **Abbey Theatre** and had a three-month run. This was followed in 1909 by his play *The Cross Roads*. At the end of that year, Robinson was appointed Play Director and Manager of the Abbey by Yeats and Lady Gregory and went to London to study theatre under Shaw, Granville Barker and the younger Boucicault.

Robinson resigned from the Abbey in 1914 following an unsuccessful Abbey tour of the United States but returned to the company again in 1919. In the interim his most successful comedy, *The Whiteheaded Boy*, was produced. In 1923 he was appointed to the board of directors, a position he held until his death. With Yeats, he founded the Dublin Drama League to bring modern European and American drama to the same theatre in which he had directed over a hundred Irish plays.

In his early days in Dublin he lived six miles outside the city in the suburb of **Foxrock** in a lodge at **Kiltieragh** on the estate of Sir Horace Plunkett. This area had magnificent marine and mountain scenery. In 1925 he bought **Sorrento Cottage** which was situated on an incline in **Dalkey** overlooking Killiney Bay. It had terraced gardens where he staged Greek plays. The following year he established the Abbey School of Acting at the Peacock Theatre on **Lower Abbey Street**, of which he was a talented teacher and Director for a number of years. At the Peacock, with Yeats he assisted Ninette de Valois in opening a School of Ballet.

On 8 September 1931, he married Dorothy Travers Smith, granddaughter of Professor Edward Dowden, in London. He was awarded an honorary D.Litt. by the **University of Dublin (Trinity College)** in 1948.

Robinson's book *Ireland's Abbey Theatre* was published in 1951, the same year that the Abbey was badly damaged by fire. The Abbey Players moved to the Queen's Theatre in **Pearse Street** which they leased until the new Abbey, designed by Michael Scott, opened on the original but slightly larger site in **Abbey Street** in 1966. This included the **Peacock Theatre**, used for smaller productions. (The original Peacock had been constructed in 1925 adjoining the Abbey.) Robinson, an astute and witty man known as Ireland's 'man of the theatre', who had been associated with the Abbey Theatre for almost half a century, did not see the building of the new Abbey.

His last home was at **20 Longford Terrace** in **Monkstown** where he died on 14 October 1958. He is buried not far from the tomb of Dean Swift in the grounds of **St Patrick's Cathedral**.

Sir Walter Scott
1771–1832

Sir Walter Scott, creator of the historical novel, visited Dublin in July 1825 and received a tumultuous welcome. The *Freeman's Journal* of 16 July reported, 'In a word there is no Prince, except our own that should be welcomed to this island, with greater enthusiasm than Walter Scott, for there is no author who has been more generally read and admired in Ireland than he has been.' He was accompanied by his daughter Ann and John Lockhart (later his son-in-law) who kept a detailed account of the visit in his *Memoirs of the Life of Sir Walter Scott*.

Scott stayed at **9 St Stephens Green** (now the Stephen's Green Club) with his son who was an officer in the 15th Hussars, stationed at that time in Dublin. Lockhart recounts that they reached Dublin on Thursday 14 July in time for dinner, and found young Walter and his bride established in one of those large and noble houses in St Stephen's Green. He could never forget the joy and pride with which Sir Walter looked around him as he sat for the first time at his son's table.

Scott had barely arrived at the house before visitors and invitations started to arrive. That evening a deputation arrived from the Royal Dublin Society (founded in June 1731 as the Dublin Society) inviting Scott to a public dinner. The following morning a letter arrived from Dr Kyle, the Provost of **Trinity College**, with the news that the University wished to confer on him a degree of Doctor of Laws by diploma. Other visitors included Dr Magee, the Archbishop of Dublin; William Cunningham Plunkett who was

Attorney-General; and the Right Hon. Anthony Blake, who brought a message from the Marquis of Wellesley, then Lord-Lieutenant of Ireland, inviting Scott to dine at his residence, **Malahide Castle**, in Malahide, County Dublin. (The castle is now open to the public.)

Dressed in a blue coat and white jacket, Scott walked through several of the principal streets. When Scott's carriage was recognised in the streets it was followed by cheering crowds: 'The watchword was passed down both sides like lightning, and the shopkeepers and their wives stood bowing and curtsying all the way down; while the mob and boys huzza'ed as at the chariot-wheels of a conqueror.'

Scott's visit to the theatre was the cause of great excitement. The *Freeman's Journal* reported that, 'The signal having been given, the entire audience rose "en masse", those on the pit standing on the seats, and three distinct cheers were given for Sir Walter Scott amid the waving of hats and handkerchiefs.'

Scott had breakfast with the son of his friend, Charles Maturin, recently deceased, and spoke a great deal about him to his son, inquiring about him and the family's present circumstances. He later called on his widow, and gave her a purse full of sovereigns.

Scott visited **St Patrick's Cathedral** to see Swift's tomb (he had edited *The Works of Swift: with a Life*) and then called to nearby **Marsh's Library** in **St Patrick's Close**, where he saw the desk at which Maturin had written several of his novels, and the copy of Clarendon's *History of the Rebellion* with Swift's remarks written in pencil in the margins: 'Very savage as usual upon us poor Scots everywhere.' They called to the deanery where Dr Ponsonby gave them a courteous reception and luncheon.

Other places visited were the Bank of Ireland in **College Green**, which was the late Parliament House. Here the Governors went to great trouble to show Scott everything in proper style. Coming out from the visit, he remarked, 'These people treated me as if I was a Prince of the Blood.' Scott found the **Phoenix Park** 'very noble'.

With his great interest in Irish antiquities, Scott spent several mornings scanning through the book barrows along the Quays. Before he left the city, he spent the considerable sum of sixty pounds on books in Mr Milliken's in **Grafton Street**.

Scott was received at **Trinity College** by the Provost in a splendid drawing room. He received his diploma and was brought on a tour through the halls and libraries. One of the librarians remarked to Scott, 'I have been so busy that I have not yet read your

Redgauntlet.' He answered, very meekly, 'I hve not happened to fall in with such a work, Doctor.'

In a letter to Maria Edgeworth, Scott said that Dublin was splendid beyond his utmost expectations.

George Bernard Shaw
1856–1950

'My sentimental regard for Ireland does not include the capital.'

One of the greatest playwrights and wits of the English stage in this century, George Bernard Shaw, was born on 26 July 1856, in a modest brick house in 3 Upper Synge Street (now **33 Synge Street**), which is situated just off Harrington Street in the south inner suburbs of the city. It is now a Shaw museum open to the public.

56. 3 Upper Synge Street, birthplace of George Bernard Shaw.

219

The third child and only son of George Shaw and Elizabeth (née Gurly), he was 'the fruit of an unsuitable marriage between two quite amiable people who finally separated in the friendliest fashion and saw no more of one another after spending years together in the same house without sharing one another's tastes, activities or interests.' Shaw explained that he and his two sisters had to find their own way in a household where there was neither hate nor love. He said that as a child, no one particularly cared about him. The children had their meals in the kitchen, 'mostly of stewed beef, badly cooked potatoes, sound or diseased as the case may be, and much too much tea out of brown delft teapots left to draw on the hob until it was pure tannin.'

Shaw's father was a partner in a milling business, and had a warehouse in **Rutland Avenue**, on the Grand Canal. Sometimes, before breakfast, Shaw accompanied him, as he liked to play under the waterwheel by the millpond and in the adjoining field. This area has since been built over.

When Shaw was a child, a servant, who was supposed to bring him around the elegant squares and along the banks of the canal for his airings, instead used to bring him to visit her friends who lived in the squalid tenements in the slums. Shaw never forgot this and it gave him a lifelong hatred of poverty: 'I saw it and smelt it and loathed it.'

Mr Shaw conducted family prayers at home and brought the children to Sunday School to the **Molyneux Church**, now known as **Christchurch**, in **Upper Leeson Street**, 'to sit motionless and speechless in your best suit in a dark stuffy church . . . hating the clergyman as a sanctimonious bore, and dreading the sexton.'

The works of Verdi, Gounod, Beethoven and Mozart were constantly being rehearsed in the drawing room in Synge Street, as Mrs Shaw was extremely musical and possessed a fine mezzo-soprano voice. Under the stage name of Hilda, she sang in the **Antient Concert Rooms**. Shaw first met George Vandaleur Lee, a man of magnetic vitality and force, when he was aged six. Lee was his mother's music tutor and Shaw was deeply influenced by him. He had lived nearby at **2 Portobello Place** and later at **16 Harrington Street**, with professional rooms at **11 Harrington Street**. He soon inveigled his way into the Shaw house by holding rehearsals in the drawing room and giving Mrs Shaw music lessons.

In 1864, Lee moved from Harrington Street to **1 Hatch Street** on the corner of Leeson Street. He also leased **Torca Cottage, Dalkey**, on the coast nine miles south of the city, to which he and the Shaws moved.

'I had one moment of ecstatic happiness in my childhood when my mother told me we were going to live in Dalkey [and move] from the street which I was born in, half of it faced with a very unpicturesque field which was soon obscured by a hoarding plastered with advertisements, to Torca Cottage, high on Dalkey Hill, commanding views of Dublin Bay from the Island to Bray Head, and a vast and ever-changing expanse of sea and sky far below and far above.' He writes of the cottage, 'I lived on a hill top with the most beautiful view in the world. . . I had only to open my eyes to see such pictures as no painter could make for me.'

Torca Cottage, which is privately owned, is situated on **Torca Road**, halfway up Dalkey Hill. It is marked with a plaque which records that Shaw lived there from 1866 to 1874. The cottage may be approached from either Torca Road via Dalkey Avenue or by a long flight of steps leading up from the Vico Road.

After the first year at Torca, the Shaws used it during the summer months only, returning for the rest of the year to **1 Lower Hatch Street**, a large Georgian house, which they now shared with Lee. According to Shaw, 'The arrangement was economical for we could not afford to live in a fashionable house, and Lee could not afford to give lessons in an unfashionable one.' It was a corner house with no garden but it had eight rooms besides the spacious basement and pantry accommodation, as against five in Synge Street.

In 1865, aged nine, Shaw attended his first school, the Wesleyan Connexional (now demolished), which was located within walking distance of his home at **94 St Stephen's Green**. His results were so bad, however, that he was withdrawn from Wesley at the end of 1868. 'I may add that I was incorrigibly idle and worthless as a schoolboy, and am proud of the fact.'

By February 1869 he was attending the **Central Model Boys' School** in **Marlborough Street** – but he left it after seven months. 'It was an enormous place, with huge unscaleable railings and gates on which for me might well have been inscribed, "All hope abandon, ye who enter here", for that the son of a Protestant merchant-gentleman and feudal downstart should pass those bars or associate in any way with its hosts of lower middle class Catholic children, sons of petty shopkeepers and tradesmen, was inconceivable from the Shaw point of view . . . I lost caste outside it and became a boy with whom no Protestant young gentleman would speak or play.' He hated school and 'learnt nothing of what it professed to teach'. Shaw was so ashamed at attending this school that he did not reveal it until seventy years later!

In 1872, Lee left for London, followed by Mrs Shaw and her daughters. Shaw attended the **Dublin Scientific and Commercial Day School** in **Aungier Street**, adjacent to Whitefriar Street Church. In October 1871, he then commenced work in the offices of Messrs Charles Uniacke and Thomas Courtney Townshend, Land Agents, of **15 Molesworth Street**. He did well and was made Chief Cashier.

Shaw and his father then moved to lodgings at **61 Harcourt Street**. Shaw remained at this address for two years, during which time he frequented the theatre, the concert halls and the **National Gallery of Ireland** in **Merrion Square**. 'I am one whose whole life was influenced by the Dublin National Gallery for I spent many days of my boyhood wandering through it and so learned to care for art.'

In 1876 Shaw followed his mother over to London, determined to become a novelist, and returned to Ireland thereafter only for occasional short visits. He was awarded the Nobel Prize for Literature in 1924 and was made an honorary Freeman of Dublin in 1946. He is commemorated with the Shaw Room, which contains his statue in the **National Gallery of Ireland**, to which he left a third of the royalties from his published works.

Percy Bysshe Shelley
1792–1822

In January 1812, Percy Bysshe Shelley started a correspondence with William Godwin, a dissenting minister and philosopher who became his mentor. In a letter dated 16 January, he wrote, 'In a few days we set off for Dublin. Our journey has been settled for some time. We go principally to forward, as much as we can (viz. Harriet, Eliza and myself), the Catholic Emancipation.'

On 12 February 1812, the tall, stooped, nineteen-year-old Percy Bysshe Shelley arrived, after a tedious journey of twenty-eight hours tossed in a gale, on the first of his two visits to Dublin. The visit lasted until 4 April. He was accompanied by Harriet, his wife, whom he had married the previous August, and his sister-in-law, Eliza Westbrook. On arrival they stayed at lodgings at 7 Lower Sackville Street (now **O'Connell Street**). Shelley's mission was to procure a repeal of the Act of Union of 1800 by means of an association of philanthropists, and to forward Catholic Emancipation.

While staying in Dublin, he had 1,500 copies printed of a

pamphlet which he had written in England, entitled *An Address to the Irish People*. Consisting of twenty-two pages, badly printed on coarse paper, it dealt with Catholic Emancipation and Repeal of the Act of Union. From the window of his lodgings, he flung copies down on passers-by who seemed like suitable candidates. With the help of Harriet, he also distributed them in the streets. A further pamphlet comprising eighteen pages followed. This was entitled *Proposals for an Association of those Philanthropists who, convinced of the inadequacy of the Moral and Political State of Ireland to produce Benefits which are nevertheless attainable, are willing to unite to accomplish its Regeneration*. In a letter dated 24 February, Shelley wrote that he had wilfully vulgarised the language in the pamphlet, in order to reduce the remarks it contained to the taste and comprehension of the Irish peasantry, who had been too long brutalised by vice and ignorance. He had no conception, he said, of the depth of human misery until now. 'The poor of Dublin are assuredly the meanest and most miserable of all. In their narrow streets thousands seem huddled together – one mass of animated filth. With what eagerness do such scenes as these inspire me!'

The Shelleys stayed on the south of the river at **17 Grafton Street**, which was close to Catherine Nugent who lived at **101 Grafton Street**. A member of the United Irishmen, she was so impressed when she read Shelley's *Address* that she made herself known to him. They found they had a lot in common and became friends.

Shelley attended a meeting at the **Fishamble Street Theatre** at which Daniel O'Connell, known as the Liberator, made a speech concerning Catholic Emancipation. Shelley also spoke at the meeting, making his first public speech. A description of him said that he 'looked wild, intellectual, unearthly; like a spirit that had just descended from the sky'.

There was one meeting of philanthropists at which Shelley made a speech and proposed his scheme, but it was unsuccessful. William Godwin managed, through his correspondence with Shelley, to dissuade him from continuing his work in Dublin as he felt he was too young and inexperienced for the job he was undertaking. Shelley felt despondent by his lack of achievement and left Dublin.

Shelley and his wife paid a second visit to Ireland in May the following year and stayed in **Great Cuffe Street** (now **Cuffe Street**) where they either visited or stayed with John Lawless who lived at number **35**. Harriet Shelley wrote a letter to Hookham from this address. Lawless, known as 'Honest John Lawless', was a leading member of the Liberal party during the agitation for Catholic

Emancipation. During this visit, which had no political objective as the former visit had, the Shelleys travelled to Killarney and stayed in a cottage on an island in the lake. Shelley wrote about the perilous navigation of the lakes; of sudden gusts and treacherous whirlwinds. This was his final visit to Ireland.

Richard Brinsley Sheridan
1751–1816

Richard Brinsley Sheridan, dramatist and statesman, was born on 30 October 1751 at **12 Dorset Street** (now demolished), one of the many fashionable areas in the city in the early eighteenth century, both north and south of the Liffey. This was close to Mountjoy Square with its splendid houses.

Sheridan had a brilliant literary and theatrical background. His mother Frances (née Chamberlaine) was a novelist and a playwright. His grandfather Thomas Sheridan was a friend of Jonathan Swift. His father, also Thomas, was a godson of Swift and was an actor and manager of the famous **Smock Alley Theatre** in Smock Alley (now **West Essex Street**). Under his management, the 1745–6 season is described as unequalled in Dublin until the twentieth century. During this time he engaged brilliant actors such as Spranger Barry, Mrs Bellamy and David Garrick. Later, in England, he became a friend of Dr Samuel Johnson. When Sheridan compiled a dictionary, Johnson became irritated and said to Boswell, 'Why sir, Sherry is dull, naturally dull; but it must have taken him a great deal of pains to become what we now see him. Such an excess of stupidity is not in nature.'

Richard was the youngest of five children; his siblings were Thomas, Charles, Betsy and Alicia, who later married Joseph Le Fanu, the grandfather of the novelist, Joseph Sheridan Le Fanu. He was christened Richard Brinsley Butler at **St Mary's Church** in **Mary Street** (no longer used as a church). Both Richard and his brother Charles attended the Academy run by their relation Mr Whyte. George Stokes wrote of him, 'It is stated of Mr Whyte that of all the schoolmasters of his time, none gave more attention to the moral training of his pupils. Being himself a man of the highest character, and with all the old chivalrous manners of the Irish gentleman of the day, he never lost an opportunity of inculcating the love of truth and the shamefulness of equivocation.' **Mr Whyte's**

Academy and house were in **Grafton Street**, on the site of the present Bewley's restaurant, where a plaque commemorates the association. The schoolrooms, however, were nearby in **Johnston's Court**, an area which figured prominently in the scandalous chronicles of Dublin in the first thirty years of the reign of George III.

In 1754, after the Smock Alley Theatre was wrecked during a political riot, Thomas Sheridan emigrated to England. The family followed a short time later. For seven years Richard attended Harrow Public School where, according to a contemporary, he 'formed no particular attachments, nor left behind him any pleasing remarks of remembrance'. His mother died in 1766, and on leaving Harrow, he had a private tutor at his father's house in London.

By 1770, Thomas Sheridan had moved to Bath where he had an Academy for teaching elocution. It was in Bath that Richard met and fell in love with the beautiful young singer, Eliza Linley, with whom he eloped to France. They were married in April 1773, and in the interim Sheridan was engaged in a couple of duels with an unworthy admirer of Eliza, Captain Matthews.

Sheridan's play *The Rivals*, which brought him instant success, was produced at Covent Garden in 1775. This was followed by his farce *St Patrick's Day* and his operatic play *The Duenna*. The play which is considered his best, *The School for Scandal*, was produced at Drury Lane in 1777. The same year he was elected as a member of the Literary Club on the motion of Dr Johnson. He became owner of the Drury Lane Theatre which he purchased from David Garrick who was retiring from the stage. This was burned down in 1809, and Sheridan consequently lost much of his income. Thomas Moore, in his *Memoirs of the Life of the Right Honourable Richard Brinsley Sheridan*, wrote that on the occasion, Sheridan is reputed to have said, 'A man may surely be allowed to take a glass of wine by his own fireside.'

The Critic, Sheridan's last major play, was produced in 1779. The following year he became a Member of Parliament and over the next few years he distinguished himself as an orator and wit. He took an interest in the political affairs of Ireland, and was opposed to the Act of Union. W.E.H. Lecky affirms that he fought 'a hopeless battle in opposition with conspicuous earnestness and courage'.

When Sheridan died in reduced circumstances on 7 July 1816, he had no equal as a playwright among his contemporaries. His obituary in *The Times* read, 'Throughout a period fruitful of able men and trying circumstances [he was] the most popular specimen in the British senate of political consistency, intrepidity, and honour.'

Following quite a spectacular funeral with four lords as pall-bearers and attended by many notable citizens of London, Sheridan was laid to rest in the Poets' Corner at Westminster Abbey.

Mrs Parkhurst, a friend of the Sheridans in London, wrote to Dublin to Mrs Le Fanu, his eldest sister, a fortnight after his death to say that Sheridan had been well cared for during his final illness. He had his family in attendance, three of the finest physicians and the Bishop of London. She added, 'He took away with him a thousand charitable actions, a heart in which there was no hard part, a spirit free from envy and malice, and he is gone in the undiminished brightness of his talent, gone before pity had withered admiration.' A fitting epitaph for such a man.

Annie M.P. Smithson
1873–1948

Annie M.P. Smithson, the best-selling Irish romantic novelist of her era, was born into a Protestant household at 22 (now number **42**) **Claremont Road** in **Sandymount**, the home of her maternal grandparents, Captain and Mrs Carpenter. This road runs from Sandymount Green to Tritonville Road and Serpentine Avenue. Annie's father, Samuel Smithson, had died when she was very young and although she lived with her widowed mother and her unmarried uncle, John Smithson, in **Baggot Street** where he had a business, she always regarded Claremont Road as her home. This was because grandfather Carpenter was 'the best beloved of my childhood'. They used to walk together to the lovely old stone-built **St Matthew's Church** in **Irishtown** to attend service, where they shared the same hymn book.

In her autobiography entitled *Myself – and Others* (1944), which is dedicated 'To the Memory of my Dear Grandfather', Annie recalls the house in Claremont Road with its front garden which in spring and summer was a mass of brightly-coloured flowerbeds. The back garden had mostly fruit trees and vegetables and a long bed of London Pride. There was a large cherry tree at the end of the garden just beside the summer house.

When Annie was a little girl she spent most of her time at Claremont Road. In the evenings, she walked as far as the pillar-box in **Tritonville Road** to await her grandfather's return from work. Captain Carpenter, who was Harbour Master of Dublin for thirty years, was a figure well known to the captains of ships from all over the world who called to the port of Dublin. He had sailed around the world three times in his own ship, bringing back all sorts of souvenirs from the various places he had visited including effigies of heathen deities. The result was that the house resembled a museum. There were prints on the wall including one of the Duke of Wellington which Annie thought was a portrait of her grandfather; they were quite alike, having similar noses. There was a large comfortable kitchen where the cockatoo lived. He, along with a monkey named Jacko, had been brought to the house by Annie's Uncle William, Captain Carpenter's eldest son who had served in India with his regiment.

Mrs Carpenter died when Annie was very young but she remembers her grandmother sitting in the drawing room 'in a voluminous silk gown, her soft hair covered with the usual cap of the period'.

In the summer, Captain Carpenter would sometimes rent a house by the sea at **Seapoint** near **Dun Laoghaire** or in **Howth** on the other side of Dublin Bay. Here Annie would stay with her young cousins and they would bathe together at Balscadden, explore the caves and stroll around the famous cliff walk.

Annie's paternal grandfather, John Smithson, had a business in the chandlery line in **Capel Street**. His three sons were: Thomas, who entered his father's business; Samuel, who read for the Bar (Annie's father); and John, who set himself up in a business in Baggot Street. Grandfather Smithson lived in an old house named Cloragh. **Cloragh Road** lies between **Whitechurch**, Rathfarnam, and **Tibradden** in the foothills of the Dublin Mountains, and has not changed since he lived there. At that time there were no buses or trams in the area and each day he set off for work in his carriage. He and the house feature in Annie's novel *The Weldons of Tibradden* (1940).

Annie's happy childhood days in **Sandymount** ended when her uncle John Smithson died on 24 April 1879 in Baggot Street, and she and her mother went to stay with cousins in England. In 1881 Mrs Smithson remarried, with a Mr Peter Longshaw who owned a chemical works at Warrington in Lancashire. The move from Dublin and the second marriage of her mother proved traumatic and upsetting for Annie. She hated Warrington and disliked her stepfather.

Mr Longshaw took a large house in Penketh just outside Warrington and Annie attended a school in West Derby. Aged nine, she discovered the great joy of reading when she was given a copy of a book entitled *The Wide, Wide World* as a birthday gift. She found reading a source of pleasure which never palled.

The family returned to Ireland for a summer holiday in 1882 when they rented the **Abbey House** in **Howth**. The house was so named as it was situated just beside the old Abbey in Howth village. Tragedy struck the family when her stepbrother, aged only six months, died during their holiday here.

In 1885, Captain Carpenter was taken ill in **Claremont Road** and Annie and her mother returned immediately, but by the time they arrived he had already died. Annie was devastated. He left her a hundred pounds to be paid yearly until she came of age, when she would receive a lump sum of six hundred pounds. A friend of the late Captain Carpenter, named Mr Dockrill, who had rooms at Trinity College, acted as her trustee.

In January 1887 a daughter was born to the Longshaws. Luck did not hold out for Mr Longshaw and his business in Warrington failed miserably. Annie was removed from school and the family moved to Ireland where Mr Longshaw worked as a commercial traveller on small earnings. Annie's mother had a small income from some property she had inherited, but rents were low and she did not receive much from them. She was in the habit of living on credit and Annie thought that if her mother had been a little less extravagant and managed her finances better, they could have lived in relative comfort. In 1888 another daughter, Kathleen Louisa, was born. At this time the family were living in the suburb of **Rathmines** and Annie had not attended school for eighteen months. Her mother hired a German governess with the idea of opening her own school. She was unsuccessful with this venture, however, and Annie acted as a home help and a nurse to her two younger sisters. She attended meetings of the Plymouth Brethren and the Sunday afternoon services for young people which were held in **Grosvenor Hall** in Rathmines. These were the only social meetings that she had at this period in her life and she looked forward to them.

The family moved to a house in **Dargle Road** in **Bray**, County Wicklow. Living in Bray was pleasant for Annie. In the winter she loved the storms with the big waves lashing up against the seafront and the regatta and the military bands were a great feature in the summer.

To her delight, her formal education resumed. She attended a school on the nearby **Meath Road** and did well with her studies, winning first prize for her English essay for the Junior Grade Intermediate Examination. She was awarded ten shillings with which she purchased a pair of Lily Langtry shoes with high heels and large buckles. In the spring of 1889 she was preparing for the Middle Grade Intermediate Examination when she was called home one day from school. Her mother had given birth to another daughter and required Annie's full-time help in the home. She was disappointed at being forced to leave school but had no choice in the matter.

In the early autumn of 1889, her stepfather died and the family moved back to Dublin where they remained for a couple of years before moving to a house called **Marie Lodge** near the railway line in **Barnhill Road, Dalkey**, County Dublin. This road runs from Dalkey Avenue to Killiney Road. The children swam at nearby **Sandycove** and enjoyed the music from the band recitals which were held in **Sorrento Park** and attended by fashionably-dressed people.

The improvident Mrs Longshaw was deeply in debt and living on credit, but it did not worry her as she realised that her daughter would inherit six hundred pounds in a short time when she came of age. Annie's time in Dalkey gave her a horror of debt which never left her. When she received her legacy, her trustee Mr Dockrill strongly advised her against allowing her mother to handle it, but the grocer's bills had to be paid. Her mother moved to another house nearby, named **Torcaville**, with the idea of starting a poultry farm, which proved a costly failure.

In the spring of 1895, on the advice of her doctor, Annie went for a change of air to live for several months with cousins in **Orchardstown House**, situated at the top of **Butterfield Avenue** in **Rathfarnham**. At the time this was a narrow country road with only six houses. This area has changed with housing developments.

In the early autumn of 1896, Annie had only thirty pounds remaining out of her legacy. Her fortune had been blown in two years. Being of independent mind, she left home for London where she trained for fifteen months as a nurse at the Chelsea Hospital for Women. She continued her training at the Royal Infirmary at Edinburgh for a further two years. In October 1900 she returned to Dublin and trained for a further six months at St Patrick's Nursing Home at **101 St Stephen's Green South**. St Patrick's Home supplied trained nurses to the sick poor. (Numbers 101–104 St Stephen's Green South now form Russell Court.)

Annie M.P. Smithson was now a qualified District Nurse and

Midwife and worked in different parts of Ireland which included Counties Clare, Donegal, Mayo and Waterford. But she returned to Dublin as she missed the bustle of city life and worked as a Child Welfare Nurse amongst the poor of Dublin whom she loved. Her district included the areas around **Mercer Street** and **York Street** and she recounts in her autobiography details about Mercer Street, with its memories of Mary Mercer, who was so fond of cats that the 'cat holes' which she had made in the hospital for the convenience of the animals could still be seen. Mercer's Hospital has since been demolished. Annie visited the house at number **6 York Street** (now demolished) where James Clarence Mangan once lived and she never went up or down those tenement stairs without feeling beside her the presence of the poor 'Nameless One'.

Her first novel, entitled *Her Irish Heritage*, was published in 1917 and is still in print. She was in her forties when she started to write fiction and had over twenty novels published between 1917 and 1946. The backgrounds for her novels include Dublin, Kilkenny, Wicklow and Mayo. In 1924 she contributed a series of articles on Child Welfare to the *Evening Mail*.

She worked diligently at her profession as well as her writing and in July 1929 she became Secretary and Organiser of the Irish Nurses' Union, a position she held until December 1947. She lived at various addresses on the south side, starting at **Rathmines** and moving to **Harcourt Street, Upper Pembroke Street, Harold's Cross** and **Nassau Street** before returning to **Rathmines**.

She became an ardent Nationalist and converted to Catholicism after an unhappy love affair with a doctor. During the Civil War of 1922–3 she took the Republican side and was involved in a four-day siege in **Moran's Hotel** at **71–73 Lower Gardiner Street**. The hotel is still there under a different ownership. In her book *The Marriage of Nurse Harding* she gives a description of this dramatic time.

Annie M.P. Smithson died on 21 February 1948 aged seventy-four and is buried in the well-kept cemetery of **Whitechurch** parish church. Her grave is situated in the grounds to the left at the rear of the church.

Smithson's novels include *The Walk of a Queen*, *Norah Connor*, *By Strange Paths*, *By Shadowed Ways*, *Wicklow Heather*, *Leaves Of Myrtle*, *The Laughter of Sorrow* and many more. Several of these are still in print.

Thomas Southerne
1659–1746

Thomas Southerne, dramatist, was born the son of Francis Southerne in the **Oxmantown Road** area of Dublin in 1659. This is an interesting part of the city named from the Danes or 'Ostmen',

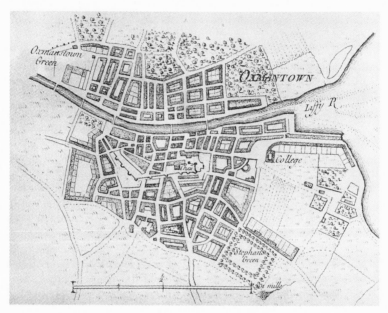

57. Oxmantown from Moll's Map of Dublin, 1714.

whose town was Ostmantown or Oxmantown. They had removed from the city and in 1095 had built **St Michan's**, the first parish church on the north side of the river Liffey. In 1635 the area of **Oxmantown Green** was to be 'kept for the use of citizens to walke and take the open air by reason this cittie is at present growing very populous'. The district started to develop in the second half of the seventeenth century with smart houses, a market and the construction of the hospital and free school of Charles II, known both as the King's Hospital and the Blue-Coat school.

Before 1670, there was only one bridge spanning the Liffey,

231

which meant that there was plenty of business for the ferry boats crossing at various points along the river. With the advent of the second bridge, which provided a link between Oxmantown Green and the west end of **Usher's Island**, trouble arose among the proprietors of the ferry which had been superseded by the new wooden bridge. They incited some apprentices to try to demolish it and a fight ensued between them and some soldiers which eventually resulted in four deaths. This occurrence resulted in its taking the name Bloody Bridge. It is now **Rory O'More Bridge**.

When he was attending **Trinity College**, Southerne would have crossed this way, or via what was then known as The Old Bridge which was further downstream. It is now known as the **Father Mathew Bridge**. On his graduation in 1680, he went to London to continue his education at the Middle Temple and settled there. Like three other dramatists with Dublin connections, Richard Steele, William Congreve and George Farquhar, all born between the years 1659 and 1678, the theatre in London provided him with an opening.

Southerne joined the army during the reign of James II (1685–8), but his military career was destroyed by the revolution of 1688, when William of Orange came to England on the invitation of the Bishop of London following King James' support for Catholics. Southerne then turned his thoughts towards drama and writing. He was a friend of Dryden, for whose plays he wrote prologues and epilogues. Southerne possessed a certain business acumen and always insisted on the author's right to a share of the second and third nights' profits from a play. In this way he made five hundred pounds from *The Spartan Dame*. He wrote a number of comedies, but he is best remembered for his highly successful tragedies, *The Fatal Marriage* and *Oroonoko, or the Royal Slave*. With these and two other plays, Drury Lane is said to have survived for over two years.

Southerne was very popular and received accolades from his friends on account of his pleasant manners and many other good qualities. He attended church regularly, and was interested in encouraging the efforts of younger playwrights and poets. In 1733, Swift reported to Pope that Southerne had visited Dublin. Pope in turn refers to Southerne's wit and to his Irish birth.

William Oldys, the editor of *Harleian Miscellany*, remembered Southerne as 'a grave and venerable old gentleman'. Thomas Southerne, the gentle man from Oxmantown, died in London aged eighty-seven, in 1746.

Edmund Spenser
c.1552–99

'A most beautiful and sweet country as any under Heaven.'

The bearded Edmund Spenser, described as a little man with short hair, wearing little bands, and little cuffs, was appointed Secretary to Arthur Grey, 14th Lord Grey de Wilton, in July 1580. Grey was then on his way to Ireland as Lord Deputy. At this time, Spenser had already started writing his greatest work, *The Faerie Queene*, having completed Book I and part of Book II.

On 12 August 1580, Lord Grey landed in Dublin accompanied by Spenser and was sworn in as Lord Deputy on 7 September. (He remained in Ireland until July 1582.) In November Spenser accompanied Grey on his journey to Kerry with Sir Walter Raleigh and the Earl of Ormond. He witnessed the massacres of the Spanish-Italian force at Smerwick and relates these vividly in his *View of the Present State of Ireland*.

Although Spenser revisited England twice, Ireland was to remain his home until the end of 1598. As Secretary, he was well paid for his work, which entailed the transcribing and collating of official documents. Among the Irish State Papers, dating between 1581 and 1589, eight of them have Spenser's signature. One of these relates to the plantation of Munster.

On 22 March 1581, he was appointed clerk of the Irish Court of Chancery, a position he held for seven years. In 1582, he took a six-year lease on Lord Baltinglass's house in Dublin and also a lease of New Abbey in County Kildare, at which he often resided. Spenser then became 'undertaker' for the settlement of Munster and in 1588 moved to his estate of Kilcolman three miles from Doneraile in County Cork, taking up his work as Clerk of the Munster council. He devoted all his spare time to writing *The Faerie Queene* and when Walter Raleigh, who was residing in Youghal, visited him, Spenser showed him the draft of his first three books of it. He also confided in Raleigh his sense of desolation. He wrote *Colin Clouts Come Home Again*, an account of his court and travel experiences, and sent the manuscript to Raleigh with a letter 'dated from my house of Kilcolman, 27 December 1591'.

233

Spenser married Elizabeth Boyle on 11 June 1594 in Cork. She was the daughter of a property owner from near Youghal.

In September 1598, he was appointed to the position of Sheriff of Cork and was described in the royal letter as 'a gentleman dwelling in the county of Cork who is well known unto you all for his good and commendable parts, being a man endowed with good knowledge and learning, and not unskilled or without experience in the wars.' In October the same year, rebellion broke out in Munster and Kilcolman Castle was destroyed by fire over the poet's head. One of his children is said to have perished in the fire. Spenser, his wife and remaining children escaped to Mallow. On 9 December, Sir Thomas Norris, the President of Munster, sent Spenser to London to brief the government on the situation. After suffering much distress Spenser was in poor health and died a month after his arrival there.

This 'Prince of Poets in his tyme, whose Divine Spirrit needs noe othir witnesse then the Works which he left behinde him' was buried in Westminster Abbey.

Richard Stanyhurst
1547–1618

Richard Stanyhurst was one of the first Dubliners to write poems in English. He was born in the medieval city in 1547, just three years before the first Irish printing press was set up in Dublin by Humphrey Powell. At that time, following the dissolution of the monasteries in 1536–40 by Henry VIII, the development of Dublin was declining.

From the fourteenth to the eighteenth century, the Stanyhurst family was established at Corduff, near **Blanchardstown** in County Dublin. One of his ancestors, also Richard Stanyhurst, was Lord Mayor of Dublin in 1489. The writer's grandfather, Nicholas Stanyhurst, who was reputed to be 'a great and good householder', was also Lord Mayor in 1542. Stanyhurst's father, James, was a prominent city official, being both the Recorder of the City and Speaker of the Irish House of Commons. He worked in the Parliaments of 1557, 1560 and 1568. Interestingly, he recommended to Parliament a proposal for the establishment of grammar schools throughout the country and the founding of a university at Dublin such as Trinity College, established in 1591 by Queen Elizabeth I on the site of the old Augustinian monastery of All Hallows, dissolved by Henry VIII.

As Recorder of the City, James Stanyhurst worked at **Dublin Castle**, which was built in 1204. One of the towers near the Castle was known as the **Stanyhurst Tower**, but unfortunately, nothing remains of it now except a slight bulge in the wall in **Little Ship Street**. Little remains of medieval Dublin apart from the Castle and a section of the wall at **Lamb Alley** and **St Audoen's Arch** in Cook Street, the sole surviving gate of the old city.

58. The remains of Stanyhurst's Tower (*to the left*) set into the wall in Little Ship Street.

James Stanyhurst died on 27 December 1573 aged fifty-one years. He was survived by his three children, Richard, Walter and a daughter Margaret, who married Arnold Ussher and was mother of Archbishop James Ussher, a distinguished scholar and archbishop of Armagh. Richard commemorated his father in a Latin elegy in the appendix to his translation of *Virgil*.

Richard received his early education from Peter White who had a school in Waterford. In 1563 he went to University College, Oxford and graduated in 1568. He then studied law at Furnivall's Inn and later at Lincoln's Inn. It was at Oxford that Edmund Campion, a fellow of St John's College, was his tutor. Campion became a Jesuit on the death of his wife and accompanied Stanyhurst back to Dublin where, under his influence and that of his father, Stanyhurst turned his attention to Irish history and geography.

Campion had already agreed to write the history of Ireland for the *Chronicles*, which Raphael Hollinshed was preparing between 1573 and 1577. Stanyhurst, under Campion's guidance, contributed a description of Ireland. He also compiled a history of Ireland during Henry VIII's reign (1509–47), carrying on his tutor's work on earlier periods. A few passages which offended the Queen and her ministers were removed. His *Description of Ireland*, which he dedicated to Sir Henry Sidney, and his portion of the *History of Ireland* appeared in the first volume of Hollinshed's *Chronicles* in 1577.

In the meantime Stanyhurst had married Janet Barnewall, daughter of Sir Christopher Barnewall, and had gone to live in Knightsbridge in London. Janet died in 1579, aged nineteen, following childbirth, and Stanyhurst left for the Netherlands, never to return. In 1582, he translated the first four books of Virgil's *Aeneid* into English heroic verse which proved somewhat burlesque. He dedicated this to his brother-in-law, Lord Dunsany. Two years later he published *De Re Rebus in Hibernia Gestis*, a discourse in Latin on the early history of Ireland.

Some time prior to 1585, Stanyhurst married Helen Copley, a staunch Roman Catholic, whose sister Mary later became the Superioress of the Abbey of Louvain in 1637. Helen died in 1602, following the birth of her second son. Stanyhurst became a Catholic, took holy orders and became chaplain to the Archduke Albert, the ruler of the Netherlands. Both his sons were later to become Jesuits.

Despite his years abroad, Stanyhurst did not lose contact with Ireland. He corresponded regularly with his relations and particularly his nephew James Ussher, to whom he wrote requesting a copy of his *Margarita*, 'presuming on that natural bond of love which is knit betwixt us'. His description of his native city in Hollinshed's *Chronicles* reads, 'Dublin, the beauty and eye of Ireland, is superior to all other cities and towns in that realm in pleasant situation, in gorgeous buildings, in the multitude of people, in martial chivalry, in obedience and loyalty, in the abundance of wealth, in largeness of hospitality and in manners and civility'.

Richard Stanyhurst died in Brussels in 1618.

Richard Steele
1672–1729

Described by Thackeray as 'undoubtedly an Irishman', Richard Steele, playwright and essayist, was born in March 1672 in **Bull Alley Street**, just a few paces north of St Patrick's Cathedral. Bull Alley appears on *Speed's Map of Dublin* (1670), between the gate-towers of St Nicholas and Pole just south of the city walls. At the time, the population numbered around nine thousand. Most of the dwellings were single-storey cabins though a number of three- and four-storey houses from the reign of Elizabeth I survived to the mid-eighteenth century, indicating that Dublin was not dissimilar to London before the Great Fire.

On 12 March 1672, Richard Steele was baptised in St Bride's (or St Bridget's) Church, then situated on the corner of Bride Street and Bride's Alley (now **Bride Road**). This was one of the six parish churches outside the city walls. In 1898, this church, which was one of the oldest and most important parishes in the city, was demolished. Its bell was transferred to St Werburgh's Church nearby and its organ to the National Museum.

Steele's father, also Richard Steele, one-time sub-sheriff of Tipperary, was a prosperous attorney who had a country house at Monkstown in County Dublin. His mother Elinor Symes (née Sheyles), from an old Irish family, was a widow when she married Steele and was described as being 'a very beautiful woman, of a noble spirit'.

Richard Steele was almost five years old when his father died. It seems unlikely that his mother survived much longer, as the child was taken into the care of his uncle, Henry Gascoigne, who worked as private secretary to James Butler, the first Duke of Ormonde, responsible for much of the development of the city of Dublin. Through the influence of the Duke, Steele secured a place in the Charterhouse School in London and left Dublin in his early teens to study there. It was here he first met Joseph Addison, who became a life-long friend. Steele later dedicated one of his plays to Addison, 'as no improper memorial of an inviolable friendship'. They attended Oxford University together, though Steele left in 1694 before obtaining his degree, to the regret of 'the whole society'.

He joined the Lifeguards under the command of the second Duke of Ormonde. In December 1694, Queen Mary II died from smallpox; Steele attended her funeral and wrote a poem about it entitled 'The Procession' which he dedicated to Lord Cutts, Colonel of the Coldstream Guards. As a result he became the Colonel's Secretary, joined the Coldstream Guards, and by 1700 had attained the rank of Captain. In 1701, he married Mary Scurlock, his second wife, and published *The Christian Hero*. *The Lying Lover* and *The Tender Husband* were published in 1703 and 1705 respectively. After thirteen years, Steele, who was a likeable and courteous man, but extravagant and therefore often in debt, left the army to become a courtier to Prince George of Denmark.

Steele was a member of London's famous Kit-Cat Club. Founded in the early eighteenth century by eminent Whigs, its members included Jacob Tonson, Alexander Pope, Joseph Addison, William Congreve and Sir John Vanbrugh. Steele's portrait was later painted by Sir Godfrey Kneller for the Club.

Steele was associated with three successive papers; with the assistance of Addison he ran the *Tatler* from 1709 to 1711; again with Addison, he ran the *Spectator* from 1711 to 1712, and he was then connected with the *Guardian* to which Pope, Berkeley and Addison all contributed. In 1713, he was elected MP for Stockbridge and, aided by the counsels of Addison and others, wrote a pamphlet, *The Crisis*, which approved of the Hanoverian succession. Swift's reply to this led to Steele's dismissal from the House of Commons in March 1714. George I, who succeeded as Elector of Hanover in 1698, had not been to England until he became King in 1714. With his accession, the tide turned for Steele. He was knighted in 1715, and secured the position of supervisor of the Theatre Royal of Drury Lane which brought him a sizeable income. In his humorous pamphlet, *Mr Steele's Apology for Himself and his Writings*, he cleared himself of his previous actions. He was elected MP for Boroughbridge in Yorkshire, and kept himself occupied with pamphlets, politics and writing. His last comedy, *The Conscious Lovers*, which he dedicated to George I, was a huge success. It included 'some things almost solemn enough for a sermon'.

In 1718, Steele obtained the patent for an innovative enterprise named the 'Fish-pool', which involved transferring live salmon from Ireland to England in a well-boat. Unfortunately it proved unsuccessful and in 1724, due to financial constraints, he left London for Wales. He died in Carmarthen, aged fifty-seven, on 1 September

1729, survived by two of his four children. He is buried there at St Peter's Church, where a memorial was erected to him in 1876.

James Stephens
1880–1950

'Dublin is less an aggregation of buildings than a collection of personages.'

James Stephens, poet and man of letters, was born on 9 February 1880 at **5 Thomas Court**, a narrow street off the busy trading street of Thomas Street in part of the old Liberties, which were areas under separate jurisdictions within the city. This little street runs alongside St Catherine's Church which was built in 1769 and outside of which a plaque marks the spot of the execution of Robert Emmet in 1803. Now deconsecrated, the church is being restored.

James, of Protestant parentage, was the second son of Francis Stephens, a van-man, and Charlotte (née Collins). Shortly after his birth (which he liked to say was two years later, at the same hour and on the same date as his friend of later years, James Joyce, born on 2 February 1882) the family moved across the river to **5 Artisan's Dwellings**, off **Buckingham Street**. Mr Stephens died at this address on 6 May, when James was two years old.

The next move was to **8 St Joseph's Road**, off **Prussia Street**, which was then a bustling area with cattle dealers, auctioneers, valuers and livestock all milling about, as the Dublin Cattle Market was close by.

Mrs Stephens seems to have been devoid of any maternal instincts and displayed little interest in her son. At the age of six, he was committed to the **Meath Industrial School**, for begging. It seems that he was poverty-striken and half starved, as he later claimed that he had fought with a dog over a crust of bread.

The Meath Protestant Industrial School for Boys was in **Carysfort Avenue, Blackrock**, where it accommodated a hundred pupils. The grey building still exists but is now used for other purposes. Once Stephens entered this school, it is probable that he never saw his mother again. Each boy had a number, and Stephens was number 279. He was to spend the next ten years here; he received an education and seems to have liked the school. He was interested in sport and gymnastics which suited his physique and his extrovert personality. He was four foot ten inches in height and on account of his antics he was nicknamed 'Fiddler'. He was very agile and it was one of his early ambitions to become an acrobat 'like one of Dan Lowry's acrobats on the Olympia stage'. Among his school friends were the Collins brothers, Tom and Dick, who were placed in the school as their father was ill. Any time they returned home to **8 Albert Road** in Kingstown (now **Dun Laoghaire**), Stephens was invited and welcomed there by Mrs Collins. Thanks to her, he had at least some home life.

Mrs Collins moved to **30 York Street** in Dublin, and when Stephens left school he was invited to lodge there with the family. At the time, around 1896, the street was in a shabby condition and had several tenements in it, although it also contained the homes of some professional people. The Collins family were at the good end of the street in one of the more respectable tenements, which they shared with several other families. By all accounts it was a lively household and Stephens got on well with the other tenants, especially the children, whom he loved. He read avidly and taught himself shorthand and typing, at which he became very proficient. His first job was as a junior clerk with a solicitor, Mr Wallace at **9 Eustace Street**. He then had other jobs, including one at **18 Exchange Street** to which he wore a shabby dark-brown suit and a big collar to hide his goitre. During the winter he attended the Dawson Street Gymnastic Club in the Engineer's Hall at **8 Dawson Street** with Dick and Tom Collins. Their team won the Irish Shield for gymnastics in 1901. At this time, he had an address at **14 Portobello Road** alongside the Grand Canal and later moved to **Essex Street**. Already he was writing and had sent one of his early stories to George Bernard Shaw. Shaw's reply to him on a postcard was not encouraging.

In 1905, Stephens sent his story 'The Greatest Miracle' to Arthur Griffith's weekly newspaper, the *United Irishman*. The paper was suppressed the following year for its revolutionary tendencies, but reappeared as *Sinn Fein* shortly afterwards. Stephens contributed poems to it on a regular basis, and this marked the start of his literary career. Griffith encouraged him and brought him to the notice of other writers. In *Hail and Farewell*, George Moore describes how Æ (George Russell) used to scan *Sinn Fein* every Thursday evening to see if he could discover anyone to rival Yeats' protégé, J.M. Synge. There is an amusing description of Æ going to the lawyer's office in **Merrion Square** where Stephens worked: 'A great head and two soft brown eyes looked at him over a typewriter, and an alert and intelligent voice asked him whom he wanted to see. Æ said that he was looking for James Stephens, a poet, and the typist answered, "I am he." '

Stephens later met Yeats, Lady Gregory, George Moore and many others. One evening he found himself in the **Bailey**, in **Duke Street**, in the company of Tom Kettle, Arthur Griffith, Seumas O'Sullivan and Oliver St John Gogarty and had what he termed his 'first adventure in that air, oxygen and gin, which we call wit, and which I watched as a cat watches a mouse, meaning to catch it'. He recalled that for the first time he heard poetry spoken of with the assured carelessness with which a carpenter talks of his planks and of the chairs and tables he plans to make of them.

Around this time Stephens moved to lodgings at **17 Great Brunswick Street** (now **Pearse Street**) with a couple named Kavanagh. Mr Kavanagh worked as a stagehand and doorkeeper at the Tivoli Theatre, a Music-hall on Burgh Quay. Not long afterwards, the Kavanaghs split up and Mr Kavanagh departed, leaving his pregnant wife. Stephens was about to leave as well when Mrs Kavanagh asked him to stay as she depended on his rent. He remained and was soon to inform his friends that he had a wife and family. Cynthia, a charming lady with Titian hair, hazel eyes and a strong will, was to prove a marvellous wife to Stephens.

Stephens' only son, James Naoise, was born in 1909. The same year, Æ helped him with the publication of his collection of poems, *Insurrections*. This was followed in 1912 by two novels, *The Charwoman's Daughter*, a portrait of Dublin slum life and poverty, and *The Crock of Gold*, considered to be his finest work.

In 1913, he resigned his post as a clerk and went to live in Paris until August 1914. On his return he and his family lived at **2 Leinster Square** in **Rathmines**. The following year he was appointed Registrar of the **National Gallery of Ireland**. This gave him some security which enabled him to continue writing, and he moved nearby to an apartment on the top floor of **42 Fitzwilliam Place**. One day Shaw invited himself around for tea. Stephens forget about the appointment and arrived back at 6.00 p.m. to find Shaw on the doorstep, just leaving. Annoyed at Stephens' unpunctuality, he remarked, 'I don't like Parisian Irishmen,' to which Stephens retorted, 'And I hate Cockney Irishmen.'

In 1916, Stephens published *The Insurrection of Dublin*, an eyewitness account of the Easter Rising. In 1923, he was awarded the Taillteann Gold Medal for his novel *Deirdre*, and with Æ he was chosen as a judge in the poetry section of the Tailltean Games in

59. The National Gallery. Merrion Square, where James Stephens was Registrar. (Note the statue of Shaw, now in the Shaw Room, who left one third of his royalties to the Gallery.)

1924. At the end of that year he resigned from his post in the National Gallery. He did not like the atmosphere of post-revolutionary Ireland. After a lecture tour in the United States, organised for him by Padraic and Mary Colum, he moved with his family to a house in Wembley and established himself as a broadcaster with the BBC. He moved in the London literary circles and returned to Dublin on visits; he gave a poetry recital in the **Abbey Theatre** in the winter of 1931–2 which was most successful.

On Christmas Eve in 1937 he had a devastating blow when his son James Naoise was killed in an accident. After this time, he withdrew into himself and never referred to his son again. His last book, *Kings and the Moon*, was published in 1938. In 1942 he was put on the British Civil Pension List. He was awarded a D.Litt. by the **University of Dublin (Trinity College)** in October 1947.

Loved by all, this popular, fun-loving and sensitive man, who opposed cruelty of any description to man or beast, died on St Stephen's Day 1950 and was interred in Kingsbury Old Graveyard in north London.

Bram Stoker
1847–1912

Bram (Abraham) Stoker, novelist and theatrical manager, is best remembered for his book *Dracula*.

One of seven children, he was the son of Abraham Stoker, a mild-mannered civil servant employed at Dublin Castle, and Charlotte, a strong-minded Sligo woman, twenty years his junior. Bram was born on 8 November 1847 at **15 Marino Crescent, Clontarf**, an exclusive terrace of twenty-six houses overlooking a private park, a few paces from the seafront. William Carleton was a neighbour at the time and lived at number 2. There is an unusual story attached to these houses. In 1792, a builder named Ffoliot had acquired the land and commenced building houses on it. Lord Charlemont, who did not wish to have his seaview from Marino House obliterated, tried to stop the builder by obliging him to pay heavy dues on materials which passed through his toll gate. The builder's retort was to have the goods brought by barge across the bay, and to complete his revenge, he built the houses in such a way that they entirely wiped out the view of the sea from Marino House. One of the Dublin newspapers reported that the Crescent was 'the most expensive hate fence in the country'.

Stoker was delicate from birth and had not been expected to live. Because of his ill health he was confined to bed for the first eight years of his life and it was at his bedside that his education began. He then had a teacher, the Reverend William Wood, who had a private day school, and under his tuition and guidance Bram made sound progress. He availed himself of his father's well-stocked library and shared his interest in the theatre, listening intently to his numerous theatre stories of bygone years. At his mother's knee he heard about her Sligo childhood and the horrific stories about the cholera epidemic of 1832, which in some cases wiped out entire families, almost whole streets. Bram asked his mother to write down her experiences of the cholera epidemic for him. Part of it is quite gruesome: 'One action I vividly remember. A poor traveller was taken ill on the roadside some miles from the town, and how did those Samaritans tend him? They dug a pit and with long poles pushed him living into it, and covered him up quick, alive.' She told him how she had heard the Banshee wail before her own mother's death, and many other stories bordering on the macabre. Being at an impressionable age when he heard these stories, Bram remembered them long afterwards.

60. Marino Crescent, Clontarf.
Bram Stoker was born in number 15 (*third from left*).

As he grew up, Bram's main interests lay in the daily newspapers and the Dublin theatre, a passion inherited from his father. On reaching his teens, he became interested in writing. By this time, his older brother William had already left home to study medicine, but Bram had plenty of companions left among the remaining children. With the family growing up, his mother had more free time, and, using her energy and determination, she became involved in some of the social issues of the day. Her voluntary work included being a workhouse visitor, and she wrote about her experiences for the Dublin newspapers.

In the autumn of 1864 Bram entered **Trinity College**. Despite his earlier illness, he had developed into a tall, handsome youth and in the space of two years became athletic champion of the University. He was a capped footballer and an unbeatable road walker. He joined the college Philosophical Society and was a lively contributor to all its debates. He read his first essay to it, entitled 'Sensationalism in fiction and society'. Later he became President of the Society.

Abraham Stoker (senior) retired in debt, after working fifty years in the civil service. He received a pension of six hundred and fifty pounds per annum which in those days was a very large sum of money. His wife was a spendthrift, however, and seemed quite incapable of running the household at Marino Crescent and taking care of her seven children, three of whom were now attending university, without running into debt. She remained steadfast that the boys should not be left short and in 1867 Bram took a week's holiday to London where he went to various theatrical productions. On his return, he went to the Theatre Royal in **Hawkins Street** (demolished in 1962) as often as he could afford it, to see performances by the most renowned actors of the day. These included Mr and Mrs Charles Kean, Charles Dillon, T.C. King, Mr and Mrs Charles Mathews and Mr and Mrs Herman Vezin. It was here, too, that Bram saw the famous Shakespearean actor Henry Irving perform, when Louisa Herbert and her company, the St James' Theatre from London, presented Richard Brinsley Sheridan's *The Rivals* in which Irving played the part of Captain Absolute.

In the spring of 1870, Bram graduated from **Trinity College** with an honours degree in science and commenced work as a civil servant in **Dublin Castle**, as his father had before him. Bram found the job dull and boring compared to his university days and started to write down ideas for articles and stories. But he did not sever his links entirely with Trinity College, where he obtained his MA degree. He was later called to the Bar, though he never practised law.

In 1872, on his twenty-fifth birthday, Stoker had the honour of being elected Auditor of the Historical Society at **Trinity College**; this made him unique as he now held the highest office in both the Historical and the Philosophical Societies. His inaugural address, entitled 'The necessity for political honesty', received substantial coverage in the Dublin newspapers, and doors were opened for him. He was now included on the invitation lists of such people as Sir William Wilde, the eminent eye and ear specialist whose son Oscar had just entered Trinity College. Oscar took him home to **1 Merrion Square**, where Bram created a favourable impression with Lady Wilde. She was especially interested in his theatrical links and welcomed him into her circle of friends. During Bram's frequent visits to the house, Sir William discussed his early travels and his explorations in Egypt.

Bram's interest in the theatre was refuelled in 1876 with the return to Dublin of Henry Irving with a company from the Vaudeville Theatre. They presented *Two Roses*, which had just completed a successful London run and for which Irving had received good notices. During its two-week run in Dublin, Bram saw it three times. Included in the audience on one occasion was George Bernard Shaw, then aged twenty. Bram searched the Dublin papers for a review of the play and was incensed when he discovered none had been written. He complained, and as a result secured an unpaid post as Drama Critic for the *Dublin Evening Mail*, a post he held for a number of years.

On the domestic front, Abraham and Charlotte Stoker were heavily in debt and, seeing no way out, decided to sell the family home at **15 Marino Crescent** and move to the continent, where they would be able to live at less cost until such time as they had paid off their debts. Their two daughters Matilda and Margaret accompanied them. By this time their sons could fend for themselves. William was a doctor, Tom was in the Indian Civil Service, and Richard and George were studying medicine. Bram was left with the task of collecting his father's monthly pension, paying off instalments on the debts and posting the balance to the family on the continent. With the break-up of the home, all the family effects were sold off except for a large trunk filled with family papers. These Bram brought with him to his new apartment at **30 Kildare Street** in the city. His apartment, which was sublet to him by an artist, was on the top floor of the house. (It is now commemorated with a plaque.)

Bram chose and bought the carpets, curtains and furniture. On hearing this, his father wrote and warned him that the artist might make off with all the new furnishings which he had invested in. Bram had 'A. Stoker, Esq.' placed above the door bell. It was a convenient address for him as he was in the centre of the city. He was leading life to the full, working in the **Castle**, attending meetings at the Philosophical Society in **Trinity College**, going to the theatre and writing his reviews for the *Evening Mail*.

Stoker was promoted in the civil service to Inspector of Petty Sessions. His salary was increased and the promotion also meant that he was not tied to his desk as he had to attend the courts. His experiences there resulted in his first book, *Duties of Clerks of Petty Sessions in Ireland*.

Later in 1876, Henry Irving returned again to Dublin and on seeing Bram's review in the *Evening Mail*, as a result of which the company's production of *Hamlet* was a major success, he asked to be introduced to him. This meeting was to set the course for Stoker's life. The two became firm friends and in 1878, when Irving asked Bram if he would give up his job in the civil service and join him as his manager, Bram agreed.

Stoker moved apartment from Kildare Street to **16 Harcourt Street**, off St Stephen's Green (c. 1876). Irving often spent evenings with him here on his visits to Dublin in 1876, 1877 and 1878. Bram Stoker's biographer, Ludlam, states that it was here that Stoker met Florence Balcombe, when Lieutenant-Colonel James Balcombe moved with his family to the house next door to him in Harcourt Street. Coincidentally, the Balcombe family had also been neighbours of the Stokers in Clontarf as they had lived in **1 Marino Crescent**. Florence, a tall graceful girl, formerly courted by Oscar Wilde who thought her 'exquisitely pretty', was to marry Bram on 4 December 1878 in **St Ann's Church** in **Dawson Street**. According to *Wright's Dublin*, 'The parishioners [of St Ann's] are rather of the higher classes of society, as it is in a most respectable and fashionable neighbourhood.' The same month, the couple emigrated to London, where Stoker became manager of the Lyceum Theatre and acted as a loyal friend and Secretary to Henry Irving for the next thirty years. Ellen Terry, the actress, said that Bram was one of the most kind and tender-hearted of men and that he filled a difficult position with great tact.

In May 1897, *Dracula*, the world's best-known vampire story, was published. A review in the *Daily Mail* read that *Dracula* was even more appalling in its glossy fascination than either *Frankenstein*, *Wuthering Heights* or *The Fall of the House of Usher*. His mother wrote to Bram, 'My dear, it is splendid, a thousand miles beyond anything you have written before, and I feel certain will place you very high in the writers of the day. I have read much but I have never met a book like this at all.' *Dracula* was followed in 1906 by *Personal Reminiscences of Henry Irving*, two volumes covering the period from the day he met Irving to the latter's death. This book was followed by *The Lair of the White Worm*.

61. The author of *Dracula*.

Bram Stoker died on 20 April 1912, aged sixty-four, leaving £4,723. His funeral took place at London's Golders Green Crematorium. Sadly, most of his personal papers and diaries were lost. His obituary in *The Times* praised him for the work he had done for Irving, and ended with the words, 'Bram Stoker was the master of a particularly lurid and creepy kind of fiction, represented by *Dracula* and other novels.'

Florence survived to see *Dracula* become a play and a film, and to this day it remains a universally popular book. The short stories Bram had been selecting before his death were published in 1914 with the title *Dracula's Guest and Other Weird Stories*.

L.A.G. Strong
1896–1958

'House sold, meadow gone
And garden too, to build upon.'
'The Forty Foot: A Retrospect'

Walmer Villa, one in a line of three cottages which once stood in **Glasthule**, on the main road from Dun Laoghaire to Dalkey, held a special place in the heart of the novelist Leonard Alfred Strong.

Strong was born the son of Leonard Ernest Strong and Marion (née Mongan) at Hartley near Plymouth on 8 March 1896. He thought it strange that his Irish mother 'whose world was bounded by her family and whose interest stretched no further' should have met two of the greatest Irishmen of her generation, Oscar Wilde and George Bernard Shaw. She visited Shaw's mother at Linden Gardens in Bayswater, London. She was frightened of Shaw and disapproved of him for 'living off his mother instead of going out and getting a job in an office'. She also encountered Edward Carson who lived in **Monte Alverno** at the corner of Sorrento Road in **Dalkey**. He was often to be seen strolling around Sandycove.

Strong first came to **Sandycove** in 1897 as a babe in arms. His mother, who was originally from the area, brought him over to her parents who lived in Walmer Villa. In his novel *The Garden*, he recalls his grandmother meeting them at the boat at the **North Wall**, wearing her black bead cape and hat tied under her chin with wide black ribbons. They travelled over the cobbles in the swaying carriage to **Westland Row** where they took the train to Sandycove – Grandpa would be waiting for them at the gate.

An unusual feature of Walmer Villa was Paddy the pet monkey who died of grief when banished to the zoo for eccentric behaviour. He was donated by a black neighbour who had to leave the country after he suffered adversely from the Irish climate. 'Paddy-monkey! Paddy-monkey! At the croon of a voice a chain rattled, and a handsome black monkey bounded out from the kennel. A second bound took him to the roof.'

Paddy Kennedy, a simple, upright and honest man described in *The Garden*, worked for Strong's grandparents, and was Strong's close friend for many years, accompanying him on his fishing expeditions to the pier and sea wall, to the circus and to all the other places which children like to visit. In the winter, Kennedy used to write to him at school, even sending him shamrock on St Patrick's day.

When the family was living in Plymouth, Strong attended Hoe Preparatory School and it was here that he began to feel the power of poetry, with Tennyson his favourite poet. Once, when he was ill, he read fifteen of Dickens' novels, an experience which he said marked him for life. At thirteen, he was writing mock Chaucerian verse which was published by Basil Blackwell. A year later he sat for three scholarships, got first place in two of them, and chose to go to boarding school in Brighton.

Strong returned to Ireland frequently, and these summer visits in his childhood were the highlight of the year to him. He wrote, 'In Walmer Villa, the Dickensian era still obtained, as it did in the inland avenues, the gardens, and the back streets of Kingstown [now Dun Laoghaire].' The area around **Sandycove** was the place where Strong spent many of his happiest childhood days and he was deeply influenced by his surroundings.

Everything to do with Walmer Villa was beautiful and strange. Much has been written about gardens down the ages and Strong's description of the garden in Walmer Villa is among the best. 'When he heard the story of the Garden of Eden, he decided at once it must have been like Granny's garden. Indeed, the two were soon confused in his mind. It was necessary for him to identify any place of which he heard with a place he actually knew.'

The garden may now be gone, but in the minds of Strong's readers it will always remain, golden and drowsed beneath the sunlight, heavy with the scent of many different flowers, and the drone of the bees. It had everything that a garden should have – nooks, a rustic seat, innumerable arches, a sundial, an unkempt croquet lawn, a summer house, a swing and long-disused iron posts for holding the tennis net. Then there was the vast manure heap so essential to every garden, the gooseberry and currant bushes, and behind, the meadow.

The big field which stretched behind the meadow for a quarter of a mile to the 'red houses in Glenageary' has vanished. It has been replaced by houses. Strong spent much of his time romping and playing near the sea which was only three hundred feet from his front door. This he describes in his novel *Sea Wall*. The ritual was always the same. As soon as he had finished his breakfast, he would be off, down the little main street of Glasthule, off sharp to the right of the Metals, and down the winding, clattery steps to the baths. **The Metals** is an interesting railside walk which stretches two miles from Dun Laoghaire as far as Dalkey.

The sea wall stretched for about a mile from Newtownsmith to Ballygihen, but disappeared when **Marine Parade** was built in 1921. Many of the landmarks of Strong's day are vanishing with the filling in of the sea rocks in **Scotsman's Bay**.

As a child, Strong recalled seeing J.M. Synge outside the house where he stayed with relatives in **Croswaithe Park** in **Dun Laoghaire**: 'He wore a broad-brimmed hat, which for some reason caught my attention and I stared at it until I became aware that the dark saturnine face beneath it, with its heavy brows and dark moustache, had softened into a smile of amusement.' This meeting resulted in Strong's poem 'A Memory':

> When I was as high as that
> I saw a poet in his hat
> I think the poet must have smiled
> At such a solemn gazing child.
>
> Now wasn't it a funny thing
> To get a sight of J.M. Synge
> And notice nothing but his hat?
> Yet life is often queer like that.

Holidays were also spent with his Uncle Dick who lived at **8 Sorrento Terrace** in **Dalkey**. This incomparable terrace of large houses, constructed in 1874, affords one of the finest views in Ireland. To Strong, the house was one of the world's wonders with its balcony, balustrade and cliffs. Like Shaw, Strong was taken by the view of **Killiney Bay** and wrote of the house, 'built on the southernmost point above Dalkey Sound, it looks across the Bay of Killiney to Bray and the Wicklow Mountains. The outline is of astonishing beauty, rising peak by peak, with a foreground of beautifully proportioned hills and foothills, a level wooded plain, and the long curved arm of Killiney Hill; the slopes of Vico, which are dotted with houses painted in gay, clean colours that give a Mediterranean effect to the steep hillside and the small crumbled cliff.'

Due to an injury he had received at college, Strong was not accepted for military service during the First World War, though many of his closest friends enlisted and were killed in action. Instead, he won an open Classical scholarship to Oxford where he met T.S. Eliot, the Woolfs and Siegfried Sassoon. He also met Robert Graves whose subsequent friendship meant a great deal to him. Some of Strong's poems were published in *The Varsity*, to which Aldous Huxley contributed under the pseudonym Aloysius Whalebelly. Strong described him as 'shy, myopic, the astringent ferocity of his writing contradicted by the gentleness of his manners'. A new periodical, *The Coterie*, also published Strong's work together with that of T.S. Eliot, R.C. Trevelyan, A.E. Coppard and Wilfred Childe.

The days spent at Oxford were happy and interesting ones, and, as one of the favoured young undergraduates, Strong was invited to Lady Ottoline Morrell's famous house, Garsington Manor, near Oxford, where his fellow guests were Bertrand Russell and W.B. Yeats. He remarked that it was his good fortune to have known Yeats for the last twenty years of the latter's life.

In 1919 and the early 1920s, while living in Oxford, Yeats kept open house on Monday evenings, but only for the invited. Strong recalled that the subjects most frequently discussed at these gatherings were psychic research, magic and the occult, writing in general and stories about poets and writers; Yeats had a liking for the unseemly and many of his own stories were Rabelaisian. In argument he was scrupulous and adroit. He devoted a great deal of ingenuity to paying off old scores against George Moore, about whom he had a great many stories which illustrated his delight in mischief and which at times he brought to absurd lengths. When Strong asked him for advice about his future Yeats told him that he would find his true strength as a writer in returning to the images of his childhood.

When Strong graduated in 1920, he took a job as a schoolmaster at Summer Fields, a north Oxford preparatory school. Cecil Day-Lewis taught in the same school and in his biography he described Strong as being a well-informed but unmalicious gossip, endlessly kind to his friends, a tireless encourager of the young and in the end, maybe, too interested in people to work hard enough at his writing.

Strong remained at Summer Fields until 1930; after this time he lived entirely on what he earned by his writings. *Travellers*, his book of short stories, won him the James Tait Black award. He once made an interesting remark to R.L. Megroz: 'I see a novel as a landscape first, with hills and perhaps a sea-coast and bays and promontories. There are one or two clouds obscuring features of the picture. Presently the clouds begin to clear away, and then I have the main events, represented by the chief landmarks.' This attachment to place, which is an Irish characteristic, is evident in Strong's novel *Sea Wall*. He describes a favourite place – the **Forty Foot**, a famous bathing place for men situated close to the Joyce Tower in **Sandycove**, which stands like a full stop at the bend of the

62. The Forty Foot Bathing Place, Sandycove, subject of a poem by Strong, and where many a literary character took the plunge.

bay. Many a literary character took the plunge here, like Buck Mulligan in *Ulysses* who capered before Stephen Dedalus and Haines, 'down towards the forty foot hole, fluttering his winglike hands leaping nimbly, Mercury's hat quivering in the fresh wind that bore back to them his brief birdlike cries'. The assortment of swimmers is described by Strong: 'Rich businessmen having their morning dip before going into the city, local tradesmen, school-boys, postmen, working men, priests, policemen coming off their beat', and as Paddy Kennedy, himself an occasional member, put it, 'When a man was in his pelt, sure only God Almighty could tell who was the gentleman then.'

In his poem entitled 'The Forty Foot: A Retrospect' from his collected poems, *The Body's Imperfections*, Strong reminisces about the place and the swimmers:

Well, that's ten years ago and more,
And I am far from Kelly Shore
And Ring Rock: no one that I love
Is left at all in Sandycove.

Strong had a keen interest in colloquial speech and dialect and this is reflected in some of his poems. A varied and prolific writer, he wrote poetry, film scripts, detective stories and children's books, as well as some fine biographies such as those on Thomas Moore and John McCormack, and in 1938 he became a Director of the London publishing house of Methuen, under which imprint a lot of his own work was published. His novels include *The Bay*, *Dewer Rides*, *Corporal Tune*, *The Garden*, *Sea Wall* and *The Hill of Howth*, which is dedicated to Micheál MacLiammóir.

It is easy to see why this gentle man loved and wrote about the area of Dun Laoghaire, Sandycove and Killiney. Some lines from *The Captain and other Stories* give some insight to his character: 'I am a quiet little man, little given to hate or anger but may I always have the strength to say, "My curse on all who set good men at odds, that waste the high brilliant life and the gentle understanding life, and spill on the ground the brains that might have lit our world." '
Strong died in Guildford, Surrey, on 17 August 1958.

A presentment, vague yet real, bade me walk slowly, look long and carefully. At the orchard gate I turned, and once more let the beloved scene soak into my sight. Then I closed the garden gate forever.

Green Memory

Jonathan Swift
1667–1745

Jonathan Swift was born at 7 **Hoey's Court** in the parish of St Werburgh's on 30 November 1667, seven months after the death of his father. He was the son of Jonathan Swift and Abigail (née Erick) of Leicester, and the grandson of Thomas Swift, the well-known Royalist vicar of Goodrich in England.

The houses in Hoey's Court, within the old city walls, were built in the seventeenth century by Sir John Hoey, who came with Lord Mountjoy from England in 1599. Many of these Dutch-gable-style houses were inhabited by the more important lawyers in Dublin. Number 7 was no exception, being the residence of Swift's lawyer uncle, Godwin Swift, an elder brother of Swift's father, who had come to Ireland some years before.

This area has altered considerably and nothing now remains of this house or indeed of Hoey's Court. The name is commemorated on a plaque at the junction of **Little Ship Street** at the South West Gate of Dublin Castle, a stone's throw from St Patrick's Cathedral in Patrick Street. The house which Swift pointed out as his birthplace now only exists in a drawing by Sir William Wilde.

When Swift was a year old, he was taken to England by his nurse who had an ailing relative there whom she wished to visit. He was returned four years later to his uncle Godwin, his widowed mother having returned to her native Leicester some years before.

From the ages of six to fourteen, Swift was sent as a boarder to Kilkenny College, considered to be one of the finest schools in Ireland at the time. According to Richard Stanyhurst, 'from it sprouted many proper impes'. William Congreve was one of Swift's contemporaries here.

From 1682 to 1689, Swift attended **Trinity College** in Dublin, to study for his BA degree. The University was then set amidst green fields on the edge of the city. It had been founded in 1591 by Queen Elizabeth I on what had been the site of the monastery of All Hallows. There were three hundred students attending the college when Swift was there. None of the buildings which were there in Swift's time still remain, the oldest surviving building in Trinity being the Rubrics, a range of red-brick apartments which date from 1700. According to the College records, Swift was an unsatisfactory student who obtained his degree only by 'special grace'. He seems to have been miserable both at school and at university, where his experiences confirmed in him that savage melancholia which lasted all his life. His education was financed by his uncle Godwin, who died in 1695 and was buried in **St Werburgh's Church** in Werburgh Street.

In 1689, Swift visited his mother in England. The same year, he became Secretary to Sir William Temple, at Moor Park, near Farnham in Surrey. Swift lived here for several years during three periods in his life. It was here that he first met Esther Johnson, known as Stella, the daughter of a companion of Temple's sister. Following his ordination, Swift worked as clergyman in Kilroot, near Carrickfergus in County Antrim. Sir William Temple died in January 1699 and, at Swift's suggestion, Stella, accompanied by

Rebecca Dingley, who was first cousin once removed of the Temples, left for Ireland.

From 1700 to 1710, Swift was the incumbent of the village of Laracor, near Trim, in County Meath. Stella lived nearby with Mrs Dingley. The three of them spent long periods with their school-master friend Dr Patrick Sheridan at Quilca in County Cavan, where Swift later wrote much of his longest and most famous ironic masterpiece, *Gulliver's Travels* (published in 1726). Mrs Dingley and Stella also spent time in Dublin in lodgings in Stafford Street (now **Wolfe Tone Street**) which overlooks St Mary's Church where Dr Sheridan had gallery seats for his pupils. The building remains but is no longer in use as a place of worship.

Swift first met Vanessa (Esther Van Homrigh), whose liaison with him is related in *Cadenus and Vanessa*, in Dunstable in 1707. Her father, Bartholomew Van Homrigh, had been Lord Mayor of Dublin in 1697 and in 1714 Vanessa came to live in the Abbey, in Celbridge, County Kildare. She also spent time in Dublin at the Van Homrighs' house at Turnstile Alley (now **Foster Place**), **College Green**. When she died in 1723 aged thirty-six, she was buried near her father and sister in **St Andrew's Church** on the corner of **Andrew Street** and **Suffolk Street**. This parish was founded in the eleventh century, with the original church at the corner of Dame Street and Church Lane. A new church was erected between 1670 and 1674, dedicated to St Andrew the Apostle, but it was destroyed by fire in 1860 and replaced by the present church which opened in 1866. (This is no longer used as a place of worship. It was sold recently by the Church of Ireland and has been converted as the city's main Tourist Information Centre.)

Swift wished to further his career in London where he was soon known as a powerful pamphleteer and became friends with Richard Steele, Joseph Addison, Alexander Pope and William Congreve. His *Journal to Stella* was written during his London stay between 1710 and 1713. He published *The Tale of a Tub* and *The Battle of the Books* anonymously, and wrote political pieces on behalf of the Tory Party. Owing to the party's downfall in 1713, he decided to accept the position of Dean of **St Patrick's Cathedral** in Dublin where he remained until his death in 1745.

St Patrick's Cathedral and some of the surrounding buildings are the main point of interest in Swift's Dublin. The Deanery, where he lived and died, was rebuilt on its old lines following a fire in 1781, but its kitchen quarters are preserved intact. Here Swift held daily prayers with his staff.

St Patrick's Cathedral was founded in 1191 and built between 1220 and 1254. It is Ireland's largest cathedral church. It contains Swift's death mask, his wooden pulpit, the semi-circular communion table from Laracor, the certificate for the Freedom of the City of Dublin granted to Swift in 1730, a marble bust presented by

63. St Patrick's Cathedral, Dublin, where Jonathan Swift was Dean from 1713 to 1745.

his publisher, and Swift's and Stella's epitaphs and graves. There is also a memorial on the wall erected to the memory of his servant, Alexander McGee, which reads:

> Here lies the body of Alex McGee, servant to Dr Swift, Dean of St Patrick's. His grateful Master caused this monument to be erected in memory of his discretion, fidelity and diligence in that humble station.

Swift was persuaded with difficulty to omit the words 'and Friend', which he had written after 'Master'.

The Duke of Schomberg, the Huguenot leader killed while in command of the Huguenot cavalry regiment at the Battle of the Boyne, was buried in the Cathedral. A marble slab, erected to his memory some forty years later by Dean Swift, can be seen on the wall of the North Choir Aisle with a Latin inscription which bears witness to a row behind the scenes.

Stella remained Swift's affectionate friend for the rest of her short life. She died on 28 January 1728 in the care of Lady Eustace at **Arbour Hill**, close to the main entrance of the Phoenix Park, or the Deer Park as it was then known. Swift did not go to her funeral, 'which my sickness will not suffer me to attend'. He moved to another room in the Deanery so that he would not see the light of St Patrick's Cathedral as they buried her. Later he wrote about Stella, 'This was a person of my own rearing and instructing from childhood; who excelled in every good quality that can possibly accomplish a human creature.' Swift spent the last thirty years of his life in gloom, an embittered man, but he continued to write and to help the poor.

One of the places which he frequented was **Marsh's Library**, to the south-east of the Cathedral. Founded about 1702 by Archbishop Marsh, it is the oldest public library in Ireland. In the library's collection may be seen a folio edition of Clarendon's *History of the Great Rebellion* with notes and comments written by Swift in the margins. This Queen Anne-style building designed by William Robinson has changed little since Swift's time. It is open to the public. (St Patrick's Park, which is adjacent, contains the reputed site of the well where St Patrick baptised many of the local inhabitants in the fifth century AD.)

Another place with Swift connections is **Fishamble Street**, off Christchurch Place. In October 1741, the new Musick Hall designed by the Huguenot architect Cassels was opened in Fishamble Street. This is one of the oldest streets in Dublin, appearing on Speed's Map of 1611. Handel, with the help of his friend Matthew Dubourg, organised an orchestra and choir for the first performance of his *Messiah* here, which was scheduled for 13 April 1742. This was not easy as Dean Swift, who was by then suffering severely from Ménière's Disease, resulting in the decay of his faculties, had written requesting his 'Sub-Dean and Chapter to punish such vicars as should appear at the Club of Fiddlers in Fishamble Street as songsters, fiddlers, pipers, trumpeters, drummers, drum-majors, or in any sonal quality, according to the flagitious aggravation of their respective disobedience, rebellion, perfidy, and ingratitude.'

One of the performances was held 'for the relief of the prisoners in the several gaols and for the support of Mercer's Hospital, in Stephen's Street, and of the Charitable Infirmary in Inn's Quay'. Handel was pleased with the choirs from Christchurch and St

Patrick's Cathedrals which took part. St Patrick's Cathedral Choir School, which was founded in 1432, is still in existence today.

During his later years Swift continued to work with the poor of Dublin, spending a third of his income on charities. **St Patrick's Hospital** in **Bow Lane**, off James' Street, was founded in 1745 for the treatment of mental illness with funds bequeathed by Swift (the bulk of his estate) for the purpose. In his own words:

> He gave the little wealth he had,
> To build a house for fools and mad,
> And showed by one satiric touch,
> No nation wanted it so much.

64. The bust of Dean Swift in the west end of the nave of St Patrick's Cathedral.

He died aged seventy-seven in the autumn of 1745, having survived Stella by seventeen years. He is buried beside her in the West End of the Nave of **St Patrick's Cathedral**, beneath the Latin epitaph which he composed himself, and which translated means, 'He has gone where savage indignation can lacerate his heart no more.'

J.M. Synge
1871–1909

'Still south I went and west and south again,
Through Wicklow from the morning till the night,
And far from cities, and the sights of men,
Lived with the sunshine, and the moon's delight.'

'Prelude'

John Millington Synge was born in the county of Dublin, but always regarded himself as a Wicklowman. He had an interesting family background. In the year 1765, John Hatch – whose father was agent

65. John Millington Synge in 1905 from a drawing by John B. Yeats.

for Jonathan Swift's patron, Sir John Temple – married a Synge. Their two daughters both married their first cousins, the sons of their mother's brother Edward Synge from Syngefield, Birr, County Offaly. One brother, Francis, built the family seat, Glanmore Castle in County Wicklow, at the beginning of the nineteenth century. Their neighbours were the Parnells of Avondale.

Synge's maternal grandfather, Dr Robert Traill, was born in County Antrim in 1793. He became the Protestant rector of Schull, a small village on the seaboard of south-west Cork, where he died of famine fever in 1847, caught amongst the people with whom he worked. His widow and family moved to Dublin where their fourth daughter, Kathleen, married John Hatch Synge, a barrister and landlord, in 1856. They lived for some time in a house at **1 Hatch Street** (named after an ancestor), later moving to number **4** where Robert, Edward and Ann were born. Leaving number 4, they moved to **Newtown Villas** in **Rathfarnham**. This was a large, grey, semi-detached house standing in its own grounds, with a fine view of pasturelands against a backdrop of the Dublin hills. Time has, however, transformed this tranquil pastoral area into built-up Dublin suburbs. Two more children were born here, Samuel on 15 March 1867 and John Millington on 16 April 1871. Just a year later, on 13 April 1872, Mr Synge died aged only forty-nine, from smallpox which he had caught when visiting a sick neighbour.

Fortunately, Mrs Synge had an income of four hundred pounds a year from property in Galway which helped her to bring up her four sons and daughter and give them a good education. She moved with her family to **4 Orwell Park** in **Rathgar**, to be next door to her mother, Mrs Traill, who lived in number **3**. The family remained here for sixteen years. Situated only half a mile from **Newtown Villas**, it was close to the river Dodder with its high, wooded banks on which the children played, and to **Rathfarnham Castle** with its densely wooden demesne where the children roamed. The castle had an imposing entrance in the form of a Roman triumphal arch built by Charles, Lord Ely. The ownership passed through various people, including Lord Chancellor Blackbourne, who gave the Synge children his permission to use the estate. The last owners of the Castle were the Jesuits. Now, all that remains of the former demesne is about four acres of land, the castle having been passed on to the State.

Synge had a happy childhood in Orwell Park, where the family kept an assortment of animals. He had a bicycle with wooden wheels which he rode around Churchtown, then a rural area.

During the summer holidays, Mrs Synge brought the children on holiday to County Wicklow. Before the death of Uncle Francis, she took the family to **Glanmore Castle** which was situated in an idyllic location just beside Avondale House, home of the Parnells. On such occasions, she and the children took the train to Rathnew Station. Here they were met by their uncle Francis and travelled back to the house with him in his four-in-hand.

Many of the holidays in County Wicklow after that were spent at **Greystones**, a small fishing village on the east coast eighteen miles south of Dublin. The family continued to holiday here from 1874 for the next sixteen years.

As a child, Synge was somewhat delicate and did not take part in the normal activities of a child of his age like swimming and games at school. His illnesses were never terribly serious, however, and did not seem to prevent him from riding his pennyfarthing bike for a distance of over sixty miles a day in later years.

He received a somewhat disconnected education, attending various schools including Mr Harrick's Classical and English School at **4 Upper Leeson Street**. When the weather was fine, John and his brother Sam walked to school, and when it was wet, they travelled part of the journey by the horse tram. At the age of fourteen, John was withdrawn from school because of his health and studied under a private tutor until he was ready for college in 1888.

From early childhood, Synge was passionately drawn to nature and was especially interested in ornithology. He also collected different varieties of moths and butterflies and in 1885 became a member of the *Dublin Naturalists' Field Club*. It was around this time that he read Darwin and suffered a crisis of faith. He had a great love for music and in 1887 started to study the violin, to which he devoted much of his time. He was rather talented and composed several pieces, most of which, unfortunately, did not survive. He attended the **Royal Irish Academy of Music** at **36 Westland Row** where he studied the violin, musical theory and counterpoint. He was unable to take up playing the violin as a career due to his extreme nervousness and shy disposition when playing before an audience.

In 1890, Mrs Synge's daughter Ann and her husband Harry Stephens, an ambitious young solicitor whose business was expanding, decided to move from their apartment in the family home 'to some neighbourhood more fashionable than the quiet blind alley of Orwell Park'. They moved to **29 Croswaithe Park West**, Kingstown (now **Dun Laoghaire**) which was beside the sea. Mrs Synge moved to number **31**, the house next door, as she wished the family to remain close together. At this time Synge was already studying at **Trinity College**, which he had entered in 1888.

In 1891, Synge was awarded a scholarship in counterpoint by the Royal Irish Academy of Music. He joined the orchestra in the Academy and played in his first concert in the **Antient Concert Rooms**, the theatre which played so great a part in the history of the Irish Revival. The first performance of the Irish Literary Theatre, situated in Brunswick Street (now **Pearse Street**), was given here in 1899.

After obtaining his degree in 1892, Synge went to Germany, partly for a holiday, where he remained for almost a year to pursue his musical studies. It was at this point that he decided to drop music as a possible career, 'seeing that the Germans were so much more innately gifted with the musical faculties than I was' and he took to literature instead.

In the summer of 1894, Cherrie Matheson, a friend of one of Synge's cousins, who lived at **25 Croswaithe Park**, joined the family holiday in Wicklow. Synge proposed marriage to her some time later, but on account of her religious beliefs (she was Plymouth Brethren), she did not accept. This affected him deeply and in the autumn of 1894 he went to Paris, moving from there to Italy the next year to study Italian. He spent the next six winters in Paris, returning to Ireland for six months of the year.

Synge first visited the Aran Islands off the coast of Galway in 1898; he went to learn Gaelic and to live among the peasants. He was an unobtrusive person and conversed easily with the local people in their native tongue. He played his fiddle in their kitchens and blended in well with their way of life, getting fresh lively images and assimilating their colourful culture as he did so. The same year he visited Lady Gregory in Coole Park and met Edward Martyn. The following year when he was back in Paris staying in the Hôtel Corneille, he met W.B. Yeats who told him with uncanny insight to give up an alien culture and go back to the Aran Islands to live there as one of the people and 'express a life that has never found expression'.

For five summers in succession Synge returned to Aran. In 1901 he completed his book entitled *The Aran Islands*, which concerns his experiences among the fishermen and their families, but it was rejected by the publisher Grant Richards. (Illustrated by Jack B. Yeats, it was published in 1907.) Lady Gregory also rejected his play *When the Moon has Set* for the Irish Literary Theatre, the forerunner of the Abbey Theatre (founded in 1904). *In the Shadow of the Glen*, which he wrote in 1902, was his first play to be produced, opening on 8 October 1903. *Riders to the Sea* followed in 1904, after which came *The Well of the Saints* in February 1905 and *The Playboy of the Western World* which opened at the **Abbey Theatre** on 26 January 1907, and was the cause of riots in Dublin.

Halfway through the third act, demonstrations began, with the audience reacting to what they regarded as Synge's blasphemous language and slur on the purity of Irish womanhood. A group in the audience began hissing and muttering when the word 'shift' was used and the interruptions continued until the final curtain. The critic for the *Freeman's Journal* wrote that the play was 'a libel upon Irish peasant men, and worst still upon Irish peasant girlhood', while the *Irish Times* wrote that it was 'a brilliant success marred by "indiscretions" '. Demonstrations continued throughout the following performances despite the fact that W.B. Yeats had called in the police to protect the company.

Synge was the first playwright in Ireland to write for an Irish audience about Irish matters. Other playwrights like Oscar Wilde and George Bernard Shaw had catered more for the tastes of an English audience. Critics accused Synge of using flowery language

66. (*left*) The old Abbey Theatre.

67. (*above*) The new Abbey Theatre.

The theatre was rebuilt in 1966 after the original building was badly damaged by fire in July 1951.

and his plays were condemned as being pseudo-Irish, which is of course untrue. Some of his sentences are formed on pure Gaelic constructions and therefore would sound strange to a person who had no knowledge of the Irish language. Synge said that in writing *The Playboy of the Western World* he used only one or two words that he had not heard among the country people of Ireland, including a certain number of phrases which he had heard from the fishermen and herdsmen along the coast from Kerry to Mayo, or from beggar-women and ballad singers nearer Dublin.

In order to be nearer to the city, and more specifically to the Abbey, Synge left Croswaithe Park and took a flat at **15 Maxwell Road, Rathmines**, followed shortly by another nearby at **57 Rathgar Road**. His sister and her husband, the Stephens, had moved to Silchester House, on the corner of **Silchester Road** in **Glenageary** and Mrs Synge to nearby Glendalough House in **Adelaide Road**. Synge often stayed here and this is where he finished writing *The Playboy*.

In 1906 Synge fell in love with Molly Allgood, an actress fifteen years his junior, who had joined the Abbey Theatre Company the previous year as Máire O'Neill. Synge was by then involved in the management of the theatre and was impressed by Molly's performance as Cathleen in *Riders to the Sea*, shortly followed by Nora Burke in *In the Shadow of the Glen*. The two became secretly engaged. The following year, Synge took a cottage for a month in the summer in Glencree, County Wicklow, and Molly stayed in nearby **Enniskerry** with her sister Sarah. The month that Synge spent here is supposed to have been one of the happiest times in his life.

The following September, Synge was admitted to hospital for an operation. In 1908, he took a flat at **47 York Road, Rathmines**, where he planned to live after his marriage to Molly, but his stay here was of short duration, lasting only from February until May when he was admitted for the second time to Elphis Nursing Home at **19 Lower Mount Street**. The marriage was postponed. Synge's doctors discovered a malignancy about which, unfortunately, they could do nothing, but he left the hospital in July thinking it was only a matter of recuperation before he was restored to his full health again. He was very weak and had to limit his outings to short walks. He wanted to go to County Kerry and the Blasket Islands for a holiday but his doctors advised against this, so instead, on 5 October, he went to Germany. While he was there, his mother, to whom he was deeply attached, died in Glendalough House. Synge felt too weak to travel home immediately for the funeral. Coincidentally, the day his mother was buried, *The Well of the Saints* was revived at the Abbey Theatre.

On 7 November the same year, Synge returned to his mother's residence at **Glendalough House**. He worked hard on his play *Deirdre*, eager to get it finished, but his health was deteriorating rapidly and he was forced to give up writing for some time. Molly visited him regularly and read extracts of his plays to him.

On 2 February 1909, Synge entered the Elphis Nursing Home for the last time, taking with him the manuscript of *Deirdre* (which he decided to call *Deirdre of the Sorrows*) in case he felt well enough to work on it. He asked to be moved to another room from which he would be able to see his beloved hills once again – the hills where he had loved to wander since his childhood, and about which he wrote with so much feeling. When his nephew visited him, Synge asked him if he had heard the blackbird yet.

He died on 24 March 1909 and was buried in **Mount Jerome Cemetery**, Harold's Cross. His epitaph reads:

A Silent sinner, nights and days,
No human heart to him drew nigh,
Alone he wound his wonted ways
Alone and little loved did die

and Micheál MacLiammóir said of him:

The minor dramatist echoes his age; the dramatist of genius is he who stands outside his age or, it may be, creates it. John Millington Synge came close to creating an age in Ireland.

William Makepeace Thackeray
1811–63

On 4 July 1842, William Makepeace Thackeray, author of *Vanity Fair* and some of the finest satirical novels in the English language, disembarked from a steamer on a visit to Ireland. Twenty-one years before, on 3 September 1821, George IV had disembarked at the same port, and the name of the town was changed to Kingstown; it has now reverted to **Dun Laoghaire**. Thackeray noted a 'hideous obelisk, stuck upon four fat balls and surmounted with a crown on a cushion' which commemorated the spot at which George IV left Ireland. (This can still be seen.)

The Kingstown to Dublin railway was already in existence, but Thackeray chose to travel into the city by horse cab after a relaxed carman with a straw in his mouth said he would take him to Dublin 'in three quarthers . . . As to the fare, he would not hear of it – he said he would leave it to my honour; he would take me for nothing.' Thackeray could not refuse such a genteel offer!

Along the road to Dublin, which Thackeray observed was in extremely bad condition, he passed through the suburbs which contained examples of both low-sized cottages and numerous handsome houses with fine lawns and woods. He thought that the continual appearance of this sort of wealth made the poverty more striking. He found the entrance to the capital very handsome, as he passed 'old-fashioned, well-built, airy stately streets and through Fitzwilliam Square, a noble place, the garden of which is full of flowers and foliage. The leaves are green, and not black as in similar places in London; the red brick houses tall and handsome.' The car pulled up outside the **Shelbourne Hotel**, 'in that extremely large square', **Stephen's Green**. Here Thackeray was accommodated in a 'queer little room and dressing-room on the ground floor, looking towards the Green'.

The daily newspapers, the *Morning Register* and *Saunder's Newsletter*, accompanied Thackeray's breakfast of broiled herring, and browsing through these gave him an idea of how the Irish amused themselves in the city. He came to the conclusion that the love for theatrical exhibitions was not very great when he discovered what was on in the various theatres – most of the pleasures of the evening were importations from England – and recorded: 'Theatre Royal – Miss Kemble and the Somnambula, an Anglo-Italian importation. Theatre Royal, Abbey Street – The Temple of Magic and The Wizard. Adelphi Theatre, Great Brunswick Street – The Original Seven Lancashire Bell-ringers: a delicious excitement indeed! Portobello Gardens – "THE LAST ERUPTION BUT SIX" says the advertisement in capitals. And, finally, "Miss Hayes will give her first and farewell concert at the Rotunda, previous to leaving her native country." '

Having read the papers, Thackeray went to see the town, 'and a handsomer town, with fewer people in it, it is impossible to see on a summer's day'. He went through **St Stephen's Green**, observing two nursery maids 'in the company of the equestrian statue of George I' (no longer in existence) and passed the **Kildare Street Club** where he saw eight gentlemen looking at two boys playing leapfrog. This club was once housed in one of Dublin's most distinguished nineteenth-century buildings. The inside has now been gutted but the fascinating carvings of the exterior stonework still exist.

Thackeray then went to **Trinity College** where six lazy porters in jockey-caps were sunning themselves. He admired the great public buildings of the **Bank of Ireland** (almost opposite the College) and the Royal Exchange (now **City Hall**), while the view along the quays to the **Four Courts** reminded him of the quays in Paris. He describes the view walking towards what is now **O'Connell Bridge**: 'You have on either side of you, at Carlisle Bridge, a very brilliant and beautiful prospect: the **Four Courts** and their dome to the left, the **Custom House** and its dome to the right; and in this direction seaward, a considerable number of vessels are moored, and the quays are black and busy with the cargoes discharged from ships. Seamen cheering, herring-women bawling, coal-carts loading – the scene is animated and lively.'

Of Sackville Street (now **O'Connell Street**) he wrote, 'The street is exceedingly broad and handsome; the shops at the commencement rich and spacious; but in Upper Sackville Street, which closes with the pretty building and gardens of the **Rotunda**, the appearance of wealth begins to fade somewhat, and the houses look as if they had seen better days.' With the Act of Union in 1800, many large houses, particularly those on the north side of the river, were left vacant while those on the south side were bought by the emerging professional classes.

After this summer day in Dublin, Thackeray left the city for a tour around Ireland, described in his *Irish Sketchbook* which he dedicated to his friend Charles Lever.

Thomas Tickell
1686–1740

'He is said to have been a man of gay conversation, at least a temperate lover of wine and company, and in his domestic relations without censure,' wrote Samuel Johnson of the poet Thomas Tickell.

Tickell, who was educated at Queen's College, Oxford, came to Dublin on 1 June 1724 and was given the position of Secretary to the Lords Justice when the new Lord-Lieutenant, Lord Carteret, testified to his 'ability and integrity'. He first resided at **Dublin Castle** where he had his own apartment. He was friendly with Jonathan Swift whom he met frequently.

Tickell married Clotilda, the daughter and co-heiress of Sir Maurice Eustace of Harristown, County Kildare. Her uncle, also Sir Maurice Eustace, was Lord Chancellor of Ireland under Charles II. The marriage took place on 23 April 1726 in **St James's Church**, in **James Street**. The present St James's Church is the third church on that site and was built in 1858–60. It was closed for public worship in 1963 and is now used for commercial purposes. It has an interesting old cemetery adjoining it.

On his marriage, Tickell gained his wife's property in Carnalway in Kildare and the couple lived there for some years. Tickell was industrious and set to work on the house and improved the land by drainage. They had four children, John, Thomas, Margaret and Philippa, and moved to the Dublin suburb of **Glasnevin** in 1736 to be closer to the city. Tickell took out an initial lease on the property for eighteen years but was only to enjoy this lovely location for four. During these years he was a close friend of his neighbour, Dr Patrick Delany, then a widower, whose house **Delville** was close by. When Tickell was abroad, Delany looked after his land and wrote to him in great detail about the progress of his work on it.

Tickell died on 23 April 1740 at Bath in England but his body was brought back to Ireland and buried in the churchyard of **St Mobhi's** near to Dr Delany in **Glasnevin**. This is situated at the end of Church Avenue, just off the Ballymun Road.

Tickell wrote a number of poems and was a contributor to the *Guardian* and *Spectator*. His ballad 'Lucy and Colin' was admired by Goldsmith and Gray who thought it one of the best in the language. He was literary executor to Addison and edited Addison's *Works*, publishing in the first volume (1721) a very fine elegy on Addison's death.

68. Thomas Tickell's House, dating from c.1736, which is now the Director's House in the Botanic Gardens, Glasnevin.

Tickell is commemorated by a tablet in **St Mobhi's Church** which reads, 'Sacred to the memory of Thomas Tickell Esq. He was sometime Under Secretary in England, and afterwards for many years, Secretary to the Lords Justices of Ireland: but his highest honour was that of having been the friend of Addison.'

The magnificent **Botanic Gardens**, which were founded by the Dublin Society in 1795, are on what was formerly Thomas Tickell's property in **Glasnevin** and his house is now the Director's residence.

Anthony Trollope
1815–82

Anthony Trollope, who established the novel sequence in English fiction, was aged twenty-six when he came to Ireland. It was to remain his home for almost two decades. He had worked as a postal clerk for seven years in the General Post Office in London, years which he said were neither creditable to himself nor useful to the public service – he was always in trouble, and constantly on the verge of dismissal. He was in debt for most of the time, lived on borrowed money and was in constant misery.

Trollope landed in Dublin on 15 September 1841 without knowing anybody and with only two or three letters of introduction from a clerk in the Post Office, 'but from the day on which I set foot in Ireland all these evils went away from me. Since that time who has had a happier life than mine?' He received a poor reference from his former superior, and in the General Post Office in Dublin he was informed by his new master that he would be judged by his own merits. Before the year was up he had passed as a thoroughly good public servant. His salary was one hundred pounds per annum, with fifteen shillings for each day he was away from home, and sixpence for each mile covered. Sometimes he rode up to forty miles a day on Post Office business. His income after paying his expenses was four hundred pounds, which he said was the first good fortune of his life.

Trollope carried out a lot of work for the Surveyor, which included inspecting post offices all over the country, charting new postal routes and investigating complaints. Through his travels, he came to know every part of the country. He lived in Banagher, County Offaly; Clonmel, County Tipperary; Mallow, County Cork; Belfast and Dublin. He took up hunting, even though he was overweight and poorly sighted. It was to become one of the great joys of his life and nothing ever stood in its way, be it work for the Post Office or the writing of books. He came to 'love it with an affection which I cannot fathom'. After a short time in Ireland, he developed an affection for the people and 'found them to be good-humoured, clever – the working classes very much more intelligent than those of England – economical and hospitable'.

In 1842, Trollope met the small and witty Rose Heseltine, in Kingstown (now **Dun Laoghaire**) and they became engaged. She was the daughter of a bank manager from Rotherham in Yorkshire and was several years his junior. As he had a few debts to pay off, including that for the purchase of a horse, they delayed their marriage and were married two years later on 11 June 1844. They went to live first in Banagher, and then in High Street, Clonmel, where their two children were born, Henry in 1846 and Frederick in 1847.

Trollope had never put pen to paper before coming to Ireland. He wrote that he wished from the beginning to be something more than a clerk in the Post Office and to make an income on which he and those belonging to him might live in comfort. It was in Ireland that he commenced his career as a novelist and completed the initial volume of his first work, *The Macdermots of Ballycloran*, before he was twenty-nine. It was on a visit to Drumsna in County Leitrim that he came across a ruined manor house in which he fabricated the plot. This was published in 1847 and was followed by *The Kellys and the O'Kellys* in 1848. While Trollope was writing a travel book, *La Vendee*, famine was raging through the country. Trollope's fourth novel, *The Warden*, which is the first of the Barchester series, was published in 1855 and his name came to the notice of the literary world. His career with the Post Office was improving also, as he had been promoted to the position of Surveyor the year before.

After living for eighteen months in Belfast the family moved to **6 Seaview Terrace, Donnybrook**, Dublin, where they lived for five years. It was at this address that Trollope finished *Barchester Towers* and wrote *Castle Richmond*.

Trollope left Ireland in 1859. About his life in Ireland he wrote, 'In Ireland it had constantly been happy. I had achieved the respect of all with whom I was concerned, I had made for myself a comfortable home, and I had enjoyed many pleasures.'

Trollope became one of the most prolific of all English writers, publishing forty-seven novels and a number of travel books and biographies, as well as various short stories. During his thirty-three

69. 6 Seaview Terrace, Donnybrook, where Trollope finished *Barchester Towers.*

years with the Post Office, his achievements included major contributions to the organisation of the postal system and the introduction of the pillar-box for letters, the first one of which he had permission to put at St Helier in Jersey.

Katherine Tynan
1861–1931

Katherine Tynan, poet, novelist and journalist, was born in Dublin on 23 January 1861 into an upper-middle-class Catholic home. She was one of a large family and 'baby succeeded baby rapidly in the home of my childhood till we were eleven'. Her first home was at **25 South Richmond Street**, then the Portobello Dairy. It remained a dairy for a number of years, and was named after the interesting area of **Portobello** which originally had a canal harbour to provide space for boats moored at Portobello House.

Katherine's education commenced at a school about a mile away, across the Grand Canal at **3 Charleston Road** in **Rathmines**. It was run by a Miss or Mrs McCabe who was well connected, her sister

273

being a governess at the Court of Napoleon III.

Like many well-off families in those days, the Tynan children had nurses who took them out for walks and on various excursions. Unknown to their parents, just like George Bernard Shaw, they were brought to the most unusual places not really suitable for children. These included visits to **Kilmainham Gaol** to see the drop (gallows) and to hospital morgues to view the corpses.

After a bout of measles, Katherine's eyes became damaged. Ulcers developed and a number of doctors were consulted, but although Dr Biggar of nearby Harcourt Street eventually treated her with some success, she remained short-sighted all her life and described herself as 'purblind'. She never let this handicap interfere with her reading.

In 1868, the family moved from the city to the rolling country fields of a farm named White Hall, near **Clondalkin**, which her father Andrew Tynan had purchased. It comprised sixty-four acres and the house, which was originally a cottage, had extensions added to it later. It was an idyllic place for the Tynan children. In her *Memoirs*, Katherine later recalled her first few months living there: 'It must have been one of the few great summers that come to Ireland. The cottage was wrapped up in roses and woodbine.' She also referred to it in her poetry:

> My cottage at the country's edge
> Hath sweetbriar growing in its hedge.
>
> 'Thanksgiving'

Aged eleven, she was sent as a boarder to the Dominican Convent of St Catherine of Siena in Drogheda, County Louth, which she loved. She found that the convent library was limited, however, and read the novels of Maria Edgeworth at home. She finished her formal education aged fourteen and remained the rest of the time at Clondalkin until her marriage. Her older sisters made an effort to teach her household management but Katherine much preferred to spend her time observing nature, roaming the fields and reading out of doors. This is reflected in her poetry, much of which is religious in theme, about the beauty of her surroundings, nature, trees and birds.

The comfortable Tynan home was always welcoming to visitors, and many interesting people called, such as the journalist and agrarian agitator Michael Davitt, John O'Leary, Douglas Hyde and many others. Katherine's father provided her with her own salon in which to write and entertain her visitors.

The short-lived Ladies' Land League, the first political association in Ireland organised by women, was founded in 1881 by Anna Parnell, a sister of Charles Stewart Parnell. He was a hero to Katherine and it was under Anna's influence that she became a member. When Parnell was imprisoned in **Kilmainham Gaol** in October 1881 after his election as President of the Land League, Katherine visited him and the other political prisoners associated with the land movement. (The Gaol, on Inchicore Road, is open to the public.)

The *Irish Monthly*, a magazine of a literary and religious character which was started in 1873, had as contributors many of the writers of the Irish Literary Revival. Father Matthew Russell, SJ, was the Editor and became a friend of Tynan through publishing her poetry. It was through him that she met the English writers Wilfred and Alice Meynell who were to remain lifelong friends. On a visit to London in 1884, she visited Lady Wilde and met Oscar. She later contributed articles to *Woman's World*, a magazine edited by Wilde.

Literary recognition came to Katherine at an early age. Her first poem was published when she was seventeen and her first collection, *Louise de la Vallière and Other Poems*, was published in June 1885. It proved an immediate success. Around this time she met W. B. Yeats who was brought to White Hall by Charles Herbert Oldham, who was then editing the *Dublin University Review*. In her memoirs, *Twenty-Five Years*, she recalls finding two young men sitting in the bay window of her drawing room. She describes the poet as, 'tall and lanky, and his face was as you see it in that boyish portrait of him by his father in the Municipal Art Gallery. At that time he was all dreams and gentleness.' Yeats became a frequent visitor to White Hall and often returned to Dublin in the Tynans' milk van. They shared mutual friends such as the poets Rose Kavanagh and Æ (George Russell), Douglas Hyde and the Sigerson family. John Butler Yeats, the poet's father, painted a portrait of Katherine in 1886 at his studio at **7 St Stephen's Green**. This is now in the **Hugh Lane Gallery of Modern Art** in **Parnell Square**.

Katherine recalls in *The Middle Years* how, in 1893, she said goodbye to the old happy irresponsible life and left Ireland for London to marry Henry Albert Hinkson, a writer and Classical scholar. The couple had three children and remained in London for eighteen years. Katherine commenced her career in journalism and contributed to such periodicals as the *Illustrated London News*, the *Pall Mall Gazette*, the *English Illustrated*, the *Irish Stateman*, the

Boston Pilot and *Catholic World*. She had a wide circle of friends, many of them other writers such as Christina Rossetti, Hilaire Belloc, Francis Thompson, Lionel Johnson and of course Wilfred and Alice Meynell.

On returning to Ireland, she spent the summer of 1911 in a house in Greystones, County Wicklow before moving in September to a rented house in **Sorrento Terrace** in **Dalkey**, County Dublin, where the family remained until May 1912. From their house there was a superb view of Killiney Bay and the hills in the background. The family often climbed nearby Killiney Hill to 'gaze over the quiet hinterland between us and the mountains on one hand, and the glorious sea and mountain on the other'.

They then moved to Clarebeg (now **Thomond**) in Corbawn Lane, **Shankill**, in the Vale of Shangannagh. This was then in a quiet, select rural area which has since been transformed with new housing developments. Clarebeg was a fine house with steps leading up to an arched porchway over the front door. It had been unoccupied for some time before they moved in and the garden was overgrown. A famous gardener had lived in the house before them and they rediscovered a really delightful old garden with a Japanese tea-house.

During the three years spent at Clarebeg, some of Katherine's old friends, such as Father Russell, called. The couple also made a new circle of friends and had visits from Æ (George Russell), Padraic and Mary Colum and Seumas O'Sullivan. James Stephens and his wife joined them for Christmas one year, and on the way from the railway station in Shankill lost their way. They took a wrong turning on the long, dark, unlit narrow road, ended up in a wet ditch and arrived at the house a woeful pair. After a change of clothing, however, Stephens delighted the children with his joyful antics with the paper hats and crackers.

In the autumn of 1914, the family moved to the West near Claremorris when Henry Hinkson was appointed Resident Magistrate to South Mayo, by Lord Aberdeen, the 'Home Rule' Viceroy. The First World War had broken out and there was political unrest at home which caused Katherine to have divided loyalties. There was an occasional visit to Dublin. In 1916 she received first-hand accounts of the Easter Rising in Dublin, which she recounts vividly in *The Years of the Shadow*.

After the death of Henry Hinkson in January 1919, Katherine left Mayo with her daughter Pamela, and for the remainder of her life she moved between Ireland and England. She had two homes in

Dublin, **Kenah Hill** in **Killiney** and **Sylvanmount** in **Shankill**, both areas with which she was familiar. Of necessity, she wrote more at this period and had a tremendous output in her last ten years. She died on 2 April 1931 in Wimbledon, Surrey, and was buried in Kensal Green Cemetery.

Æ (George Russell) wrote of Tynan, 'She was a born singer, almost everything she has written seeming effortless. The earliest singer in that awakening of the imagination which has been spoken of as the Irish Renaissance, I think she had as much natural sunlight in her as the movement ever attained.'

On International Women's Day, 8 March 1993, the Irish President Mrs Mary Robinson unveiled a plaque to commemorate Katherine Tynan. It is on the wall of the Dominican Priory in the old village of **Tallaght**, near to her former childhood home.

> All in the April evening,
>   April airs were abroad;
> I saw the sheep with their lambs,
> And thought of the Lamb of God.

'Sheep and Lambs'

Oscar Wilde
1854–1900

Oscar Wilde was one of the great dramatists to emerge in Dublin in the late nineteenth century. He was born on 16 October 1854 at **21 Westland Row**. He was the second son of Sir William Wilde, the noted eye surgeon, and Jane Francesca (née Elgee), a poet and woman of letters who wrote under the pseudonym of Speranza. Oscar was christened on 26 April 1855 in **St Mark's Church** in **Brunswick Street** (now **Pearse Street**) by his uncle the Revd Ralph Wilde, rector of Kilsallaghan.

In June 1855, the family moved to a fine Georgian residence at **1 Merrion Square**. These well-proportioned terraced houses, built to the design of John Ensor with stucco work and fine marble chimney-pieces, were in what was then one of the most fashionable residential areas of the city. The Wildes' house was in a good position on the north side of the square, on the corner of Lower Merrion Street. It has a graceful wrought-iron balcony and a sun room adjoining the first floor. It was here that Lady Wilde held her famous salons frequented by many famous Irish names, such as Sheridan Le Fanu; Charles Lever, who had attended medical school with William Wilde; Sir Rowan Hamilton, the mathematician; George Petrie, the antiquarian and artist; Isaac Butt, the barrister and politician; and Samuel Ferguson who later wrote William Wilde's elegy. Amongst the household staff were a German governess, a French maid and six other servants.

70. 1 Merrion Square, home of the Wilde family, where Lady Wilde held her famous salons.

Isola, the Wilde's third child and only daughter, was born here in 1858. She survived only nine years. Her death had a devastating effect on Lady Wilde: 'A sadness is on me for life – a bitter sorrow that can never be healed.' Oscar had also been devoted to her and some years later commemorated her in 'Requiescat', one of his most quoted poems. He kept a lock of her hair which was found in an envelope when he died.

The children received their early education at home and were taught to speak both German and French. Following in his brother William's footsteps, the nine-year-old Oscar went as a boarder to Portora Royal School in Enniskillen, County Fermanagh, where he remained for seven years.

During their summer holidays, the two brothers would leave Merrion Square and go to the country; initially, they went to

Dungarvan in County Waterford. In 1854 or 1855, Lady Wilde took a house in the beautiful Glencree Valley, near the newly opened Glencree Reformatory in County Wicklow. She became friendly with the Revd Fox, a convert to Catholicism, and the Reformatory Chaplain, who visited them. She always had a longing to become a Catholic and thought of having the boys received. Father Fox later wrote, 'It was not long before she asked me to instruct two of her children, one of them being that future erratic genius, Oscar Wilde. After a few weeks I baptised these two children, Lady Wilde herself being present on the occasion.' When their father was told, he remarked, 'I don't care what the boys are so long as they become as good as their mother.'

The brothers also spent holidays at both Sir William's home in Moytura, close to Lough Corrib in Galway and said by Oscar to be situated 'in the most romantic scenery in Ireland', and his fishing lodge at Illaunroe on Lough Fee in Connemara which he had bought in 1853. Here they enjoyed the wildlife and became proficient anglers. They accompanied their father on his walks in search of ruins and antiquities in the area.

Oscar's brother William seemed to outshine him at school. In his final year, however, Oscar won the school prize for Greek Testament, a Gold Medal in Classics, and a scholarship to Trinity College, Dublin.

In the autumn of 1871, he matriculated at **Trinity College** and decided to study Classics. During his first year at university he stayed with his parents at **1 Merrion Square** and for his second and third years he moved into the university living quarters where he shared rooms with his brother. Their rooms were on the first floor of house number **18** in the cobbled quadrangle named **Botany Bay**. One of his fellow students at Trinity was Edward Carson whom Wilde was to meet again at his trial in 1895.

Oscar had a brilliant academic career at Trinity, crowned by his winning the Berkeley Gold Medal, the highest award for Classics. His father was justly proud and invited Sir John Gilbert, the President of the Royal Irish Academy, to 1 Merrion Square to celebrate.

Professor John Pentland Mahaffy, the Greek scholar who was later to become Provost of the College, was one of Oscar's tutors, and he was taught Greek by Professor Robert Tyrrell. Later Oscar said of them, 'Mahaffy and Tyrrell. They were Trinity to me.' During the summer of 1874, he spent much of his time at Mahaffy's home, **Earlscliff**, in **Howth**, County Dublin, where the the pair of them were working on the proofs of Mahaffy's book *Social Life in Greece from Homer to Menander*. 'He has a charming house by the sea here, on a place called the Hill of Howth (one of the crescent horns that shuts in the Bay of Dublin), the only place near town with fields of yellow gorse, and stretches of wild myrtle, red heather and ferns.' He continued his friendship with Mahaffy after university and they went on expeditions together to Italy and Greece.

In 1874, Oscar won a scholarship to Magdalen College, Oxford, where he took a double first and won the Newdigate Prize for his poem 'Ravenna'. When he was in his second year at Oxford, however, tragedy again struck the family. Sir William Wilde died, leaving hefty mortgages on some of his properties which were soon sold off. Oscar's brother William was left **1 Merrion Square** and the Moytura property in Galway, while Oscar was left numbers **1–4 Esplanade Terrace** in **Bray**, County Wicklow, and a share in Illaunroe with Dr Henry Wilson, a natural son of Sir William. Lady Wilde moved from 1 Merrion Square and took lodgings in Kensington in London.

Oscar fell madly in love with a beautiful young girl, Florence Balcombe, who lived at **1 Marino Crescent** in **Clontarf**. She was later to marry Bram Stoker, a civil servant and the author of *Dracula*, who had lived at **15 Marino Crescent**. On her engagement to Stoker, Oscar wrote to her, 'Though you have not thought it worthwhile to let me know of your marriage, still I cannot leave Ireland without sending you my wishes that you may be happy; whatever happens I at least cannot be indifferent to your welfare; the currents of our lives flowed too long beside one another for that.' He also requested her to return the little gold cross which he had given her. 'We stand apart now, but the little cross will serve to remind me of bygone days, and though we shall never meet again, after I leave Ireland, still I shall always remember you at prayer.' She married Stoker in 1878 by which time Oscar had left Ireland.

Wilde returned only on two brief visits. Once was to lecture at the **Gaiety Theatre** in **South King Street** in Dublin when he stayed in the **Shelbourne Hotel** on **St Stephen's Green**. On this occasion, Constance Lloyd, the daughter of Horace Lloyd, QC, whom he had met in London, was in Dublin also, visiting her maternal grandmother Mrs Atkinson nearby at **1 Ely Place**. It was in this house that Wilde proposed marriage to her.

On 29 May 1884, by which time Wilde was already a celebrity, the handsome young couple were married in St James's Church in Paddington. They spent their honeymoon in Paris and then led an extravagant life (mostly on Constance's money) in Chelsea. They had two sons, Cyril born in 1885 and Vyvyan born in 1886.

Wilde made his mark in British theatre and dominated the Victorian scene with his wit and personality. His first great theatrical success, *Lady Windermere's Fan* (1892), resulted in his becoming the most fashionable and talked-about playwright in London. Florence Balcombe attended on the first night, looking radiant, accompanied by her husband who was managing the Lyceum Theatre. The play was followed by *A Woman of No Importance* (1893), *An Ideal Husband* (1895) and what is generally accepted to be the best light comedy in English, *The Importance of Being Earnest* (1895).

71. Oscar Wilde at the height of his success, sporting his traditional green carnation.

Wilde was also beginning to achieve notoriety through his constant companionship with Lord Alfred Douglas, whom he had met in 1891, and the latter two plays were both playing in London when Wilde was arrested and imprisoned for homosexual offences in 1895. Constance left England and changed her name and that of her sons to Holland, but when Lady Wilde died while Oscar was still in Reading Gaol, Constance returned from Italy to break the news to him. He wrote in his apologia, 'De Profundis', which was written as a long letter to Lord Alfred Douglas, 'No one knew how deeply

I loved and honoured her. Her death was terrible to me; but I, once a lord of language, have no words in which to express my anguish and my shame.'

Wilde was released in 1897. He went to France, taking the name of Sebastian Melmoth from the romance by Charles Maturin, a relation of his mother. Constance Wilde died in 1898 and Oscar died in Paris on 30 November 1900 at the Hôtel D'Alsace in the Rue des Beaux Arts. He was buried in Bagneux cemetery but some time later his remains were removed to the Père Lachaise cemetery in Paris. He rests beneath an unusual tomb sculpted by Sir Jacob Epstein, which bears the epitaph:

> And alien tears will fill for him
> Pity's long broken urn.
> For his mourners will be outcast men
> And outcasts will always mourn.

William Wilde
1815–76

William Wilde, writer, archaeologist, father of Oscar Wilde, and one of the foremost eye and ear specialists of his day, was born in Kilkeevin, Castlerea, in County Roscommon. He was one of three sons of Dr Thomas Wilde and Emily Fynne. He studied medicine at the **Royal College of Surgeons in Ireland** on **St Stephen's Green**. This neo-classical building, the foundation stone of which was laid in 1806, was designed by Edward Parke and built partly on the site of an old Quaker burial ground, and later enlarged. It has interesting connections. Abraham Colles, famous for his anatomical discoveries and after whom the Colles ligament and fracture were named, held the chair of surgery from 1806 to 1836.

After his graduation in 1837, Dr Wilde took the opportunity to travel and accompanied a wealthy businessman as his personal physician on a cruise resulting in his two-volumed *Narrative of a Voyage to Madeira, Tenerife and along the Shores of the Mediterranean*. His salary from this position enabled him to pursue further his studies concerning diseases of the eye and ear at London, Vienna and Berlin. His medical books *Epidema*, *Opthalmia* (1851) and *Aural Surgery* were the first of the modern textbooks on their subjects and remained standard works for many years.

In Dublin, he lived in 199 Brunswick Street (now **Pearse Street**) and subsequently set up practice at **15 Westland Row**. In 1851, aged thirty-six, he married the six-foot-tall Jane Francesca Elgee, a woman of letters and a poet. She was the daughter of a Wexford lawyer, granddaughter of Archdeacon John Elgee, Rector of Wexford, and niece of Charles Maturin, the novelist. A woman of great courage, she frequently contributed features under the pseudonym Speranza to the well-known periodical the *Nation*, among others.

William Wilde, known for his generosity, set up a dispensary for poor people in a converted stable, which was the precursor of **St Mark's Ophthalmic and Aural Hospital** in **Lincoln Place**, founded in 1844. This was situated close by at the rear entrance to Trinity College. (It was once frequented by the young Sean O'Casey.) The site has now been redeveloped and the Hospital has moved to **Adelaide Road**.

As Dr Wilde prospered, he moved house to **21 Westland Row**, where his two sons, William and Oscar, and his daughter, Isola, were born. He had also fathered three children before his marriage, of whom the first was a son named Henry Wilson who was born in 1836. Wilde did not shirk his duties and educated Henry who later joined him in his medical practice. His daughters, Emily and Mary Wilde, born in 1847 and 1849 respectively, lived in County Monaghan with his brother, the Revd Ralph Wilde who had adopted them as his wards. Both died tragically when they were trapped in a fire at a ball in November 1871. Dr Wilde was grief-stricken.

As Commissioner for the 1851 Census, Wilde compiled statistics on the incidence of diseases and malfunctions of the eye and ear, the first ever compiled in the country. In 1862, King Oscar I of Sweden conferred on Dr Wilde the Order of the Polar Star. In 1863, he was appointed Surgeon Occulist to the Queen in Ireland.

Dr Wilde's reputation as a surgeon increased and in 1864 he was knighted for his services to statistical sciences. During this same year, however, his fortunes turned. One of Sir William's patients, a Miss Mary Travers, claimed that he had given her chloroform and then raped her. She had withheld her allegations for two years but public recognition of the Wildes on occasions such as Sir William's knighthood on 28 January 1864 spurred her into action and she issued a pamphlet which gained wide publicity. To protect his family against the ensuing scandal Wilde moved them out to **Esplanade Terrace** in **Dray**, County Wicklow, a maritime town twelve miles from Dublin. He had built houses numbers **1 to 4** some years before. Miss Travers continued her tirade on the family and eventually, following a trial, she received a farthing in compensation. Dr Wilde, who had entailed huge legal costs, ended up ruined. His practice gradually fell into decline over the next decade. He spent more time in his house at Moytura on Lough Corrib and at his fishing lodge, Illaunroe, in Connemara. His book, *Lough Corrib and Lough Mask*, was published in 1867. The same year, the British Medical Association met in Dublin and Dr Wilde brought them on a tour of the Boyne Valley. He was a noted archaeologist and knew the area intimately, having published *The Beauties of the Boyne and the Blackwater* some years previously. His catalogue of the Royal Irish Academy's collection of antiquities is described as 'a milestone in the history of Irish Archaeology'. Among his other books are *The Closing Years of Dean Swift's Life* and a *Memoir of Gabriel Beranger*.

Dr Wilde died on 19 April 1876 and was buried in **Mount Jerome Cemetery** in Harold's Cross, Dublin.

Jack Butler Yeats
1871–1957

Jack Yeats, the premier Irish painter of the twentieth century, was also a playwright and novelist. He was born in London on 29 August 1871, the youngest of five children of John Butler Yeats, the notable portraitist, and Susan (née Pollexfen). At the age of eight he went to Sligo to live with his maternal grandparents and he remained there until he was seventeen. He returned to London to study at the Westminster, South Kensington and Chiswick Schools of Art. He said he became a painter because he was 'the son of a painter'.

In 1894, he married a fellow art student, Mary Cottenham White, and three years later they settled in Devon. He commenced his working career as a black-and-white illustrator contributing to various periodicals, and in the late 1890s, he began to devote himself to Irish subjects. During his lifetime he illustrated more than thirty books and a large number of articles and stories for magazines. He held a number of one-man exhibitions of his watercolours and drawings in New York, and was the first Irish artist to hold such exhibitions at the Tate and National Galleries in London.

He visited Ireland frequently, and finally returned with his wife in 1910, staying some time with his sisters, Lily and Lolly, at their lovely house **Gurteen Dhas** on **Lower Churchtown Road**. (Sadly, Gurteen Dhas has been rebuilt and extended and bears little resemblance to what it was. It is at **100 Lower Churchtown Road**.) They then settled at **Red Ford House**, near **Greystones** in County Wicklow. Yeats used the glass house here as his studio. In the autumn of 1917, the couple moved to **61 Marlborough Road**, in **Donnybrook**, Dublin, which was in a less lonely area and more convenient for meeting friends. They then moved to a large first-floor apartment in a Georgian house at **18 Fitzwilliam Square** where he also had his studio. Each Thursday he held an 'afternoon' and invited guests to drink Spanish wine and discuss literature and art. Among the regular guests were Austin Clarke and Padraic Colum, and Samuel Beckett attended when he was in Dublin.

72. 18 Fitzwilliam Square, home and studio of Jack B. Yeats.

During the 1930s, Yeats wrote a number of prose works and plays which include *Sligo* (1930), *Sailing, Sailing Swiftly* (1933), *The Amaranthers* (1936) and *The Careless Flower* (1947). Three of his plays were produced at the **Abbey Theatre**: *Apparitions* (1933), *La La Noo* (1942) and *In Sand* (1949).

In 1950 Yeats retired periodically from time to time to the **Portobello Nursing Home** overlooking the Grand Canal, where he took a room at the top of the house overlooking the roofscapes. He liked to walk up the canal to see the swans and ducks. When he became frail, he travelled around by taxi accompanied by a nurse. In 1955, he removed completely from Fitzwilliam Square and remained in the nursing home, rarely going out, though he had many friends who called to see him. Thomas McGreevy was one who often remained talking to Yeats well into the night and the story goes that the patient in the room adjoining his complained that Yeats never switched off his wireless, even after midnight!

Jack B. Yeats died on 28 March 1957. His funeral service was held at **St Stephen's Church, Mount Street Crescent** and he was buried at **Mount Jerome Cemetery**, in Harold's Cross, Dublin.

William Butler Yeats
1865–1939

The marriage of Susan Mary Pollexfen, a quiet, sensitive girl from Sligo, and John Butler Yeats, talented painter and conversationalist, took place in St John's Church, Sligo, on 10 September 1863. The young couple spent their honeymoon in Galway and then set up home at **5 Sandymount Avenue**, in a semi-detached, six-roomed, eighteenth-century house, known also as **1 George Villas**. It is marked with a plaque. They were to remain here for about a year and a half. They bought most of the furniture at auctions, with the exception of their drawing-room carpet, the bedsteads and the bedding.

At the time of his marriage, John Butler Yeats was studying law and Susan understood that he had a bright career ahead of him as a successful barrister.

Their first child, named William Butler, born in **1 George Villas** on 13 June 1865, was to become the dominant poet of the English-speaking world. He was baptised at **St Mary's Church, Donnybrook**, which is situated at the junction of Simmonscourt Road and Anglesea Road, a straight line from Sandymount Avenue on the far side of the Merrion Road. On one of the first outings in his pram, William's nurse took him to Sandymount Castle and she reported that the baby was very frightened by the deer. (Yeats is now commemorated by a bust in **Sandymount Green**.)

Yeats was brought to Sligo at an early age, and he later said he always considered the place to be his home. He had a number of relations there and his great-grandfather, the Revd William Butler Yeats, had been rector in the parish of Drumcliffe.

73. 5 Sandymount Avenue,
birthplace of William Butler Yeats.

John Butler Yeats, who had no sense of financial commitment, abandoned his career as a barrister and took up portrait-painting instead, much to the dismay of his wife and her family. As a result, in the early years of their marriage, the family was constantly on the move between London and Dublin, with Sligo being the principal domicile. Their first home in London was at 23 Fitzroy Road, Regent's Park, where they lived for seven years.

When Yeats was aged nine, in 1874, the family moved to a house in West Kensington. Susan Yeats detested London and was most unhappy. She missed Sligo, to which she had an intense attachment, and often spoke to her children about it, telling them stories and fairytales set in that bit of countryside. On arrival in London, John Butler Yeats took over the education of his son. Two years later the family moved to Bedford Park and Yeats' formal education began when he went to Godolphin School in Hammersmith – he did not particularly like it and did not distinguish himself as a student.

Late in 1880, for financial reasons, John Butler Yeats returned to Dublin. He took lodgings for himself at **90 Gardiner Street** and rented a studio at **44 York Street** (now demolished), and the family followed some months later when he was given the loan of **Balscadden Cottage** in **Howth** for the winter. This was situated on the cliffs on Kilrock Road near the baths (now disused), just below in Balscadden Bay. The sea spray came through the windows and sometimes drenched their beds. After six months, they moved to a small house called **Island View** on **Harbour Road** where they remained until the autumn of 1883. They had a view of the old harbour of Howth and of the fishermen's single-masted sailing vessels passing by. (At that time, fishing was still the principal occupation of the permanent inhabitants of the area.) The ailing poet Samuel Ferguson lived nearby and Lily Yeats, William's sister, often left him fresh fish. The family settled well into their new environment with the cliffs and sea, and Susan Yeats felt quite at home exchanging stories with the fishermen's wives over a cup of tea in her kitchen.

Howth forms a peninsular promontory, occupying the north side of Dublin Bay and joining the mainland by a low sandy isthmus half a mile in width. The harbour, built in 1807, was originally the chief packet station. It was also a popular watering place with hot and cold baths. Howth demesne, famous for its rhododendrons, was close to Island View and Yeats sometimes trespassed there at dead of night. He also explored the wooded areas and dells on the hill of Howth and it was here that he began formulating his aesthetic theories.

In 1881, Yeats started at High School (now demolished) in **Harcourt Street** and each morning father and son would leave Howth for the eight-mile train journey into the city centre. They would breakfast together at the studio, and Yeats would return there for his midday meal of bread and butter. He attended this school from October 1881 to December 1883, from the ages of sixteen to eighteen. At this time, Yeats was already writing poetry. One of his fellow pupils was William Magee, who later wrote under the pseudonym of John Eglington. The school was five minutes from his father's studio which acted as a nerve centre for art and philosophy in the city, with Sarah Purser and Edward Dowden frequent visitors. In late 1883, John Butler Yeats moved studio to **7 St Stephen's Green**. Katherine Tynan, the poet and novelist, gives a description of it in her *Reminiscences*: 'Everybody who was anybody in Dublin, or visiting Dublin, seemed to find his way there . . . It was a delightful place, its atmosphere permeated by the personality of Mr J.B. Yeats, the quaintest and most charming of men. Canvases were stacked everywhere round the walls. They were used to conceal many things – the little kitchen and tea-table arrangement at one end, Mr Yeats' slippers and the dressing-room of the family.'

When he finished school, Yeats studied painting at the **Metropolitan School of Art** in **Kildare Street** where he met Æ (George Russell), the mystic poet who encouraged his interest in the occult and became a lifelong friend.

In 1884, due to lack of finance, the family left their airy Howth home for 10 Ashfield Terrace (now **418 Harold's Cross Road**). It was closer to the city and more convenient in that respect. At that time Harold's Cross was a suburb, with a green which was later taken over by the Rathmines Commissioners and converted into a public park, behind which is Mount Jerome Cemetery. Æ often called to the house and he and Yeats would share a meal and chant their verses to each other.

Professor Edward Dowden, who lived in **Highfield Road** in **Rathgar**, often invited John Butler and his son for breakfast and would listen to the young Yeats reading out his verses after they had eaten.

John Butler Yeats was invited to become a member of the **Contemporary Club** which held discussions and debates on literary and political subjects at **116 Grafton Street**. He brought his son with him. Here were gathered many of Dublin's intelligentsia including John F. Taylor, Thomas Rolleston, George Sigerson, Michael

Davitt, the Gaelic scholar Douglas Hyde, Stephen Gwynn and John O'Leary, the Fenian hero, who had returned to Dublin after a twenty-year exile. O'Leary had a deep interest in Irish literature and his presence had a profound influence on the young Yeats, while the older man immediately recognised the latter's genius and encouraged him from the start. It was through him that Yeats joined the Young Ireland Society and said that, from the Society's debates, 'from O'Leary's conversation and from the Irish books he lent or gave me has come all I have set my hand to since'.

Yeats published his first poems in the *Dublin University Review* which was founded in 1885. He became artistically and politically aware of Irish history and literature and these were soon the inspiration for and theme of his writings. He had expanded in several directions – 'in a form of literature, in a form of philosophy, and a belief in nationality'.

In 1887 the family moved back to London and from then on Yeats lived between both cities. In London, he met other poets and publishers and joined the Blavatsky Lodge of the Theosophical Society. In January 1889, John O'Leary sent the legendary beauty Maud Gonne, a passionate advocate of Irish freedom, to the Yeats home at Bedford Park. Yeats, who was twenty-three, fell desperately in love with her and shortly afterwards he wrote, 'From this time the troubling of my life began.' *The Wanderings of Oisin*, a series of ballads and poems, was published the same year.

In 1891 Yeats founded the Irish Literary Society in London and the following year the Irish National Literary Society. In 1893 he wrote *The Countess Cathleen*.

From the early 1890s until 1918, Yeats lived most of his time in England. When he visited Dublin, he stayed at different addresses such as **Lonsdale House**, a boarding house in **St Lawrence's Road, Clontarf**; the **Nassau Hotel** in **South Frederick Street**; **Morrison's Hotel, Dawson Street**; and **53 Mountjoy Square**.

In 1896 his friendship with Lady Gregory began and he spent long periods at her home in Coole Park in Galway. With the help of Edward Martyn, they began a movement for an Irish Literary Theatre which was founded in 1898, and whose aim was for Irish playwrights to write plays about Irish themes for an Irish audience. The first productions, which were given in the **Antient Concert Rooms** in Brunswick Street (now **Pearse Street**) in 1899 were Yeats' *The Countess Cathleen* and Martyn's *The Heather Field*. Yeats wrote *Cathleen ni Houlihan* which was produced in 1902 with Maud Gonne in the lead role. (Maud married John McBride in the following year.) The Irish Literary Theatre gained permanent premise in the **Abbey Theatre** in 1904, opening with *On Baile's Strand* by Yeats and *Spreading the News* by Lady Gregory.

After his marriage to Miss George Hyde-Lees in 1917, Yeats spent more time in Ireland, returning in 1918, as he wanted his first child to be born there. They stayed in Maud Gonne's house at **73 St Stephen's Green**, and about this time he bought a Norman tower, Thoor Ballylee, near Gort, in County Galway, which he restored as his summer residence. They then lived in Oxford from 1920 until 1922 when Yeats was made a Senator of the Irish Free State. He spent the summer at Thoor Ballylee and bought a fashionable Georgian mansion close to Leinster House in Dublin, at **82 Merrion Square**, in which he remained until 1928. He was awarded the Nobel Prize for Literature in 1923.

There is a cartoon portraying Yeats, who lived at **82** Merrion Square, and Æ, who had his office at number **84**, passing number **83** simultaneously on their way to visit each other. Neither sees the other, as each is in characteristic stance, Yeats with his head in the air and Æ with his lowered.

74. 'Chin-angles, or How the Poets Passed': cartoon by Mac of W.B. Yeats and Æ.

Yeats lived for a brief spell in a rented house named **Brooklawn** in Dun Griffan Road, **Howth**, and then in a top-floor apartment at **42 Fitzwilliam Square**, before moving to his final home in Ireland in 1934 at **Riversdale House, Rathfarnham** (on the Ballyboden Road), set in four acres of beautiful, well-kept garden. Yeats played croquet on the lawns here with his children Michael and Anne. Directly through the gateway, there was a stone bridge over a small river, but this entrance is now defunct, having been bypassed by another one.

Yeats died on 28 January 1939 at Cap Martin on the French Riviera, and was buried at Roquebrune. After the Second World War, his wish to be laid to rest in Ireland was fulfilled and his remains were brought back and buried in Drumcliffe Churchyard, County Sligo, as he had requested.

> Cast a cold eye
> On life, on death.
> Horseman, pass by!
>
> 'Under Ben Bulben'

A Selection of
Literary and Historical Pubs
in Dublin

Within the city of Dublin there are more than seven hundred public houses. The pub is an institution in Ireland, a haven from the slings and arrows of outrageous fortune; a place for deep philosophical discussion where God, religion and politics can be explained and put to rights; where post mortems on sporting events can be held; or where one may go alone to read a newspaper or have a quiet drink. One may be elated or depressed when going into a pub but the one thing that is not necessary to have is a thirst – this is only incidental.

There are all sorts of pubs in the city – quiet or noisy; calm or rowdy; singing or disco pubs. The clients also vary – there are literary pubs, journalists' pubs, yuppie pubs, dockers' pubs, civil servants' pubs, students' pubs and at least one gravediggers' pub. The literary pubs of Dublin are legendary. A surprisingly large number have survived over the years although their appearance in some cases may have changed. Many still have the original bar furnishings and oak-panelled interiors.

Of necessity, only a small selection can be given below but each pub listed has its own particular character, atmosphere and, sometimes, charm. Many of these are on or adjacent to the Literary Routes contained in the book.

The oldest pub is the **Brazen Head**, at **20 Lower Bridge Street**, which dates from 1666. It is on the site of Standfast Dick, an inn founded in 1210, which was then within the city walls. Today, the Brazen Head retains much of its old-world atmosphere. Over the past centuries Irish revolutionaries have gathered here, including Robert Emmet, who led the insurrection of 1803. It is incorrectly referred to by Corley in Joyce's *Ulysses* as 'The Brazen Head over in Winetavern Street'.

The Bleeding Horse, 25 Upper Camden Street, founded in 1649, is a pub which was frequented by James Clarence Mangan and is mentioned in the works of Sean O'Casey. It has been refurbished since Joseph Sheridan Le Fanu gave the following description of it in *The Cock and the Anchor*, published in 1845: 'There stood at the southern extremity of the city, near the point at which Camden Street now terminates, a small, old-fashioned building, something between an alehouse and an inn. It occupied the roadside by no means unpicturesquely; one gable fitted into the road, with a projecting window, which stood out from the

293

building like a glass box held together by a massive frame of wood; and commanded by this projecting gable, and a few yards in retreat, but facing the road, was the inn door, over which hung a painted panel, representing a white horse, out of whose neck there sprouted a crimson cascade and underneath, in large letters, the traveller was informed that this was the genuine old Bleeding Horse. At the time, the proprietor was the middle-aged, corpulent, Tony Bligh, who was as pale as tallow and with a sly ugly squint.' The Bleeding Horse also appears in the Eumaeus episode in Joyce's *Ulysses*. Corley says, 'I saw him a few times in the Bleeding Horse in Camden Street, with Boylan, the billsticker.'

The Bailey, 2–3 Duke Street, which was an eighteenth-century tavern, has been a restaurant since 1837. Rebuilt in Georgian coffee house-style, it is one of Dublin's most historic taverns and one with a great literary tradition. Charles Stewart Parnell and members of the Irish Party frequented it. It has been rebuilt into the Marks & Spencer building.

The door of **7 Eccles Street**, the home of Leopold Bloom, the protagonist in Joyce's *Ulysses*, was preserved here. It was unveiled by the poet Patrick Kavanagh on 16 June 1967. Kavanagh drank here, as did James Stephens, Brendan Behan, Thomas Kettle, Padraic Colum, Liam O'Flaherty, Brian O'Nolan, Brinsley McNamara, Seumas O'Sullivan and Oliver St John Gogarty. Because it was frequented by so many writers and poets, the Bailey receives many references in their works; Gogarty remembered it as 'the place with the best whiskey and the best steak in Dublin' while James Stephens recounts his first visit there: 'Upon an evening I found myself sitting in the Bailey in front of a drink. I had my first adventure in that air, oxygen and gin, which we call wit, and which I watched as a cat watches a mouse, meaning to catch it, and, for the first time, I heard poetry spoken of with the assured carelessness with which a carpenter talks of his planks and of the chairs and the tables and oddments he will make with them.' The Bailey, though one of Joyce's favourite pubs, is not mentioned in *Ulysses*. (Door of **7 Eccles Street** is now at the James Joyce Cultural Centre.)

Across the street from the Bailey at **21 Duke Street** is **Davy Byrne's**, named after the Wicklowman who bought it in 1873 when he was in his mid twenties. It is known as 'Davy Byrne's moral pub', after the description in *Ulysses* which reads, 'He entered Davy Byrnes. Moral pub. He doesn't chat. Stands a drink now and then. But in leap year once in four. Cashed a cheque for me once.' Many famous people frequented the place, including politicians such as Michael Collins, known as 'the Big Fellow', and Arthur Griffith of Sinn Fein; poets, such as Padraic O'Conaire and F.R. Higgins, a founder member of the Abbey Theatre; the painter Sir William Orpen; and the playwright, Brendan Behan, whose father-in-law, Cecil Salkeld, a noted Irish artist, was responsible for a series of murals in the pub.

Davy Byrne's is the scene of Bloom's lunch during the Lestrygonians episode in *Ulysses*: 'Mr Bloom ate his strips of sandwich, fresh clean bread, with relish of disgust pungent mustard, the feety savour of green cheese. Sips of his wine soothed his palate. Not longwood that. Tastes fuller this weather with the chill off. Nice quiet bar. Nice piece of wood in that counter. Nicely planed. Like the way it curves there.'

Davy Byrne's is popular with business people and a haven for the literary tourist. Oysters and other seafood are offered all year round.

Close by at **9 Duke Street** is **The Duke**, which was a favourite with Brendan Behan and Patrick Kavanagh.

McDaid's at **3 Harry Street**, off Grafton Street, has an unusual history.

75. McDaid's pub in Harry Street, frequented by
Patrick Kavanagh, Brian O'Nolan and Brendan Behan.

It was originally the city morgue; it then became a church but lost its cloistered air when it became a pub. It was a popular watering-hole for Patrick Kavanagh, Brian O'Nolan and Brendan Behan. Gainor Christ, on whom the hero of J.P. Donleavy's *Ginger Man* is based, was a regular customer, as were most of the literati of the late forties and fifties.

Mulligan's of **Poolbeg Street** was founded in 1782. It is popular with journalists and retains much of its original character and decor. It is also another of the well-known pubs mentioned by Joyce; the parlour at the back was used as the venue for a scene in his *Dubliners* story, 'Counterparts', where Mr Farrington, the solicitor's clerk, used to drink. Mulligan's pub was frequented by Brendan Behan.

Larry O'Rourke's on the corner of **Eccles Street** and Dorset Street has been refurbished. Gone are the engraved glass door panes which once bore the interlocking initials, LOR. In the Calypso episode in *Ulysses*, Bloom passes it on his way from 7 Eccles Street to Dlugacz's, the pork butcher: 'He approached Larry O'Rourke's. From the cellar grating floated up the flabby gush of porter. Through the open doorway the bar squirted out whiffs of ginger, teadust, biscuitmush. Good house, however: just the end of the city traffic.' It is a good place to stop for a pint.

Grogan's (the Castle Lounge) at **15 South William Street** has remained relatively unchangedd since its foundation in 1899. When Paddy O'Brien, the famous barman, moved from McDaid's in Harry Street to Grogan's, many of the regulars moved with him. This pub was frequented by Brendan Behan.

Neary's, 1 Chatham Street, the back door of which is opposite the stage door of the Gaiety Theatre, is the haunt of actors, whether resting or working. It was a favourite drinking place of Brian O'Nolan. It is a good place for a pint of Guinness with smoked salmon and brown bread.

The **Horseshoe Bar** in the fashionable **Shelbourne Hotel** on **St Stephen's Green** has been the centre of Dublin life for over a century. The hotel has for a long time been frequented by successful writers such as Elizabeth Bowen, William Thackeray, Rudyard Kipling and George Moore, who set his novel *A Drama in Muslin* there.

The next three pubs are in close proximity.

O'Donoghue's, 15 Merrion Row, is a popular pub, well known for its frequent impromptu sessions of Irish traditional music and song. It is where the Dubliners group started their career.

Toner's, 139 Lower Baggot Street, was founded more than one hundred and seventy years ago. It retains its old-world atmosphere, together with the original pump beer handles and old storage drawers for groceries and tea. This, it is alleged, is the only Dublin pub in which W.B. Yeats ever had a drink, having been brought there by Oliver St John Gogarty. When Yeats had finished his sherry he rose to his feet and said, 'I have seen a pub now, will you kindly take me home?'

Doheny and Nesbitts, 5 Lower Baggot Street, contains its original Victorian fittings, including the snugs. It is popular with writers, broadcasters, raconteurs, artists and academics who, according to Brian O'Nolan, may be heard to speak of God as though he worked in the offices next to theirs. Doheny and Nesbitts features in David Hanly's novel *In Guilt and in Glory*: 'Haslam sat at one of the wall tables, black, cast-iron tripod and Kilkenny marble top, and ordered a pint . . . And he loved this pub.'

The **Palace Bar, 21 Fleet Street**, is much the same as it was during the 1930s, when it was a favourite meeting place for journalists, poets and writers. It was a convenient venue for Robert M. Smyllie, the legendary editor of the *Irish Times*, to meet F.R. Higgins, Brinsley MacNamara, Austin Clarke, Patrick Kavanagh, John Betjeman and others. Smyllie held court here from five o'clock each evening.

The **Norseman, 29 Essex Street East**, located on the corner with Eustace Street, is a small cosy little place in the heart of the lively Temple Bar or 'Left Bank' area of the city. It was formerly J.J. O'Neill's, Wine and Tea Merchant (Publican). It is mentioned in the Wandering Rocks episode in *Ulysses* when Lenehan and McCoy check the time at O'Neill's clock. In the *Dubliners* story 'Counterparts', Farrington leaves his firm of employment, Crosbie and Alleyne's, and goes for a drink 'in the dark snug of O'Neill's shop'. The snug no longer remains but the pub has changed little and still contains some of its original fittings.

The **Castle Inn, 5 Lord Edward Street** was built on the site of what was formerly 3 Fishamble Street, the birthplace of the poet James Clarence Mangan in 1803. This has been refurbished in medieval style with stonework, a wooden-beamed ceiling and memorabilia of the period such as an open cart, the sides of which serve as a place to put your drink! There are interesting photographs on the wall of the excavations of old Dublin which took place at nearby Wood Quay. It is spacious and has a welcoming open fire and is an ideal location in the heart of old Dublin to stop for lunch or just a drink.

The **Lord Edward, 23 Christchurch Place**, is situated in the heart of old Dublin, and is close to Dublin Castle, St Werburgh's Church and Christchurch Cathedral. Rebuilt in 1904, it was deemed one of the most modern pubs in the city at that time. Everything in it was Irish-made, including slates from a Wicklow quarry and granite from Newry. In the 1950s some alterations were carried out but the pub retains much of its original character and charm and is certainly worth a visit. The lounge, which is upstairs, contains memorabilia pertaining to Lord Edward Fitzgerald, the Irish patriot.

The Viceregal Cavalcade in the Wandering Rocks episode in *Ulysses* would have passed **Ryan's** of **28 Parkgate Street** en route to the Royal Dublin Society showground. Situated on the north side of the Liffey, between the Phoenix Park and the Croppies' Acre, Ryan's dates from 1896 and is really one of the finest Victorian pubs in the city. It still contains its original fittings which include two snugs, antique engraved mirrors, a central carved oak and mahogany bar, stained-glass windows and brass gas lamps. It serves traditional ploughman's and hot pub lunches. In an area associated with Rudyard Kipling's visit to Dublin, it is well worth a visit.

Kitty O'Shea's, 23–25 Upper Grand Canal Street, one of Dublin's most popular pubs, is named after Charles Stewart Parnell's beloved Katherine, whose divorce was responsible for ending Parnell's political career. It is a lively bustling place and excellent for lunch or Sunday brunch.

The Mullingar House Inn, at Chapelizod Bridge, **Chapelizod**, south of the Phoenix Park, was established in 1694. It was formerly an old coaching inn and the stage coaches from Mullingar used to stop here. Originally there were stables behind in which the horses were rested and rubbed down.

This pub has strong Joycean associations, figuring prominently in *Finnegans Wake*. Humphrey Chimpden Earwicker, the hero, lived with his family in Chapelizod, where he was the publican in the Mullingar House: '. . . owns the bulgiest bung-barrel that ever was tiptapped in the privace of the Mullingar Inn; was born with a nuasilver tongue in his mouth.' A plaque on the building commemorates the connection:

> Home of all
> Characters and elements
> In James Joyce's novel
> *Finnegans Wake.*

John Stanislaus Joyce, father of James Joyce, spent three or four years from 1877 working as secretary for the local Distillery Company. He took part in the local jollifications as he was a friend of the Broadbent family who owned the Mullingar Hotel.

The Oval Pub, 78 Middle Abbey Street, was situated near the offices of the *Freeman's Journal* and *National Press*. Ned Lambert and Mr Dedalus drink in the Oval Pub in the Wandering Rocks episode in *Ulysses*. The Oval also features in Beckett's novel *More Pricks than Kicks*.

There has been a pub on the site of the **Brian Boru–Hedigan's Pub, 1 Prospect Terrace, Prospect Road, Glasnevin**, for over two hundred years; the present building dates from the 1850s and the front façade is virtually unchanged. It has been in the same family since July 1904 when Patrick Hedigan, a native of Limerick, purchased it.

The pub always did a great trade from the funerals at Prospect Cemetery (now Glasnevin). In the Hades episode in *Ulysses*, the funeral cortege passes over Crossguns Bridge at the Royal Canal: 'They drove past Brian Boroimhe house', while Sean O'Casey in *Pictures in the Hallway* writes, 'The Brian Boru nicely stuck in the way to or from a burial in Glasnevin.' Paddy Hedigan was renowned for his special 'Power's White Label' whiskey which he bonded, blended to his own recipe and served straight from the wood.

The pub has a conservatory and beer garden, and a good menu.

Kennedy's, 31–32 Westland Row on the corner of Lincoln Place, was formerly Conway's which appears in the works of both Samuel Beckett and James Joyce.

The Horse and Tram, 3 Eden Quay, was formerly Mooney's and is referred to as 'Mooney's sur mer' in *Ulysses*. It was a stopping place for Stephen Dedalus on his way to the library. It is popular with journalists.

Kavanagh's Pub, Prospect Square, Glasnevin, has been in the same family for eight generations. During this time it has changed little, retaining its original stone floor and snug. Known as the Gravediggers' Pub, it is a real little gem and has been featured in various films. It is an ideal location for a pint either before or after a tour of Glasnevin Cemetery.

The Stag's Head, 1 Dame Court, has remained virtually unchanged since it opened in 1895. It has some fine carvings, stained glass and brass lamps.

The Long Hall, 51 South Great George's Street, so called on account of its shape, was built in the 1880s. It contains a collection of antiques ranging from a 250-year-old clock to a brass bed warmer. It has a fine Victorian bar and is worth a visit.

Joxer Daly's, 103 Upper Dorset Street, was founded around 1816. Joxer Daly appears as a character in Sean O'Casey's play *Juno and the Paycock*. This pub is an ideal place to stop for lunch or refreshments when walking Route 4.

The Guinness Hop Store in **Crane Street** off James's Street has a permanent exhibition which takes visitors through each stage of the brewing process.

'We have highest gratifications in announcing to pewtewr publikumst of pratician pratyusers, genghis is ghoon for you.'

and

'Ghinees hies good for you.' *Finnegans Wake*

The Irish Whiskey Corner at Bow Street Distillery, **Smithfield**, consists of a Museum and Heritage Centre concerning the history of distilling in Ireland. The tour, which usually takes an hour and fifteen minutes, comprises an audio-visual presentation, a visit to the Ball O'Malt Bar where there is an opportunity to taste various Irish whiskeys, and then a wander around the museum which contains artifacts associated with the whiskey industry in Ireland.

On the subject of Irish whiskey, Raphael Hollinshed the famous chronicler, wrote in 1577:

> It keepeth the reason from stifling,
> the stomach from wambling,
> the heart from swelling,
> the bellie from wirtching,
> the guts from numbling,
> the hands from shivering,
> the sinews from shrinking
> the veines from crumpling,
> the bones from aking,
> and the marrow from soaking.
> And trulie it is a sovereigne liquor
>   if it be orderlie taken.

Suggested Literary Routes

These tours are designed as walking tours and each includes just some of the places with literary associations in a particular area mentioned in the text. Sunday is the best day to take a walk, as there is an absence of traffic and the city is therefore seen to advantage.

Numbers in square brackets refer to locations on the maps.

1. G.B. Shaw House, 33 Synge Street/Shaw/Vandaleur Lee

2. 16 Harrington Street/Shaw/Vandaleur Lee

3. 11 Harrington Street/Shaw/Vandaleur Lee

4. 2 Portobello Place/Shaw/Vandaleur Lee

5. CBS, Synge Street/O'Nolan

6. 33 Emorville Avenue/Æ

7. 14 Portobello Road/Stephens

8. Portobello Nursing Home/John B. Yeats

9. 25 South Richmond Street/Katherine Tynan

10. 4 Harcourt Terrace/MacLiammóir/Edwards
    5 Harcourt Terrace/Æ's *Deirdre*

11. Harcourt Street Railway Station/Beckett

12. Site of the High School/W.B. Yeats

13. 1 Lower Hatch Street/Shaw

14. 60/61 Harcourt Street, Harcourt Hotel/Shaw

15. 17 Harcourt Street/Newman

16. 16 Harcourt Street/Newman/Stoker

17. 79/82 Harcourt Street/Site of the
    Standard Hotel/Lady Gregory

18. 14 Harcourt Street/Barrington

19. 6 Harcourt Street/Newman

20. Site of Wesleyan Connexional/Shaw

21. University Church/Newman

22. Newman House/Newman/Hopkins/Joyce/
    Colum/Pearse/Kettle

23. Joyce seat

24. Iveagh House/Mrs Delany

25. Earlsfort Terrace/University College/O'Nolan
    /MacDonagh

26. Site of Alexandra College/Ingram

27. 41 St Stephen's Green East/Irwin

28. 1 Ely Place/O. Wilde

29. 3 Upper Ely Place/Æ

30. 4 Upper Ely Place/G. Moore

31. Site of 15 Upper Ely Place/Gogarty

32. Ely House/Thornley Stoker

33. 32 St Stephen's Green/Gogarty

34. The Shelbourne Hotel/Thackeray/Bowen/Kipling

35. 30 Kildare Street/Stoker

36. National Library/Metropolitan School of Art

37. 39 Kildare Street/Lady Morgan

38. Kildare Street Club (formerly)/Edward Martyn

39. Nassau Street/Joyce/Smithson/Gregory

40. South Frederick Street/Barrington/W.B. Yeats

41. Site of Morrison's Hotel/Dickens/W.B. Yeats

42. 8 Dawson Street/Stephens

43. Molesworth Street/Shaw (number 15)

    (also Lever/Hyde/Bowen)

44. St Anne's Church/Hearn/Hemans

45. 21 Dawson Street/Hemans

46. 21 St Stephen's Green North
    (now Stephen Court)/Johnston

47. 9 St Stephen's Green North/Scott/Newman

48. 8 St Stephen's Green North/Standish O'Grady

49. 7 St Stephen's Green North/John B. Yeats

50. 79 Grafton Street (Bewley's)
    /Samuel Whyte's Academy/
    Brinsley Sheridan/T. Moore

51. MacDaid's, Harry Street

52. Duke Street/The Bailey and Davy Byrne's

53. College of Surgeons/ W. Wilde

54. York Street/Maturin/Mangan/Stephens
    /John B. Yeats/Smithson

55. Cuffe Street/Shelley

56. 12 Aungier Street/T. Moore

57. Site of St Peter's Church/Maturin

58. Camden Row Churchyard/T. Moore's parents

59. Meath Hospital/Mangan/Gogarty/Behan

60. The Bleeding Horse/Mangan

ROUTE 1

This route starts at the **Shaw House** and finishes at the **Bleeding Horse**, Upper Camden Street.

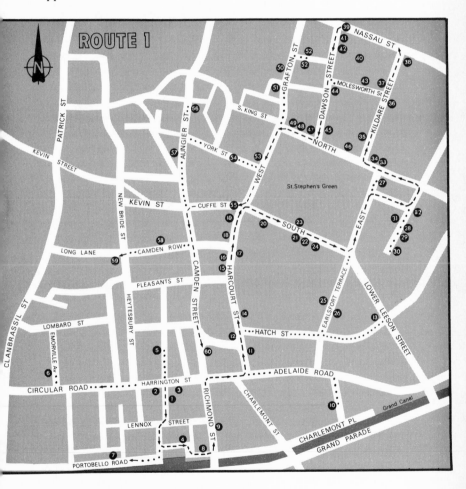

STARTING POINT: The **George Bernard Shaw House, 33 Synge Street** [1] (open to the public). A number of houses in this area have connections with Shaw and his mother's music teacher, Vandaleur Lee. From the Shaw House proceed north to **Harrington Street**. Vandaleur Lee lived at **16 Harrington Street** [2]. At the junction of Synge Street with Harrington Street turn left and it is three doors up on the left-hand side. He used number **11** which is situated close by in the same street for his professional Music Rooms [3]. He moved to Harrington Street from **2 Portobello Place** [4], which is off Portobello Harbour.

Diversions: The Christian Brothers School at numbers 12–16 Synge Street [5] was the first school which Brian O'Nolan attended.

*Æ's (George Russell's) first home in Dublin and where he lived for seven years until 1885, was nearby at 33 Emorville Avenue [6], off the South Circular Road, from where he attended Mr Power's School in **Harrington Street**.*

*James Stephens, the writer, had lodgings in 1901 at 14 Portobello Road [7], which runs alongside the Grand Canal. Jack B. Yeats died in 1957 in the **Portobello Nursing Home** [8], which overlooks the canal, and which features in Beckett's poem 'Enueg'. The house is now a business college.*

Katherine Tynan lived nearby at **25 South Richmond Street** [9] from 1861 to 1868.

Continue north-east to **Harcourt Street**.

Diversion: Micheál MacLiammóir shared a house with Hilton Edwards at 4 Harcourt Terrace [10] from 1944 to 1978. In the rear of the garden of number 5, the adjoining house, the world premier of Æ's (George Russell's) play Deirdre *was performed on 2 January 1901.*

Proceed down Harcourt Street passing the old **Harcourt Street Railway Station** [11] on the right-hand side. This was used by Samuel Beckett when he attended Earlsfort House School at 63 Adelaide Road. Beckett refers to the station in his play *That Time*.

Almost opposite the station was the **High School** [12] (now demolished and redeveloped) which W.B. Yeats entered in 1881.

Diversion: The Shaw family shared a house with Vandaleur Lee at 1 Lower Hatch Street [13], on the corner of Leeson Street. Augusta Persse (Lady Gregory) married Sir William Gregory in St Matthias's Church (now demolished) in Upper Hatch Street, on 4 March 1880.

Numbers **60–61 Harcourt Street** [14] comprise the building where G. B. Shaw and his father had lodgings from 1874 to 1876. Their stay here is commemorated with a plaque. It is now the Harcourt Hotel.

Cardinal Newman lived for a couple of years at numbers **16 and 17** [15, 16] where his friend, Dr James Quinn, ran a boarding school and where Newman rented a room. Two decades later, Bram Stoker had an apartment in number **16** when he moved from Kildare Street. Number **17**, known as Clonmel House, was the home of the Municipal Gallery of Modern Art from 1908 to 1932. Cardinal Newman, after a couple of months at Dun Laoghaire, moved into number **6** [19].

Lady Gregory stayed at the Standard Hotel, **79–82 Harcourt Street** [17]. Now demolished, it has been replaced by offices. It was situated on the right-hand side at the intersection of **Clonmel Street**. Here she gave her famous tea parties for Yeats and his contemporaries.

Jonah Barrington, the diarist, lived almost opposite at **14 Harcourt Street** [18], the house with the first-floor bow window. His *Personal Sketches and Recollections* are the standard and very racy account of high life in late eighteenth-century Ireland.

Turn right into **St Stephen's Green South**. Numbers **101–104** now comprise Russell Court which is a new development. Former houses which stood here were number 102, the Russell Hotel, which Lady Gregory used as her Dublin headquarters, and number 101, St Patrick's Nursing Home, where Annie M.P. Smithson trained in 1900–1. Number **94**, now replaced by offices, was the Wesleyan Connexional [20], Shaw's first school, which he attended briefly and loathed. Continue to the **University Church** of SS Peter and Paul [21] founded by Cardinal Newman and opened in 1856. Adjoining are numbers **85–86** which comprise **Newman House** [22], the old Catholic University where John Henry Newman was rector from 1854 to 1858; where Gerard Manley Hopkins was Professor of Greek and Latin from 1884 to 1889; and where James Joyce was a student from 1898 to 1902. Many other writers, such as Denis Florence MacCarthy, Thomas Kettle, Austin Clarke, Patrick Colum, Thomas MacDonagh and Patrick Pearse had connections here. Newman House is open to the public.

Opposite Newman House is a seat [23] commemorating 'John Stanislaus Joyce, Corkman' and his son 'James Joyce, Dubliner'.

The statuary in the park of **St Stephen's Green** records some of Ireland's history and poetry. There are many memorials to writers, including one to James Joyce which faces Newman House and others to James Clarence Mangan, Thomas Kettle and a bronze tribute to W.B. Yeats by Henry Moore.

On the same side of St Stephen's Green South as Newman House are numbers **80–81** which comprise **Iveagh House** [24], now the Department of Foreign Affairs. Mrs Delany, then Mary Pendarves, stayed at number **80** in 1731–3, when it was the town house of Robert Clayton, Bishop of Killala.

*Diversion: To the right is **Earlsfort Terrace**. Most of the faculties of University College Dublin [25] were situated here from 1914 (when they were moved from St Stephen's Green) until they were transferred to Belfield Campus, Stillorgan, in the 1960s. Writers who studied here included Brian O'Nolan and Donagh MacDonagh. Opposite is the original site of Alexandra College [26] (now demolished) which John Kells Ingram helped to found.*

Turn left and continue along **St Stephen's Green East**.

Diversion: Thomas Caulfield Irwin lived in number 41 [27], the house next to the Bank of Ireland. It is situated in the stretch beyond the intersection of Hume Street.

Turn into **Hume Street** and turn right into **Upper Ely Place**, to what was formerly known as Smith's Buildings (1829), comprising numbers 1–5. These are fine houses, each with four storeys over a basement. Æ (George Russell) lived in number 3 [29] when it was the headquarters of the Dublin Theosophical Society and found number 4 [30] for his friend George Moore. Opposite is the Royal Hibernian Academy Art Gallery at number 15 [31], on the site of a Queen-Anne style house, now demolished, where Oliver St John Gogarty lived. Continue down to **Ely Place,** to number 8, Ely House [32], now the offices of the Knights of St Columbanus and formerly the home of Sir Thornley Stoker, a leading surgeon and brother of Bram Stoker. Oscar Wilde proposed marriage to Constance Lloyd who would become his wife in number 1 [28] which is the last house on the right-hand side. The entrance to number 1 has been relocated to around the corner, and the house has therefore been renumbered to 149 Lower Baggot Street.

Turn left from Ely Place into **Merrion Row** and **St Stephen's Green North**. In number 32 [33], now owned by the Shelbourne Hotel, Gogarty rented consulting rooms between 1915 and 1917. The house is marked with a plaque. Adjoining is the **Shelbourne Hotel** [34] where George Moore spent the winter of 1883–4 and wrote most of *A Drama in Muslin*. Elizabeth Bowen, Rudyard Kipling and William Makepeace Thackeray stayed there and Thackeray described it in his *Irish Sketchbook* as a 'respectable edifice' while Bowen described it as 'an architectural cuckoo'.

Turn right down **Kildare Street**, the street where Padraic Colum had his first job in an office and where Bram Stoker had a top-floor apartment in number 30 [35] on the left-hand side. Further up on the opposite side is the **National Library** [36] which Lady Gregory used when working on her translations. This is where James Joyce studied and where he met Gogarty in 1902, and the discussion on *Hamlet* in *Ulysses* is set here. Behind this was the Metropolitan School of Art, where W.B. Yeats studied painting and where he probably first met Æ (George Russell).

Lady Morgan lived for eighteen years in number 35 (now **39**), the site of Setanta House [37]. It is marked with a plaque.

On the right-hand side at the junction with **Leinster Street** [38] is the building where the Kildare Street Club, which Edward Martyn frequented, and of which John Betjeman was elected as an overseas member, was formerly sited. Notice the carved animals around the window ledges, by Charles Harrison. (The Club has amalgamated with the University Club and is now housed at 17 St Stephen's Green.)

Continue along **Nassau Street** [39], the street where Annie M.P. Smithson lived and where James Joyce and Nora Barnacle first met, in 1904. Pass the end of **South Frederick Street** [40] where numbers **16** to **20** comprised the **Nassau Hotel** (now demolished). Lady Gregory rented rooms here when she first came to Dublin in connection with the Abbey Theatre and W.B. Yeats stayed here occasionally. Jonah Barrington lodged at a boarding house in this street also. Turn left into **Dawson Street**. Morrison's Hotel, where Charles Dickens, Charles Stewart Parnell and W.B. Yeats stayed, was sited on the corner where the Lombard and Ulster Bank now stands [41]. Number **8** [42] was formerly the Engineer's Hall where the Dawson Street Gymnastic Club, which James Stephens attended, held its meetings.

*Diversion: Linking **Dawson Street** to **Kildare Street** is **Molesworth Street** [43] where, as a child, Elizabeth Bowen attended dancing classes at Molesworth Hall, 39–40 Molesworth Street (now demolished) and where George Bernard Shaw held a job as cashier in number 15, in the offices of Messrs Uniacke and Courtney. The building dates from 1755. In the early 1820s, Charles Lever stayed in a boarding house at number 33 and in 1892 Douglas Hyde gave his lecture at the Leinster Hall 'On the necessity for de-Anglicising the Irish people'.*

Continue up **Dawson Street** to St Ann's Church [44] where Lafcadio Hearn's great-great-grandfather, Daniel Hearn, was rector. Bram Stoker, author of *Dracula*, married Florence Balcombe here on 4 December 1878. There is a memorial here to the poet Felicia Hemans who is buried in one of the vaults. She died in 1835 in her home at **21 Dawson Street** [45], on the top left-hand side. In 1894, Percy French lived in a studio on this street.

On reaching **St Stephen's Green North** turn left for number **21** (now redeveloped as Stephen Court), the site of St Andrew's School [46] where Denis Johnston went to school. In 1833 Felicia Hemans lived in number **36** (now demolished) before she moved to 21 Dawson Street. Retrace your steps and cross the top of Dawson Street to **9 St Stephen's Green North** (now the Stephen's Green Club) [47] where Sir Walter Scott was entertained by his son, Captain Scott in 1825. Newman had considered joining the Stephen's Green Club in order to use it for dining purposes. Standish O'Grady lived in number **8** [48] and John

B. Yeats, artist and father of W.B. Yeats, had his studio in number **7** [49], almost opposite the Fusiliers' Arch.

Diversion: **Grafton Street** *was the birthplace of Samuel Lover in 1797. Number 79, where Bewley's Café now stands [50], was* **Samuel Whyte's Academy** *where Richard Brinsley Sheridan, Thomas Moore and Robert Emmet were among the notable pupils. In 1812, Percy Bysshe Shelley and his wife lived at number 17 and pamphleteered in the area. Walter Scott bought books in Mr Milliken's in Grafton Street and Rudyard Kipling and his wife shopped there. There are three literary pubs in the vicinity: McDaid's in* **Harry Street** *[51] and Davy Byrne's and The Bailey in* **Duke Street** *[52].*

Continue to **St Stephen's Green West**, past the **Royal College of Surgeons** [53] where Sir William Wilde took his licentiate in 1837.

Diversion: Look up **York Street** *[54]. All the original houses have been demolished. The street contour is still the same as when Mangan lived in number 6 in 1822; James Stephens had lodgings in number 30 around 1896; Charles Maturin died in number 37 in 1824; and John Butler Yeats rented a studio at number 44 in the early 1880s. Annie M.P. Smithson covered this area as a district nurse.*

Continue along St Stephen's Green West and turn right down **Cuffe Street** [55]. As in York Street, all the houses have been demolished. Shelley stayed at number **35** with Mr John Lawless on his second visit to Dublin in 1813.

Diversion: Turn right for **12 Aungier Street** *[56], the birthplace of Thomas Moore, which is situated at the corner of* **Little Longford Street.** *Also in Aungier Street is the site of the former* **St Peter's Church** *[57] where Maturin was curate and where he was later buried.*

Turn left off Cuffe Street up **Wexford Street**.

Diversion: In St Kevin's Churchyard in **Camden Row** *[58] is the grave of John Moore and Anastasia Codd, Thomas Moore's parents. Before returning back up Camden Row, see the* **Meath Hospital in Heytesbury Street** *[59] where, in 1911, Oliver St John Gogarty was appointed as ear, nose and throat surgeon. James Clarence Mangan died here in 1849 and Brendan Behan in 1964.*

Continue up **Camden Street** and finish at the end of the street in the **Bleeding Horse** [60], a pub founded in 1649. This was frequented by Mangan, and features in Le Fanu's *The Cock and the Anchor*, O'Casey's *Pictures in the Hallway* and Joyce's *Ulysses*. (See Literary Pubs section.)

Route 1 takes approximately 2 hours (main route only).

ROUTE 2

This route starts at the **National Gallery** and finishes at **Toner's** pub, 139 Lower Baggot Street.

STARTING POINT: The **National Gallery of Ireland, Merrion Square West** [1]. In the Gallery, there is a room dedicated to George Bernard Shaw who bequeathed one third of the royalties from his published works to it. The statue of Shaw by sculptor Paul Trubetzkoy (1866–1938) that once stood outside the main entrance is now in the Shaw Room.

Proceed down Merrion Square West and turn left into **Clare Street** where Jonah Barrington had one of his first Dublin addresses. **Greene's bookshop** [2], which features in Beckett's *Dream of Fair to Middling Women*, is on the left-hand side, while across the street is number 6 which was the office of Beckett and Medcalf [3]. Beckett lived for a time in the garret.

Before turning into Lincoln Place see **1–2 Leinster Street** [4] on the corner, formerly the site of Finn's Hotel where Joyce's Nora Barnacle worked as a chambermaid in 1904. It is a four-storey, red-bricked building overlooking College Park where, now as then, the quarter-mile flat handicappers start in pursuit around the track.

Continue into **Lincoln Place** where Edward Martyn had rooms. Adjoining the back entrance to Trinity College is number **32**, formerly St Mark's Ophthalmic and Aural Hospital [5] founded by Sir William Wilde. This building has been demolished and the area has been redeveloped. It was at St Mark's that the young Sean O'Casey had his eyes treated. A few paces further on is **Kennedy's** pub, which is mentioned in Beckett's works. Opposite is **Sweny's** chemist shop. Joyce's character Leopold Bloom was right in his thoughts that 'chemists rarely move', since it was here that he bought his cake of 'sweet lemony soap' for 4d in 1904.

Diversion: 21 Westland Row [6] was the birthplace of Oscar Wilde. Opposite this house is St Andrew's Church [7] where Brendan Behan married Beatrice Salkeld in 1955 and where Bloom, in the 'Lotus Eaters' episode in Ulysses, watched the priest celebrate Mass. Behind the Church in Cumberland Street South [8] is the Christian Brothers School (known as the CBS in Westland Row, just to confuse matters) which Patrick and Willie Pearse attended.

Return southward to **1 Merrion Square** [9], home of the Wilde family and where Oscar spent his youth. It was outside this house that James

309

1. National Gallery/Shaw
2. Greene's Bookshop/Beckett
3. 6 Clare Street/Beckett
4. 1/2 Leinster Street/Joyce
5. St Mark's Hospital/W. Wilde/O'Casey
6. 21 Westland Row/O. Wilde
7. St. Andrew's Church/Behan
8. CBS South Cumberland Street/Pearse
9. 1 Merrion Square North/Wilde family
10. 84 Merrion Square South/Æ
11. 82 Merrion Square South/W.B. Yeats
12. 70 Merrion Square South/Le Fanu
13. 42 Merrion Square East/Barrington
14. National Maternity Hospital/Behan/Joyce
15. 19 Lower Mount Street/Synge
16. Lower Grand Canal Street/Sir Patrick Dun's Hospital/Lever
17. 11 Warrington Place/O'Leary
18. 15 Warrington Place/Le Fanu
19. 25 Herbert Place/O'Nolan
20. 12 Herbert Place/Bowen
21. Parson's Bookshop/Kavanagh
22. 35 Haddington Road/Kavanagh
23. The Waterloo/Kavanagh
24. Searson's/Kavanagh
25. 38 Upper Baggot Street/MacCarthy
26. 110 Baggot Lane/Kavanagh
27. 62 Pembroke Road/Kavanagh
28. 19 Raglan Road/Kavanagh
29. St Bartholomew's Church/Bowen

30. 54 Wellington Road/Johnston
31. 18 Waterloo Road/Behan
32. 119 Upper Leeson Street/Kettle
33. 35 Upper Leeson Street/Kavanagh
34. Christ Church (Methodist)/Shaw
35. 4 Upper Leeson Street/Synge
36. Mespil Flats/O'Connor
37. 35 Mespil Road/French
38. Patrick Kavanagh seat
39. Percy French seat
40. Kavanagh bronze
41. 1 Wilton Place/Kavanagh
42. Court Flats/O'Flaherty/O'Connor
43. 67 Lower Baggot Street/Davis
44. 15 Herbert Street/Behan
45. St Stephen's Church/Bowen/French/Jack Yeats
46. Pike Theatre/Behan/Beckett
47. 37 Upper Mount Street/Kavanagh
48. 38 Upper Mount Street/Ingram
49. 50 Upper Mount Street/Betjeman
50. United Arts Club, 3 Upper Fitzwilliam Street
51. 18 Fitzwilliam Square South/Jack Yeats
52. 60 Fitzwilliam Square North/Johnston
53. 42 Fitzwilliam Square West/W.B. Yeats
54. 13 Fitzwilliam Place/the Catacombs
55. 42 Fitzwilliam Place/Stephens
56. 133 Lower Baggot Street/the Misses Yeats
57. 139 Lower Baggot Street/W.B. Yeats/Gogarty

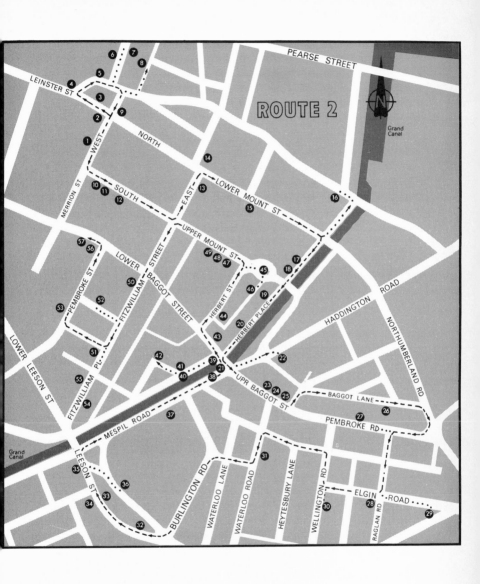

ROUTE 2

Joyce arranged his first assignation with Nora Barnacle. She didn't keep the appointment.

Proceed up **Merrion Square West** turning left into **Merrion Square South**. Æ (George Russell) lived in number **84** [10], W.B. Yeats in number **82** [11] from 1922 to 1928, and Joseph Sheridan Le Fanu in number **70** [12]. All are marked with plaques.

Proceed down **Merrion Square East**. Jonah Barrington lived in number **42** [13] which he purchased in 1793.

The **National Maternity Hospital** on **Holles Street** [14], birthplace of Brendan Behan, is facing you. Most of the 'Oxen in the Sun' chapter of *Ulysses* takes place here.

Turn right into **Lower Mount Street**. It was in Mr Mangan's school on this street that Thomas Davis had his early education. J.M. Synge died in number **19**, then the Elphis Nursing Home and now the students' residence of the American College in Dublin [15]. One of Synge's last requests was to be lifted to the window so that he could see once more his beloved mountains. The Elphis Nursing Home also features in Beckett's work *More Pricks than Kicks*. It is on the right-hand side of the street and is easily discernible as there is an American flag flying over the portico.

Continue down Lower Mount Street to the Grand Canal.

*Diversion: Charles Lever studied medicine nearby at Sir Patrick Dun's Hospital in **Lower Grand Canal Street** [16] (no longer used as a hospital).*

On reaching the canal, turn right into **Warrington Place** where Thomas Davis lived when his family moved from Cork in 1818. John O'Leary's last address was number **11**, now John O'Leary House [17]. In 1845 Le Fanu moved to number **1** and a year later to number **15** [18].

Continue alongside the canal to **25 Herbert Place** [19] where Brian O'Nolan lived when the family moved in from Inchicore. Number **12** was Elizabeth Bowen's birthplace [20] and where she spent her first seven winters. On the opposite side of the canal is Percy Place, where Patrick Kavanagh shared a flat with his brother in the early 1940s.

On reaching the junction with Baggot Street, turn left over Baggot Street Bridge. The red-bricked building on the right-hand side [21] is Bridge House, the former home of **Parsons Bookshop** which was frequented by Patrick Kavanagh. Upper Baggot Street and the Pembroke township make an area primarily associated with Patrick Kavanagh and Elizabeth Bowen.

*Diversion: Turn left to **35 Haddington Road** [22] where Kavanagh had a flat. It is the seventh house in the terrace of houses on the right-hand side. Its door knocker is the head of a fox.*

Continue along to **Upper Baggot Street**, where Elizabeth Bowen went shopping with her governess. Pass the **Waterloo** [23] and

Searson's [24], pubs frequented by Kavanagh. Next door to the Waterloo is number **38** [25], where Denis Florence MacCarthy lived. Turn left into **Eastmoreland Place** and right into **Baggot Lane** where Patrick Kavanagh lived at number **110** [26] in 1959–60. Turn right and right again, to the junction of Pembroke and Raglan Roads.

Diversion: Kavanagh lived in 62 Pembroke Road [27] from 1946 to 1958.

Turn left up **Raglan Road**. Situated at the right-hand corner on the junction with Elgin Road is **19 Raglan Road** [28] where Kavanagh lived when he moved from Pembroke Road. The house is marked with a plaque. Frank O'Connor lived in a basement flat on this road in 1933.

Diversion: St Bartholomew's Church [29] in Clyde Road was used as a place of worship by the Bowen family. The wide tree-lined roads concentrated in this area are what Bowen termed as the 'Red Roads'. These include Raglan, Clyde, Elgin, Wellington and Waterloo Roads.

Proceed up **Elgin Road** towards Wellington Road.

Diversion: Turn left in Wellington Road to see the house where Denis Johnston lived at number 54 [30], which is on the left-hand side.

From **Elgin Road** turn right into Wellington Road, left into Pembroke Lane, then turn left into **Waterloo Road**, where the garden flat of number **18** [31] was Brendan Behan's first home after his marriage. Cross to **Burlington Road** which is directly opposite number 18. Traverse **Waterloo Lane**, bearing left along Burlington Road.

Diversion: Turn left into Upper Leeson Street and cross the street to see where Lafcadio Hearn lived as a child in number 73, the third house down on the left-hand side of this fine terrace. The house is marked with a plaque and there is a pillar-box outside the entrance.

Turn right and proceed into **Upper Leeson Street**. Continue along to number **119** [32], the address to which Thomas Kettle wrote home from the battle front. Down a few paces on the same side is number **136** [33] where Patrick Kavanagh lived in 1965. This is on the right-hand side past a cluster of shops and almost opposite **Christchurch Methodist Church** [34] (formerly known as **Molyneux Church**) where Mr Shaw brought his children to Sunday school. Number **4** on the left-hand side [35] near Leeson Street Bridge was **Mr Harrick's Classical and English School** which J.M. Synge attended.

Diversion: On the right-hand side up Sussex Road is the entrance to Mespil Flats [36] where Frank O'Connor lived in the winter of 1958–9.

On reaching the canal, don't cross the bridge, but turn right down **Sussex Terrace** straight into **Mespil Road**. Continue to number **35**, one-time home of Percy French [37]. This stretch of the canal between

313

Leeson Street and Baggot Street bridges was a favourite with Kavanagh who is commemorated by a seat [38] on the Mespil Road side of the canal beside the lock by **Baggot Street Bridge**. His poem 'Lines Written on a seat on the Grand Canal' is engraved on it.

Cross the little footbridge over the lock which leads to the seat commemorating Percy French [39]. Just to confuse matters, the Percy French seat is on the site where Kavanagh wrote the poem 'Lines Written on a seat on the Grand Canal'!

Diversion: On the same side, a few metres further up on the canal bank, tarry awhile at the life-size seated bronze statue of Kavanagh by sculptor John Coll [40]. This is on the spot claimed by Kavanagh as the site of his rebirth as a poet. Engraved on it are some lines from his poem 'Canal Bank Walk'. After living for a short time in 110 Baggot Lane, Kavanagh moved to 1 Wilton Place [41] in 1960. Nearby in Court Flats, Wilton Place [42], Liam O'Flaherty and Frank O'Connor spent their latter years.

Turn left over Baggot Street Bridge and proceed along **Lower Baggot Street**. Cross the street to number **67** [43], the house where Thomas Davis died in 1845. A stone profile of him marks the house.

Turn right into **Herbert Street** where Samuel Beckett's mother died in the Merrion Nursing Home at number **21** in August 1950. Brendan Behan lived in number **15** [44]. Continue up to the junction with **Upper Mount Street**.

Diversion: Turn right into Mount Street Crescent for St Stephen's Church [45] with its fine neo-Grecian façade. It is known as the Peppercannister. Elizabeth Bowen attended service here with her parents. It is also where Percy French and Ettie Armitage Moore were married in 1890 and where Jack B. Yeats' funeral service was held in March 1957. Turn right into Herbert Lane, a narrow lane running behind the houses in Herbert Street, accessible from both Mount Street Crescent and Herbert Street. It was in this lane that the tiny Pike Theatre [46] was located, where the first production of Behan's The Quare Fellow was staged in 1954 and Beckett's Waiting for Godot was produced in 1955.

Proceed along **Upper Mount Street**. Patrick Kavanagh lived in number **37** [47] for a short time and John Kells Ingram lived in number **38** [48] when the street was in its heyday. Number **50** [49] was where John Betjeman had his office when he was posted in Dublin as Press Attaché from 1941 to 1943.

Turn left and proceed along **Upper Fitzwilliam Street** where number **3** is the United Arts Club [50], gathering place of writers, musicians and painters through the years. Among its members were W.B. Yeats, Lennox Robinson and Percy French. Continue to **18 Fitzwilliam Square South** [51] where Jack B. Yeats lived and worked.

Diversion: Denis Johnston lived in 60 Fitzwilliam Square North [52].

W.B. Yeats had an apartment at **42 Fitzwilliam Square West** [53] before he moved to Riversdale in Rathfarnham.

*Diversion: The **Catacombs** was in the basement of **13 Fitzwilliam Place** [54] and this was where the Bohemian set met in the 1950s after the pubs closed.* It features in Anthony Cronin's novels The Life of Riley *and* Dead as Doornails, *and also in J.P. Donleavy's* The Gingerman. *James Stephens had a top-floor apartment in **42 Fitzwilliam Place** [55].*

Continue down **Pembroke Street** and turn left into **Lower Baggot Street**. Just at the corner is number **133** where the Misses Yeats had the Cuala Press [56].

Just along the street, finish at **Toner's** at number **139** [57], where Oliver St John Gogarty bought W.B. Yeats his one and only drink in a pub!

Route 2 takes approximately 2–2½ hours (main route only).

1. St Patrick's Cathedral/Swift/Lover/Ferguson/Hyde/
Robinson/Scott/Johnston

2. Marsh's Library/Swift/Maturin/Joyce/Scott

3. St Patrick's Park/Literary Parade

4. Bull Alley/Steele/Brown

5. Chancery Lane/Mangan

6. Little Ship Street/Stanyhurst Tower

7. Hoey's Court/Swift

8. St Werburgh's Church/Dr Delany

9. Dublin Castle/Addison/Tickell/Stoker/Poetry Ireland
/Austin Clarke

10. 5 Lord Edward Street/Mangan

11. Fishamble Street/Handel/Swift/Delany/Owenson

12. West Essex Street/Smock Alley Theatre/Sheridan/
Farquhar/Church of St Michael and St John

13. Parliament Street/Kickham/O'Leary

14. Cecilia Street/Joyce/Gogarty
Crow Street/Carleton/Owenson

15. St Andrew's Church/Swift/Esther Van Homrigh

16. Foster Place/Swift/Vanessa

17. Bank of Ireland/De Quincey

18. 21 Fleet Street, the Palace Bar

19. Site of the Pearl Bar, Fleet Street

20. 9 D'Olier Street/Lover

21. Hawkins Street/Theatre Royal/Boucicault/Lover

22. Poolbeg Street/Mulligan's/Joyce

23. Trinity College

24. 27 Pearse Street/Pearse's birthplace

25. St Mark's Church/O. Wilde

26. Site of the Antient Concert Rooms/Synge/Joyce

ROUTE 3

This route starts at **St Patrick's Cathedral** and ends beyond **Trinity College** at Pearse Street. Encompassing some older parts of the city, it includes places associated with many of the earlier writers such as Stanyhurst, Swift, Addison, Tickell, Mangan and Carleton.

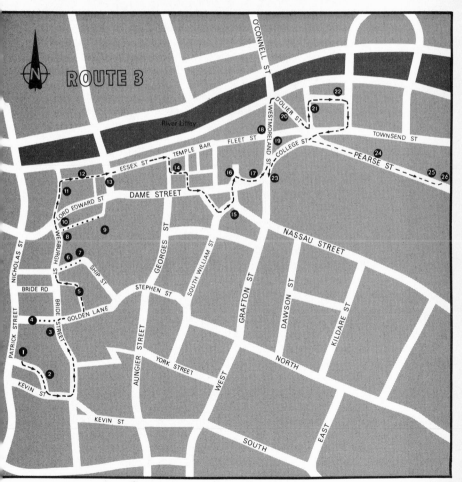

STARTING POINT: **St Patrick's Cathedral, Patrick Street** [1]. St Patrick's Cathedral is the focal point of interest in Dean Swift's Dublin. In the **west end of the nave** are the graves of Swift and Stella, Swift's bust and epitaph and the memorial to Stella. (Sir Walter Scott visited the Cathedral in 1825 to see Swift's tomb.) In the **north aisle** is the marble memorial to Samuel Lover. The **north transept** has Swift's Corner containing his pulpit, table and chair, a collection of his works and a scroll which he received as Freeman of the City of Dublin. The **north choir aisle** contains the grave of the Duke of Schomberg, slain in 1690 at the Battle of the Boyne. It has an inscription written by Swift.

In the **south transept** is Swift's memorial to his faithful servant, Alexander McGee. Also of interest in the same area is a memorial to the Revd Charles Wolfe, author of *The Burial of Sir John Moore*. In the **south aisle** a memorial to Douglas Hyde, the first President of Ireland, can be seen. His inauguration as President was held in the Cathedral in 1938, and his funeral service was held here in 1949. Beside this is a memorial to Sir Samuel Ferguson, poet and antiquarian, who was President of the Royal Irish Academy and Deputy Keeper of the Public Records in Ireland.

Outside the Cathedral, in the **Close**, Lennox Robinson and Denis Johnston are buried in adjoining plots. Johnston's grave is easy to find as a little unicorn marks the back of his gravestone, in recognition of his play *A Bride for the Unicorn*, staged in the Gate in 1933.

Proceed to **Marsh's Library** [2], in **St Patrick's Close**. Built in 1705 to house the library of Archbishop Narcissus Marsh, its interior is still the same as when William Carleton, Charles Maturin, James Joyce and others both read and wrote here. Among the library's collection is a folio edition of Clarendon's *History of the Great Rebellion*, containing Swift's comments in the margins. Sir Walter Scott visited the library and saw the desk where Maturin wrote several of his novels, and William Maturin, son of the writer, was librarian here around 1860.

*Diversion: Carleton lived in nearby **Francis Street**, west of Patrick Street, and in the early years of his marriage he lived in **The Coombe**.*

Continue from Marsh's Library to **Kevin Street Upper** and turn left into **Bride Street**. This has been redeveloped since James Clarence Mangan had his last dismal lodgings here. In **St Patrick's Park** [3], inside the boundary adjoining Bride Street, is a **Literary Parade**, which

318

consists of a memorial to honour ten distinguished Irish writers: Swift, Mangan, Wilde, Shaw, Yeats, Synge, O'Casey, Joyce, Behan and Beckett. It was erected by Dublin Corporation for the Dublin Millennium in 1988.
Continue along Bride Street to the junction with **Golden Lane**.

*Diversion: On the left is **Bull Alley Street** [4]. It was in this area that Richard Steele was born in 1672. Christy Brown attended the Cerebral Palsy Clinic here.*

Turn right into **Golden Lane** and left off this into **Chancery Lane** [5] where Mangan's family had accommodation consisting of two wretched rooms at the back of an old house. All the houses in this street have been demolished.

*Diversion: The remains of the **Stanyhurst Tower** [6], shown only by a slight protrusion in the wall, may be seen in **Little Ship Street**. Further down Little Ship Street, at the junction with **Great Ship Street**, a plaque marks **Hoey's Court** [7]. Number 7, Swift's birthplace (now demolished), was about a hundred feet north-west of this spot.*

Continue up **Werburgh Street**, where Mangan attended school at Mr Courtney's Academy in Darby Square (now demolished), which was on the left-hand side. Pass by **St Werburgh's Church** [8] where Dr Patrick Delany, the husband of Mary Delany, and confidant of Swift, preached.

*Diversion: To the right, up **Castle Street**, is **Dublin Castle** [9] where Joseph Addison lived during his time in Dublin. Thomas Tickell had an apartment in the Castle and Bram Stoker worked here as a civil servant. **Poetry Ireland**, which houses the Austin Clarke Library, is situated in the **Bermingham Tower** in **Upper Castle Yard**.*

The site of Mangan's birthplace is nearby. Demolished in 1944, it is where the Castle Inn now stands at **5 Lord Edward Street** [10], which in Mangan's time was in Fishamble Street.
Cross Christchurch Place and proceed down **Fishamble Street** [11], where the site of the old Musick Hall, designed by the Huguenot architect, Cassels, is still to be seen. It was here that the choir of St Patrick's Cathedral took part in the first performance of Handel's *Messiah* on Tuesday, 13 April 1742. A plaque is on the house which adjoins the site of the Musick Hall. At a later date, Mr Owenson, the Irish actor and father of Sydney Owenson (later Lady Morgan) lived in the Musick Hall with his family so as to be close to Crow Street Theatre.
Continue almost to the end of **Fishamble Street** and turn right up **West Essex Street** [12]. Formerly named Smock Alley, it was where the famous **Smock Alley Theatre** was situated, for which Thomas Brinsley Sheridan, father of Richard, was an actor and manager. Here too, George Farquhar performed in *Othello*. The theatre pit was said to be

on the site of the burial vaults of the Church of St Michael and St John.

Diversion: On the right is **Parliament Street** *[13]. The* Irish people *newspaper, with which Charles Kickham, John O'Leary and Thomas Caulfield Irwin were connected, had its offices at number* **12**.

Continue into **Essex Street East**, passing the **Norseman** pub which appears as O'Neill's shop in Joyce's story 'Counterparts' in *Dubliners*, and turn right into **Temple Lane**, then left to **Cecilia Street** [14]. The large square building here, Cecilia House, was once the Medical School of the Catholic University which James Joyce and Oliver St John Gogarty attended for a time. Adjoining Cecilia Street is **Crow Street**. The **Crow Street Theatre and Music Hall** (sited where the Medical School was later built) was opened by Spranger Barry in opposition to the nearby **Smock Alley Theatre**. Carleton was a frequent visitor here, often spending his last shilling on the upper gallery. Robert Owenson, Lady Morgan's father, acted here.

Continue to **Dame Street**. Cross this, continue up **Trinity Street** and turn left into **St Andrew's Street** to **St Andrew's Church** [15] where Swift's Vanessa (Esther Van Homrigh) is buried near her father and sister.

Continue down **Church Lane** to **College Green** and cross to **Foster Place** [16] where Vanessa stayed in the Van Homrigh's house. Foster Place was then called Turnstile Alley.

Continue past the old Parliament House (now the **Bank of Ireland**) on the left where, in 1800, Thomas De Quincey attended the last sitting of the House of Lords [17].

Continue down **Westmoreland Street**, passing on the left-hand side the **Palace Bar** [18] near the corner of Fleet Street. The **Pearl Bar** [19], now closed, may be seen in Fleet Street on the right-hand side of Westmoreland Street. R.M. Smyllie, Brinsley McNamara, F.R. Higgins, Brian O'Nolan and others of the literati met in both these pubs (joined by John Betjeman during his time in Dublin).

Continue round to **9 D'Olier Street** [20], the home of Samuel Lover in the early 1830s. This is situated near the *Irish Times* clock.

Turn left into **Hawkins Street** [21], where once the **Theatre Royal**, which staged Boucicault's *Arrah-n-Pogue* in 1864, and the Royal Dublin Society House, where Samuel Lover exhibited his paintings, were situated. Turn right into **Poolbeg Street** [22] for **Mulligan's** pub.

Turn right again, cross to **College Street** and follow the wall of **Trinity College** [23] on your left to the Front Gate. Statues of Goldsmith and Burke flank the entrance. Trinity College has associations with most of the writers in this book. The Book of Kells may be seen in the **Long Room** of the **Old Library**.

Retrace your steps back via **College Street** and proceed down **Pearse Street** (formerly Brunswick Street) where Patrick Pearse was born in number **27**. A stone memorial with the profiles of Patrick and Willie

Pearse is on the front of the house [24] placed between the windows on the first floor. James Stephens also lived in this street.

Further up on the same side is **St Mark's Church** [25] where Oscar Wilde was christened in 1855. Close by, near the junction with **Westland Row** and **Lombard Street**, is the building of the former **Antient Concert Rooms** [26], where the Irish Literary Theatre staged its first productions. James Joyce once shared a platform here with the singer John McCormack and J.M. Synge played in a concert. Shaw's mother, who had a fine mezzo-soprano voice, sang here under the stage name Hilda.

Route 3 takes approximately 1½–2 hours (main route only).

1. 18/19 Parnell Square North/Dublin Writers' Museum

2. 5 Parnell Square East/Gogarty

3. Gate Theatre/MacLiammóir/Edwards/Longford/
   Johnston – Rotunda Rooms/Newman/Dickens/O'Flaherty

4. 20 North Great George's Street/Ferguson

5. 35 North Great George's Street/James Joyce Cultural Centre

6. 38 North Great George's Street/John Pentland Mahaffy

7. 2 Great Denmark Street/Lever

8. Belvedere College/Joyce/Clarke/Plunkett/DonaghMacDonagh

9. 53 Mountjoy Square West/W.B. Yeats/O'Leary

10. 2 Belvedere Place/Joyce

11. 34 Fitzgibbon Street/Joyce

12. North Richmond Street/Joyce (number 17) CBS/Joyce/Gogarty/Kettle

13. Richmond Place, 609 and 617 North Circular Road/Joyce

14. Russell Street/Behan

15. 21 Great Charles Street/Mangan

16. 14 Temple Street/Fanny Parnell

17. Hardwicke Street/Joyce/Plunkett/Martyn/T. MacDonagh

18. Site of 85 Upper Dorset Street/O'Casey's birthplace

19. Site of 12 Upper Dorset Street/Brinsley Sheridan's birthplace

20. Gardiner Street Upper/St Francis Xavier's Church/Newman/Hopkins

21. 47 Gardiner Street Lower/Boucicault
    48 Gardiner Street Lower/Hearn

22. 9 Innisfallen Parade/O'Casey

23. 32 Glengariff Parade/Joyce

24. Mountjoy Gaol/Behan

25. 422 North Circular Road/O'Casey

26. Larry O'Rourke's/Joyce

27. Site of 7 Eccles Street/Joyce

28. 2 Nelson Street/Le Fanu

29. Berkeley Road Church/Clarke

30. 44 Fontenoy Street/Joyce

31. 15 Mountjoy Street/Clarke

32. The Black Church/Clarke

33. Lower Dominick Street/O'Casey (number. 20) also Le Fanu/Owenson

ROUTE 4

This route starts at the **Dublin Writers' Museum** and ends nearby in **Dominick Street**. It covers Dublin city north of the Liffey, an area which has associations with, among others, Southerne, Tickell, Berkeley, Delany, Burke, Sheridan, Morgan, Lover, Mangan, Lever, Ferguson, Le Fanu, Boucicault, Gogarty, O'Casey, Joyce, Clarke, MacLiammóir and Behan.

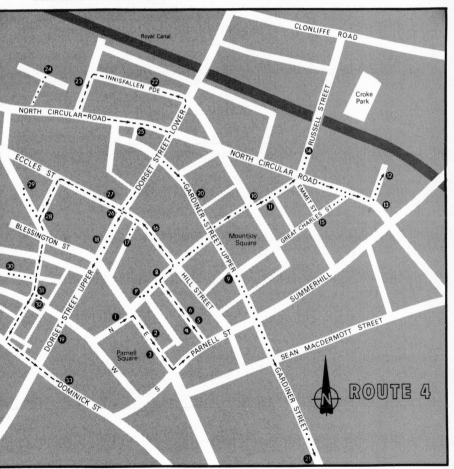

STARTING POINT: **Dublin Writers' Museum, 18–19 Parnell Square North** [1].

Proceed to **5 Parnell Square East** [2] where Oliver St John Gogarty was born in 1878 (when it was named Rutland Square). The house is marked with a plaque.

A few paces down in **Cavendish Row**, on the opposite side, is the **Gate Theatre** [3], which has associations with Hilton Edwards, Micheál MacLiammóir, Lord and Lady Longford, Denis Johnston and numerous other playwrights. It is where Orson Welles gave his first professional performance as an actor at the age of sixteen. Adjacent to the Gate is what was formerly the **Rotunda Rooms**, where John Henry Newman gave a series of lectures in 1852 and where crowds thronged to hear Charles Dickens read from his works during his visits to the city in 1858 and 1867. Liam O'Flaherty, in a protest with some unemployed dockers, took over the Rotunda Rooms in 1921.

Turn left into **Parnell Street** and left again into **North Great George's Street**. Number 22 (now demolished) was Major Swan's house; Le Fanu's mother visited it in order to retrieve a dagger belonging to Lord Edward Fitzgerald. Number **20** [4] was the home of Samuel Ferguson, where he held his literary gatherings attended by, amongst others, Lady Morgan, Le Fanu and Lever. Number **35**, the former home of Denis J. Maginni, Professor of dancing who appears in *Ulysses*, is now the **James Joyce Cultural Centre** [5]. (Officially opened in 1994, its aim is to promote interest in Joyce's life, works and Dublin background.) Number **38** [6] was the home of John Pentland Mahaffy, Oscar Wilde's tutor at Trinity College. In number **44**, Lady Morgan's father, Mr Owenson, died at the home of his son-in-law, Sir Arthur Clarke. (Numbers 44 and 45 have been replaced.)

Continue to the junction with **Great Denmark Street**.

Diversion: Charles Lever attended school in 2 Great Denmark Street [7], to the left.

Turn right into **Great Denmark Street**. On this street, facing down North Great George's Street, is **Belvedere College** [8] which James Joyce, Austin Clarke, Joseph Plunkett and Donagh MacDonagh attended. Continue to the junction with **Temple Street**.

*Diversion: Proceed straight up **Gardiner Place**. At the south-west end of **Mountjoy Square** is number 53, where W.B. Yeats and O'Leary lodged [9]. Cross over to Mountjoy Square North and into **Belvedere***

Place, where number 2 was the home of the Sheehy family, frequented by Joyce [10]. O'Casey lived in 35 **Mountjoy Square South** *(now demolished) and this is where he later set his play* The Shadow of a Gunman. *Proceed to* **34 Fitzgibbon Street** (formerly number 14) where the Joyce family lived for almost a year [11]. Continue down to the traffic lights on the **North Circular Road**, *bear right and then take the third turn on the left into* **North Richmond Street** *[12]. Number 17, where the Joyce family lived, is on the right-hand side. Opposite is the* **Christian Brothers School** *which was attended by Tom Kettle, Oliver Gogarty and James Joyce. Retrace your steps to the* **North Circular Road** *and turn left for numbers* **609** *and* **617***[13]. These were formerly numbers 17 and 21* **Richmond Place** *respectively, James Joyce's last addresses in Dublin in 1912. In the same area, Brendan Behan lived in* **Russell Street** *[14] at number 14 (now demolished), and Mangan was employed in the Ordnance Survey Office at* **21 Great Charles Street** *[15]. His friend George Petrie lived in the same house from 1835 to 1850. The house is marked with a plaque.*

From **Great Denmark Street**, turn left into **Temple Street**. O'Leary lived at number **17** (now demolished) and Fanny Parnell, who wrote poetry for the *Irish People*, lived at number **14**, which is now part of Temple Street Childrens' Hospital [16].

St George's Church in Hardwicke Place, a crescent, was designed by Francis Johnston in 1802. Bloom heard its chimes in *Ulysses*, as did the O'Caseys from nearby Dominick Street.

Diversion: Facing St George's Church is **Hardwicke Street** *[17]. The Joyce family lived in number 29 (now demolished) in early 1893. Joyce's short story in* Dubliners, *'The Boarding House', was set at* **Waverley House**, *which still operates as a boarding house at number* **4***. Joseph Nannetti, foreman of the* Freeman's Journal, *who appears in* Ulysses, *also lived in this street. In 1914, Thomas MacDonagh, Edward Martyn and Joseph Plunkett founded the* **Irish Theatre** *here.*

Continue along **Hardwicke Place** to the junction with **Dorset Street**.

Diversion: In 1880, Sean O'Casey was born in **85 Upper Dorset Street***[18], to the left. A branch of the Bank of Ireland now occupies the site of his birthplace, which is marked with a plaque. Richard Brinsley Sheridan was born at number* **12** *[19].*

From **Hardwicke Place**, turn right along **Lower Dorset Street**.

Diversion: In May 1852, John Henry Newman took lodgings in Dorset Street as it was convenient for the Jesuit Church, **St Francis Xavier's** *in* **Upper Gardiner Street** *[20], where he celebrated Mass. Gerard Manley Hopkins' requiem Mass was held here before his burial in Glasnevin Cemetery in June 1889. This church is noted for its coffered ceilings, and contains Dublin's finest Italian high altarpiece. Dion*

Boucicault was born further down at 47 Lower Gardiner Street [21], and, as a boy, Lafcadio Hearn stayed next door at number 48. John B. Yeats had lodgings at number 90.

Continue along **Lower Dorset Street**, cross the **North Circular Road** and continue until you come to **Innisfallen Parade** on the left. The O'Casey's lived at number **9** [22], after they moved from Upper Dorset Street. Innisfallen Parade links up with **Glengariff Parade** where the Joyce family lived in number **32** [23] in 1901–2.

Diversion: The backdrop to Glengariff Parade is Mountjoy Gaol [24] where Brendan Behan wrote his first play.

Turn left into the **North Circular Road** where O'Casey lived at number **422** [25]. Retrace your steps down **Lower Dorset Street** and turn right into **Eccles Street**. **Larry O'Rourke's** pub [26], which is featured in *Ulysses*, is on the corner and makes an ideal place to stop and rest. Number 7 Eccles Street [27], the home of Leopold Bloom in *Ulysses*, stood roughly where the main entrance to the private clinic of the Mater Hospital is situated. It is marked with a plaque which reads:

At the housesteps of the 4th of the equidifferent uneven numbers, number 7 Eccles St, he inserted his hand mechanically into the backpocket of his trousers to obtain his latchkey.

Turn left up **Nelson Street** where Joseph Sheridan Le Fanu lived in number **2** after his marriage to Susan Bennett [28].

Diversion: As a child, Austin Clarke was familiar with the streets around this area and attended Mass in Berkeley Road Church [29] where he made his first confession.

Cross **Blessington Street** and continue up for **Mountjoy Street**.

Diversion: Turn right up Blessington Street for the Basin, entering through the main gate. Bear left around the Basin and exit at the first gate. Proceed straight up Primrose Street and take the second turn left to 44 Fontenoy Street [30] where the Joyce family lived.

Austin Clarke lived in **Mountjoy Street** at number 15 (now derelict). This is the second-last house [31] on the left-hand side of Mountjoy Street at the junction where the Western Way and St Mary's Place converge.

Diversion: Nearby is the church known as the Black Church [32] in St Mary's Place, which fascinated Austin Clarke. Also in St Mary's Place is the former Christian Brothers School which Clarke attended.

Proceed along Mountjoy Street to **Dominick Street** [33]. The birthplace of Joseph Sheridan Le Fanu was at number 45 (now demolished). Sean O'Casey lived with his mother and sister in the attic flat at number **20** and attended St Mary's Infants School in the same building. He then went to St Mary's National School in the same street. Sydney Owenson (later Lady Morgan) worked here as a governess with the Featherstonehaugh family, and in 1903, Austin Clarke attended a private school in the same street run by the Holy Faith Sisters.

Route 4 takes approximately 2 hours (main route only).

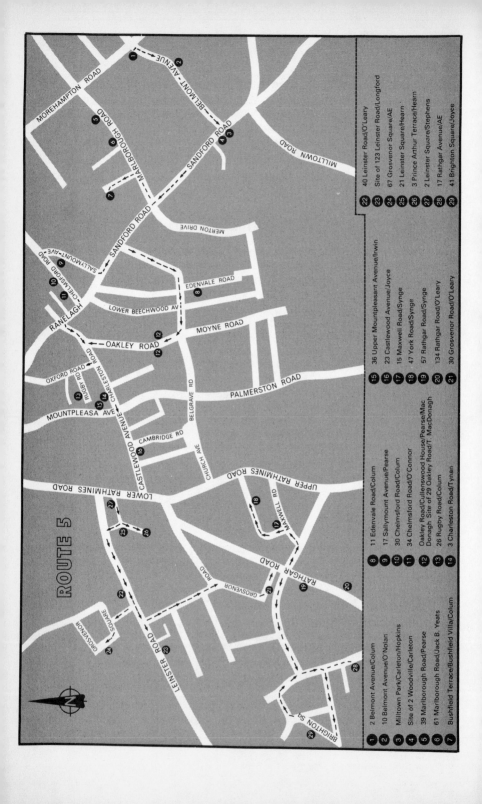

ROUTE 5

Legend:

1. 2 Belmont Avenue/Colum
2. 10 Belmont Avenue/O'Nolan
3. Milltown Park/Carleton/Hopkins
4. Site of 2 Woodville/Carleton
5. 39 Marlborough Road/Pearse
6. 61 Marlborough Road/Jack B. Yeats
7. Bushfield Terrace/Bushfield Villa/Colum

8. 11 Edenvale Road/Colum
9. 17 Sallymount Avenue/Pearse
10. 30 Chelmsford Road/Colum
11. 34 Chelmsford Road/O'Connor
12. Oakley Road/Cullenswood House/Pearse/Mac Donagh Site of 29 Oakley Road/T. MacDonagh
13. 26 Rugby Road/Colum
14. 3 Charleston Road/Tynan

15. 36 Upper Mountpleasant Avenue/Irwin
16. 23 Castlewood Avenue/Joyce
17. 15 Maxwell Road/Synge
18. 47 York Road/Synge
19. 57 Rathgar Road/Synge
20. 134 Rathgar Road/O'Leary
21. 30 Grosvenor Road/O'Leary

22. 40 Leinster Road/O'Leary
23. Site of 123 Leinster Road/Longford
24. 67 Grosvenor Square/AE
25. 21 Leinster Square/Hearn
26. 3 Prince Arthur Terrace/Hearn
27. 2 Leinster Square/Stephens
28. 17 Rathgar Avenue/AE
29. 41 Brighton Square/Joyce

ROUTE 5

There are a number of locations scattered around the south city suburbs of **Ranelagh, Rathmines** and **Rathgar.** The route is best devised by the individual reader, for which reason the map has been left unmarked for the most part, with the exception of a few guidelines.

If starting from point [1] at **Belmont Avenue,** take a number 11 bus southbound from O'Connell Street. This passes through **Ranelagh** and across the top of Belmont Avenue. The number 14 bus from College Street passes through **Rathmines** and **Rathgar,** as do the numbers 15a and 15b also from College Street.

Padraic Colum lived at **2 Belmont Avenue,** Donnybrook [1], for two years after his marriage to Mary Gunning in June 1912. Number **10** was the home of Brian O'Nolan[2].

Milltown Park[3], the Jesuit house on **Sandford Road,** was visited by William Carleton and Gerard Manley Hopkins. The site of 2 **Woodville, Sandford Road**[4], where Carleton died in January 1869, is situated approximately where numbers **83** and **85** now stand.

The Pearse family moved to **39 Marlborough Road** [5] in 1902 and remained at this address for three years. Jack B. Yeats moved to number **61** in the autumn of 1917 and had his studio there[6].

From 1909 to 1911, Padraic and Mary Colum lived in **Bushfield Villa, Bushfield Terrace** [7], off **Marlborough Road.** The house stands on its own at the end of the road on the left-hand side.

Number **11 Edenvale Road, Ranelagh**[8], was Padraic Colum's last address in Dublin. The house is marked with a plaque.

In 1907, the Pearse family moved to Brookville, **17 Sallymount Avenue, Ranelagh**[9]. The house has been demolished and site redeveloped.

Padraic Colum lived at **30 Chelmsford Road** [10] from 1905 to 1909. Frank O'Connor lived a few doors up on the same side in number **34** [11].

In 1908 Patrick Pearse founded **St Enda's School** in **Cullenswood House, Oakley Road**[12]. Directly opposite was number **29** where Thomas MacDonagh lived when he was teaching at St Enda's. The original house has been replaced.

Padraic Colum lived at **26 Rugby Road** [13] with his family before he was married. The house is situated near the end of the cul-de-sac on the right-hand side.

Katharine Tynan attended school at **3 Charleston Road** [14]. Thomas Caulfield Irwin lived just around the corner at **36 Upper Mountpleasant Avenue** [15].

329

James Joyce lived as a child at **23 Castlewood Avenue, Rathmines**[16], from 1884 to 1887. This was his second Dublin address. J.M. Synge lived at **15 Maxwell Road** [17]. This house is situated on the corner at the intersection with York Road. It was close to the flat at **47 York Road** [18] which he took in 1908 and where he planned to live after his marriage to the actress Molly Allgood. In between, he had lived at **57 Rathgar Road** [19].

In the autumn of 1889, John O'Leary moved to **134 Rathgar Road** [20] and the following year to **30 Grosvenor Road, Rathmines** [21]. In 1885 he had lived at **40 Leinster Road, Rathmines** [22]. This house was the meeting place for young Irish poets and writers such as W.B. Yeats, Tynan, Rolleston and Hyde. Further down **Leinster Road** is the redeveloped site of number **123**, the former residence of Lord Longford [23].

Æ (George Russell) lived at **67 Grosvenor Square** [24] from 1885 to 1891. The square is situated off **Leinster Road**.

Going towards the Rathmines end of **Leinster Road**, on the right-hand side there are some unobtrusive steps leading up to **Leinster Square** [25] where Lafcadio Hearn lived at number **21**. A few paces further on is **3 Prince Arthur Terrace** [26] where Hearn also lived. James Stephens lived at **2 Leinster Square** [27] on his return from Paris in 1914.

William Carleton lived in **Rathgar Avenue** at number **1** (now demolished) and a plaque marks number **17** where Æ lived and held his famous literary soirées [28].

James Joyce was born on 2 February 1882 at **41 Brighton Square, Rathgar** [29].

Mount Jerome Cemetery

Buses to **Mount Jerome, Harold's Cross**, to the south-west of Dublin, include numbers 16 and 16a from O'Connell Street, number 54a from Eden Quay, and number 155 from College Street.

To find the locations of writers' graves in the cemetery, it is easiest if the directions given below are followed. Many of the paths in the cemetery are overgrown with bushes and briars making it difficult to locate the graves, and it is not possible to show every path on a map of this scale. The number against each name is the map reference number, and the codes shown on the map are the official grave numbers.

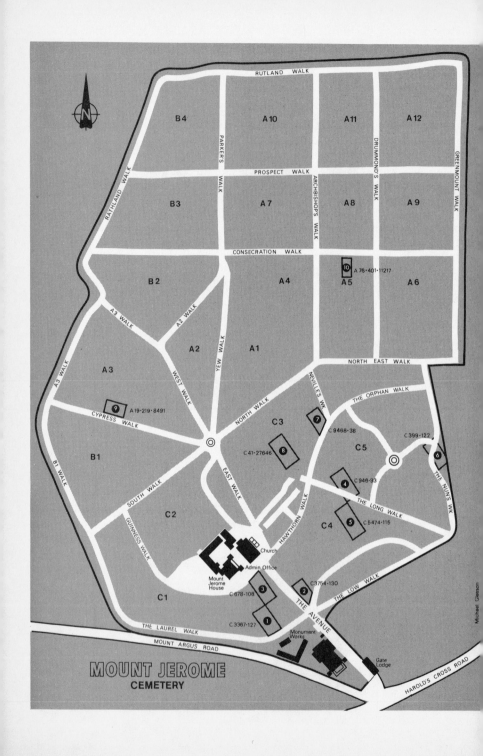

RUTLAND WALK

N

B 4   A 10   A 11   A 12

PARKER'S WALK

PROSPECT WALK

RATHLAND WALK

B 3   A 7   A 8   A 9

ARCHBISHOP'S WALK

DRUMMOND'S WALK

GREENMOUNT WALK

CONSECRATION WALK

B 2   A 4   A 5   A 6

10 A 76·401·11217

A3 WALK

A2 WALK

YEW WALK

A 2   A 1

A 3   NORTH EAST WALK

A3 WALK

WEST WALK

NORTH WALK

NEVILLE'S WK.

THE ORPHAN WALK

9 A 19·219·8491

CYPRESS WALK

C 3   7

EAST WALK

C 9468·38

C 399·122

B 1   8 C 41·27646   C 5   6

C 946·93   THE NUNS WK.

B1 WALK   4

SOUTH WALK   THE LONG WALK

GUINNESS WALK   C 2   C 4   5 C 5474·115

HAWTHORN WALK

Church

Admin Office

Mount Jerome House

C 678·108   3   2 C 3754·130

C 1   THE LOW WALK

THE AVENUE

C 3367·127   1

THE LAUREL WALK

Monument Works

MOUNT ARGUS ROAD

Gate Lodge

HAROLD'S CROSS ROAD

MOUNT JEROME
CEMETERY

Michael Gleeson

[1] JOHN KELLS INGRAM
Take the first left turn inside the main entrance which is the **Laurel Walk**. Continue to the first bend and turn right at the headstone for James Samuel Wauchope Craig on the right-hand side. Take the second turn right after this. Ingram's grave is the fourth on the left-hand side.

[2] WILLIAM CARLETON
Proceed up the **Avenue**. Take the first set of little steps on the right-hand side. The William Carleton Memorial is second on the left.

[3] SIR WILLIAM WILDE
Proceed to the top of the **Avenue** and turn left at the church. Wilde's headstone is the third on the left-hand side.

[4] THOMAS CAULFIELD IRWIN
From the **Avenue**, turn right at the church for **Hawthorn Walk**. Continue along and turn right to the **Long Walk**. Approximately seventy yards away, the thirty-sixth grave down on the left-hand side is the memorial to Irwin, which is a limestone cover on a granite plinth.

[5] THOMAS DAVIS
The easiest way to reach the grave of Thomas Davis is to proceed to Irwin's memorial as directed above. On reaching it, turn right and opposite is a similar type of grave with the name Beasley on it. Proceed straight up the narrow pathway beside this, passing the headstone to Sir Rowan Hamilton, the mathematician, on the right-hand side. Take a right turn between the headstones for Bradley and Sherrard. The Celtic cross marking Davis' grave is the first on the left-hand side.

[6] JOSEPH SHERIDAN LE FANU
Take the first turn right inside the main entrance which is the **Low Walk** and continue to the **Nun's Walk**. At the bend marked on the map there is a white limestone headstone to Kathleen Keane. Le Fanu's grave, a flat vault with a limestone top, is to the left of this.

[7] JOHN MILLINGTON SYNGE
Proceed up the **Avenue** from the main entrance and turn right at the church for the **Hawthorn Walk**. At the junction with the **Long Walk**, bear slightly left at the corner. (Note: the part of the **Long Walk** directly on the left no longer exists, having been filled in almost completely to a

short cul-de-sac.) On the left-hand side is a headstone for Wynne; follow the narrow concrete pathway, passing at intervals on the left-hand side the headstones for Norton, Smyth and Dallas. Some bushes cross the path. A headstone for Bolster is directly ahead. Synge's headstone is second to the left of this.

[8] JACK B. YEATS
Proceed up the **Avenue** and turn right at the church for the **Hawthorn Walk**. Continue straight to the fork, taking the left for **Neville's Walk**. After the first tree, take a sharp left. Yeats' grave is the sixteenth in on the right-hand side.

[9] ETHEL ARMITAGE FRENCH
Proceed up the **Avenue** and up the **East Walk**. Bear ahead and left to **Cypress Walk**. (Cypress Walk is not marked, but the headstones at the entrance are Captain Joseph Bolland on the left and Gertrude Quinn on the right.) The grave of Ettie, wife of Percy French, is 120 yards up on the right-hand side, three headstones in from the pathway.

[10] GEORGE WILLIAM RUSSELL (Æ)
Proceed up the **Avenue** to the church and turn right for the **Hawthorn Walk**. Fork left up **Neville's Walk** and continue up **Archbishop's Walk**. Turn right at the junction with **Consecration Walk**. As a guide, the headstone on the left corner is for McGrail. Twenty-five graves down on the right, there is a narrow pathway between the headstones for O'Rourke and Cooling. Æ's grave, a flat stone on the ground, is the fifth row in on the right.

Glasnevin Cemetery

Buses to **Glasnevin Cemetery**, north of the city centre, include numbers 40, 40a, 40b and 40c from Parnell Street.

The following directions will assist readers in locating the writers' graves. The number against each name is the map reference number, and the codes shown on the map are the official grave numbers.

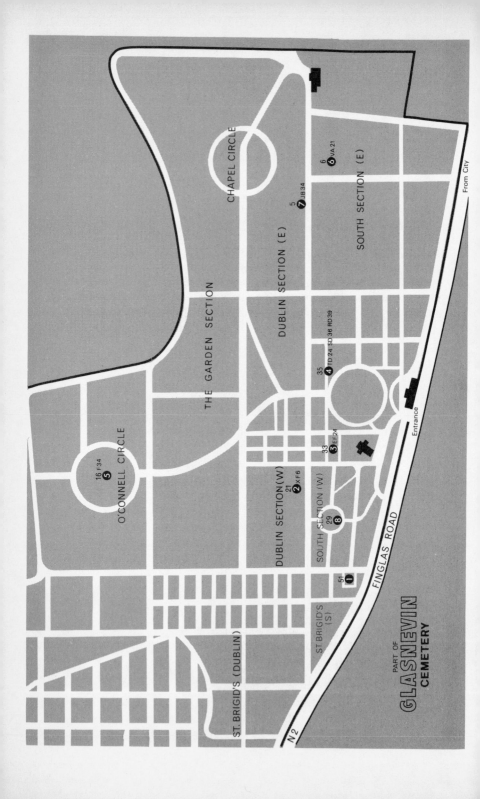

PART OF
GLASNEVIN
CEMETERY

O'CONNELL CIRCLE

16 F·34
5

CHAPEL CIRCLE

THE GARDEN SECTION

DUBLIN SECTION (E)

5 JB34
7

6 VA 21
6

SOUTH SECTION (E)

35
4 TD 24 SD 36 RD39

33
3 EF24

DUBLIN SECTION (W)
21
2 XF6

SOUTH SECTION (W)
29
8

51
1

ST BRIGID'S (S)

ST. BRIGID'S (DUBLIN)

FINGLAS ROAD

Entrance

From City

N 2

[1] GERARD MANLEY HOPKINS, SJ
Bear left inside the main entrance gate, towards the chapel. At the chapel turn right and then take the first turn left. The large granite crucifix in the enclosed **Jesuit Plot** is clearly visible about fifty metres directly ahead, on the plinth of which, along with other names, can be read the inscription, 'P. Gerardus Hopkins obiit Jun. 8 1889 aetat. an. 44.' Hopkins is buried to the left of the plot's entrance gate in an unmarked grave.

[2] JOHN STANISLAUS JOYCE AND MARY JANE JOYCE
Bear left inside the main entrance gate. At the chapel turn right and then take the third turn left. Approximately fourteen graves down on the right-hand side is a headstone to Walter Ahern. James Joyce's parents' grave, marked with a gleaming white marble headstone, is third in to the left of this.

[3] MAURA LAVERTY
Bear left inside the main entrance gate and proceed towards the chapel. Take the right turn *before* you reach it and then the second turn on the left. Walk on a few yards and the grave is the first on the left-hand side.

[4] CONSTANCE MARKIEVICZ, MAUD GONNE MCBRIDE and JOHN O'LEARY are all buried in the section marked as number 4 on the map. Turn right at the round tower commemorating Daniel O'Connell just inside the main entrance gate, and follow the circle to the Boland Memorial Vault on the left-hand side.

Constance Markievicz (SD36 Snc)
Almost directly to the right of the Boland Memorial Vault is the **Republican Plot** where Countess Markievicz (née Gore-Booth), the revolutionary, is buried. Her grave is marked in the kerbstone surrounding the Republican Plot.

Maud Gonne (TD24 all, 25 ½ Snc)
After the Boland Memorial Vault, instead of continuing around the circle, proceed straight on. Maud Gonne's grave is the tenth down on the left-hand side.

John O'Leary (RD39 all, Snc)
This grave is marked with a large Celtic cross on the near side of the **Republican Plot**, to the right-hand side of the Boland memorial Vault.

337

[5] DORA SIGERSON

Dora Sigerson (1866–1918), poet and designer, was the daughter of Dr George Sigerson, physician and scientist. She married Clement Shorter, editor of the *Illustrated London News*. She designed the 1916 memorial in Glasnevin Cemetery. To reach her grave, bear left inside the main entrance and right before the chapel. Continue straight down this path, going over two sets of main crossroads, to reach the **O'Connell Circle**. Continue up some steps and turn right, and about twenty yards on the right is a covering stone to Dora Sigerson with a grass verge leading into the vaults.

[6] BRENDAN BEHAN

Bear right at the main entrance and proceed straight down the avenue past the administration offices. Take the second-last turn to the left and continue straight on. Brendan Behan's grave is on the right-hand side almost at the end of this avenue. It has an unusually shaped granite stone with a bronze inset. (Just opposite, on the left-hand side, two graves in, is the headstone of Francis Sheehy-Skeffington, who was murdered in Portobello Barracks on 26 April 1916.)

[7] JAMES CLARENCE MANGAN

From Brendan Behan's grave, go to the end of this little avenue and take a left turn. Continue to the grave on the right-hand side with a surround of black railings. (JB is marked on the back of some of the gravestones in this row.) Turn right here and proceed down through the grass past the headstones marked for Nicholas Synott on the left. Count nine headstones down after this and the back of Mangan's headstone is almost directly opposite.

[8] CHARLES STEWART PARNELL

At the main entrance bear left and take the right after the chapel, then first left. Parnell's grave, marked with a large stone of Wicklow granite, is just on the right, enclosed by a railing, in the **Parnell Circle**.

CHRISTY BROWN

From the main entrance cross **Finglas Road** to **St Paul's** section. Proceed up the main avenue to the crossroads, at which turn right and continue a couple of hundred metres. A black marble headstone to Delma Lawler is on the left and Christy Brown's grave is seven in from this (IF50, St Paul's).

EDWARD MARTYN

Martyn is buried in an unmarked grave in the area known as the **General Poor Ground**, which is located in the north-east of the cemetery near Violet Hill.

The Dart

The DART (Dublin Area Rapid Transit), which runs between **Howth** and **Bray**, may be used as a quick, convenient and scenic route around Dublin Bay. Below are listed some of the stops, together with those writers associated with the districts within walking distance of the stations. Refer back to the main entry for each writer for precise information.

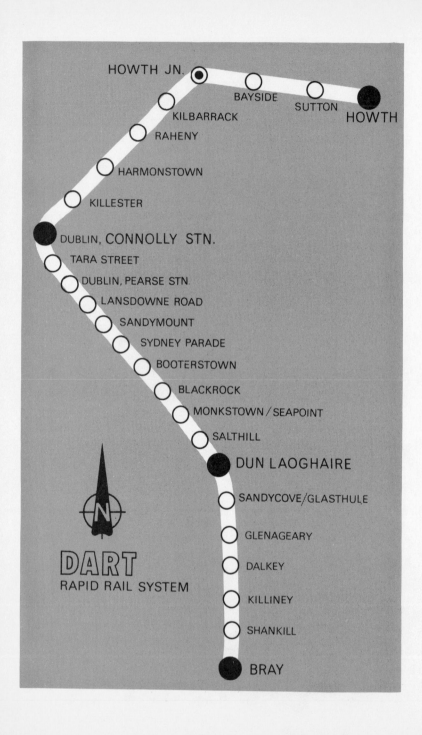

The Dart

Howth:	Samuel Ferguson, W.B. Yeats and Annie Smithson.
Landsdowne Road:	Denis Johnston.
Sandymount:	James Joyce, Donagh McDonagh, T.C. Murray, Frank O'Connor, W.B. Yeats, Annie Smithson, Patrick Pearse and Christy Brown.
Blackrock:	James Joyce, Emily Lawless, Brian O'Nolan and James Stephens.
Monkstown/Seapoint:	Charles Kickham and Annie Smithson.
Dun Laoghaire:	Samuel Beckett, James Joyce, J.M. Synge, John Henry Newman and W.M. Thackeray.
Sandycove/Glasthule:	Padraic Colum, Oliver St John Gogarty, Monk Gibbon, Denis Johnston, James Joyce, Sean O'Faoláin, L.A.G. Strong.
Glenageary:	J.M. Synge.
Dalkey:	James Joyce, Denis Johnston, Denis Florence MacCarthy, John Henry Newman, Lennox Robinson, G.B. Shaw, Katherine Tynan and Annie Smithson.
Shankill:	Katherine Tynan.
Bray:	James Joyce, Sir William Wilde, Oscar Wilde and Annie Smithson.

Useful Information

Transport
DART

For information on the Dublin Area Rapid Transit which runs between **Howth** and **Bray**, see pages 340–1.

DUBLIN BUS (BUS ATHA CLIATH)
There are a number of bargain fares available, on a daily, weekly and monthly basis, which are excellent value. For fares and other useful information, such as a guide to Dublin Services, see the *Dublin Bus Timetable*. For full details contact **Dublin Bus, 59 Upper O'Connell Street, Dublin 1. Tel: 01–872 0000.**

Places
The following places appear throughout the text.

ABBEY AND PEACOCK THEATRES, Lower Abbey Street, Dublin 1. Tel: 01–878 7222.

BOTANIC GARDENS, Glasnevin, Dublin 9. Tel: 01–837 4388. Open all year. **Buses:** 13 and 19 from O'Connell Street or 34 from Middle Abbey Street (also convenient for the Bons Secours Hospital on the site of Delville, former home of Mary Delany).

DOUGLAS HYDE GALLERY, Trinity College, Dublin 2. Tel: 01–608 1116.

DUBLIN CASTLE, Dublin 2. Tel: 01–677 7129. State Apartments open all year. See point [9] on Route 3.

DUBLIN WRITERS' MUSEUM, 18–19 Parnell Square, Dublin 1. Tel: 01–872 2077. See point [1] on Route 4.

GAIETY THEATRE, South King Street, Dublin 2. Tel: 01–677 1717.

GATE THEATRE, 1 Cavendish Row, Dublin 1. Tel: 01–874 4045. See point [3] on Route 4.

GLASVENIN CEMETERY Buses: 40, 40a, 40b, 40c from Parnell Street. See separate map and information, pages 335–8.

GUINNESS HOP STORE, Crane Street, Dublin 8. Tel: 01–453 8364. Open Monday to Friday from 10.30 a.m. to 3.30 p.m.

Useful Information

IRISH MUSEUM OF MODERN ART, Royal Hospital Kilmainham, Dublin 8. Tel: 01–612 9900. Open all year. **Buses:** 51, 51b, 68, 69, 78a, 79 from Aston Quay; DART Feeder Bus from Connolly and Tara Street Stations to Heuston Station nearby.

IRISH NATIONAL WAR MEMORIAL PARK, Islandbridge. Buses: 51 and 51b from Aston Quay.

IRISH WHISKEY CORNER, Bow Street Distillery, Smithfield, Dublin 7. Tel: 01–872 5566.

JAMES JOYCE CULTURAL CENTRE, 35 North Great George's Street, Dublin 1. Tel: 01–878 8547. See point [5] on Route 4.

JAMES JOYCE TOWER MUSEUM, Sandycove, County Dublin. Tel: 01–280 9265 (if no reply: 01–872 2077). Open May to September. Other times by appointment. **Buses:** 7 or 8 from Burgh Quay. DART to Sandycove Station.

KILMAINHAM GAOL, Dublin 8. Tel: 01–453 5984. Open all year. **Buses:** 79 from Aston Quay.

MALAHIDE CASTLE, Malahide, County Dublin. Tel: 01–846 2516/2228/2184. Open all year. **Buses:** 42 from Beresford Place.

MARSH'S LIBRARY, St Patrick's Close, Dublin 8. Tel: 01–454 3511. Open all year. **Buses:** 50, 50a from Aston Quay, or 54, 54a from Burgh Quay. See point [2] on Route 3.

MOUNT JEROME CEMETERY, Harold's Cross, Dublin. Buses: 16, 16a from O'Connell Street; 54a from Eden Quay; and 155 from College Street. See separate map and information, pages 331–4.

MUNICIPAL GALLERY OF MODERN ART, Parnell Square, Dublin 1. Tel: 01–874 1903.

NATIONAL GALLERY OF IRELAND, Merrion Square West, Dublin 2. Tel: 01–661 5133. Open all year. See point [1] on Route 2.

NEWMAN HOUSE, 85–86 St Stephen's Green, Dublin 2. Tel: 01–706 7422/7419. See point [22] on Route 1.

PEARSE MUSEUM, St Enda's Park, Rathfarnham, Dublin 14. Tel: 01–493 4208. Buses: 16 from O'Connell Street or 47b from Hawkins Street.

POETRY IRELAND, The Bermingham Tower, Upper Castle Yard, Dublin Castle, Dublin 2. Tel: 01–671 4632. Open all year. Contains Austin Clarke Library of 6,000 volumes. See point [9] on Route 3.

POWERSCOURT GARDENS AND WATERFALL, Enniskerry, County Wicklow. Tel: 01–204 6000. Bus: 44 from Hawkins Street.

RATHFARNAM CASTLE, Rathfarnham, Dublin 14. Tel: 01–493 9462. Buses: 16 and 16a from O'Connell Street.

ROYAL HOSPITAL KILMAINHAM, Kilmainham, Dublin 8. See **Irish Museum of Modern Art** above.

SHAW BIRTHPLACE, 33 Synge Street, Dublin 8. Tel: 01–475 0854. See point [1] on Route 1.

ST ENDA'S, Rathfarnham. See **Pearse Museum** above.

TRINITY COLLEGE, DUBLIN 2. Tel: 01–677 2941.

For visitor information and opening times to other places of interest contact the Tourist Information Office. See Telephone Directory under **Dublin Tourism**.

Select Bibliography

Æ (GEORGE RUSSELL)
Eglington, John (W.K. Magee), *A Memoir of Æ* (Macmillan, London, 1937)
Moore, George, *Hail and Farewell* (Colin Smythe, Gerrards Cross, Bucks, 1976)

BARRINGTON, SIR JONAH
Barrington, Sir Jonah, *Personal Sketches and Recollections of his Own Times* (3 vols), Colburn and R. Bentley, 1827–32)
Barrington, Sir Jonah, *Historic Memoirs of Ireland* (2 vols, London, 1933)

BECKETT, SAMUEL
Bair, Deirdre, *Samuel Beckett: A Biography* (Harcourt Brace Jovanovich, New York and London, 1978)
O'Brien, Eoin, *The Beckett Country: Samuel Beckett's Ireland* (The Black Cat Press, Monkstown, County Dublin, in Association with Faber & Faber, London, 1986)

BEHAN, BRENDAN
O'Connor, Ulick, *Brendan Behan* (Hamish Hamilton, London, 1970)

BETJEMAN, JOHN
Delaney, Frank, *Betjeman Country* (Hodder & Stoughton, London, 1983)
Hillier, Bevis, *John Betjeman: A Life in Pictures* (John Murray in association with Herbert Press, London, 1984)

BOUCICAULT, DION
Hogan, Robert, *Dion Boucicault* (Twayne, New York, 1969)

BOWEN, ELIZABETH
Bowen, Elizabeth, *Bowen's Court and Seven Winters: Memories of a Dublin Childhood* (Virago Press, London, 1984)
Glendenning, Victoria, *Elizabeth Bowen* (Weidenfeld & Nicolson, London, 1977)

CARLETON, WILLIAM
Carleton, William, *The Autobiography of William Carleton*, preface by Patrick Kavanagh (MacGibbon & Kee, London, 1968)
Kiely, Benedict, *Poor Scholar: A study of the works and days of William Carleton* (The Catholic Book Club, London, 1948)

O'Donoghue, J. D, *The Life of William Carleton* (Downey, London, 1896)

CLARKE, AUSTIN
Clarke, Austin, *A Penny in the Clouds* (Routledge & Kegan Paul, London, 1968)
—*Selected Poems*, edited and with an introduction by Thomas Kinsella (The Dolmen Press, North America: Wake Forest University Press, 1976)
—*Twice Round the Black Church* (Moytura Press, Dublin, 1990)
Irish University Review (Vol. 4, No. 1, Spring 1974)
Poetry Ireland (Nos 22, 23, Summer 1988)

COLUM, PADRAIC
Bowen, Zack, *Padraic Colum* (S. Illinois University Press, 1970)

DARLEY, GEORGE
Colles, Ramsey (ed.), *The Complete Works of George Darley* (Routledge & Sons, London, N.D.)
Ridler, Anne (ed.), *Selected Poems of George Darley* (The Merrion Press, London, 1979)

DELANY, MRS
Delany, Mrs, *The Autobiography and Correspondence of Mary Granville* (3 vols, Richard Bentley, London, 1861)

DICKENS, CHARLES
MacKenzie, N. and J, *Dickens: A Life* (Oxford University Press, 1979)
Pope-Hennessy, U, *Charles Dickens* (Penguin Books, London, in association with Chatto & Windus, 1945)

FERGUSON, SIR SAMUEL
Ferguson, Lady, *Sir Samuel Ferguson in the Ireland of his Day* (Vols I and II, Blackwood & Sons, Edinburgh and London, 1896)

GOGARTY, OLIVER ST JOHN
Gogarty, Oliver St John, *It Isn't This Time of Year at All!* (MacGibbon & Kee, London, 1954)
O'Connor, Ulick, *Oliver St John Gogarty: A Poet and his Times* (Jonathan Cape, London, 1964)

GREGORY, LADY AUGUSTA
Coxhead, Elizabeth, *Lady Gregory: A Literary Portrait* (Macmillan, London, 1961)
Robinson, Lennox (ed.), *Lady Gregory's Journals 1916–1930* (Putnam, London, 1946)
Yeats, William Butler, *Dramatis Personae* (The Cuala Press, Dublin, 1935)

HEARN, LAFCADIO
Ronan, Sean and Toki Koizumi, *Lafcadio Hearn (Koizumi Yakumo):*

His Life, Work and Irish Background (Ireland Japan Association, Dublin, 1991)

HEMANS, FELICIA
Hemans, Felicia, *Poetical Works* (Frederick Warne, London, 1897)

HIGGINS, F. R.
Clarke, Austin, *A Penny in the Clouds* (Routledge & Kegan Paul, London, 1968)
Higgins, F.R, *Island Blood* (The Bodley Head, London, 1925)

HOPKINS, GERARD MANLEY
Martin, Robert Bernard, *Gerard Manley Hopkins: A Very Private Life* (Flamingo, London, 1992)
Ruggles, Eleanor, *Gerard Manley Hopkins: A Life* (John Lane, The Bodley Head, London, 1947)

HYDE, DOUGLAS
Daly, Dominic, *The Young Douglas Hyde* (Irish University Press, Shannon, 1974)

JOYCE, JAMES
Costello, Peter, *The Years of Growth 1882–1915* (Kyle Cathie, London, 1992)
Ellmann, Richard, *James Joyce* (Oxford University Press, New York, 1959)
Igoe, Vivien, *James Joyce's Dublin Houses and Nora Barnacle's Galway* (Mandarin, London, 1990)

KAVANAGH, PATRICK
Kavanagh, Patrick, *By Night Unstarred. An Autobiographical Novel* (Goldsmith Press, The Curragh, Ireland, 1977)
Kavanagh, Peter, *Sacred Keeper. A Biography of Patrick Kavanagh* (Goldsmith Press, The Curragh, Ireland, 1979)

KETTLE, THOMAS
Lyons, J.B, *The Enigma of Tom Kettle* (The Glendale Press, Dublin, 1983)

KIPLING, RUDYARD
Kipling, Rudyard, *Something of Myself and Other Autobiographical Writings*, edited by Thomas Pinney (Cambridge University Press, 1990)
Pinney, Thomas (ed.), *O Beloved Kids: Rudyard Kipling's Letters to his Children* (Cambridge University Press, 1983)

LE FANU, JOSEPH SHERIDAN
Browne, Nelson, *Sheridan Le Fanu* (Arthur Barker, London, 1951)
Dagg, T. S. C, *Joseph Sheridan Le Fanu: A Memorial Discourse* (Dublin University Press, 1949)

LEVER, CHARLES
FitzPatrick, W.J, *The Life of Charles Lever* (Ward Lock, London, 1884)
Stevenson, Lionel, *Dr Quicksilver: The Life of Charles Lever* (Chapman & Hall, London, 1939)

LOVER, SAMUEL
Symington, A.J, *Samuel Lover* (Blackie, London, 1880)

MANGAN, JAMES CLARENCE
Mangan, James Clarence, *Autobiography*, edited by James Kilroy (The Dolmen Press, Dublin, 1968)

MATURIN, CHARLES
Lougy, Robert, *Charles Robert Maturin* (Bucknell University Press, 1975)

MOORE, GEORGE
Hone, Joseph, *The Moores of Moore Hall* (Jonathan Cape, London,1939)
Moore, George, *Confessions of a Young Man* (Heinemann, London, 1937)
—*Esther Waters* (Dent, London, 1962)
—*Hail and Farewell*, edited by R. Cave (Colin Smythe, Gerrards Cross, 1976)
—*A Drama in Muslin* (Colin Smythe, Gerrards Cross, 1981)

MOORE, THOMAS
Strong, L.A.G, *The Minstrel Boy: A Portrait of Tom Moore* (Hodder and Stoughton, London, 1937)
White, Terence de Vere, *Tom Moore: The Irish Poet* (Hamish Hamilton, London, 1977)

NEWMAN, CARDINAL JOHN HENRY
McRedmond, Louis, *Thrown Among Strangers. John Henry Newman in Ireland* (Veritas, Dublin, 1990)

O'CASEY, SEAN
O'Casey, Sean, *Autobiography* (6 vols, Macmillan, London, 1949)

O'CONNOR, FRANK
Matthews, James, *Voices: A life of Frank O'Connor* (Gill & Macmillan, Dublin, 1983)
O'Connor, Frank, *An Only Child* (Macmillan, London, 1961)

O'FAOLÁIN, SEAN
Doyle, Paul, *Sean O'Faoláin* (Twayne Publishers, New York, 1968)

O'LEARY, JOHN
O'Leary, John, *Recollections of Fenians and Fenianism* (Downey, London, 1896)

Select Bibliography

O'NOLAN, BRIAN
Clissman, Anne, *Flann O'Brien: A Critical Introduction to His Writing* (Gill & Macmillan, Dublin, 1975)
Cronin, Anthony, *No Laughing Matter: The Life and Times of Flann O'Brien* (Paladin, London, 1989)

PEARSE, PATRICK
Edwards, Ruth Dudley, *Patrick Pearse: The Triumph of Failure* (Gollancz, London, 1977)

ROBINSON, LENNOX
O'Neill, M.J, *Lennox Robinson* (Twayne Publishers, New York, 1964)
Robinson, L, *Curtain Up: An Autobiography* (Michael Joseph, London, 1942)
Robinson, L. and R, and N. Dorman, *Three Homes* (Browne & Nolan, Dublin,1938)

SCOTT, SIR WALTER
Lockhart, J.G, *Memoirs of Sir Walter Scott* (Vol. VIII, Adam and Charles Black, Edinburgh, 1882)

SHAW, GEORGE BERNARD
Holroyd, Michael, *The Search for Love, Vol. 1, 1856–1898* (Chatto & Windus, London, 1988)

SHELLEY, PERCY BYSSHE
Hogg, Thomas Jefferson, *The Life of Shelley*
Trelawny, Edward John, *The Recollections of Shelley & Byron*
Peacock, Thomas Love, *Memoirs of Shelley* (Dent, London, 1933)

SHERIDAN, RICHARD BRINSLEY
Gibbs, Lewis, *Sheridan, His Life and His Theatre* (Morrow, New York, 1948)
Moore, Thomas, *Memoirs of the Life of the Right Honourable Richard Brinsley Sheridan* (Longman, London, 1825)

STEPHENS, JAMES
Pyle, Hilary, *James Stephens: His Work and an Account of His Life* (Routledge & Kegan Paul, London, 1965)

STOKER, BRAM
Ludlam, Harry, *A Biography of Dracula: The Life Story of Bram Stoker* (The Fireside Press, London, 1962)

STRONG, L.A.G.
Strong, L.A.G, *The Garden* (Gollancz, London, 1931)
—*The Body's Imperfection: The Collected Poems of L.A.G. Strong* (Methuen, London, 1957)
—*Green Memory* (Methuen, London, 1961)
Wall, Mervyn, *Forty Foot, Gentlemen Only* (Allen Figgis, Dublin, 1962)

SWIFT, JONATHAN
Johnston, Denis, *In Search of Swift* (Hodges Figgis, Dublin, 1959)
Lane-Poole, Stanley (ed.), *Letters and Journals of Jonathan Swift* (Kegan Paul, Trench, London, 1885)

SYNGE, JOHN MILLINGTON
Stephen, Edward, *My Uncle John: Life of J.M. Synge*, edited by Andrew Carpenter (Oxford University Press, 1974)
Synge, J.M, *Autobiography*, edited by Alan Price (The Dolmen Press, Dublin, 1965)

THACKERAY, WILLIAM MAKEPEACE
The Works of William Makepeace Thackeray, Vol. VII *The Irish Sketchbook* (13 vols, Smith, Elder, London, 1883)

TICKELL, THOMAS
Nelson, E.C. and E.M. McCracken, *The Brightest Jewel: A History of the National Botanic Gardens, Glasnevin, Dublin* (Boethius Press, Kilkenny, 1987)

TROLLOPE, ANTHONY
Trollope, Anthony, *An Autobiography*, edited by M. Sadleir and F. Page (Oxford University Press, 1980)

TYNAN, KATHERINE
Tynan, Katherine, *Twenty-Five Years* (Smith, Elder, London, 1913)
—*The Middle Years* (Constable, London, 1916)
—*The Years of the Shadow* (Constable, London, 1919)
—*The Wandering Years* (Constable, London, 1922)
—*The Poems of Katherine Tynan*, with an introduction by Monk Gibbon (Allen Figgis, Dublin, 1963)

WILDE, OSCAR
Ellmann, Richard, *Oscar Wilde* (Hamish Hamilton, London, 1987)
Montgomery Hyde, H., *Oscar Wilde: A Biography* (Methuen, London, 1976)
White, Terence de Vere, *The Parents of Oscar Wilde: Sir William and Lady Wilde* (Hodder & Stoughton, London, 1967)

WILDE, SIR WILLIAM
Fleetwood, John, *History of Medicine in Ireland* (Richview Press, Dublin, 1951)
Wilson, T. G., *Victorian Doctor: being the Life of Sir William Wilde* (Fischer, New York, 1946)

YEATS, JACK B.
Pyle, Hilary, *Jack B. Yeats: A Biography* (Routledge & Kegan Paul, London, 1970)

Select Bibliography

YEATS, WILLIAM BUTLER
Ellmann, Richard, *The Man and the Masks* (Faber & Faber, London, 1949)
Murphy, William M., *The Prodigal Father: The Life of John Butler Yeats (1839–1922)* (Cornell University Press, Ithaca and London, 1978)

GENERAL
Bennett, Douglas, *Encyclopaedia of Dublin* (Gill & Macmillan, Dublin, 1991)
Boylan, H., *A Dictionary of Irish Biography* (Gill & Macmillan, Dublin, 1978)
Cosgrave, D., *North Dublin: City and Environs* (Four Courts Press, Dublin, 1909)
Cowell, J., *Where They lived in Dublin* (O'Brien Press, Dublin, 1980)
Craig, M., *Dublin 1660–1860* (Hodges Figgis, Dublin, 1952)
Dictionary of National Biography
Dublin Historical Record
The Freeman's Journal
Gilbert, Sir J.T.A., *A History of the City of Dublin* (3 vols, Vol.1 James McGlashan, Dublin, 1854; Vols 2 and 3 McGlashan & Gill, Dublin, 1859)
Harrison, W., *Memorable Dublin Houses* (W. Leckie, Dublin, 1890)
Hickey, D.J. and J.E. Doherty, *A Dictionary of Irish History since 1800* (Gill & Macmillan, Dublin, 1980)
Historic Dublin Maps, compiled by Dr Noel Kissane (The National Library of Ireland, 1988)
Joyce, Weston St John, *The Neighbourhood of Dublin* (M.H. Gill and Son, Dublin, 1939)
The Macmillan Dictionary of Irish Literature, edited by Robert Hogan (Macmillan, London and Basingstoke, 1980)
McCready, C.T, *Dublin Street Names* (Hodges Figgis, Dublin, 1892)
O'Connor, Ulick, *Celtic Dawn: Portrait of the Irish Literary Renaissance* (Hamish Hamilton, London, 1984)
O'Dwyer, Frederick, *Lost Dublin* (Gill and Macmillan, Dublin, 1981)
The Oxford Companion to English Literature, edited by Margaret Drabble (Oxford University Press, 1985)
Walsh, Caroline, *The Homes of Irish Writers* (Anvil Books, Dublin, 1982)
Wright, G.N., *An Historical Guide to the City of Dublin* (Baldwin, Cradock and Joy, London, 1825)

Index

Abbey Street, 58, 87,
110, 149, 156, 197,
216, 212, 298
Abbey Theatre, xix, 47,
49, 52, 80, 87, 88, 98,
99, 112, 113, 162, 164,
171, 191, 197, 198,
200, 201, 214, 216,
242, 264, 266, 291,
294, 307, 342
Abercorn Road, 197, 198
Addison, Joseph, xv,
1–2, 18, 237, 238,
256, 270, 317, 319
Adelaide Road, 10, 113,
166, 283, 304
Adelaide Road (Dun
Laoghaire), 266
Æ (George W. Russell),
xix, 2–5, 47, 52, 53,
54, 79, 88, 97, 98, 121,
123, 124, 162, 181,
182, 183, 200, 211,
240, 241, 275, 276,
277, 289, 291, 304,
306, 312, 330, 334
Ailesbury Road, 72
Albert Road, 240
Aldborough House, 148
Allgood, Molly, 266, 330
Allgood, Sara, 216
Amiens Street, 148, 149
Andrews Street, 256, 320
Anglesea Road, 16, 200,
286
Anglesea Street, 186
Anne Street, South, 125
Antient Concert Rooms,
72, 120, 220, 290, 321
Aras an Uachtaráin, 108,
138
Aravon School, 75
Arbour Hill, 15, 164,
214, 258
Architectural Review,
The, 20

Ardilaun, Lord, 28, 180
Arnold, Thomas, 102,
130
Arran Quay, xx, 36
Artane, 128
Arts Club, The, 314
Aungier Street, 174, 184,
185, 186, 187, 222, 308
Avoca, 71
Avoca Terrace, 207, 208
Avondale, 261, 262

Baggot Lane, 125, 313,
314
Baggot Street, Lower,
26, 58, 59, 98, 226,
227, 297, 314
Baggot Street, Upper,
28, 124, 125, 126, 159,
180, 181, 312, 314
Bailey, The, 127, 241,
194, 308
Balcombe, Florence, 247,
248, 280, 281, 307
Ballsbridge, 16, 72, 112,
129, 131, 191, 200
Ballybetagh, 56
Ballymun Road, 270
Balscadden, 288
Barnacle, Nora, 121, 122,
131, 309, 312
Barnhill Road, 229
Barrington, Jonah, 5–8,
156, 305, 307, 309, 312
Barry, James, 37
Barry, Spranger, 224, 320
Basin, The, 326
Beach, Sylvia, 122, 126
Beckett, Samuel, xvii, xx,
xxi, 8–13, 285, 298,
299, 309, 312, 314, 319,
341
Behan, Brendan, xv, xix,
14–16, 125, 294, 295,
296, 308, 314, 319, 325,
326, 338

Bell, The, 15, 21, 22, 110,
200, 202
Belloc, Hilaire, 276
Belmont Avenue, 53,
208, 329
Belvedere College, 46, 47,
117, 118, 161, 213, 324
Belvedere House, 68
Belvedere Place, 130,
131, 325
Benburb Street, 138
Berkeley, George, xviii,
16–19, 238, 323
Berkeley Road, 46, 326
Berkeley Street, 146
Bermingham Tower, 319
Betjeman, John, 19–23,
124, 297, 307, 314, 320
Bickerstaffe, Isaac, 24
Black Church, The, 45,
46, 326
Blackrock, 115, 134, 141,
160, 186, 203, 207, 208,
239, 241
Blackwood's Magazine,
56, 67, 92, 153, 158
Blanchardstown, 234
Bleeding Horse, The,
147, 293, 303, 308
Blessington Street, 326
Bloody Bridge, 232
Blue Coat School, 231
Bolton Street, 15, 46, 67
Botanic Gardens, 2, 77,
271, 342
Boucicault, Dion, xix,
25–6, 143, 197, 208,
216, 320, 323, 326
Bow Lane, 259
Bow Street, 300
Bowen, Elizabeth, xxi,
26–30, 296, 306, 307,
312, 313, 314
Bowen's Court, 30
Bray, 75, 114, 228, 241,
280, 283, 339

Index

Brazen Head, The, 293
Brian Boru–Hedigan's
    Pub, The, 298
Bride Street, 168, 237,
    318
Bridgefoot Street, 40
Brighton Road, 10
Brighton Square, 113,
    330
Brooke, Henry, 30–1
Brown, Christy, xv,
    32–5, 319, 338, 341
Browning, Robert, 57
Brunswick Street, North,
    79
Brunswick Street, South,
    see Pearse Street
Buckingham Street, 41,
    239
Bull Alley, 34, 237, 319
Burgh, Thomas, 18, 138,
    151
Burgh Quay, 241
Burke, Edmund, xviii,
    xx, 35–8, 61, 82, 83,
    323
Burlington Road, 313
Bushfield Terrace, 52,
    329
Butler, James (1st Duke
    of Ormond) 138, 237
Butt, Isaac, 278
Butterfield Avenue, 229
Byron, Lord, 186

Cambridge Road, 114
Camden Row, 187, 308
Camden Street, 147, 187,
    294, 303, 308
Campion, Edmund, 235,
    236
Capel Street, 46, 227
Carleton, William, xv,
    xvi, xviii, 38–44, 134,
    159, 175, 317, 318,
    320, 329, 333
Carson, Edward, 249,
    279
Carysfort Avenue, 115,
    239
Cassels, Richard, 141,
    258
Castle Inn, The, 297, 319
Castleknock, 21

Castle Lyons, 141
Castle Street, 319
Castlewood Avenue, 4,
    114, 181, 330
Catacombs, The, 16, 315
Cathedral Street, 131
Catholic University, The,
    78, 102, 108, 118, 119,
    129, 130, 159, 192,
    193, 194, 207, 305, 320
Catholic University
    Medical School, 172,
    194, 320
Cavendish Row, 65, 324
Cecilia Street, 78, 119,
    130, 172, 193, 194, 320
Celbridge, 141
Celt, The, 132
Chancery Lane, 167, 319
Chapelizod, 144, 148,
    206, 298
Charles Street, Great,
    167, 325
Charleston Road, 273,
    329
Chatham Street, 126, 296
Chekhov, Anton, 165,
    199
Chelmsford Lane, 210
Chelmsford Road, 51,
    200, 329
Chesterfield, Lord, 24
Christ Church Cathedral,
    60
Christchurch Place, 258,
    297
Christian Brothers
    Schools, 15, 77, 117,
    129, 199, 207, 209,
    304, 309, 325, 326
Church Lane, 256, 320
Church Street, 36, 40,
    147
Churchtown, 261, 285
Cibber, Mrs, 61
City Hall, 59, 268
Claideamh Soluis, An,
    108
Clare Street, xx, 5, 11,
    12, 309
Claremont Road, 69,
    226, 228
Clarence Street, Great
    North, 96

Clarendon Street, 4
Clarke, Austin, xx, 5,
    44–9, 76, 96, 97, 98,
    285, 297, 305, 319,
    323, 324, 326, 327
Clayton, Dr Robert, 59,
    305
Cloncurry, Lord, 140
Clondalkin, 21, 181, 274
Clongowes Wood
    College, 78, 114, 129
Clonmel Street, 305
Clonskeagh, 181
Clontarf, 29, 41, 151,
    188, 205, 243, 290
Cloonyquin, 70
Cloragh Road, 227
Clyde Road, 28, 124, 313
Coldstream Guards, 238
Coliemore Harbour, 12
College Green, 19, 59,
    107, 135, 218, 320
College Street, 320, 331
Colles, Abraham, 151,
    282
Collins, Michael, 80, 294
Collinstown House, 21
Collis, Dr Robert, 33
Collisson, Dr Houston,
    72, 74
Colum, Mary, 53, 276
Colum, Padraic, xv, 5,
    49–54, 76, 162, 163,
    211, 214, 242, 276,
    285, 294, 305, 306, 341
Congreve, William, xvii,
    17, 54–5, 232, 238, 256
Conmee, Revd Father
    John, 105, 116, 117
Connolly, James, 214
Connor, Jerome, 5, 124,
    329
Convent Avenue, 119
Cook Street, 46, 235
Cooldrinagh, 8, 10, 11
Coole Park, 85, 86, 87,
    170, 263, 290
Coombe, The, 41, 318
Corbawn Lane, 276
Corkery, Daniel, 53,
    191, 199
Cosgrave, William, 80
Coulson Avenue, 4
Croppies' Acre, The,
    138, 298

Cronin, Anthony, 315
Croswaithe Park, 251, 262, 263
Croswaithe Terrace, 193
Crow Street 41, 187, 319, 320
Crow Street Theatre, 320
Cuala Press, 54, 98, 315
Cuffe Street, 223, 308
Cullen, Cardinal Paul, 191
Cullenswood House, 162, 211, 329
Cumberland Street, 209, 309
Curragh Camp, 15
Curran, John Philpot, 141, 181, 212
Custom House, 117, 207, 269

Dalkey, 80, 193, 216, 220, 221, 229, 241, 249, 251, 276
Dalkey Avenue, 160, 221
Dame Street, 2, 256, 320
Damer, An, 16
Dana Magazine, 78, 120
Darby Square, 166
Dargle Road, 228
Darley, George, 55–7
Dartmouth Square, 161
Davis, Thomas, xix, 57–9, 132, 181, 312, 314, 333
Davitt, Michael, 274, 290
Davy Byrne's Pub, 294, 308
Dawson Street, 65, 69, 72, 89, 94, 95, 189, 240, 290, 307
Deansgrange Cemetery, 161, 201
De Quincey, Thomas 63, 320
De Vere, Aubrey, 159
De Valois, Ninette, 216
Delany, Dr Patrick, 1, 60, 61, 62, 270, 319, 323
Delany, Mrs Mary, (Mary Pendarves) xv, 1, 59–63, 305, 319, 323
Delville, 60, 61, 62, 63, 270

Denmark Street, Great, 46, 67, 117, 150, 213, 324, 325
Denzille Street, 114
Dickens, Charles, xv, 15, 64–5, 95, 138, 158, 307, 324
Digges Street, 5
Dillon, John Blake, 58
Dr Steevens' Hospital, 146, 151
Dodder, River, 33, 98, 261
Dodderdale, 98
Dodder Road, Lower, 49, 98
Doheny and Nesbitt's Pub, 297
D'Olier Street, 158, 320
Dollymount, 41
Dominick Street, xx, 46, 143, 188, 196, 197, 323, 325, 326
Donnybrook, 6, 53, 112, 125, 210, 272, 285, 286, 329
Dorset Street, 192, 196, 224, 325, 326
Dorset Street, Upper, xix, 195, 326
Douglas Hyde Gallery, The, 342
Dowden, Edward, 69, 78, 216, 289
Doyne, Major, 212
Drumcliffe, 287
Drumcondra, 117, 124, 188, 191, 197
Dryden, John, 55, 65, 232
Dublin Bus, 342
Dublin Castle, 1, 49, 60, 178, 187, 235, 243, 245, 255, 269, 319, 342
Dublin Corporation, 319
Dublin Magazine, The, 22, 110, 124, 159
Dublin Morning Register, The, 58
Dublin Penny Journal, The, 168
Dublin University Magazine, The, xviii, 67, 146, 148, 152, 153, 158, 168

Dublin University Review, The, 275, 290
Dublin Writers' Museum, 323, 324, 342
Duffy, Charles Gavan, 58, 132
Duke Street, 127, 241, 294, 308
Dun Laoghaire, 12, 51, 152, 193, 227, 241, 249, 251, 254, 267, 272, 305
Dunsinea House, 21

Earl Street, 188
Earlsfort Place, 10
Earlsfort Terrace, 81, 109, 306
East Wall, 197
Eastmoreland Place, 313
Eccles Street, xx, 46, 122, 146, 207, 294, 296, 326
Eden Quay, 331
Eden Road, 50
Edenvale Road, 54, 329
Edgeworth, Maria, xviii, 42, 69, 218, 274
Edwards, Hilton, 164, 165, 324
Eglington, John, 120, 182, 289
Elgin Road, 28, 313
Ellis Street, 138
Eliot, T. S., 19, 252
Elphin, 70, 82, 83
Elphis Nursing Home, 13, 266, 312
Ely Place, 79, 80, 157, 280, 306
Ely Place, Upper, xx, 3, 4, 180, 181, 306
Emmet, Robert, 155, 185, 209, 212, 239, 293, 308
Emorville Avenue, 3, 304
Enniskerry, 56, 202, 266
Ensor, John, 64, 277
Esplanade Terrace, 280, 283
Essex Street East, 297, 320

Essex Street, West, 65, 66
Eustace Street, 240
Exchange Street, 240

Fairview, 118, 119, 121
Farney Park, 161
Farquhar, George, 65–6, 232, 319
Father Mathew Bridge, 232
Fay Brothers, The, 4, 87, 216
Ferguson, Samuel, xix, 59, 66–70, 104, 111, 278, 288, 318, 323, 324, 341
Finn's Hotel, 309
Fishamble Street, xx, 61, 166, 167, 188, 223, 258, 319
Fitzgerald, Lord Edward, 147, 186, 324
Fitzgibbon Street, 14, 116, 117, 130, 325
Fitzwilliam Place, 16, 241, 315
Fitzwilliam Square, 112, 181, 285, 286, 292, 314, 315
Fitzwilliam Street, Upper, 314
Fleet Street, 13, 16, 99, 124, 126, 297, 320
Fontenoy Street, 122, 326
Forster, E. M., 30
Forty Foot Bathing Place, 11, 79, 253
Foster Place, 256, 320
Four Courts, The, 47, 268, 269
Foxrock, 13, 216
Francis Street, 40, 318
Frankfurt Place, 52
Frederick Street, South, 6, 88, 290, 307
Freeman's Journal, The, 31, 64, 65, 99, 217, 218, 264, 298, 325
French, Ethel Armitage, 71, 72, 334
French, Percy, 70–4, 307, 313, 314

Gaelic League, The, 52, 108, 162, 197, 210, 211
Gaiety Theatre, The, 71, 108, 183, 280, 342
Gardiner, Luke, 25, 67, 195
Gardiner Place, 46, 324
Gardiner Street, Lower, 25, 89, 230, 326
Gardiner Street, Upper, 105, 159, 192, 325
Garrick, David, 24, 37, 82, 224, 225
Garsington, 252
Gate Theatre, 23, 65, 112, 148, 153, 155, 164, 324, 342
General Post Office, 214
George's Street, Great North, 67, 68, 76, 147, 189, 324
George's Street, Great South, 3
Gibbon, Monk, 74–6, 341
Gladstone, W. E., 142
Glanmore Castle, 261, 262
Glasnevin, 2, 270, 271, 299, 335
Glasnevin Cemetery, 16, 35, 63, 105, 139, 169, 172, 205, 325, 342
Glasthule, 50, 113, 341
Glenageary, 266, 341
Glencree, 266, 279
Glencullen, 10
Glengariff Parade, 119, 326
Godwin, William, 222, 223
Gogarty, Oliver St John, 53, 76–82, 120, 121, 129, 130, 157, 170, 181, 241, 297, 306, 308, 323, 324, 325, 341
Goldsmith, Oliver, xv, 24, 37, 70, 82–4, 106, 270
Gonne, Maud, 4, 107, 291, 337
Gort, 85, 88, 291
Grafton Street, 16, 28, 137, 155, 156, 158, 180, 185, 218, 223, 225, 289, 308
Granby Row, 46
Grand Canal, 13, 26, 57, 89, 124, 125, 127, 146, 166, 201, 205, 206, 220, 240, 273, 286, 312, 314
Grand Canal Street, Lower, 151, 312
Grangegorman, 47
Grattan, Henry, 186
Green Street, 40, 133
Greene's Bookshop, 12
Gregory, Lady, xix, 52, 53, 84–8, 109, 170, 171, 182, 216, 241, 263, 290, 291, 304, 305, 306, 307
Gresham Hotel, 88
Greystones, 262, 276, 285
Griffith, Arthur, 52, 171, 240, 241, 294
Grogan's Pub, 207, 296
Grosvenor Park, 155
Grosvenor Road, 205, 330
Grosvenor Square, 3, 330
Grove Terrace, 4
Guardian, The, 18, 270
Guinness Hop Store, 299, 342
Gwynn, Stephen, 290

Haddington Road, 124, 126, 312
Hamilton, Sir Rowan, 278
Handel, George Frideric, xx, 61, 188, 258
Harbour Road, 288
Harcourt Street, 6, 10, 88, 164, 181, 192, 222, 230, 247, 274, 289, 304, 305
Harcourt Terrace, 166, 304
Hardwicke Place, 325
Hardwicke Street, xxi, 22, 116, 123, 163, 171, 214, 325
Harold's Cross, xvi, 5,

59, 72, 110, 111, 148, 230, 267, 284, 287, 331
Harold's Cross Road, 289
Harrington Street, 3, 219, 220, 304
Harry Street, 16, 127, 295, 308
Hastings, Warren, 38
Hatch Street, 81, 220, 221, 261
Hawkins Street, 26, 41, 157, 245, 320
Hawthorne Terrace, 197
Hearn, Lafcadio, xv, 88–91, 313, 326, 330
Hemans, Felicia, xv, 92–5, 307
Henrietta Street, 67
Henry Street, 40, 197
Herbert Lane, 13, 16, 314
Herbert Place, 26, 27, 29, 206, 312
Herbert Street, 13, 16, 207, 314
Hermitage, The, 212
Heytesbury Street, 16, 80, 168, 308
Highfield Road, 289
Higgins, F. R., 5, 49, 95–9, 204, 294, 297, 320
Higginsbrook, 95
Hoey's Court, 254, 255, 319
Holles Street, 14, 312
Hollinshed, Raphael, 236, 300
Hollinshed's *Chronicles*, 236
Hone, Nathaniel, 182
Hopkins, Gerard Manley, xv, 99–105, 305, 325, 329, 337
Horniman, Annie, 87
Horse and Tram, The, 299
Howth, 53, 54, 67, 69, 227, 228, 279, 280, 288, 289, 292, 339, 341
Hugh Lane Gallery of Modern Art, 275
Hughes, John, 3, 182

Humbert, General, 84, 177
Hume Street, 306
Hunt, Leigh, 55
Hyde, Douglas, xv, 53, 105–9, 162, 182, 204, 210, 211, 274, 275, 290, 318, 330

Ibsen, Henrik, 119, 164, 165, 171
Inchicore, 191, 206, 275, 312
Ingram, John Kells, 109–10, 306, 314, 333
Innisfallen Parade, 196, 198, 326
Inverness Road, 119
Irish Academy of Letters, 204
Irish Agricultural Organisation Society (IAOS), 34
Irish Freedom, 214
Irish Homestead, The, 3, 183
Irish Independent, The, 58, 110
Irish Literary Society, 3
Irish Literary Theatre, 52, 87, 171, 183, 263, 290, 320
Irish Monthly, The, 275
Irish Museum of Modern Art, 138, 343
Irish National Dramatic Company, 4
Irish National Theatre, 4, 87, 182, 214
Irish National War Memorial Park, 132, 343
Irish People, The, 110, 132, 320, 325
Irish Republican Brotherhood (IRB) 132, 214
Irish Review, The, 53, 163, 214
Irish Statesman, The, 3, 123, 200, 275
Irish Theatre, The, 163, 325

Irish Times, The, 99, 208, 264, 320
Irish Volunteers, 163, 202, 214
Irish Whiskey Corner, 300, 343
Irishtown, 226
Irving, Henry, 246, 247, 248
Irwin, Thomas Caulfield, 110–11, 320, 329, 333
Islandbridge, 80, 132
Iveagh House, 60

James Joyce Cultural Centre, 68, 324, 343
James Joyce Tower, *see* Martello Tower
James's Street, 39, 259, 269, 299
Jervis Street, 143
Johnson, Lionel, 276
Johnson, Dr Samuel, 1, 24, 37, 82, 83, 84, 224, 225, 269
Johnston, Denis, 112–13, 307, 314, 318, 324, 341
Johnston, Francis, 22, 108, 149
Johnston's Court, 225
Joyce, James, xv, xvii, xx, xxi, 11, 47, 78, 113–23, 125, 130, 142, 148, 160, 207, 208, 293, 294, 296, 299, 305, 306, 308, 309, 318, 320, 321, 323, 324, 325, 326, 330, 341
Joyce, John Stanislaus, 113, 114, 115, 117, 119, 305, 337

Kandahar, 138
Kavanagh, Patrick, xx, 5, 21, 123–8, 294, 295, 296, 312, 313, 314
Kavanagh's Pub, 299
Kavanagh's Weekly, 125, 126
Kennedy's Pub, 299, 309
Kerrymount Avenue, 6
Kettle, Thomas, 78, 79, 128–132, 241, 294, 305, 313, 325

Index

Kevin Street, 318
Kickham, Charles, 132–5,
320, 341
Kiely, Dr Benedict, 44
Kildare Road, 15
Kildare Street, 3, 35, 51,
78, 88, 130, 210, 246,
247, 306
Kildare Street Club, 23,
171, 189, 268, 307
Kilkenny College, 17, 54,
255
Killala, 84
Killiney, 12, 48, 50, 51,
76, 113, 202, 216, 276,
277
Kilmainham Gaol, 67,
164, 213, 214, 274, 275,
343
Kilternan, 56
Kimmage, 32, 213
King Street, North, 18
King Street, South, 71,
108, 183, 280
King's Hospital, 231
Kings Inns, 67, 130, 210
Kipling, Rudyard, 135–9,
296, 298, 306, 308
Kit-Kat Club, 55, 238
Kitty O'Shea's Pub, 298
Kneller, Sir Godfrey, 238
Knocknaree Road, 193

Lamb Alley, 235
Lamb, Charles, 56, 57
Land League, 129
Lansdowne Road, 112,
241
Laracor, 98, 99, 256
Larkin, James, 159, 197,
198
Larry O'Rourke's Pub,
296, 326
Laverty, Maura, 139, 337
Lawless, Emily, 140–2,
341
Le Fanu, Joseph
Sheridan, xviii, xx,
143–8, 278, 293, 312,
323, 324, 326, 333
Lecky, William, 211, 225
Ledwidge, Francis, 5, 164
Lee, George Vandaleur,
220, 221, 222, 304

Leeson Street, 28, 90,
125, 127, 131, 181,
207, 220, 262, 313, 314
Leinster Road, 107, 204,
330
Leinster Square, 89, 241,
330
Leinster Street, 307, 309
Lever, Charles, xviii,
147, 148–53, 269, 278,
307, 312, 323, 324
Lewis, C. S., 19
Liberty Hall, 214
Liffey, River, 1, 36, 137,
141, 142, 146, 208,
224, 231, 323
Lincoln Place, 3, 172,
196, 309
Lissoy, 82, 83
Lloyd, Constance, 280,
306
Lombard Street, 321
Longford, Lord, 153–5,
324, 330
Longford Street, Little,
184, 308
Longford Terrace, 217
Longwood Avenue, 51
Loos, Battle of, 139
Lord Edward Street,
166, 297, 319
Lord Edward, The, 297
Lover, Samuel, xviii,
155, 159, 308, 318,
320, 323
Lutyens, Sir Edwin, 132
Lyric Theatre Company,
49
Lyttleton, Sir Neville,
138

MacCarthy, Denis
Florence, 159–60, 305,
341
McCormack, John, 321
McDaid's Pub, 16, 127,
208, 295, 308
MacDiarmada, Sean, 214
MacDonagh, Donagh,
161, 324, 341
MacDonagh, Thomas,
47, 53, 162–3, 171,
213, 214, 305, 325, 329
McGreevy, Thomas, 286

MacLiammóir, Micheál,
54, 112, 153, 164–6,
215, 254, 267, 323, 324
McMaster, Andrew, 164
McNamara, Brinsley, 97,
99, 320
MacNeice, Louis, 19
MacNeill, Eoin, 53, 108,
210
McSwiney, Terence, 191
Maginni, Denis J., 324
Mahaffy, John Pentland,
68, 69, 78, 182, 279,
280, 324
Malahide, 129
Malahide Castle, 218,
343
Mangan, James
Clarence, xviii, xix,
xx, 147, 166–9, 230,
293, 297, 305, 308,
317, 319, 323, 325, 338
Manor Street, 44, 45
Maretimo, 141
Marine Parade, 251
Marino Crescent, 42,
243, 245, 246, 247, 280
Markievicz, Countess, 4,
141, 337
Marlborough Road, 210,
285, 329
Marlborough Street, 47,
150, 156, 171, 193, 221
Marsh, Archbishop, 41,
258, 318
Marsh's Library, 41, 175,
218, 258, 318, 343
Martello Terrace, 114
Martello Tower,
Sandycove, 78, 80,
121, 343
Martin, Violet, 88
Martyn, Edward, 23, 87,
162, 163, 170–2, 180,
182, 211, 263, 307,
309, 325, 338
Mary Street, 40, 47, 224
Mary's Lane, 40
Maturin, Charles
Robert, xviii, xx, 41,
143, 168, 173–7, 189,
218, 282, 283, 308, 318
Maunsel and Company,
53

Maxwell Road, 266, 330
Maynooth College, 159
Meath Hospital, 16, 80, 168, 308
Meath Industrial School, 239
Meath Road, 75, 229
Mercer Street, 230
Mercer's Hospital, 230, 258
Merrion Road, 200, 286
Merrion Row, 306
Merrion Square, 4, 5, 6, 29, 147, 148, 180, 240, 246, 277, 278, 279, 288, 291, 309, 312
Merrion Street, 34, 277
Mespil Flats, 201, 313
Mespil Road, 72, 74
Messiah, xx, 61, 258, 319
Metals, The, 251
Methuen, 254
Metropolitan School of Art, 3, 210, 289, 306
Meynell, Wilfred and Alice, 275, 276
Millbourne Avenue, 117
Milltown, 109
Milltown Park, 43, 329
Mitchel, John, 167
Molesworth Street, 29, 108, 151, 222, 307
Monasterevin, 103
Monkstown, 3, 217, 341
Montpelier Place, 134
Moore, George, xix, xx, 5, 53, 79, 86, 88, 98, 107, 170, 240, 241, 252, 296, 306
Moore, Thomas, xviii, 157, 158, 184–7, 254, 308
Moore Street, 40
Moran's Hotel, 230
Morehampton Road, 125
Morgan, Lady (Sydney Owenson), xviii, 68, 187–90, 307, 319, 320, 323, 324, 327
Morrell, Lady Ottoline, 252
Morrison's Hotel, 65, 290, 307
Mosse, Bartholomew, 211

Mount Jerome Cemetery, xvi, 5, 44, 59, 72, 110, 111, 148, 267, 284, 286, 289, 331, 343
Mount Merrion Avenue, 160, 208
Mount Street Crescent, 29, 71, 286, 314
Mount Street, Lower, 13, 58, 146, 266, 312
Mount Street, Upper, 21, 29, 109, 125, 146, 180, 314
Mountjoy Gaol, 15, 16, 133, 196, 326
Mountjoy Square, 14, 117, 198, 205, 224, 290, 324, 325
Mountjoy Street, 45, 46, 47, 326
Mountpleasant Avenue, Upper, 4, 5, 111, 329
Mulligan's Pub, 296
Mullingar House Inn, The, 293
Mungret College, 47, 77
Municipal Gallery of Modern Art, 305, 343
Munster Fusiliers, 199
Murray, T. C., 190
Musick Hall, 61, 319

Na gCopaleen, Myles, *see* Brian O'Nolan
Nassau Hotel, 290, 307
Nassau Street, 65, 121, 172, 230, 307
Nannetti, Joseph, 116, 325
Nation, The, xix, 43, 58, 109, 110, 132, 168, 283
National Gallery of Ireland, 168, 222, 241, 242, 308, 343
National Library, 78, 88, 109, 120, 130, 210, 306
National Literary Society, 107
Nationalist, The, 130
Neary's Pub, 126, 296
Nelson Street, 146, 326
Newbridge Avenue, 133, 209

Newman, Cardinal John Henry, xv, 129, 130, 159, 191–4, 207, 324, 325, 341
Newman House, 129, 159, 163, 193, 305, 343
Newtownsmith, 251
Norseman Pub, The, 297, 320
North Circular Road, 14, 15, 47, 111, 119, 123, 198, 325, 326
North Strand Road, 121
North Wall, 197, 249
Northumberland Road, 131

Oakley Road, 162, 211, 329
O'Brien, Flann, *see* Brian O'Nolan
O'Casey, Sean, xvi, xvii, xix, 47, 80, 88, 195–9, 283, 293, 299, 309, 319, 323, 325, 326
O'Conaire, Padraic, 98, 294
O'Connell, Daniel, 141, 223
O'Connell Street, 21, 22, 88, 125, 149, 159, 202, 214, 222, 269
O'Connor, Frank, xx, 5, 21, 124, 199–201, 313, 314, 329, 341
O'Connor, Ulick, 76, 82
O'Donoghue's Pub, 296
O'Donovan Rossa, Jeremiah, 132, 133, 163
O'Faoláin, Sean, xx, 21, 125, 201–2, 341
O'Flaherty, Liam, xx, 203–4, 294, 314, 324
O'Leary, John, 107, 110, 132, 204–5, 274, 290, 312, 323, 324, 325, 330, 337
O'Nolan, Brian (Flann O'Brien, Myles na gCopaleen), xx, 125, 161, 206–8, 294, 296, 306, 312, 320, 341
Orpen, William, 294

Orwell Park, 261
Osborne, Walter, 182
O'Sullivan, Seumas, 5,
    22, 48, 53, 98, 124,
    162, 241, 276, 294
Otway, the Revd Caesar,
    42
Oval Pub, The, 298
Oxmantown Green, 231,
    232
Oxmantown Road, 231

Palace Bar, 49, 99, 124,
    126, 208, 297, 320
Palastrina Choir, 171,
    172
Paradise Place, 46
Parke, Edward, 282
Parkgate Street, 298
Parliament Street, 110,
    133, 320
Parnell, Charles Stewart,
    16, 115, 275, 294, 307
Parnell, Fanny, 325, 338
Parnell Square, 32, 76,
    150, 324
Parnell Street, 40, 67,
    335
Patrick Street, 255, 318
Peacock Theatre, 164,
    216, 217, 342
Pearl Bar, 16, 49, 208,
    320
Pearse Museum, 343
Pearse Park, 213
Pearse, Patrick, 209–13,
    214, 305, 320, 329
Pearse Street (formerly
    Brunswick Street), 72,
    90, 209, 210, 216, 241,
    277, 283, 317, 320, 341
Pembroke Road, 124,
    125, 181, 313
Pembroke Street, xx, 93,
    125, 230, 315
Peninsular Wars, 89, 92
Percy Place, 125, 312
Peter Street, 41
Petrie, Dr George, 167,
    185, 187, 278, 325
Phibsborough, 119
Phoenix Park, 21, 24, 33,
    60, 64, 108, 138, 144,
    218, 258, 298

Pike Theatre, 13, 16, 314
Plunkett, Joseph Mary,
    162, 163, 213–14, 324,
    325
Plunkett, Sir Horace,
    320, 216
Poetry Ireland, 49, 319,
    343
Pollexfen, Susan, 286
Poolbeg Street, 296, 320
Pope, Alexander, 18, 30,
    55, 61, 62, 232, 238,
    256
Portland Street, 111
Portobello, 273
Portobello Barracks, 74
Portobello Nursing
    Home, 13, 286
Portobello Place, 220,
    304
Portobello Road, 240,
    304
Portora School, 10, 278
Powerscourt Gardens
    and Demesne, 21, 343
Powerscourt House, 31
Prince Arthur Terrace,
    90, 330
Prior, Thomas, 17
Prospect Road, 298
Prospect Square, 299
Prussia Street, 239
Purser, Sarah, 211, 289
Pussy's Leap, 33

Queen's Theatre, 72

Raglan Road, 28, 124,
    125, 200, 313
Ranelagh, 51, 54, 162,
    200, 329
Rathcoole, 34, 35
Rathfarnham, 49, 53, 74,
    98, 229, 261, 292
Rathfarnham Castle,
    261, 344
Rathgar, xx, 4, 113, 261,
    289
Rathgar Avenue, 4, 5,
    43, 97, 330
Rathgar Road, 205, 266,
    329, 330
Rathmines, 3, 4, 47, 89,
    90, 107, 111, 114, 155,

204, 205, 208, 228, 230,
    241, 273, 329
Rathmines Road, Lower,
    89
Rathmines Road, Upper,
    52
Ratra, 108
Red Cow Lane, 47
Reynolds, Sir Joshua, 24,
    37, 83
Richmond Avenue, 119
Richmond Hospital, 79
Richmond Place, 123, 325
Richmond Street, North,
    77, 118, 129, 325
Richmond Street, South,
    273, 304
Ringsend, 1
Roberts, George, 53
Roberts, Lord (Field
    Marshal) 136
Robinson, Lennox, 79,
    161, 201, 202, 215–17,
    314, 318, 341
Robinson, William, 41
Rolleston, T.W., 107,
    182, 204, 289, 330
Rory O'More Bridge,
    138, 232
Rosmeen Park, 202
Rotunda Hospital, 22, 32,
    33
Rotunda Rooms, 64, 65,
    171, 178, 192, 203, 268,
    324
Roxborough House, 84,
    86
Royal Canal, 197
Royal College of
    Surgeons, 80, 282, 308
Royal Dublin Fusiliers,
    131
Royal Dublin Society, 17,
    26, 129, 217, 320
Royal Hibernian
    Academy, 157
Royal Hibernian Military
    School, 144
Royal Hospital
    Kilmainham, 136, 138,
    344
Royal Irish Academy, 69
Royal Irish Academy of
    Music, 262, 263

Royal Terrace, 119
Rugby Road, 51, 329
Russell, George, *see* Æ
Russell, The Revd
    Matthew, 275, 276
Russell Street, 14, 325
Rutland Avenue, 220
Rutland Square, *see*
    Parnell Square
Ryan's Pub, 298

Sackville Street, *see*
    O'Connell Street
St Agatha's School, 15
St Alban's Terrace, 47
St Andrew's Church
    (Andrew Street), 256,
    320
St Andrew's Church (All
    Hallows, Westland
    Row), 16, 309
St Andrew's School, 112,
    307
St Ann's Church, 89, 95,
    247, 307
St Audoen's Arch, 31,
    46, 235
St Bartholomew's
    Church, 313
St Catherine's Church,
    155, 185, 239
St Colman's College, 162
St Columba's College, 74
St Enda's School, 53,
    162, 211, 212, 213,
    329, 344
St Fintan's Cemetery, 54,
    166
St Francis Xavier's
    Church, 325
St George's Church, 22,
    149, 196, 325
St George's Place, 44
St James's Church, 269
St John's Road, 71
St Joseph's Road, 239
St Kevin's Churchyard,
    187, 308
St Laurence Road, 206
St Mark's Church, 277,
    321
St Mark's Ophthalmic
    and Aural Hospital,
    196, 283, 309

St Mary's Church (Mary
    Street), 143, 195, 224,
    256
St Mary's Church
    (Donnybrook), 286
St Mary's Hospital, 144
St Mary's Place, 45, 46,
    326
St Mary's Pro-Cathedral,
    47, 131, 171
St Matthew's Church,
    226
St Matthias' Church, 86,
    304
St Michael's and St
    John's Church, 65
St Michael's Terrace, 206
St Michan's Church, 36,
    147, 231
St Mobhi's Church, 62,
    270, 271
St Nahi's Cemetery, 76
St Patrick's Cathedral,
    xvii, 70, 109, 113, 158,
    173, 217, 218, 237,
    255, 256, 257, 258,
    259, 317, 318
St Patrick's Close, 41,
    175, 218, 318
St Patrick's Home, 229,
    305
St Patrick's Hospital, 259
St Patrick's Park, 318
St Patrick's Training
    College, 191
St Paul's Church, 18
St Peter's Church, 174,
    175, 308
St Peter's Road, 119
St Saviour's Church, 46
St Stephen's Church, 29,
    71, 286, 314
St Stephen's Green, 12,
    28, 29, 47, 60, 79, 80,
    88, 94, 102, 104, 111,
    112, 129, 132, 137,
    159, 163, 164, 169,
    178, 179, 180, 182,
    192, 193, 207, 217,
    221, 229, 268, 280,
    289, 301, 305, 306,
    307, 308
St Werburgh's Church,
    60, 237, 255, 319

Sallymount Avenue, 211,
    329
Salmon, Dr George, 69
Sandford Road, 43, 52,
    329
Sandycove, 12, 50, 79, 80,
    121, 229, 249, 250, 253
Sandycove Road, 75, 76,
    341
Sandymount, 71, 121,
    130, 161, 209, 210, 226,
    227, 341
Sandymount Avenue, 34,
    133, 191, 210, 286
Sandymount Green, 200,
    287
Santry, 97
Sarsfield Road, 206
Scalp, The, 56
Scott, Sir Walter, xviii,
    66, 139, 175, 176, 177,
    217, 219–22, 307, 308,
    318
Scotsman Bay, 251
Seafield Crescent, 201
Sean McDermott Street,
    67
Seapoint, 227
Seapoint Avenue, 3, 341
Seaview Terrace, 272
Shanganagh Terrace, 48
Shankill, 276, 277, 341
Shaw, George Bernard,
    xvii, xix, xxi, 53, 88,
    111, 112, 204, 219–22,
    240, 249, 265, 274, 304,
    305, 307, 309, 319, 321,
    341
Shaw House, 303, 304,
    344
Shelbourne Hotel, 29,
    121, 137, 178, 268, 280,
    296, 306
Shelbourne Road, 121
Shelley, Percy Bysshe, xv,
    110, 111, 222–4, 308
Sheppard, Oliver, 3
Sheridan, Richard
    Brinsley, xvii, 143, 147,
    185, 195, 224–6, 308,
    323
Sheridan, Thomas, 1, 30,
    61, 319
Sheridan's Academy, 30

Ship Street, Great, 319
Ship Street, Little, 5,
  235, 255, 319
Sigerson, Dora, 338
Sigerson, George, 107,
  134, 275, 289
Silchester Road, 266
Simmonscourt Road, 286
Sir John Rogerson's
  Quay, 151
Sir Patrick Dun's
  Hospital, 151
Skeffington, Francis
  Sheehy, 74, 78, 130
Smithfield, 47, 300
Smithson, Annie M.P.,
  226–30, 305, 307, 308,
  341
Smock Alley, 224
Smock Alley Theatre,
  65, 224, 225, 319, 320
Smyllie, Robert M., 49,
  99, 297, 320
Somme, Battle of the,
  131
Sorrento Park, 229
Sorrento Road, 80, 113,
  249
Sorrento Terrace, 251,
  276
South Circular Road, 351
Southerne, Thomas,
  231–2, 323
Spectator, The, 233, 234,
  270
Spenser, Edmund, 31,
  233
Springhill Park, 76
Stag's Head Pub, The,
  299
Standard Hotel, 88, 305
Stannaway Road, 32
Stanyhurst, Richard, xv,
  234–6, 255, 317
Stanyhurst's Tower, 235,
  319
Steele, Richard, 1, 18,
  232, 237–8, 256
Stephens, James, xix, 5,
  53, 79, 162, 239–43,
  276, 294, 307, 308
Stephen's Green Club,
  192, 307, 315
Stillorgan, 153, 200

Stoker, Abraham, xviii,
  79, 143, 146, 243–8,
  305, 306, 319
Stoker, Sir Thornley, 79,
  181, 306
Stokes, William, 69, 151,
  168
Stonybatter, 45
Strindberg, August, 165
Stradbrook Road, 134
Strand Road, 121, 161
Strong, L.A.G, 249–54,
  341
Suffolk Street, 256
Summer Field, 252
Sussex Road, 313
Sundrive Road, 32
Sutton, 35, 166
Swift, Jonathan, xvii, 1,
  15, 17, 18, 30, 31, 54,
  55, 60, 62, 77, 99, 154,
  218, 224, 232, 254–9,
  269, 317, 318, 319, 320
Swords, 12
Synge, J.M., xvii, xix,
  88, 142, 162, 198, 199,
  240, 260–7, 312, 313,
  319, 321, 330, 341
Synge Street, 207, 219,
  220, 221, 304, 333

Talbot Street, 151, 156
Tallaght, 277
Taney, 74, 76
Tatler, The, 2
Temple, Sir William, 55,
  255
Temple Lane, 320
Temple Street, 205, 324,
  325
Templeogue, 33, 48, 98,
  152
Tennyson, Lord, 72, 110
Terenure, 181
Thackeray, William
  Makepeace, xv, 153,
  267–9, 296, 306, 341
Theatre Royal, 25, 41,
  187, 245, 320
Thomas Court, 239
Thomas Street, 39, 46,
  155, 185
Thomastown, 16

Thompson, Francis, 213,
  276
Thoor Ballylee, 170, 291
Tibradden, 227
Tickell, Thomas, 1,
  269–70, 317, 323
Tivoli Theatre, 241
Todhunter, Dr John, 72
Tolka, River, 1
Tone, Wolfe, 209
Toner's Pub, 296, 309,
  314
Torca Cottage, 220, 221
Torca Road, 221
Trench, Samuel
  Chenevix, 70, 121
Trinity College, 6, 11,
  13, 17, 23, 27, 30, 35,
  37, 38, 49, 54, 56, 58,
  62, 65, 67, 69, 70, 77,
  78, 79, 82, 84, 89, 103,
  105, 106, 108, 109,
  137, 142, 146, 151,
  152, 155, 157, 160,
  165, 167, 174, 186,
  196, 204, 216, 217,
  218, 232, 234, 243,
  245, 246, 247, 255,
  263, 268, 279, 309,
  317, 320, 324, 344
Trinity Street, 320
Tritonville Road, 227
Trollope, Anthony, xv,
  271–3
Tulira Castle, 23, 87, 170
Tynan, Katherine, xxi,
  74, 88, 103, 107, 134,
  204, 273–7, 289, 329,
  330, 341
Tyrell, Dr Robert
  Yelverton, 78, 279

United Irishman, The,
  52, 240
University Church, 193,
  305
University Club, 307
University College, 47,
  53, 131, 161, 194, 203,
  306
Usher's Island, 232
Ussher, Archbishop
  James, 235, 236

Van Homrigh, Hester, 18, 256
Viceregal Lodge, 138
Vico Road, 202, 221
Volta Cinema, 47, 122
Vonolel, 138

Walpole, Horace, 61
Warrington Place, 26, 57, 146, 205, 312
Waterloo Bar, 126
Waterloo, Battle of, 145, 212
Waterloo Road, 16, 28, 124, 313
Watling Street, 46
Wellesley, Arthur, 185
Wellington Road, 112, 124, 313
Wentworth, Sir Thomas, 65
Werburgh Street, 60, 166, 255, 319
Wesleyan Connexional School, 221
Westland Row, 12, 16, 139, 152, 196, 210, 249, 262, 277, 283, 309, 321
Westmoreland Street, 320

Westport, Lord, 63
Wexford Street, 308
Whitechurch, 49, 98, 162, 227, 230
Whitefriar Street, 222
Whyte's Academy, Samuel, 185, 187, 224, 308
Wilde, Lady (Speranza), 43, 275, 277, 278
Wilde, Oscar, xvii, xviii, xix, xxi, 72, 78, 79, 165, 178, 249, 265, 275, 277–82, 306, 309, 321, 324, 341
Wilde, Sir William, 151, 246, 255, 277, 280, 282–4, 308, 309, 333, 341
William Street, North, 15
William Street, South, 31, 149, 296
Wilton Place, 28, 125, 201, 204, 314
Windsor Avenue, 118, 119
Winetavern Street, 46, 47, 293
Wolfe Tone Quay, 138

Wolfe Tone Street, 143, 195, 256
Woolf, Virginia, 30
Wordsworth, William, 95

Yeats, Jack B., 54, 88, 263, 284–6, 314, 329, 334
Yeats, John B., 104, 182, 275, 284, 286, 289, 307, 308, 326
Yeats, Lily, 76, 285, 288, 315
Yeats, Lollie, 76, 285, 315
Yeats, W.B., xv, xvii, xix, xx, xxi, 3, 4, 52, 53, 76, 79, 80, 87, 88, 98, 103, 107, 113, 124, 162, 165, 170, 171, 178, 180, 182, 191, 198, 199, 204, 205, 211, 240, 241, 252, 263, 265, 275, 286–92, 297, 305, 306, 307, 308, 312, 314, 324, 330, 341
York Road, 266, 330
York Street, xx, 41, 168, 174, 175, 189, 230, 240, 288, 308